MYSTICAL THEOLOGY

Entombment of Christ
• —Peter Paul Rubens

MYSTICAL THEOLOGY
A Layman's Guide

The Collected Works of
Dom Savinien Louismet, OSB

Vol. 2

The Mystery of Jesus
Mystical Initiation
The Burning Bush

MEDIATRIX PRESS
MMXXIII

ISBN: 978-1-953746-19-1

The Mystery of Jesus, Mystical Initiation, and *The Burning Bush* were published in 1922, 1923, 1926 by PJ Kennedy and Sons.

Cover art:
The Supper at Emmaus
—Paolo Veronese

Mediatrix Press
607 E 6th Ave.
Post Falls, ID 83854
www.mediatrixpress.com

Adprobationes

The Mystery of Jesus
Visa relatione Censoris deputati, concedimus ut quintum hocce volumen de Oratione mystica, a R. P. D. SAVINIANO LOUISMET, O.S.B., Monasterii Buckfastriensis Monacho conscriptum, typis mandetur, si cœteris, quorum interest, ità videbitur.
Datum Sublaci, ex Asceterio S. Specus, in festo S. Joannis Evang. 1921.
D. BENEDICTUS GARIADOR, O.S.B., Abbas Generalis.
D. VINCENTIUS GOOSEMANS, O.S.B., Pro.-Con. a secratis.

Nihil Obstat
F. THOMAS BERGH, O.S.B.,
Censor Deputatus.
Imprimatur:

EDM. CAN. SURMONT,
Vic. Gen.

Mystical Initiation

Visa relatione Censoris deputati concedimus ut sextum hocce volumen de Oratione mystica, a R.P.D. Saviniano Louismet, O.S.B. Monasterii Buckfastriensis Monacho conscriptum, typis mandetur, si caeteris, quorum interest, ita videbitur.

Datum Subiaci, ex Asceterio S. Specus, die 21 Maii 1923.

D. BENEDICTUS GARIADOR, O.S.B.,
Jus Generalis.

Nihil Obstat:
F. THOMAS BERGH, O.S.B., *Censor Deputatus.*
Imprimatur:
EDM. CAN. SURMONT,
Vicarius Generalis.
Westmonasterii,
die 2 *Octobris* 1923.

The Burning Bush

Visa relatione Censoris deputati concedimus ut sextum hocce volumen de Rubo Ardenti, a R.P.D. Saviniano Louismet, O.S.B. Monasterii Buckfastriensis Monacho conscriptum, typis mandetur, si caeteris, quorum interest, ita videbitur.

Datum Subiaci, ex Asceterio S. Specus, die 16 Junii 1926.

D. BENEDICTUS GARIADOR, O.S.B.,
Jus Generalis.

Nihil Obstat:
F. THOMAS BERGH, O.S.B., *Censor Deputatus.*
Imprimatur:
EDM. CAN. SURMONT,
Vicarius Generalis.
Westmonasterii,
die 2 *Octobris* 1923.

TABLE OF CONTENTS

BOOK V: THE MYSTERY OF JESUS

PART I: PRELIMINARIES

Quo Vadis Domine?
—Annibale Carraci

BOOK V

THE MYSTERY OF JESUS

PREFACE

THIS new volume is the fifth in the series of treatises on mystical theology which wisely or perhaps foolishly I began publishing a few years ago, and still fondly hope, with God's grace and the help of the many prayers of my brethren, to bring to completion within a few more years.

In the preceding treatise, on DIVINE CONTEMPLATION FOR ALL, my aim has been to give a general idea of the first and most important function of the mystical life. Now, in the further development of this subject of divine contemplation, the logical order demands that, from the abstract and general, we should come down to the concrete; that is to say, that we should proceed to treat of the very object of contemplation.

This object is twofold, namely: first, in the order of dignity, the mystery of the Blessed Trinity, and then, secondly, that of the Sacred Humanity of Our Lord.

In the present volume we treat only of this second object, reserving the first for another volume, because in the order of execution the loving contemplation of Our Lord takes precedence, as it paves the way to that of the Blessed Trinity. "*I am the Way*" says Our Lord.

From our title it must not be inferred that we are here presenting to the public a learned or technical treatise. Indeed, the purpose of this little book is not science—not even the science of Jesus for its own sake—but love: honey-sweet, delectable, inebriating, all consuming love. Whatever we say herein must be turned exclusively to the purposes of love.

The treatise is divided into three distinct parts, thus:

I. Preliminaries.
II. The amazing human life of Christ on earth.
III. Mighty sequels, in time and eternity, to the human life of Christ on earth.

Here and there, though sparingly, I have ventured to give free rein to my own feelings on so entrancing a subject; and, at times, I have also drawn upon the mystical experiences of others of which I have been either the confidant or, even in a way, the happy witness: thinking that it might be some help to souls of good will. I hope people will not, in consequence, conceive any high opinion of me, or on the other hand, accuse me of having betrayed *the secret of the King*, The things I have set down in these pages are only on the fringe of the contemplation of Jesus. They are not it, but they certainly proclaim its near approach: just as, of old, in the temple of Jerusalem, the tiny golden bells, around the high-priest's robes, betrayed his approach by their melodious jarrings and jinglings.

There is infinitely better than what can be set down in writing. As long as the mystical experience can be expressed, it is not much: there still remains what can never be told in human speech.

Lord Jesus, thou knowest how dissatisfied I am with this last production of my pen, the puny result of nearly three years of hard work and intense prayer; how I feel its falling so short of the high mark I had aimed at. Twice did it write it all over, the first draft displeasing me utterly, whilst I can hardly say whether this second one be much better. However, I must be content to give it to the public as it now stands, for there are ever so many of the readers of my former treatises who are clamoring for it and I ought not to disappoint them much longer.

For one thing I may rejoice; however great be the shortcomings of this little book, Thy sweet name, O my dear Lord, is written all over it. Then, also, the unworthiness of my discourse is often relieved by generous quotations of Thy Holy Writ. And I know that Thy grace will help pious readers to find more in these pages than I have actually set down. For, indeed, how could a sinful man, in his mortality, express Thee, my Lord, who art the eternal joyful wonder of the angelic hosts?

PART I
PRELIMINARIES

"Sweeter delight I know not than in my heart to sing
Thee Jesu, whom I love, a song of Thy praise."
— Richard Rolle
The Fire of Love, Book 2, ch. xii.

CHAPTER I

THE MYSTERY WHICH IS CHRIST

RAYING . . . that God may open unto us a door of speech to speak the mystery of Jesus, (Col. 4:3.)
We speak the wisdom of God in a mystery which is hidden, which God ordained before the world unto our glory, (1 Cor. 2:7.) *The mystery which was kept secret from eternity.* (Rom. 16:25.) *The mystery which is Christ, which has been hidden from ages and generations, but now is manifested to his Saints,* (Col. 1:26-27.)

Mysteries, both natural and supernatural, surround us, press us and penetrate us on all sides. We are simply steeped in mysteries. We are to our very selves, and each one of the brethren is to us, a mystery or rather a sheaf of mysteries. The material universe we are in is an enormous congeries of mysteries: in the inscrutable depths of the firmament, in the atmosphere which envelops our planet, above and beneath the surface of the earth, in the oceans, are found mysteries upon mysteries and mysteries within mysteries.

Each tiny particle of matter, animate or inanimate, is a little world and a formidable abyss which our short-sighted reason cannot fathom. Science has demonstrated that a single atom of matter has a more complicated structure than any Gothic cathedral. The last word as to its internal laws is yet to be said, and will very likely never be said by man this side of the grave. The more advance is made in the exploration of the infinitesimally small, the more also the goal of all researches, perfect knowledge, seems to recede and elude our grasp.

Then, infinitely transcending these natural mysteries, there are the supernatural ones of the realm of grace and of that of glory.

Innumerable as these also are, they may still be reduced for convenience sake to three most comprehensive ones in which all

1

the others are included as circles within circles, *rota in rotam,* says Ezechiel. Thus:

First and foremost the mystery of the Most Holy Trinity of the Divine Persons.

Then, the mystery of Our Lord Jesus Christ.

Finally, the mystery of the Church of Christ, in time and eternity.

Even these three distinct mysteries so intermingle or interpenetrate each other, and are so involved in each other, that at least to the eyes of our created intelligence they seem ultimately to run into just one huge mystery, namely the mystery of Jesus. For, indeed, the mystery of the Church of Christ is still the mystery of Jesus, since it is, in the main, the mystery of the extension of Jesus in all souls of good will, in this life and in the next.

On the other hand, Jesus being the Son of God, one and the same God with the Father and the Holy Ghost, we cannot exclude Him from the mystery of the Blessed Trinity. Thus the mystery of Jesus stretches out into all things divine and human and reaches out from eternity even unto eternity. Our Lord is in Himself the whole supernatural order, and He moreover takes unto Himself and sanctifies and transfigures the whole natural order. Whatever is outside of Him and refuses to become one with Him, is doomed; although the process of elimination and separation from Jesus comes not from Him, but from reasonable creatures, whether angels or men, making a wrong use of their freedom to choose.

We have been told, in books purporting to unfold to us the divine plan, that the supernatural order is built upon the natural. It so appears at a first glance, when we look at things as they are mirrored in the medium of our prejudiced mind, instead of viewing them as they really stand in their mutual relations. We are, then, victims of the same illusion as the man who, looking at a landscape reflected in a lake, would persuade himself that the world is upside down. But, if we place ourselves at the right view-point, which is that of God, we shall realize that God has created all things in Christ and for Christ, in close dependence and strict subordination to Him.

The sacred humanity is the *primum volitum,* the very first object God had in view in creating the world. It is in Jesus Christ and in reference to Him that God has willed the rest of created things, this world of angels and men and lower beings. It is in him that God has loved us from all eternity and has brought us into actual existence and has co-ordinated the entire providential plan of things: *in Christ* as St. Paul is so fond of repeating, "in Christ" and not otherwise.

Now, as the whole supernatural order is built upon the person of Our Lord—to be more precise, upon His sacred humanity—it follows that even the natural order rests upon the same sacred humanity, and has been created for its sake. All things visible and invisible, angels, men and inferior creatures are in an absolute dependence on the sacred humanity of Our Lord and exist only for His sake: *I am Alpha and Omega, the beginning and the end, saith the Lord God, who is and who was and who is to come, the Almighty. ... I am the first and the last, and alive and was dead and behold I am living for ever and ever, and have the keys of death and of hell.* (Apoc. 1:8-18.)

O, dear Lord Jesus, thou art truly the first and the last word of God, the first and the last word of the whole universe of things visible and invisible, the first and the last word of all in time and eternity: be Thou also the first and the last word of Thy poor servant, every day of his life, in all his undertakings, but most particularly at the time of recollection and prayer. I want to contemplate this sublime mystery which Thou art, I want to grow more and more enamored of it; to live upon it; to inhale its delectable, substantial perfume, and to breathe it out all around me, until Thou at last be pleased to call me to the beatific vision of Thy glory with the Father and the Holy Ghost in heaven.

Jesus! sweet Lord and Love! Oh! may it please Thine infinite goodness to shed upon me the radiance of Thine adorable countenance, of Thy five Wounds, of Thy gracious eyes, of Thy loving Heart, of Thy dear Soul, of Thy Godhead! Then shall I fall at Thy Feet as dead. Then wilt Thou lay Thy right hand upon me saying: *Fear not.* . . . Then will the unutterable take place.

CHAPTER II

HOW TO BEGIN THE LOVING CONTEMPLATION OF OUR LORD

ESUS answered and said to the Samaritan J woman: If thou didst know the gift of God and who he is that saith to thee, Give me to drink, thou perhaps wouldst have asked of him, and he would have given thee living water, (John 4:10.)

Now, the contemplation of Jesus is often inaugurated just like that.

There is a seemingly casual meeting of Our Lord with some soul, perhaps actually in a state of great unreadiness. But the hour of grace has struck. The two confront each other. There is Jesus who is the gift of God to us men, *for God so loved the world as to give it His only begotten Son* (John 3:16), and there is that poor sinful or lukewarm Christian, who hitherto has but little appreciated this gift of the Father.

Let the soul whom Jesus meets thus, only listen to what He has to say. Now He says in the depth of her heart: *Give me to drink*—not indeed a drink of earthly water out of an earthen vessel, but out of the cup of thine own heart, the generous wine of all thy affections. The poor soul is quite overcome at such an unexpected request. She replies: "How is this, that you being sanctity itself should speak to such an unworthy sinner as I am?" But Jesus does not mind the interruption. He pursues: "If you only knew Me in My true character of a loving and merciful Savior! However, give Me the drink I ask of you, and see what I shall give you in return: the living water of My own sweetest, dearest love in time and for all eternity."

Who would not be that happy soul? O, my brother, it is for us to be it. You know where you can meet Him, and speak with Him. You know what He will want of you and what He will press upon you in exchange. Now all this is the work of contemplation. The inspired writer exhorts us in these words: *Seek ye his face evermore.* (1 Paral. 16:11.)

The face of my Jesus in the Blessed Sacrament! The white species within the span of a narrow circle! That is all I can see of Him there, and it is only His veil, not His sweet self, only the veil behind which He hides His tremendous majesty, that I may approach Him without fear and receive Him. But oh! can anything more touching and moving be imagined than such a presentation of Himself by *the King of Glory?* How I must love to contemplate Him thus and pour out to Him all the treasures of tenderness and affectionateness of my heart.

O Salutaris hostia!

It is not difficult even at all hours of the day and night, with the eyes of faith, to penetrate behind the closed doors of the tabernacle and see Him as He is there, and pour out to Him our love.

Nor is it difficult, after a time, with a very slight exercise of the imagination, to discover within the circle of the sacred species of bread, a tiny representation of Our Lord in the very mystery of His which we may be contemplating at the time. For in His Blessed Sacrament, Jesus has contrived to make Himself into a living memento and a breathing monument of all and each of His mysteries. Says the Psalmist: *"He hath made a remembrance of His wonderful works, being a merciful and gracious Lord; He hath given food to them that fear Him."* (Ps. 110:4-5.)

Seek ye His face evermore in the Gospel story. The face of the tiny Babe of Bethlehem, the eager, joyful face of the little Christ Child, the thoughtful face of the sweet boy of twelve among the doctors; the face of the young carpenter growing into manhood, the face of the *Son of Man* preparing for His public work which is at hand; the face of the preacher of the Gospel of the Kingdom, of the good Shepherd, of the friend of poor sinners!

Then the face of my Jesus in His terrible agony in the garden; and a little after, the face of my Jesus buffeted, spat upon, crowned with thorns, covered with trickling blood. Then at the end of His three hours on the cross, the face of my Jesus wan, absolutely bloodless, surrendered to death. Ah! let me seek His face evermore in all these mysteries of His beautiful life and of His cruel death!

And then, the face of my Jesus risen from the dead, appearing to His sweet Mother, and to His special friend Mary Magdalen, and to His Apostles, and conversing with them so sweetly and so lovingly. Then also the face of my Jesus in glory, seated at the right hand of His Heavenly Father. If you be risen with Christ, seek ye the things that are above where Christ is sitting at the right hand of God. (Col. 3:1.)

Now, all these successive contemplations of the one object of our passionate love under various aspects, will finally lead us up, even during these days of our exile, to a certain obscure contemplation of His face as *the Only Begotten Son who is in the bosom of the Father* (John 1:18), thus giving us a foretaste of the beatific vision in paradise. This is the living water Jesus promises to whomsoever will give Him to drink.

If you ask me: When thus contemplating my Lord, what acts shall I produce? I would answer: Never mind trying to produce deliberately any particular acts: simply let yourself go, let your heart speak; say what comes; and if nothing comes, be content to stay thus simply gazing at Him, silently adoring Him.

CHAPTER III

THE FIRST POINT IN THE MYSTERY OF JESUS

I N the great mystery of Jesus we can consider three distinct sets of mysteries, namely, (1) The mysteries of His sacred Flesh and Blood; (2) Those of His blessed human soul; and (3) Those of His pure Godhead.

It is the contemplation of the sacred humanity of Our Lord, that is to say, of His human body and soul which will engross our attention in these pages. Nevertheless we must needs take our starting-point from this paramount feature in Jesus Christ, that He is God, and that according to the magnificent expression of St. Paul, *in Him dwelleth dll the fulness of the Godhead corporally.* (Col. 2:9.)

We shall return in a subsequent volume to the consideration of His Godhead for its own sake; for the present we notice it only in its relation to His sacred humanity; nevertheless we must at the outset give due prominence to this marvelous, all-entrancing fact of His being a divine person.

This historical personage, Jesus Christ, whose coming into the world, and whose human life, death, resurrection and after-life we are about to consider, is GOD.

He is God from all eternity. He is God before His Incarnation and during it and after it, God uninterruptedly and for evermore.

Jesus is God from the first moment of His Incarnation; God in His human soul and in His human body, God in all His human acts.

He is, to use the words of the Nicene Creed, " the only begotten Son of God, born of the Father before all times, God of God, light of light, true God from true God, begotten not made, consubstantial with the Father, by whom all things have been made."

From whatever angle we view our Lord, whichever of His mysteries we are contemplating, we must never lose sight of this splendid fact that He is God. We could not prescind from it, even for the sake of argument, without the greatest risk of lapsing into material heresy.

Jesus being a divine person, it would seem as though when we have stated this supreme characteristic of His, nothing more could be added; as though no new feature of loveliness could be put on the brow of the infinitely lovely; but Our Lord has found the means of presenting Himself to our contemplation with increased loveliness, not indeed by adding anything to His native majesty, but rather by an inverse process, namely by putting away something of His own, and thus making His sweet Self nearer and more accessible to all and each of us.

He has made Himself obedient, and fulfilled the command of His Father who sent Him to us on earth. He has put on our human nature, taking upon Himself all our infirmities, sin excepted. Innocent and infinitely holy as He is, He allowed the very splendor of His sacred humanity to be obscured by the sufferings and ignominies of His passion and death.

In His holy sacrifice of the Mass and Eucharistic Sacrament, He puts away even the semblance of our human nature, thus to become our victim of oblation and the bread of our souls.

Now each one of these successive acts of His ought to add some new feature to His native loveliness as it is given to us to perceive it.

O, Jesus, thou art indeed, as the Word, *the brightness of eternal light and the unspotted mirror of Gods majesty, and the image of his goodness* (Wisd. 7:26), *Thou art* indeed *the only begotten Son who is in the bosom of the Father* (John 1:18); but at present it is more to our liking and within the scope of our ability to contemplate Thee as the *Son of Man* and as the *Man of Sorrows,* as *the Lamb of God who taketh away the sin of the world,* and as *the clean oblation offered in every 'place to the name of the Lord* (Mal. 1:11) as the *living bread which came down from heaven* (John 6:41), as our *Emmanuel, God with us, the Word made flesh.*

CHAPTER IV

THE WAY TO PROCEED IN THIS CONTEMPLATION

T had been commanded to the Israelites of old, in regard to the paschal lamb: *You shall eat the head with the feet and entrails thereof.* (Ex. 12:9.) This was in figure of the contemplation of Our Lord, this true Lamb of God: the head standing for His divine nature, the entrails for His sacred human soul, the feet with all the rest of the lamb for His sacred flesh and blood.

The right order of this contemplation is that we should exercise our loving attention, first of all, upon the mysteries of His sacred flesh and blood and His whole sensibility as summed up in His Sacred Heart; then upon the mysteries of His most holy human soul; then upon the mysteries of His Godhead, which will introduce us to the contemplation of the Blessed Trinity. Thus Jesus in His sacred humanity shows Himself truly *the way* that leads to the Father, the door which gives us access to the holy of holies of the Blessed Trinity, *the* very *key* that opens to us the treasury of the infinite perfections.

Indeed, before we can hope to see and taste how sweet the Lord God is in His pure essence, we must learn first to taste and see how sweet the sacred humanity of His divine Son is; we have to taste and see how sweet Jesus is in the mysteries of His life, death, resurrection and glory.

Now we must realize that we are not alone in this work of the contemplation of Jesus. There are two persons concerned in it: firstly, the Christian who, roused by the grace of God, sets about this work, and then, secondly, Jesus whose sacred humanity is to be contemplated and who uses it as an instrument with which to act upon the soul of the contemplative. There are two energies at work: that of man seeking Our Lord, and that of Our Lord seeking the man of good will, meeting him more than half way, laying hands on all his faculties and communicating Himself to him with unspeakable tenderness.

So Jesus is not only the object of my contemplation, but He is all the while vitally acting upon my soul, and acting upon it with His own body and blood and heart and human soul; with His own life and doctrines and the virtues that emanate from Him. All this simply on condition that I go to Him not as to a lifeless model painted on the wall or sculptured on a pedestal, but as to my living and loving master, a marvelous teacher who does not only speak to the ears and to the eyes but to my inmost soul. Then Jesus takes me in hand and proceeds with my spiritual education. Can anything more desirable be thought of?

God had already conversed familiarly and lovingly with the first man in the garden of Eden and taken in hand the work of his supernatural education, when Adam, by his prevarication, brought this divine undertaking to a sudden stop. Now, the Lord God, in His loving kindness, makes a new venture; but to be sure of a welcome on our part, He becomes man, our brother by flesh and blood and human love. It is in this new capacity of the Word made flesh, that He now attempts our new education if only we will respond to His sweetly compelling invitations.

Behold Adam is become like one of us (Gen. 3:22), said God derisively of the first man after he had eaten of the forbidden fruit and thereby forfeited for himself and us all the privileges of primitive innocence. We have now our revenge, sweet revenge, provided by the Lord God Himself in the incarnation of his divine Son.

Behold God is become like one of us, we may exultantly cry out when we see the tiny infant Jesus at His virgin-mother's breast, or the little child Jesus innocently disporting with other children of His age, or the fair boy playing truant to those who will so terribly miss Him, or the delicate and beautiful youth earning His livelihood by the sweat of His brow at the carpenter's bench, or the man in the full development of His noble personality preaching His gospel of love, bravely mixing with all sorts of people, good and bad, friends and foes, healing the sick, doing good everywhere; or finally hanging naked on the cross, every bone protruding, His sacred lips parched by an intolerable thirst, whilst even His sacred soul is so absolutely desolate that He cannot but cry out to His heavenly Father: *"My God, my God, why hast thou forsaken me?"* (Matt, 27: 46). *Behold the Son of God is indeed become as one of us!*

Oh! be Thou welcome among us, dear Son of the living God, Jesus, our brother, Thou the Word made flesh. May all men welcome Thee rapturously. May they all take Thee to their heart of hearts, and allow Thee to make them holy and happy. As for myself, after a long life of sin and tepidity and resistance to thy grace, behold at last I want to surrender myself completely to Thy masterful love, in the contemplation of the mysteries of Thy sacred humanity.

CHAPTER V

THE SACRED BODY OF OUR LORD

A BODY hast thou fitted to me. (Heb. 10:5.) These are the very first words of Our Lord, in coming into the world. So speaks to His Divine Father the Word made man: "O Father, a body hast Thou fitted to Me: what shall I do with it? To what uses shall I apply it?

"I will use it as a tool for the hard work of reparation that is due to Thy offended Majesty for the sins of the world, and for the building up of the edifice of My Church. I will make of it a high-pitched trumpet with which to proclaim loudly Thy Gospel of peace. I will turn it into a flag of brightest white and ruddy colors unfurled on high on the flag-pole of the cross, compelling all men to see it, soliciting all hearts to love it, *drawing all things to Myself;* a rallying sign to all men of good will. *Wheresoever the body shall be, there shall the eagles also be gathered together.* (Matt, 24:28.)

"It will also be a musical instrument melodiously sounding forth Thy praises. It will be a spotless mirror of Thy sweetness and loveliness as well as of Thy Majesty. But above all it will be, in My hands, an oblation, a victim, a victim of sacrifice, of a sacrifice that is to be without end, without interruption during time or eternity: *juge sacrificium.* (Dan. 8:11.)

O my soul, let us worship with the worship of adoration this Body of Christ, this flesh of our Jesus, this Victim which is no other than God Himself, no other than the Word made man. *"Ave, verum corpus,*—Hail, thou true human body that wast born of the Virgin Mary, that wast truly to suffer and be immolated on the cross for man's sake. I hail Thee in the womb on the day of Thy conception, I hail Thee on the straw of the stable of Bethlehem on the day of Thy nativity; I hail Thee growing and waxing strong and filled with grace and loveliness; I hail Thee on the Cross! I hail Thee in the Blessed Sacrament; I hail Thee on

15

the Altar of heaven. *O Salutaris hostia!* with worship of adoration do I worship Thee!"

Is that all I have to do?

No indeed. Let us bear in mind that we, too, are the body of Christ, the very flesh and blood of our Jesus who has incorporated us with Himself, and made us His living members, evidently with a purpose. We seem to hear Him repeating: "*A body Thou hast fitted to Me.* O Father, Thou hast fitted to Me this mystical body, the flesh and blood and souls of My faithful, and what shall I do with it? To what uses shall I apply it? I will make of this mystical body, even as of Mine own personal body of flesh, a victim, a victim of sacrifice. Only, for this I require their consent and their cooperation."

Thou shalt have it, my Lord, at least, as far as I can speak for myself, counting upon the help of Thy grace. Yes, let me be with Thee an oblation, a victim of sacrifice to be smitten with Thy divine chastisements: to be struck down and bled to death and skinned alive and pierced through and through, and cut into pieces and burned up and consumed—by the violence of illness and infirmities, by the enmities of men, by voluntary austerities; even as Thy martyrs, even as the saintly penitents, as all Thy dear saints, treading in the footsteps of the Queen of Martyrs, Thy sweet Mother, who suffered all these torments, not indeed in her own virgin flesh, but in Thine and in her own Mother's heart: and this proved a still more terrible experience. Yea, even as Thyself. With this last word, all is said: what more could be added?

But what a joy is this! What? Can I, even I, aspire to be and become in reality, thanks to my poor body of flesh, so misused and sin- stained, an oblation, a victim? Even so, if I join myself to the great victim, to Thee, my Jesus, and if I say also with Thee, taking for my own Thy very words: *Corpus aptasti mihi . . . ecce venio:* "O Father, a body hast Thou fitted to me; here I am." I know now for what purpose I have a body of flesh and to what uses I am expected to apply it: I must make of it *a living sacrifice, holy, pleasing unto God* (Heb. 12:1). This body of mine and with it the spirit that animates it, I must unite to the human Body and Soul of my Lord during all His life on earth and especially during His sorrowful Passion.

My dear Guardian Angel, does it not look as though I had the advantage of you, in this at least, that a body God has fitted to me?

CHAPTER VI

THE SACRED BLOOD OF OUR LORD

IS there any lyrical production from the pen of men that can compare with this prophetic outburst of Isaiah:

Who is this that cometh from Edom, with dyed garments from Bosra, this beautiful one in his robe, walking in the greatness of his strength?

I that speak justice and am a defender to save.

Why, then, is thy apparel red, and thy garments like theirs that tread in the wine-press?

I have trodden the wine-press alone, and of the Gentiles there is not a man with me. I have trampled on them in my indignation and have trodden them down in my wrath, and their blood is sprinkled upon my garments and I have stained all my apparel: for the day of vengeance is in my heart, the year of my redemption is come. I looked about and there was none to help: I sought and there was none to give aid; and my own arm hath saved for me and my indignation hath helped me. And I have trodden down the people in my wrath, and have made them drunk in my indignation, and have brought down their strength to the earth. (Isaiah 63:1-7.)

Looked at from the point of view of Jewish history, that is to say in its literal meaning, this page of Holy Writ is a vivid description of the intervention of God in behalf of His chosen people and of the awful destruction He was soon to make of their enemies. Such is the literal, historical meaning; but looked at from the Christian point of view, that is to say, in its symbolical sense, this passage is all about the Sacred Blood of Our Lord and the part it has played in the work of our redemption.

Blood is liquid flesh, a stream of life that courses through the veins and arteries: it is the great builder and beautifier of the human body, the great feeder of its energies, the great restorer of its constantly decaying fabric. If a man loses some of his blood through a wound he grows faint in proportion; if he loses all his blood he dies.

A decree had gone forth from the infinite justice and wisdom of God that *without effusion of blood there could be no redemption.* (Heb. 9:22.) That great truth was revealed to mankind from the very dawn of its history after the fall, and it explains the fact of bloody sacrifices in all religions: sacrifices, not only of all sorts of animals, but even sometimes of human creatures, of prisoners of war, of maidens, nay (horror of horrors!) of little children. This was a fearful mistake of the false religions, and yet it served to bring into evidence that universal belief of mankind that without effusion of blood there can be no remission of sin. The Jewish religion had many sacrifices of oxen and goats and lambs and doves, but even these had in themselves no efficacy. The blood of only one Person could serve, that of the true Lamb of God, and so He came to put an end to all former sacrifices and shed His own blood on the altar of the cross.

We ought greatly to honor the diverse bloodsheddings of our dear Savior.

Ah! He did not wait long after his birth to shed the first drops of it. Only eight days after, when he was circumcised. Let us shed tears with Mary and Joseph over the cruel tearing of the delicate flesh of the child-God. After that, for thirty-three years, we have only to admire the work of the sacred blood in the building up gradually of the body of the divine Victim.

Then come within the space of one night and one day the great sheddings of that sacred blood, in the Agony in the garden, the scourging, the crowning with thorns, the tearing open of all His wounds several times by the putting on and the taking away of His garments, by the crucifixion and finally, after His death, by the stroke of the centurion's lance.

The first of these blood-sheddings, that in the garden of Olives, ought particularly to retain our attention. The others are caused by the malice of men let loose upon the Lamb of God to inflict on him tortures which baffle imagination; but in the Agony, the blood-shedding is caused by Our Lord Himself allowing the whole weight of the sins of the world and at the same time the whole weight of the anger of his Divine Father to come upon Him and press down upon His heart and crush it as the grape under the wine-press.

Thus did Jesus pay the ransom of the world, and particularly the ransom of my soul, with all His blood. It seems He should rest satisfied with this mighty deed of His love. No, that is not enough for Him: He must give us His flesh to eat and His blood to drink in the holy sacrifice of the Mass, daily and hourly celebrated all over the world. *This is my blood, drink ye all of it.* (Matt, 26:27.) O dear Lord, we will.

I have noticed, with great joy, that many Protestants, Nonconformists as well as Anglicans, have a marked veneration for the Sacred Blood and sing hymns in its honor. With such parts of the Bible as they have preserved without interpolation, this much at least they have in common with us. Any particle of faith and love of our blessed Lord retained by them is to us a matter of sincere congratulation. But the great pity is that they only speak of the Divine Blood, they do not get it applied to their souls as we do in the seven sacraments, principally in the blessed Eucharist.

I have had the happiness of bringing some of them back to the true fold of Christ by this sole consideration. Only in the Catholic Church can they be sure that they *wash their garments in the blood of the Lamb.* (Apoc. 7:14.) Only there can they really bathe their souls in it. Only there can they drink of the chalice of the new and eternal Covenant.

Oh, Christ Jesus, dear Redeemer, eternal thanks be to Thee for being so lavish in the gift of Thy most precious blood!

CHAPTER VII

THE SACRED HEART OF OUR LORD

HOSOEVER pays loving reverence to the person of our Lord Jesus Christ, the Word made flesh, pays also loving reverence to His most Sacred Heart. It does not matter whether he realizes this or not, or actually thinks of it or not.

This consideration is very sweet and comforting. It shows that the devotion to the Sacred Heart has been at least implicitly practiced by the Church and all her children from the very beginning. Even heretics, when pious and in good faith, as is the case with a certain number of them, Practice this devotion in spite of themselves and at the very time that they are condemning it in the Catholic Church.

Conversely, whosoever honors explicitly and with special worship the Sacred Heart of Jesus, certainly honors at the same time His whole divine person, both in His Godhead and in His humanity. It is in order to give due prominence to this doctrine that the Church does not permit the representation of the Sacred Heart separately from the whole body of the divine Savior.

Our Lord wants us now to render express and explicit worship to His Sacred Heart, and has attached wonderful blessings to the practice. The better to enter into the spirit of it let us try to unravel the fundamental idea of this devotion.

Seeing that we would not understand the infinitude of His divine love in itself, that it would hardly make an impression on us, that it would even frighten us away from Him, on account of the distance there is between His infinite majesty and our littleness, and still more on account of our sinfulness, God said: I will make Myself their very own brother by flesh and blood, I will take unto Myself a man's heart with which to love them; I will love them with human love; a human love that will have behind it the whole tremendous force of My divine love. *I will draw them with the cords of Adam, with the bands of love.* (Osee. 11:4.) I, their God, will love them passionately, even to the breaking of My human heart, even unto death. Thus in all the mysteries of His incarnation and of His human life our Lord is pulling at our heart's strings, appealing to us and to each one of us as man to man, the brotherly love of His heart calling for the brotherly love of our own.

The cataract of Niagara, with its immense weight of waters pouring continually over its brink, has scooped out at its base an abyss of which it is impossible to gauge the immense depth. Infinitely more so is it with the floodgates of divine love poured out from the highest heaven of the Blessed Trinity into the human heart of our beloved Lord.

He Himself warns us in the Apocalypse to be on our guard against *the depths of Satan* (Apoc. 2:2, 4); depths of malice and perversity which, indeed, far exceed all we can imagine. But, O my Jesus, how much more immeasurable are the depths of loving tenderness of Thy Sacred Heart!

All the Scriptures of both Testaments endeavor to give us some idea of it and fail. The holy Gospels are the books that come nearest to achieve this. Next to them in this connection comes the Canticle of Canticles; but one must obtain permission of one's spiritual father before venturing to read it, and one must be sure to read it aright.

After the Scriptures and in the light of their revelation nothing can surpass the compelling virtue of the revelation of Our Lord to Saint Margaret Mary Alacoque.

That human heart of my Savior loved me as soon as it was formed by the Holy Ghost in the mystery of the Incarnation. It loved me throughout all His earthly life and in every incident of His cruel passion. It loved me at the moment of His death. It loved me ever since His glorious resurrection during the centuries that intervened till my coming into the world. It has loved me throughout all the incidents of my sinful life, hating my sin but full of compassion for me the sinner. He loves me at this moment. He loves me as though I was the only one in existence;

loves me for my own sake, not collectively with the others, but personally; not in a platonic way, but most tenderly. Oh! this love is ineffable!

Man shall come to a deep heart, and God shall be exalted, (Ps. 63:7.) The deep heart spoken of here is that of Our Lord. No sooner have we come to it than we become skilled in the praise of God, skilled in the sublimest contemplation. The poor sinner, the poor sinful woman, draw near to that heart: they have no sooner looked into it than they are seized with a sort of giddiness; they cast themselves body and soul into its abysmal depths, and instead of crushing themselves to death, they find therein life, health, joy, purity, security, confidence, love, love inexpressible.

I admire the boldness of expression of St. Paul proclaiming to his dear Corinthians the greatness of his apostolic love for them: *Our mouth is open to you, O ye Corinthians, our heart is enlarged. You are not straitened in us.* (2 Cor. 6:11-12.) As though he would lodge them all within his heart. What with the Apostle was only an eloquent figure of speech, becomes a mystical reality as far as the Sacred Heart of Jesus is concerned in regard to all the just on earth and in purgatory and all the blessed ones in paradise, as well angels as men. The heart of Jesus is for them all a dwelling place, a paradise within a paradise, a garden of delights far more pleasant than that of our first parents.

This, then, is what ought to constitute our contemplation of the Sacred Heart. We ought to be incessantly trying to realize the depths of THE HUMAN LOVE OF OUR LORD. The depth of His human love for God the Father, for the Divine Word to whom it is united in the person,[1] for the Holy Spirit who has filled it to overflowing with the fulness of His gifts. Then His human love so tender and so filial for His sweet virgin-mother Mary. Then His human love for the nine choirs of His blessed angels and all

---

[1] *Or hypostatically united.* Both expressions are really hard for the average reader as they equally stand for the whole treatise *De Incarnatione Verbi.*

the different orders of His saints already in paradise, or still in purgatory or pilgrims on earth; also for poor sinners and finally, even for me, the worst of all.

Here is, indeed, a feast for contemplative souls, enough to satiate their keenest hunger and thirst. *Eat, O friends, and drink and be inebriated, my dearly beloved.* (Cant. of Cant, 6:1.)

CHAPTER VIII

THE HUMAN SOUL OF OUR LORD

INCE Our Lord, the Son of the living God, has taken unto Himself a human soul like our own, since that human soul is the most noble that can ever be, being in itself absolutely the master-piece of creative Omnipotence and, moreover, united to the person of the Word of God and filled with the fulness of the Holy Spirit; since finally Our Lord has spoken to us of His soul: *My soul is sorrowful even unto death* (Matt, 26:38), He said to His Apostles on entering the garden of Gethsemani: I want to contemplate this most holy human soul of the Son of God and my Savior and keep my own soul constantly in touch with it.

In the contemplation of the creatures to which we are so naturally drawn, the sight of their exterior charms of body but too often prevents our penetrating to the very soul: the folds of the flesh hide from us the pure, immortal essence of the spirit that is within. The reverse of this ought to be the case in our loving contemplation of Our Lord. The mysteries of His sacred flesh are but a transparent veil, which attracts our eyes only to lead us beyond it and enable us to penetrate to that which it covers. The delicate and tender mysteries of the flesh of Jesus ought to serve to lift the mind of the Christian out of the low region of the senses and place him suddenly face to face with the most marvelous created mirror of the Godhead, the human soul of the Son of God. In this mirror, the devout Christian will come gradually, and, of course, dimly, to discover with the eyes of faith, the Word of God and with Him and through Him the whole blessed Trinity. Thus is the contemplation of the soul of Our Lord the immediate preparation for the contemplation of the pure essence of the Godhead.

The soul of Jesus, then, is that human soul which found itself at the very first moment of its existence possessed and

27

appropriated by the Divine Word, made one with Him in person, for all times and all eternity. It is the soul of that sacred body and blood which was to be the victim and ransom of the whole human race. It is the soul of the Lamb of God born of the Virgin Mary, the new Adam.

Therefore two marvelous things cling to that soul: on the one hand the second person of the Blessed Trinity whose own human soul it is, and on the other the flesh and blood of Our Lord of which it is the substantial form: hence it follows that during the pilgrim days of Jesus on earth, there were in His soul, by a beatific vision such as was never granted to the highest seraph in glory, reverberations of the infinite happiness of the Word of God, and at the same time echoes of all the labors and fatigues of His body, from His childhood to his last day, and of all the torments of His sacred flesh during His passion and death on the cross.

But there is even more, oh! much more than this. In the passion of our Savior, besides what is particularly, so to say, the passion of His sacred flesh, such as the torment of His scourging at the pillar, the crowning with thorns, the nailing and hanging on the wood of the cross, there is also what we may describe as more particularly the passion of His sacred soul, that is: His agony in the garden, the treason of Judas, the thrice-repeated denial of Peter, the ignominious comparison Pilate made of Him with the assassin Barabbas, the rejection of Him by His people, their clamoring for His blood, their horrible blindness which made them cry out: *His blood be upon us and upon our children* (Matt, 27:25); the cruel taunts and blasphemies of His enemies whilst He was in agony on the cross, the distress of His sweet Mother at the foot of the cross, the seeming dereliction of Himself by His Father at this climax of all His sufferings.

We must also understand that this passion of the soul of our beloved Lord took an amplitude and an intensity unimaginable, from the fact that the mind of Our Lord, with the divine knowledge that was communicated to it by His union in person with the Word of God, took in at a glance, but all distinctly and separately, the sins of the whole human race. Thus behind Judas the traitor, in the act of betraying Him with a kiss, the soul of Jesus saw the multitude of misers who would sell their soul and sell their God for the coveted gold, also the multitude of sacrilegious communicants stretching forth all along the centuries. Behind the cowardly denial of Peter He saw and deplored all the sins that would be committed through human respect. Behind the despair of Judas and the evil death of the bad thief, He discerned the countless multitude of those who would not be saved, in spite of His love for them and His terrible passion; and He grieved over the eternal loss of each of them as no one else could, because no one knows as well as Jesus the price of an immortal soul.

Finally it is in the soul of Our Lord that the anger of His Father against the sins of the world with which Jesus had clad himself in order to atone for them all made itself felt. And this, joined to Jesus' own loathing for all these abominations, made His sorrows reach a sort of infinitude.

At the same time as it performs all the functions of a soul towards its body of flesh and all the intellectual and volitive operations that are proper to a rational and free agent, the human soul of Our Lord discharges another office, quite unique and unprecedented, that of building up to itself a second body, a mystical body composed of all men of good will united in his love.

This wonderful capacity of the soul of Our Lord, due to its personal union with the Word of God and consequent beatific vision and omniscience, gives us an explanation of how it came to pass that the object of its contemplation was so diversified even during the life of Our Lord on earth. Even from the first moment of his conception Jesus applied his soul, first to the contemplation of the divine essence and of the life *ad intra* of the three divine persons, even as though he were already in heaven. Then He contemplated with ineffable delight the sanctity of His sweet Mother Mary and the operations of the Holy Ghost in her, as also in St. Joseph and in all those He came in contact with, such as the infant John the Baptist still in His mother's womb, and later His Apostles and disciples, the holy women who followed Him, the little children whom He caressed and blessed, the poor sinful creatures whom He converted. He was seeing in them the first elements of His Church that will be His spotless bride after the resurrection and general judgment. Who will describe to us the transports of love with which the human soul of Our Lord yearned after each one of us, knowing full well the struggles and temptations which awaited us, the occasional defeats we should experience and the final triumph with which his grace, as we firmly hope, would crown us? Even when still in His mother's womb and afterwards at every successive phase of His life, Jesus applied his human soul with its wonderful infused knowledge to the loving consideration of each one of us, calling each by His own baptismal name, and adding to it that new name which will be given us when we reach heaven.

O soul of my Savior, I love thee, I adore thee; do thou sanctify me.

CHAPTER IX

THE MIND OF JESUS

IN Our Lord there are two natures, the divine and the human; and there are also two minds, as there are also two wills, the divine and the human. The divine mind or spirit of Our Lord is none other than his Holy Spirit of love, the Holy Ghost, which in union with the Father He breathes out eternally. Now, besides this Divine Spirit of our Lord, we are obliged to acknowledge in Him the presence of another spirit or mind, which is that of His sacred humanity, emanating from His human understanding and will, and from His experiences in His human life. It is of this mind of Our Lord that St. Paul speaks to the Philippians when he exhorts them and us in these words: *Let this mind be in you which was also in Christ Jesus.* (Philip, 2:5.)

It might seem at a first glance that it should suffice to us to have the Holy Ghost; but on closer observation it will soon become evident that unless we have at the same time the spirit or mind of the sacred humanity of Our Lord, we could not get on satisfactorily in our spiritual life.

A few moments before the miraculous taking away of Elias in a fiery chariot, his disciple Eliseus addressed to him this petition: *I beseech thee that in me may be thy twofold spirit* (4 Kings 2:9), that is to say, the gift of prophecy and that of miracles. We do not ask of Our Lord for these *gratis datae* graces, but for something far more precious which He let fall as a mantle over the shoulders of His Church when He went up to heaven on the day of His glorious ascension: both His divine spirit and His human spirit.

The human spirit of Jesus is that special mentality of His, partly infused and partly acquired, of which Our Lord shows Himself to be in possession at the successive stages of His earthly life, and which perseveres in Him now in the glory of heaven and in His Blessed Sacrament.

I say that part of this mentality of Our Lord was infused in Him, whilst the rest of it was acquired by Him in the same way in which other men come by their own proper and personal mentality, namely by the accumulated experiences of their life. On coming into this world by His conception in the womb of the blessed Virgin Mary, Jesus showed Himself, at that very first moment of His earthly life, in possession of a very definite mentality, since He utters these words: *Sacrifice and oblation thou wouldst not, but a body thou hast fitted to me; then said I: Behold I come. In the head of the book it is written of me that I should do thy will) O God* (Heb. 10:5-7.) By what previous experience, by what logical sequence of ideas, by what process of deduction of His human mind, or previous deliberation of His will did Our Lord come to think and speak and will and act in His mother's bosom? By none of these antecedent processes, since He had only just then come into existence. So we are compelled to acknowledge in Our Lord, even at that moment, the possession of an infused mentality, in virtue of which He is able to think, speak and act before any experience has brought Him its contribution. We shall be less surprised to find this to have been the case with the second Adam, when we see that it was the case even with the first. Quite miraculously, without any previously acquired knowledge, but by infused wisdom, the ancestor of the human race, fresh from the creative hands of God, showed himself in possession of a language so perfect that he could call each beast, as it passed before him, by a name which expressed the characteristics of its very nature. And when Eve is brought to him after his mysterious sleep, he begins to show a prophetic knowledge of the future, saying: *This, now, is bone of my bone and flesh of my flesh. . . . Wherefore a man shall leave father and mother, and cleave to his wife.* (Gen. 2:23-24.)

On the other hand, the same St. Paul speaks also plainly of that part of the mentality of Our Lord which was acquired by Him. He says that: *Whereas, indeed, he was the Son of God, he learned obedience by the things which he suffered.* (Heb. 5:8.) Most assuredly the mentality of Our Lord, born of His own various personal experiences, had its growth, was gradually modified, was much enriched, day by day, year by year. The Gospel clearly states the fact: *Jesus advanced in wisdom and age, and grace with God and men.* (Luke 2:52.) So there cannot be the least doubt that the human mentality of Our Lord under its experimental aspect was found to be very different, of a difference of superiority and richness at the moment of His death on the cross, in comparison with what it was at the moment of His coming into the world.

Now, for the Christian to have the mind of Christ, is to appropriate to himself the human mentality of Our Lord both infused and acquired; to think, to speak, to act interiorly and exteriorly even as Christ was wont to do whilst on earth, even as He would do at this hour were He in our place. What would my Jesus think of this? What would He say under such circumstances? How would He act at this particular juncture? Usually a moment's prayerful consideration will suffice to enlighten a soul of good will upon these points; especially when, through constant perusal and meditation, one has become familiar with the text of the four Gospels.

Thus to be able to discern what Jesus would say or do, were He in our place, is assuredly a great advantage already; still, this would not be a proof as yet that the mind of Christ Jesus is in us. Something more is needed. Not only must we perceive what Jesus would do, but we must bend ourselves to do it. We must not only recall to mind what He did or said under similar circumstances, but we must make His feelings and discourses our very own; we must force ourselves to say what He would say and in the manner He would say it, with that blending of sweetness, moderation and firmness which He always exhibited.

How many Christians shall we find who have risen to such perfection and maintain themselves in it? Very few. Mystics alone do so. Others have not in themselves the mind of Christ Jesus, the human mentality of Our Lord, the grace to see and to will in perfect harmony with the divine Master. There are ever so many Christians, even of those who live habitually in the state of grace, and who therefore have in them the Holy Ghost, who yet have not at the same time the human mind of Our Lord, since they are not guided in their thoughts and speech and actions by the standard of the Gospel of Jesus, but by self-love, human respect or the maxims of the world. Does not this show that indeed we must have the twofold spirit of Jesus Christ if we wish our spiritual life to proceed satisfactorily? We receive His divine Spirit, the Holy Ghost, through the efficacy of the sacraments, and with their help we must moreover acquire by divine contemplation and by our practice of all virtues His human mentality and make it our own.

Says the author of THE IMITATION:

> "Let our great occupation be to meditate on the life of Christ.
>
> "The teaching of Christ surpasses all the teachings of the Saints, and whosoever would take it to heart would find therein a hidden manna.
>
> "It happens that many persons derive but little profit from the frequent hearing of the Gospel because they have not the spirit of Christ.
>
> "But whosoever wishes fully and feelingly to understand the words of Christ, must endeavor to make his whole life conformable to His." (Book I, c. 1.)

CHAPTER X

THE MYSTERY OF THE INCARNATION ILLUSTRATED BY A HOMELY COMPARISON

T is St. Ildephonsus, Bishop of Toledo in the seventh century, in his forty-third sermon, *In diem natalem sanctae Mariae,* who seems to be the first to have brought forward in a few words the comparison of a sunbeam passing through a pane of glass, in order to give to his hearers an inkling of the wonders of the Incarnation. The same comparison occurs now and again with further developments in subsequent ecclesiastical writers. I will give it as it now presents itself to my mind.

The sunbeam proceeds from the sun in a way which we are unable to observe, because the splendor of the sun dazzles our eyes. In like manner the generation of the divine Word in the effulgence of the Godhead, in the splendors of the ineffable sanctities of the Father, is impenetrable to us. Whence Isaiah exclaims: *Who shall declare his generation?* (Is. 53:8.)

The sunbeam is as old as the sun which produces it, for the sun is never without its own resplendence. So likewise is the Son of God in regard to His divine Father: *In the beginning was the Word, and the Word was with God, and the Word was God. The same was in the beginning with God.* (John 1:1-2.) *The Lord hath said to me: Thou art my Son, this day have I begotten thee.* (Ps. 2: 7.)

The sun pours out upon all things light and warmth, and fruitfulness and beauty by means of its rays of light. The Father in heaven pours out all His gifts upon the world through His own divine Son who is *the life* as St. John declares (John 1:4) and as He Himself proclaims: *I am the life* (John 14:16); and *the light of the world* (John 8:12); *the true light which enlighteneth every man that cometh into this world* (John 1:9)—*All things were made by him, and without him was made nothing that was made.* (John

35

1:3.)

The sun in the high heaven produces its beam of light without any deterioration of itself; indeed so far from this being the case the sunbeam is the very glory and perfection of the sun. Likewise the Son of God is one and the same God with his Father and, therefore, is no cause of loss to Him, but on the contrary He is the splendor of the Father, *the brightness of eternal light* (Wisd. 7:26); *the brightness of his glory.* (Heb. 1:3.)

Although the sunbeam extends itself through space, reaching down even to our earth, it remains united to the parent sun, never leaving it for a single instant. So also the Son of God proceeding from the Father and by Him sent upon our earth, nevertheless remains in Him, *the only begotten Son who is in the bosom of the Father.* (John 1:18.) Hence He Himself proclaims: *I and the Father are one.* (John 10:30.)

The light of the sun passes through a pane of glass without breaking it either at its entrance or at its egress. Thus Christ our Lord, the Son of the living God, entered the bosom of the blessed Virgin Mary and came forth from it without breaking the seal of her virginal integrity. *Behold a* VIRGIN *shall conceive and bear a son* (Is. 7:14). And Mary said to the Angel: *How shall this be done,* BECAUSE I KNOW NOT MAN? (Luke 1:34.) *Now the generation of Christ was in this wise: when as his mother Mary was espoused to Joseph, before they came together, she was* FOUND WITH CHILD, OF THE HOLY GHOST. (Matt, 1:18.)

The sunbeam passing through a pane of glass causes it to shine with great brightness. Thus also Jesus in regard to the ever Blessed Virgin Mary. Says St. John in the Apocalypse: *A great sign appeared in heaven, a woman clothed with the sun.* (Apoc. 12:1.)—*The Holy Ghost shall come upon thee, and the power of the most High shall overshadow thee.* (Luke 1:35.)—*Elizabeth cried with a loud voice and said: Blessed art thou among women, and blessed is the fruit of thy womb.* (Luke 1:42.)—*And it came to pass as he spoke these things, a certain woman from the crowd lifting up her voice said to him: Blessed is the womb that bore thee, and the paps that gave thee suck.* (Luke 11:27.)

The sunbeam passing through stained glass takes upon itself the coloring of the glass. The Son of God passing through the blessed Virgin Mary took unto Himself our human nature: hence He loved to call Himself emphatically *The Son of Man (passim* in the Gospels and the Apocalypse). The bride in the Canticle of Canticles exclaims: *Who shall grant me, O my brother, sucking the breast of my mother, that I may find thee without and kiss thee?* (Cant, 8:1.) *I, Jesus, am the root and stock of David, the bright and morning star. And the spirit and the bride say: Come. And he that thirsteth, let him come, and he that will, let him take the waters of life, freely.* (Apoc. 22:16-17.)

The sunbeam, before it became colored in its passage through the stained glass, was indeed a sunbeam, but was not colored; but once it has assumed its color, it remains indeed what it was till then, namely a ray of light, and it becomes at the same time a colored one. Thus before His Incarnation, the Son of God was God indeed, but not man, but since the Incarnation He is for ever at the same time both God and man. *His name shall be called Emmanuel* (Is. 7:14) *—which being interpreted is God with us.* (Matt. 1:23.)—*And the Word was made flesh and dwelt among us, and we saw his glory, the glory as it were of the only begotten of the Father, full of grace and truth.* (John 1: 14.)—*I am the first and the last, and alive and was dead, and behold I am living for ever and ever.* (Apoc. 1:17-18.)

What upholds the color in the ray of light is the sunbeam itself. In the same way in Christ what upholds His human nature is the person of the Divine Word. *Amen, amen I say to you,* BEFORE ABRAHAM WAS MADE, I AM. (John 8:58.) I AM WHO AM. (Exod. 3:14.)

The light from the sun diffuses itself all over the world, but as colored it is only in the place where it passes through the pane of glass. Similarly Christ as God is everywhere: *Whither shall I go from thy spirit? or whither shall I flee from thy face? If I ascend into heaven, thou art there; if I descend into hell, thou art present. If I take my wings early in the morning, and dwell in the uttermost parts of the sea, even there also shall thy hand lead me, and thy right hand shall hold me.* (Ps. 138:7-10.) But as man Our Lord is only in heaven and in the Blessed Sacrament. *The Lord said to my Lord: Sit thou at my right hand.* (Ps. 109:1.)—*And whilst they were at supper, Jesus took bread and blessed and broke, and gave to his disciples and said: Take ye and eat,* THIS IS MY BODY. *And taking the chalice he gave thanks, and gave to them, saying: Drink ye all of this, for* THIS IS MY BLOOD. (Matt, 26:26-28.)

The father of the sunbeam is none other than the sun itself, although the beam does not derive its color from the sun; its mother, so to say, is the pane of glass, because although it does not produce the sunbeam as such, it nevertheless produces it colored. In the same way the Son of God purely as such, is produced by the Eternal Father alone: *From the womb, before the daystar I begot thee* (Ps. 109:3), but as God made man He is produced by the blessed Virgin Mary. *And it came to pass that when they were there, her days were accomplished that she should be delivered, and she brought forth her first-born son, and wrapped him up in swaddling clothes and laid him in a manger, because there was no room for them in the inn.* (Luke 2:6-7.)

The sunbeam purely as such is older than the stained glass; as colored it is younger. So also our Lord in regard to His virgin-mother: as God he is older than her, as man and her son he is younger, as is obvious.

The ray of light, purely as such, cannot be seen in the sun whence it proceeds, because there the fierce intensity of its blaze would put out our eyes; but when it presents itself to view as colored through the stained glass, far from doing our eyes any harm, it gives them pleasure. In the same way Christ as God is absolutely invisible and ineffable to his reasonable creature on earth: *If he come to me I shall not see him, if he depart I shall not understand.* (Job 9:11.)— *Peradventure thou wilt comprehend the steps of God and wilt find out the Almighty perfectly? He is higher than heaven and what wilt thou do? He is deeper than hell and how wilt thou know?* (Job 11:7.)—WHO SHALL BE ABLE TO BEHOLD THE THUNDER OF HIS GREATNESS? (Job 26:14.) But as God made man He is exceedingly sweet to contemplate, compelling our love:

*Beautiful above the sons of men: grace is poured abroad in thy lips.
. . . With thy comeliness and thy beauty, set out, proceed
prosperously and reign. . . . Thou hast loved justice and hated
iniquity, therefore God, thy God, hath anointed thee with the oil of
gladness above thy fellows. Myrrh and stade and cassia perfume
thy garments from the ivory houses.* (Ps. 44:3-9.) The garments
from the ivory houses are none other than the immaculate flesh
Our Lord took from the bosom of the Blessed Virgin Mary.

In this connection I know of nothing more wonderful than
the fifth chapter of the Canticle of Canticles. Therein the mystic
bride sets forth, in the most direct and realistic language, the
loveliness of Our Lord on the Cross, where He makes a sort of
ostentation of his Sacred Humanity. Let me quote these
entrancing verses, giving a brief paraphrase at the same time.

In the beginning of this chapter the mystic bride, that is to
say, the soul of the fervent Christian in love with our Lord Jesus
Christ, relates some of her less pleasing spiritual experiences.
Jesus, the beloved had presented Himself to her, knocking at the
door of her heart by strong impressions of interior sweetness,
and calling for a response on her part. She made the mistake of
putting Him off for a little while under slight excuses, and He
went away, that is to say, she ceased to have these sweet feelings
of devotion. Whereupon she began to stir herself to recover
them. She went first to her spiritual director, who apparently
gave her a good scolding; then she addressed herself to someone
else in authority who made matters worse by some rough
handling of her case. At last in her distress she turned to the dear
saints in heaven and earnestly prayed to them for help in this
trouble. The saints and angels are touched with compassion at
her plight and, in order to soothe her sorrow, they make her
speak of her beloved and ask from her a description of him. Here,
now, is her answer:

My beloved is white and ruddy, white with the splendor of His
infinite sanctity, ruddy with the torrents of His blood shed in His
sacred passion. *Chosen out of thousands,* nay, out of all the
million millions of angels and men, and preferred to them all.

His head is as the finest gold. The head of Jesus, according to St. Paul, is his divine nature (1 Cor. 11:3); finest gold indeed, since there is nothing so precious as the divine essence, As for the head of His body of flesh, can anything in the whole range of creation be found finer than it, with every feature of its face illumined and resplendent with the most ardent charity? *His locks ore as branches of palm trees, black as ravens;* that is to say His divine thoughts are deep and impenetrable, therefore dark to us; every hair of His sacred head is to each of His elect a token of victory even as the palms of the martyrs and of the confessors already in heaven.

His eyes as doves upon brooks of waters, which are washed with milk and sit beside the plentiful streams. The eyes are the mirrors of the soul: therefore what ineffable purity and compassion and tenderness, and all other virtues, must the eyes of Jesus have reflected in life, and do now still more in glory.

His cheeks are as beds of aromatical spices set by the perfumers. The blood trickling down from the cruel perforations of the crown of thorns on His brow made patterns and divisions on His cheeks, and the most delicate perfumes are not to be compared with the virtue that emanated from this tracery of His sacred blood.

His lips are as lilies dropping choice myrrh. What dropped from the lips of our Lord were words of the most earnest supplication for sinners. No sooner was He raised aloft on this terrible and atrocious instrument of torture, the cross, than His first prayer was for His tormentors. *Father, forgive them,* He said, *they know not what they do.* (Luke 23:34.)

His hands are turned and as *of gold, full of hyacinths.* We cannot doubt but that the hands of our Lord were the most marvelously beautiful and perfect, and after Him those of His sweet virgin-mother. They are as gold on account of the many good deeds and miracles of mercy they have performed. They are full of hyacinths by reason of the clotted purple blood which fills the wounds of Our Lord on the cross, one single drop of which would pay the ransom of thousands of worlds even more guilty than ours.

His belly as of ivory, set with sapphires. The first *Adam and Eve were both naked and were not ashamed.* (Gen. 2:25.) How much less need the new Adam, the immaculate Lamb of God, be ashamed of His nakedness on the cross? The sapphires are the wounds made by the scourging; for His tormentors spared no part of His sacred body, so that it could be said, in the words of the prophet: *From the sole of the foot unto the top of the head, there is no soundness in him.* (Is. 1:6.) But the slightest of these wounds is more precious than all the precious stones of the world.

His legs are as pillars of marble that are set upon bases of gold. Bases of gold are the two feet of Our Blessed Lord, nailed to the cross, enduring the horrible torment of supporting upon their wounds the whole weight of His sacred body. His legs are as pillars of most rare and precious marble, since they support the body of Our Lord, which is the most perfect temple of the Divine Majesty.

His form as Libanus, excellent as the cedars, that is to say, of matchless nobility and majesty, during His whole earthly life, and particularly during His sacred passion, and now in glory.

His throat most sweet: that is to say His words and discourses are full of amenity and love. His seven words on the cross are a most admirable conclusion and compendium of all His teaching; especially these words to Mary and John: *Behold thy son, behold thy mother.* (John 19:26-27).

And he is all lovely: lovely in His Godhead, lovely in His sacred humanity; lovely in His most holy soul, lovely in His immaculate flesh and blood and sacred heart.

Indeed, therefore, must we conclude, our Emmanuel, God made man "of the most pure blood of the Virgin Mary " *ex purissimis sanguinibus* as St. Thomas expresses it, is exceedingly sweet to contemplate and compels our love. He has taken all this loveliness with His own sacred humanity, from the Blessed Virgin Mary.

Thus in the mystery of the Incarnation, Mary is the crystal

door or window of paradise, through which that sunbeam, the Divine Word, came from the bosom of the Eternal Father even unto our lowliness. To Him be love and praise and rapturous thanksgiving throughout all times and all eternity!

CHAPTER XI

THE ORTHODOX LITERATURE CONCERNING OUR LORD JESUS CHRIST

CONSIDERABLE, and under certain aspects, interesting and instructive is the unorthodox literature about Our Lord Jesus Christ. I mean all those works touching our Blessed Lord, which have strayed to a greater or lesser extent from the data of divine revelation, and in consequence have been condemned by the Church.

Beginning with the gnostic heresies and the apocryphal gospels, this literature extends through all the centuries of the Christian era to our own times, and bids fair to stretch away to the end of the world. Such works are rank poison, absolutely unfit for feeding the souls of men; that is why the Church finds herself in duty bound to forbid their reading generally. However, they have had this one good effect of forcing the Church carefully to discuss every point of the doctrine concerning Our Lord, and thereby to become conscious of the treasures of light and comfort contained in it; and finally to set this doctrine in clean-cut formulas and definitions which render final the conclusions arrived at in Ecumenical Councils as well as in the ex-cathedra decisions of the Popes. In these pages we have nothing to do with this unorthodox literature about Jesus.

As for the orthodox literature, it is obviously out of the question to point out all the good books that have been written about Our Lord Jesus Christ, during these well-nigh two thousand years. Merely to record the names of the books and of their writers would be the task of a Hercules and fill enormous folios. My aim in this chapter is much more modest. It is simply to give a list of some of the books I have read and found serviceable. I do not pretend that they are all the very best that could be found, and that those I have not entered in this list are to be considered as being of an inferior quality. No, I can only assure my readers that these are very good, fairly representative, and that any of them may be of great help. I have been obliged to keep this list within reasonable limits.

The order I follow is this: beginning with contemporary books on Our Lord, I work my way up through the centuries to the very first, where we reach at last the bedrock foundation of the four Gospels and the rest of the Scriptures.

I could not use the word "Christology" in this connection, because it is too learned a word for many of my readers, and also because the words at the head of this chapter allow of a larger scope in the choice of books to be recommended.

THE TRAMP, by A. Young, a wonderful penny pamphlet of the Catholic Truth Society, containing a study of Our Lord at the age of three, so finely thought out, and so exquisitely drawn that it makes one heartily wish the author would draw up similar studies of Our Lord at different times of His life on earth.

LE RAYON, by Reynès-Monlaur, a French book larger than the preceding one, giving an impression of what must have been the winsomeness of Our Lord during His three years of public life.

BEN-HUR.—The famous work of the American Lew Wallace, gives a striking interpretation of the data of the Gospel from the birth of Our Lord to His death, interwoven in a very dramatic story of human sorrow, love and frailty.

The above three compositions are, each in its own way, fairly representative of a very large class of works on Jesus which has developed in the last half of a century. They belong to the realm of imaginative creations and yet approach the subject of Our Lord with profound reverence and some happy effects. The works which follow are of quite a different character, as their titles will show.

Abbot Vonier: THE PERSONALITY OF CHRIST, THE CHRISTIAN MIND, THE DIVINE MOTHERHOOD.

✠A. Goodier, S.J., Archbishop of Bombay: A MORE EXCELLENT WAY. Only a small pamphlet of thirty odd pages, but worth ten times its weight in gold. Price threepence, at the Manresa Press.

Rev. P. M. Northcote: GOD MADE MAN.

THE LIFE OF JESUS by different authors such as Le Camus, Didon, Veuillot, Fouard, Sister Aimée de Jésus O.C. (this last, a really marvelous production; 3 vols.)

Father Coleridge S.J. (thirty odd volumes).

Father Meschler, S.J.: MEDITATIONS ON THE LIFE OF OUR LORD.

Abbot Marmion: CHRIST, THE LIFE OF THE SOUL, CHRIST IN HIS MYSTERIES.

Mgr. Benson: FRIENDSHIP OF JESUS.

Francis Thompson: THE HOUND OF HEAVEN, ORIENT ODE.

Mgr. Sauvé: JÉSUS INTIME.

Pope Leo XIII's ENCYCLICALS: *Annum sacrum* (May 25th, 1899), on the consecration of the human race to the Sacred Heart. *Tametsi jutura prosedentibus* (November 1st, 1900), on Jesus the Redeemer, *Mirae caritatis* (May 28th, 1902), on the Holy Eucharist.

Lacordaire: CONFERENCES of the year 1846. Duquesne: L'E VANGILE MÉDITÉ.

Cardinal Franzelin: DE VERBO INCARNATO.

J. S. Arnold: L'IMITATION DU SACRÉ COEUR DE JÉSUS.

St. Alphonsus Liguori: PRACTICE OF THE LOVE OF JESUS CHRIST, and various other most devout opuscules on Our Lord's Life and Passion and the Holy Eucharist.

Olier: CATÉCHISME CHRÉTIEN POUR LA VIE INTERIEURE.

Bossuet: SUNDAY SERMONS—ELEVATIONS ON THE MYSTERIES—MEDITATIONS ON THE GOSPELS.

Pascal: PENSÉES, LE MYSTÈRE DE JÉSUS. Marie d'Agréda: LA CITÉ DE DIEU.

CATECHISMUS CONCILII TRIDENTINI. Pars 1 art. I is. ad vii inclus.

St. Ignatius: SPIRITUAL EXERCISES, 2nd, 3rd and 4th week.

THE FOLLOWING OF CHRIST. Book 1, c. I. Book 2, cc. 6 to 12. Books 3rd and 4th in full.

St. John of the Cross: THE LIVING FLAME OF LOVE.

THE LIFE OF CHRIST, by Ludolph of Saxony.

Dante's DIVINA COMMEDIA. Part 3, cant. 14, 23 and 33.

St. Bonaventure: MEDITATIONS ON THE LIFE OF CHRIST.

St. Thomas Aquinas: Summa ad Gentiles. Liber *iv.*—Summa Theologica. Part III, quaestio xxvii-lxii.—Opusculum liv, De Humanitate Christi Domini nostri.— Catena Aurea.

Petrus Lombardus: Sententiarum Liber tertius.

Richardus a St. Victore: De Incarnatione. De Emmanuele.

St. Bernard: Sermons on the Canticle of Canticles, done into English by a monk of Mount Melleray in Ireland.

St. Anselmus Cantuariensis: Cur Deus Homo.

St. Joannes Damascenus: De duabus in Christo voluntatibus.

Ven. Beda: De meditatione Passionis Christi per 7 horas.

St. Gregorius Magnus: Expositio in Cantica Canticorum.

St. Leo Magnus: Sermones de Mysteriis Domini.

St. Augustinus: De Civitate Dei. De Sermone Christi in monte. Tractatus 124 in Joannis Evangelium. Sermones. Enarrationes in Psalmos.

St. Cyrillus Alexandrinus: Quod unus sit Christus.—Scholia de Incarnatione Unigeniti Verbi Dei.—Liber de Incarnatione.—Adversus eos qui B. Virginem Nolebant Deiparam.

St. John Chrysostom: Homilies on St. Matthew, on St. John, on the Epistles of St. Paul, Demonstration against Jews and Gentiles that Christ is God.

St. Basilius Caesariensis: Homilia in sanctam Christi generationem.

St. Ephrem: Sermones 13 De Nativitate Domini.

St. Hilarius Pictaviensis: De Filii et Patris unitate.—De essentia Patris et Filii.

St. Hyppolitus Episcopus: Demonstratio de Christo et Antichristo.

Clemens Alexandrinus: Libri 3 Paedagogi. St. Irenaeus: Detectio et eversio falsi cognominatae cognitionis.

St. Ignarius M. Ep. Antiochensis: Septem Epistolae.

Many Acta Martyrum.

Iconography of the Catacombs.

The Book of Saints, being a Dictionary of Servants of God,

etc., by the Benedictine Monks of St. Augustine's Abbey, Ramsgate. J. Huby. S.J.: CHRISTUS. MANUEL D' HISTOIRE DES RELIGIONS.

DIMMLER: DAS NEUE TESTAMENT ERKLART.

CHAPTER XII

HOW TO USE THE SCRIPTURES FOR THE AFFECTIVE CONTEMPLATION OF OUR LORD

"TO ignore the Scriptures is to ignore Christ," says St. Jerome. That is as much as saying: If you want to know Our Lord you must read the Scriptures, both Testaments, prayerfully and lovingly. *Search the Scriptures,* says Our Lord to the Jews, . . . *They give testimony of me.* (John 5:39.)

It is true that recently a blasphemous publicist, at a loss what to do to keep himself in the limelight of public notoriety, has found nothing better than to swell his voice and puff his cheeks to the point of bursting, and proclaim that the old Bible is out of date. According to him the Christian Bible can no more keep pace with the advance of humanity, and, in consequence, it is time for thoughtful men to put their heads together and proceed to make a fresh Bible in full accord with the sublimer aspirations of the world.

Now let me ask him: Who will be the historical personage around whom this new Bible will revolve? Will he come after having been predicted, prefigured, ardently called for and yearned after by all the nations of the earth as has been the case with Our Lord Jesus Christ? What message better than the two commandments of love and the eight beatitudes will he bring to the world? And will this man seal his new message with his own blood and allow himself to be crucified? And, once dead, will he raise himself from the dead? For, when all has been said, we must come back to the fundamental fact that the Bible is not, like any other book, a dead thing, but living. Our Lord Jesus Christ is not only the hero of the Bible: *He is the Bible.* His enemies know this quite well, and when they wish to suppress the Christian Bible by any means their ingenuity can devise, it is not so much the book they want to put out of the way as Our Lord Himself.

What will be the fate of such a preposterous, sacrilegious attempt?

He that dwelleth in heaven shall laugh at them, and the Lord shall deride them. (Ps. 2:4.)

Of this no more need be said.

In our search after a deeper revelation of Jesus and an increased affective knowledge of Him by means of the Scriptures, we may follow this order:

Seek Him first in the four GOSPELS OF SS. MATTHEW, MARK, LUKE AND JOHN. They give us the authentic historical Christ. There He lives under our eyes, He speaks in our hearing, He lives His magnificently simple life till the age of thirty, and suddenly bursts forth into the great prophet and miracle-worker and evident Messiah. There we see Him at last die on the cross, rise from His tomb on the third day and soon after ascend into heaven.

This is the first and fundamental and necessary presentment of Our Lord: the historical one, without which all the others would be absolutely worthless. We must insist upon this great truth, as nowadays some people are quite content to make to themselves an imaginary Christ whom they can proclaim either divine or purely human as suits their convenience, but a Christ whom no one need take seriously, a Christ that does not demand the allegiance of mind and heart, nor impose any moral obligation.

From the four historical Gospels it will be good, then, to pass to what we may call the anticipated Gospels of THE PSALMS and THE PROPHETS, particularly ISAIAH and JEREMIAS. It will do us good to see every feature of our dear historical Savior, every circumstance of His incarnation, birth, life, passion and death and after-life minutely predicted and His sweet praise sung in passionate accents, which we shall make our own, and love to repeat with all the Church.

When our spiritual education is sufficiently advanced, we shall, with due approval of those in authority over us, take up what I call the *Evangelium cordis,* that is to say, the CANTICLE OF

CANTICLES, using, as is the will of God, with heart disengaged of all earthly affections, this dramatic presentation of human love, to raise ourselves to the spiritual love that ought to unite our soul to her heavenly Bridegroom. It is to be noted, however, that one may read rightly and enjoy spiritually the Canticle of Canticles, and be still full of imperfections, whilst many souls who have never read and will never read it, realize, in their intercourse with the Beloved, all that is therein set down by the inspired writer.

Then there is THE APOCALYPSE, which we may call the Gospel of Jesus in glory. Reading it with a great spirit of faith and love, do not bother about the obscure passages of prophetic announcement of events, which it would do you no good whatever to understand clearly; but lay particular stress on those whose meaning is quite clear, such as, for instance, the first and the last chapters. They will lift you up to heaven, and perfume your soul with their unearthly fragrance.

There is also the Gospel of Jesus living in His Church on earth, and in each wayfaring soul of goodwill, as adumbrated in the ACTS OF THE APOSTLES and the CANONICAL EPISTLES.

Finally, there is what I would call the LYRICAL GOSPEL, made out of all the pages in the EPISTLES OF ST. PAUL, which refer to Our Lord. St. Paul is essentially lyrical. He cannot take up his pen in order to treat of the most obscure points of the Judaic law or of the most trivial incidents in the lives of the first Christians without being drawn far beyond his original intent and suddenly soaring to immeasurable heights. Horace warns us in his ode, *Pindarum quisquis studet aemulari* not to attempt the impossible: what shall we say, then, of the inimitable boldness of the flight of the great Apostle of the Gentiles into the realm of the supernatural? His mind is lyrical, his phrases are lyrical, his expressions are lyrical, his action is lyrical, his whole person, of so mean an outward appearance, from his own account (see 2 Cor. 10:10), is lyrical. Everything in him is vibrating, and it is the love of Jesus which makes it vibrate.

Whilst the four Evangelists are writing the epic of the life of

Our Lord in the grand and simple manner of Herodotus and Thucydides, leaving these at an infinite distance behind them, Saint Paul proceeds by springs and bounds, sudden and unexpected, which of course make it rather difficult to follow him: but whosoever takes the trouble to do so, very soon finds himself richly paid for his labor.

In the other books of the Bible it is seldom, and only casually, that any of their writers' personality transpires through their composition; here, on the contrary, it is the very personality of Paul which stamps each separate page, each sentence, one might almost say each word, with its own characteristics, and gives them their life and coloring.

In these marvelous epistles we discover two distinct revelations at one and the same time: first of all, a very special revelation of Our Lord, and then also a striking revelation of the apostolic soul of St. Paul. The two revelations cling to each other, compenetrate each other and together form a literary monument quite unique of its kind: something very human and very divine at the same time, something extremely sweet and invigorating and startlingly personal.

The Holy Ghost and Our Lord make of this man, Paul of Tarsus, this former Pharisee so dramatically converted on the road of Damascus, not only their amanuensis, or their herald sent to us with a message: they make him their message itself. Paul's life is what he preaches, and he preaches what is the very life of his life. *I live now, not I,* he is able to say, *but Christ liveth in me.* (Gal. 2:20.)

In very deed, by the hand of St. Paul, Our Lord takes the trouble of explaining Himself, to make us understand the immense import of His own divine person, His doctrine, His acts. Better even than in the historical Gospel, Jesus herein tells us to what extent He is all that matters in the eyes of God the Father; to what degree He is verily all in all things and in all persons, and how truly we are in Him, one with Him and He is in us. We might perhaps call this presentation of Our Lord in the Epistles of St. Paul, the dogmatic Christ, as distinct from the historical

Christ. It is Our Lord from life, but analyzed, dissected, to make us touch as with our fingers by how many ties we are indissolubly united to Him.

I know of no writer, ancient or modern, who has done full justice to St. Paul. As far as I am aware, no one as yet has succeeded in giving a full, connected, harmonious and lucid account of the mind of St. Paul; of his intellectual vision, of the message he has brought to the world, of the revelation of Himself that Jesus has favored him with. I suppose we must be satisfied with glimpses of this, and even so the contemplative will find his piecemeal study of Christ in St. Paul a source of infinite delights.

Before closing this chapter on the study of Our Lord in the Bible, I would give this advice. Let him who only seeks to feed his own personal piety and increase his love of Jesus Christ, avoid reading works of textual criticism, even of the orthodox kind. I know of nothing more calculated to dry up the soul. It is as a wind which has swept over the desert of Lybia and lost every particle of moisture. We had better leave critical studies of the sacred text to those who have specialized in this branch of sacred study, whose special vocation it is, and who receive from God a special charisma for the purpose, and can speak *tanquam auctoritatem habentes* on those difficult matters. We can do no better than simply accept, at least provisionally, their conclusions, when they do not clash with those of the Biblical Commission instituted by the Holy See. Thereby we shall save our time and energies for the more congenial and profitable task of the loving contemplation of Our Lord.

END OF PART I.

PART II
THE AMAZING HUMAN LIFE OF CHRIST JESUS ON EARTH

THE AMAZING LIFE

CHAPTER XIII

THE MANNER OF THIS CONTEMPLATION

THE foregoing chapters in Part I ought to have enabled us now, when meditating on the life of Our Blessed Lord, to take in the whole of Him, so to say, in any one of His mysteries; to take notice at the same time of His sacred body, His blood, His heart, His soul, of the workings of His human mind and His divine personality as the Word of the Father, true God and true Man—at whatever age of His earthly life we are actually contemplating Him. We shall see, later on, that even all this is not as yet the whole Christ, the "Christus totus" as St Augustine speaks of Him in several passages of his works; it will, nevertheless, suffice us for the present purpose of contemplating Him in the mysteries of His life on earth.

How are we to proceed in this contemplation?

Let us note first that we shall not conceive a just and true idea of Our Lord and of our necessary relation to Him, if we consider Him separately from us and look upon ourselves as isolated from Him. We are one with Him and He is one with us, in His human nature, even irrespective of the fact that we are Christians. Then, as Christians, we are one with Him as the several members of the mystical body of which He is the head, as the branches are one with the vine.

He extends His divine life into each one of us and makes him *partaker of the divine nature* (2 Pet. 1:4); a true extension of Himself; *I am the vine, you the branches* (John 15:5). Can the branch be separated from the vine? To do so would be to kill it. On the other hand to consider the vine as though it had no branches would be to do it an injustice, for the branches are part of it, they bear its fruits, besides being nourished by its sap.

From this principle it follows clearly enough that, whosoever wishes to derive from the contemplation of the life of Jesus on earth all the fruits Our Lord wants him to, must approach the subject with his whole self, body and soul, heart and mind, and not fail to bring to bear upon it all his own personal experiences of life. Nothing will bring home to him more vividly the incidents of the life of his Savior. Moreover he must in spirit make himself the contemporary and the witness of the life of Jesus, absolutely as though it were actually being enacted under his eyes: and this he must do to such an extent as even to mix in the crowd, to follow Jesus step by step, to speak to Him, and to enter into His feelings and act a part in the drama.

Thus you will really enter into the life of Jesus and cause Him to enter into your own life and become the best part of it.

One might perhaps object: Is there not a great deal of make-believe in all this process? Certainly there is: and what of that? Provided it serves the purpose of love, provided it enables you to receive in your soul a more vivid impression of the divine realities, all is well. I do not see why we should be highly approved when we apply this marvellous and dangerous power of ours to imagine things and endow them with colour and movement and life, to all profane subjects of past history, and should deny ourselves the help this power can afford us in sacred subjects: the more so that, precisely herein, we can count upon the help of the Holy Spirit if we humbly pray for it.

The Church in the sacred liturgy is constantly appealing to our senses and imagination, urging us to make a generous use of them in divine worship. The Saints, on their part, have done so to an extent which may amaze us at first, but which is quite enchanting, and we can do no better than imitate them as much as possible. Here a decided return to the candour and simplicity of little children will stand us in good stead.

As an example in point, let us borrow a page from the little book THANKSGIVING AFTER HOLY COMMUNION of Father Villefranche, 2nd edition, p. 30.

"We can also imagine scenes. Let us hear how St. Bonaventure encouraged his novices to adopt this method:

"Imagine," said the seraphic Doctor, "that you are making a visit to the Child Jesus in Egypt. . . . The Holy Child runs to meet you; He is so winning! You kneel down and kiss His feet, and then you open your arms: He will repose within them, and for a few seconds you will taste the sweetness of His embrace. Then He will speak. Perhaps you will hear Him say, ' We have received permission to return to Judea; we are leaving to-morrow. You have come exactly at the right moment; will you accompany us?' You will answer eagerly that you are delighted with His proposal; that your wish is to follow Him wherever He goes. . . . Then He will lead you to His Mother, and He will greet her lovingly and present you to her! You will bend the knee to her, and also make a reverence to St Joseph, and take your rest beside them. . . . This way of making use of Our Lord,' adds the holy Doctor, 'may appear childish, but I assure you that it is a perfect means of nourishing our piety." (MEDITATIONS ON THE LIFE OF CHRIST. XIII.)

THE STUPENDOUS EVENT

I LIKE to represent to myself the Blessed Virgin at the moment of the Angel's visit, just as she has been quasi-miraculously depicted at the house of the Ladies of the Sacred Heart in Rome. She is seated as is proper for one who is really the Queen of Angels, receiving one of her servants. Meanwhile, as this servant of Mary is at the same time to her the ambassador of the Eternal Father, he prefaces his message by an unusual and amazing salutation. At this Mary is troubled, for she has an intuition that he is carrying out anything but a celestial visit of pure courtesy, so to speak.

Then the Archangel tells her all at once that she is not mistaken, and that he is concerned with nothing less than the raising of her to the dignity of being the true Mother of God. Then see how wise and prudent she is: notice how completely she recovers her presence of mind, and how she is considering within herself her vow of virginity to God. A pious tradition assures us that Mary already knew that the Mother of the Messiah would remain a virgin, according to the well-known prophecy of Isaiah, *ecce virgo concipiet,* Behold a virgin shall conceive (Is. 7:14), and that she at the same time had made a vow of virginity in order to merit being the servant of the Virgin Mother of God. Then, since she knew this much, why her question, *"How shall this be, seeing that I know not man?"*

Quite simply, she asks to be informed (she had now the right) of that which the prophecy of Isaias passes over in silence—the ways and means of the miracle. This interests Mary in the highest degree, since it is she who is the one chosen of God to this end. Her question has not, in itself, the smallest element of doubt or hesitation as to her acceptance. If she desires enlightenment, it is that she may utter her *fiat* with full knowledge of the case, with all the greater fervor and self-surrender.

The Archangel's reply to this question of hers is indeed of a kind to inflame the heart of Mary, and to throw her wholly, body and soul, into a transport of love befitting so great a mystery. The angel replies in substance: O Mary, this is by no means a work of the flesh. For the accomplishment of this marvel, the three Divine Persons will come unto thee in such a way as they have never come to any created being. The Father and the Son will presently make to thee a new and ineffable communication of their Holy Spirit of Love, to the end that thou mayest be wholly worthy of the sacred mystery, with thy body and thy soul, both already so pure. Then the Father, overshadowing thee in the veil of His unspeakable sanctity, will impart to thee His Divine fecundity, and the Son will be born of thee.

As soon as she heard these words, the immense import of which she took in at a glance, the eyes of her soul being powerfully illumined by the Holy Spirit, Mary stood up and then threw herself on her knees. With her eyes lifted to heaven—her arms extended as though to receive and embrace the Son of God, she said *ecce ancilla Domini: Behold the handmaid of the Lord: be it done to me according to Thy word.* (Luke 1:38.) Then she crossed her hands upon her breast, bowed her head down with the profoundest reverence, and worshipped in herself, within her chaste bosom, the *Sanctum Domini,* who was born of her, and at this very moment was making the offering of His Flesh and Blood for the world's salvation.

In a moment was the great mystery accomplished.

Let us admire the power of Mary's *Fiat!* At the beginning God had said *Fiat lux! Fiant luminaria magna ... et stellae.* And before all these fiats which organized the material universe, God had pronounced a fiat which is not mentioned in the Scriptures at all—the fiat which caused the nine shining choirs of angels to leap out of nothingness—all beautiful, innocent and holy *ab origine.* But the Fiat which the Holy Spirit places on the lips of this tender young virgin, and which He causes to take effect in her interior, is incomparably more powerful, more marvelous, since its object is no longer concerned with creatures, be they never so numerous and beautiful—it is God: it is a Divine Person: it is THE WORD! *In principio erat Verbum. ... et Verbum caro factum est. In the beginning was the Word,* and in Mary *was the Word made flesh.*

How long did Mary remain in amazement at the advent of the Son of God within her, and in the transports of her worship and thanksgiving? Many hours, most assuredly. And when she humbly returned to the course of her ordinary life, St. Joseph, without suspecting the extent of the miracle, clearly saw that something unusual and magnificent had taken place between his most holy spouse and God. With the discretion of the Saints, of whom he is presumably the greatest, St. Joseph restrained himself from putting the smallest question to his gentle spouse, until she should speak of her own accord; and on her part, Mary, with the humility befitting the Queen of all the Saints, kept the secret of the King of Heaven inviolably sealed within her heart—God would know how to reveal it in His own appointed time.

Let us who know the mystery, adore it in the white cloud of the Immaculate Virgin's flesh. Let us include St. Joseph in our veneration and in our sympathy. Let us in spirit hasten over the moment when this wonderful servant of God will have passed through the dreadful ordeal which awaits him, and when he will see in the arms of the Virgin-Mother who is his spouse, the *Sanctum Domini,* the Holy One, the thrice Holy, the Word made Flesh of his virgin spouse's flesh, the Lamb of God, the Savior of the World!

CHAPTER XV

THE INFANT GOD

ET US try to fathom the notion of an infant God.

Who amongst us would consent—whatever the consideration might be—to become a little infant again, retaining all the knowledge and feelings of a man, whilst foregoing the right to manifest them?

With full consciousness of one's self, who could wish to become once more that powerless creature, without an articulate word—an infant, in swaddling clothes, nourished at the breast, dependant, without strength, carried on a woman's arm, and counting so little in the world's life and the ordinary sequence of events?

Would the small boy of five, eight or twelve years of age like to become a babe again? Only speak to him of such an idea, and you will see with what magnificent disdain he will scout such a suggestion, not because it appears to him ridiculous and impossible, but because, were it possible, he would not have it at any price. His ambition is to become a man.

And the full-grown man in the prime of life, in complete possession of all his powers, and in the rightful pride of his dominion over the world—would he now be willing to become a little new-born child?

Remember that it is not a man, but a God who has done this. The God Who, by His infinite Wisdom, Might and Goodness, has built up the universe, preserves it and conducts it to its end—this Divine Person, the Word, Who is the substantial Wisdom of God the Father, is made flesh, is made a little Infant—a babe, and before He suffers Himself to be carried in arms, to be swaddled or suckled, is concealed within the embryo of a human body, hidden within the mother's womb.

It is a great mystery of love, worthy of my whole worship.

Now let us consider the other aspect of the same mystery.

O Infant Jesus, Thou art the Word—the Word of the Eternal Father, the Divine Word, the everlasting song which the Eternal Father chants to Himself; God of God, Light of Light, Very God of Very God, whiteness of the eternal brilliance, spotless mirror of God's Majesty, image of His excellence, supreme Good, the great I AM. O Jesus, Infant Jesus, Eternal Word, my Love!

Nothing is beautiful, nothing good or lovable but Thou, O Divine Word, who hast become a little Child for love of me—and Thy Father who begot Thee in His own likeness, and Thy Holy Spirit of Love who proceeds from the Father and from Thee. None is good but Jesus the Word of God. None is good but the Holy Spirit of Jesus and of the Father. Oh, how is the man to be pitied who knows Thee not, Infant Jesus, Word of God! Even amongst those who profess the true faith, are there not many who know Thee not? These are they who offend Thee.

No; they know Thee not.

Is it possible to know Jesus, the Word of God, and not to love Him? And if one loves Him, is it possible to offend Him?

At the very instant when the Christian commits a sin—even before he performs the act of sinning, his soul has already undergone an eclipse. Either he turns aside so as not to see Thee, or he plunges in wantonness of heart into shadowy caves, or he allows a dense cloud to intervene between his soul's gaze and this most lovable object, who all the time is his soul's light, even Thee, O my Jesus, O Word of God.

My Jesus, Infant of a few hours, as the Divine Word Thou hast ho age. Age is a measure and Thou art measureless. Age marks the beginning and succession of being, but Thou art without beginning and utterly immutable as Thy Divine Father. The eternity is not a succession; it is the ETERNAL NOW, the HODIE, incomprehensible to us, in which the Father begets Thee in the splendors of infinite sanctity: EGO HODIE GENUI TE!

O Infant Jesus, Divine Word, I worship Thee in Thine infinite perfection, in Thine Eternal Generation, in Thine immutability, in Thy full and perfect possession of sanctity which Thou receivest from Thy Father, and which is Thine Essence. But why should my stammering tongue speak of such things?

My soul, let us be still and let us worship in silence.

CHAPTER XVI

THE DAY AFTER THE NATIVITY

GO in spirit to the Cave of Bethlehem; and I inquire tenderly about the Infant Jesus.

Did He sleep well? Did He wake in the night? Has He cried and wept, or rather wailed, for He is so very small? And so, sweet Mary, you have offered Him your virginal breast. He has taken milk like any other small infant, just as I did myself at that age, and He has gone to sleep again upon your gentle bosom. Now you can say: *Dilectus meus mihi, et ego illi, qui pascitur inter lilia,* (Cant, 2:16.) He is mine; He is my own true Son, and I am His happy Mother, His too highly honoured servant; wholly His, and He finds His delight and His rest between the lilies of my virginal bosom. Again you can say, O wonderful Mother: *Fasciculus myrrhae dilectus meus mihi: inter ubera mea commorabitur.* (Cant, 1:12.) My little Jesus is to me a fragrant nosegay, which bloomed delightfully. I will always carry Him upon my breast.

I have the greatest delight in praising you, most sweet Virgin Mary, but I have one mercy to ask of you, a great mercy, a very great favour. You are smiling, dear Mother; have you guessed what is in my mind? How kind of you, O Mary; yes—it is just that, you are anticipating my wishes. I should like to see your dear little Jesus asleep.

Oh! how enchanting He is in His slumber, with His sweet little eyes tightly closed, His dear little rosy mouth half open, and His breath, lightly drawn, rhythmically raising His tender breast. Sleep, gentle Jesus, sleep. I know that Thy Heart is watching. Sleep, my infant Saviour; the time will come, speedily enough, when Thou must watch and pray for me and my fellow sinners, passing whole nights in prayer, *perno dans in oratione Dei,* (Luke 6:12.) The time will come when Thou must agonize in the Garden of Olives, then be dragged at midnight through the streets of

Jerusalem to the house of Annas and Caiphas, implacable enemies of Thine—be condemned to death as a blasphemer and deceiver by the spiritual guides of Thy people, and be denied thrice before cockcrow by the chief of Thine Apostles. O dreadful night which will usher in a day more terrible still, bloody, and tragic beyond all conception! Sleep, then, gentle Jesus, sleep whilst Thou canst. During the day I will return to see Thee awake and smiling, to take Thee in my arms and cover Thee with my kisses, if Thy sweet Mother will let me.

She *will* let me! How happy I am—and see! before letting me go she embraces me. Thank you, Mother Mary. St. Joseph, too, embraces me, and putting his hand gently on my head, blesses me. Thank you, dear, kind St. Joseph. How happy I am! I seem to be treading on air. My heart is singing within me, and my steps are springing like those of a young roe.

Returning in the morning at eleven o'clock—for I could wait no longer—I find the Holy Child fully awake, with His beautiful eyes— lovelier far than all the stars of the firmament— wide open. I could not restrain myself, I uttered joyful shouts, and, like David before the Ark of the Covenant, I began to dance—for here, indeed, is one infinitely greater than the Ark, here is the God both of the Ark and the Covenant, here God reveals Himself no more as a terrible being, but as one altogether lovely. How beautiful Thou art, my little Jesus! How enchanting! Oh! I must needs embrace Thee!

And I hasten forward, though gently, trembling with happiness. Tears of tenderness fall from my eyes. Mary is quite willing that I should lift Him up; she shows me how to hold Him, she helps me; and here I am at last, with this light burden on my arm and upon my heart. Is not this sufficiently amazing? Truly, I bear Him who bears up the universe. After Holy Communion, Christian, thou earnest in thyself Him Who carries the universe.

Dare I venture to kiss Him?—to touch Him with my sinful lips? Most certainly, for I know that He has come for this very reason, to show Himself to poor sinners in a form that can cause them no alarm. Who could fear so small a child? In this form He wishes to charm their poor hardened hearts, to melt them into tenderness, to be covered with kisses by them and to be bathed in their happy tears. Behold then, what I am about to do, dear Infant Jesus, tender Savior, my dear Love, and my Child-God. I kiss and worship Thee. I kiss Thee and ask of Thee pardon for all my sins, for the transgressions of my whole life, for all the failures of love of which I have been guilty. I kiss Thee that I may regain purity by contact with Thine innocent Flesh. I kiss Thee that I may learn once more in Thy divine and infant school, the ways of purity and love.

Dear Mother Mary! How happy you are! How I congratulate you on being so pure and holy, so perfect and so worthy of Him! I rejoice that He has made you such a paradise of delights for Himself.

And you, dear St. Joseph, purer than the nine choirs of Blessed Angels, wondrous masterpiece of divine grace, created expressly to be the worthy protector of the Virgin Mother, and the worthy Foster-Father of the Infant God, how one is fain to admire you, to praise and bless you! Oh pray for me!

Before going away, I had taken up the dear Infant again and again, fairly devouring Him with my caresses. I had kissed not only His dear little face, but His tiny feet, His little hands, and His dear breast in which the heart of the Infant God was beating.

I was going to give Him back to His Mother with sighs of contentment and regret, when the idea seized my mind of giving up myself—my own self, as I had just done with the Infant Jesus—for the period of my whole life—to the kind care of Mary and Joseph.

O gentle Mother Mary! O great St. Joseph! Receive me, I humbly pray you, into your holy keeping, as the Infant Jesus Himself, whose least, unworthiest, and meanest servant I am. You know, for His own dear lips have uttered it: *Whatsoever ye shall do unto one of the least of these, ye have done it unto me.* (Matt, 25:40.) By the love which you bear to our dear Infant Jesus, take charge, I beseech you, of the rest of my poor life. Grant that as I advance in age, I may become as a little child, like the Infant

Jesus. Grant that I may copy the virtues of His divine Infancy, especially His entire abandonment, in your arms, O Mary and Joseph, to the providence of the Eternal Father. Say yes, I beg of you. Grant me this favor through Jesus, your sweet treasure, Amen.

Am I heard?—Yes—and in consequence I trouble no more to look after myself. I am the adopted son, foster-child, pupil, ward of Mary and Joseph. These are the two who are taking charge of me; they will see to it that I be in want of nothing; they will lead me in the paths of life; they will sympathize with all that concerns me. Joseph and Mary are to me, as to the Child Jesus, both Father and Mother. They assent to it. Never will I forsake their holy guardianship.

Be of good cheer, then, O my soul: we are now in good hands: take courage, let thyself go; think no more of self than does the Divine Child Jesus. Abandon thyself, as He does, in the most absolute way, to the care of divine providence, in the arms of Mary and Joseph.

O ecstatic joy! And it all comes from a visit to the crib.

CHAPTER XVII

THE PURIFICATION AS CELEBRATED BY BLESSED HENRY SUSO

AT the time of the Purification of the Virgin, in order to make himself ready to receive her devoutly in the Temple, Brother Henry would set apart the three days which preceded this feast, and he then honoured symbolically the virginity, the humility and the maternity of Mary, by burning a three-branched candle, and by reciting the 'Magnificat' thrice a day.

"On the morning of the solemnity, before the people came to Church, he would go to prostrate himself before the high altar, and there he meditated on the glories of Mary, just at the moment of her approaching to bring her dear Son into the Temple: then he raised himself up, and imagining that she had arrived at the Church door, he called all the friends of God, and together with them went to the door and on the public square to receive the Holy Mother and her Divine Babe.

"When he had met her, he begged her to be willing to stay a moment with her train, to listen to a canticle which his heart wished to sing to her in the silence of his soul, with the help of all those who loved her: then with tenderness he intoned this spiritual hymn: *Inviolata, integra et casta es, Maria, quae es effecta fulgida coeli porta; suscipe pia laudum praeconia; O benigna, quae sola inviolata permansisti,* 'Thou art pure, thou art chaste and without stain, O Mary! Thou hast become the shining portal of heaven; receive the devout tribute of our praises, O compassionate Virgin, who alone hast preserved thy purity.'

"At these last words he humbly bent his head, and besought Mary to have compassion on his heart so poor and burdened with sins; then he would arise and turning towards the altar, he followed her, holding the candle whose mystic brilliance he caused to shine, in order to ask of Mary that she would never allow the light of the Eternal Wisdom and the flame of divine love to be extinguished in his heart. He then addressed all the friends of God, engaging them to sing with him the anthem *Adorna thalamum,* etc., and to receive the Savior and His Mother with the liveliest feelings of love and praise.

"On arriving at the altar, at the moment when Mary was offering her dear Son to the aged Simeon, he begged of her, humbly prostrate on the ground, with eyes and hands towards heaven, that she would show him her Child, allow him to embrace His feet and His hands, and to entrust Him for an instant to his soul. Mary consented, and Brother Henry, trembling from head to foot with joy and love, took Jesus into his arms, pressed Him to his heart, embraced Him again and again, as though he actually possessed Him. He contemplated with delight His shining eyes, His countenance pure as milk, His lovely mouth, His little hands, His body, white as snow, His childish limbs, shining with a heavenly brightness. In his transport and ecstasy, he was wholly moved, wholly astonished to see the Creator of all things at the same time so great and so small, so beautiful and so sublime in heaven, so weak and so poor on earth!

" It was in the midst of his songs, tears and thanksgiving that he gave up the divine Child to Mary, and accompanied her to the choir, and in the ceremonies of the feast " (LIFE OF BLESSED HENRY SUSO).

The more we enter—even we, with this spirit of artless simplicity, into the contemplation of the mysteries of our Jesus, the more progress we shall make in the knowledge of Him and His love. He will reveal Himself to us without the sound of words, and He will give us so powerful an impression of His divine goodness that we shall be amazed at it; and then He will introduce us into the contemplation of the Most Holy Trinity.

CHAPTER XVIII

THE FLIGHT INTO EGYPT

ASK St. Joseph permission to go with them.

I will wait upon them.

He did not venture to take upon himself to give me this permission: the Angel had said nothing on that subject. I said to him: Consult the Blessed Virgin: you will see she will say yes. Am I not also her child? I am one with the Infant Jesus: I identify myself with Him: we cannot possibly be separated.

Through her tears and anxiety, sweet Mary smiled a smile of approval. What a joy for me! How I shall strain every nerve to give them all possible help! I am going to assume the duties of a good watch-dog, of a devoted slave, of a servant, of a child of the family, of an elder brother of the Infant Jesus. If need be, I will offer myself to death to further their flight.

The first stage was a long one—indeed quite as long as they dared make it without risking the death of the poor ass upon which Mary rode. She and Joseph maintained a strict silence. They did not wish to confide their apprehensions ro each other for fear of increasing them. St. Joseph, holding the ass by its bridle, quickened its pace, looking round from time to time to see if anyone were following them. Mary pressed her Treasure to her heart, and I could clearly see that in order to seize Him they would be obliged to kill her. I shuddered at the thought. It was possible, did they so desire, to slay both the Infant Jesus and His Mother under the very eyes of St. Joseph, who was powerless to defend them. Under our eyes! My God, what should I do if this calamity should happen? Ah! I would die with them.

It was with a mind greatly preoccupied and troubled with such fears, that we rested by the roadside for the midday meal.

We had set out in haste at midnight; we had not broken our fast; we had moved on at a great pace without stopping for an instant, and now no one seemed to be hungry. St. Joseph made a pretense of eating in order to encourage Mary. Mary did likewise in order that her holy Spouse might take something, but both of them were still far too full of anxiety. They had much the appearance of two startled birds. When in this way they had made a pretense of eating, excepting the dear Child Jesus Who had drunk His milk from the virginal cup of Mary's breast, they began their advance again with the same feverish solicitude.

Evening came, and I pointed out to St. Joseph a suitable position for encamping at the verge of a thicket. There was some dead wood for a fire, grass for the ass, a running stream, and there was shelter from the wind and from inquisitive folk on the high road. I know a thing or two. It is not for nothing that I have lived for thirteen years in a wild country, and oftentimes camped in the open air.

The question was how to lodge the travelers comfortably. Poor sweet Mary! How wearied and worn out you look! It is absolutely necessary this time that you should take nourishment, for you see, unless you do so it is not only you who will suffer, but your Divine and beloved Child as well: how could you suckle Him? Leave it to me. Here are some herbs, the properties of which I know, and I am going to make you a plentiful decoction. ... There. See! It is already made, and my Queen graciously consents to receive the draught at my hands—only she first hands it to St. Joseph, and persuades him to drink part of it. What a relief it was for me to see the dear Saint completely refreshed by this simple draught! Now it is my Mother's turn, and she, too, after having taken a good draught of it, shows by the reinvigorated appearance of her lovely face, that she has gained real relief. She has left a little at the bottom of the cup. I drain it greedily with delight. That which Mary and Joseph have left; what a favour for me to receive!

CHAPTER XIX

THE CHILDHOOD OF CHRIST

ONE YEAR OLD.

He does not speak, but He is wide awake and notices many things.

He already has His little preferences, and knows quite well how to make them known. He holds out His little arms to me—this dear, tender friend of my heart—and tells me by all His movements as clearly as words themselves can do: *Pone me ut signaculum super cor tuum, ut signaculum super brachium tuum. "Place me as a seal upon thy heart, as a seal upon thy arm"* (Cant, 8:6.) Oh! I do desire it, Holy Child Jesus! I wish to impress Thee upon my heart and my entire self—to carry Thee with me everywhere.

A mother delights in holding her dear little infant on her left arm, as she goes to and fro carrying on her work with her right hand. So did Mary with her beloved Divine Child, and so may I likewise do in my own case.

O dear Child Jesus, whilst I am reading, writing, preaching, or performing whatever act of my sacred ministry, I am in spirit holding Thee reposing on my left arm and on my heart, and Thou art looking at my poor work out of Thy dear eyes, and Thy little hands are caressing my face. Oh, how sweet it is to feel these baby hands of Thine! But, is it true—that one day they will be cruelly pierced, nailed to a wooden cross, and torn by the whole weight of Thy sacred body on the Cross? I kiss these dear little hands which are doomed to suffer so terrible a torture, all because of me, and for my sake.

O my Love, my Love, my tender Love, my little Jesus! *I wish to put Thee as a seal upon my heart, as a seal upon my arm* (Cant. 8:6), and to keep Thee there for ever.

FOUR YEARS.

At the age of four the Child Jesus was growing wholly gracious. Still small enough to be taken up and carried in arms, an action which Mary and Joseph would do with unspeakable rapture—yet big enough to walk alone, and to make much happy stir in the house and round about it.

The Child Jesus began to smile, to laugh and prattle, and to enter upon an innocent and happy life, like other dear little children of that age. I cannot imagine the Child Jesus frowning. No doubt from time to time His sweet Mother and His foster-father had suddenly come upon Him and found Him rapt in a state of prayer infinitely beyond His age: but as a rule His appearance and conduct were those of the most beautiful, perfect, natural and loving little child that ever existed.

I can imagine that men—and still more, women—would love to stop Him in the street, in front of the house, both to make Him talk and to caress Him. His little companions too, unconsciously attracted to Him, would love to embrace Him, and He would show them all the marks of the most loving friendship. All would admire Him, all would love Him, all would wish that they might in some way belong to Him, and He to them, and when they would take Him in their arms, and press Him to their hearts, they would not understand, poor, blind creatures, the secret of His irresistible attractiveness. They would not understand that they were holding the supreme, absolute, indefectible Being, the source of all good, God Himself. He never manifested His Godhead to them at all, for then they would have fled away from Him, terrified! St. Peter's utterance after the miraculous draught of fishes is indeed the utterance of all fallen humanity—suddenly brought face to face with infinite holiness: *"Depart from me, for I am a sinful man, O Lord!"* (Luke 5:8.) No: they could never have ventured further, or even desired to be more familiar with Him. But Jesus, the Infant God, the Word made Man, desires that men, His brethren, should approach Him, take Him in their arms, place Him upon their heart and be familiar with Him. The Jansenists, blinded by their human way of thinking, have never been able, any more than worldly people, to understand this, but the Saints have understood it.

The Holy Child, at four years of age, was more desirous of receiving the caresses of all people, and of bestowing His own, than any of them, especially the more affectionate, could be to kiss and embrace Him. Dear Holy Child! Didst Thou not cause some of them, more highly favored than the rest, to perceive the very secret of Thy charm?

They congratulate St. Joseph and the Blessed Virgin on having a child so affectionate, so sweet, of such ravishing beauty, and they remark upon His strong likeness to Mary. Men would believe that it was from her He had derived all His charms—whereas, on the contrary, it is from Him that she had received hers. But the greatest beauty, both of Jesus and Mary is wholly interior, and hidden from the eyes of the flesh. *Omnis gloria Filiae regis* (et Filii Reginae), *ab intus.* Oh, the innermost of the Child Jesus, where burns the flame of His Deity, at the center of a human soul whose perfection is as it were infinite! And the interior loveliness of His sweet Mother, who receives the vehement communications of His grace, without ever placing the least hindrance in the way!

Yet there were occasions when this little Prince, so gentle, gave way suddenly to a storm of tears, sobs and cries. It was when He happened to see or hear men offend His Eternal Father. He gave way then to transports of grief as though His little Heart would break. All His tender bodily frame would shake convulsively, and Mary, who understood so well the meaning of His cries and sobs, must then needs take Him in her arms, mingling her tears with His, and gradually pacify Him by her gentle words.

At these times the face of St. Joseph was also bathed in tears, and falling devoutly on his knees, He would offer to his God and foster-Child every reparation which his devotion could suggest. O Joseph and Mary, let me unite myself to you! Dear Holy Child Jesus, wounded to the heart by the sins of men, I ask Thy forgiveness. I hate these hideous sins, both mine own and those of all my fellow men. Save us from our evil ways; make us wholly like unto Thee.

THE PLAYTHING OF THE CHILD JESUS

Here are some lines of unusual charm, written by one who surely was a great mystic:

> "For some time past I had been offering myself to the Child Jesus to be His little plaything. I had told Him not to keep me as a costly toy which children must be content to look at without venturing to touch, but as it were a little ball of no value, which He could throw on the ground, kick with His foot, break, leave in a corner, or press hard to His Heart, if that should please Him. In a word, I wanted to amuse the Infant Jesus, and to give myself up to His childish humors. He heard my prayer. In Rome He pierced His little toy. ... Doubtless He wanted to see what was inside—and then, content with the discovery, He let His little ball fall to the ground, and fell asleep. And what became of the forsaken ball? Jesus dreamed that He was still playing with it, that He took hold of it, and then in turn let it fall again; that He sent it rolling away to a great distance, and finally pressed it to His heart, without letting it escape from His little hand any more." (SOEUR THÉRÈSE DE L'ENFANT JÉSUS: HISTOIRE D'UNE AME, c. 6.)

And I, I have my own ambition as well. I offer myself to the Holy Child, like an old worn-out wooden-shoe, cracked, broken, useless, which St. Joseph can tie with a string, and the little Infant Jesus can drag along, making plenty of noise, and uttering joyous shouts, as I have seen country little boys do: then leave it in the dust or mud of the road, where everyone can kick it, or pitch it far away. I shall not complain. Jesus will know quite well how to recover His old worn-out shoe, some day; He will then work a miracle of renewal upon it, and at the same time make of it a beautiful ornament for the Heavenly Jerusalem.

EIGHT YEARS OF AGE.

When he is eight years old, the small boy (I speak now of any boy) is nearly a man. He affects manly ways. He plays at being a man. His father can give him no greater pleasure than to associate him—according to his little measure —in his work. We might see, then, the little man filled with pride at carrying a tool or a piece of work, trotting along at the heels, or by the side of the full-grown man, whose calm power he admires, and whom he despairs of ever being able to equal.

Meanwhile he plays at being that which one day he desires to be—at being a priest, and he says Mass on a chair, in a paper chasuble, and, perhaps, his little sister or little girl-cousin offers the cruets and makes the responses—a grave infraction of the rubrics—but the innocent cares not a jot for that!—or at being a soldier, when he sees himself a great captain, leading his little comrades on to terrible mimic fights—or at being an explorer, who risks his life in the midst of virgin forests filled with wild beasts and savage tribes—or it may be at being a ship's captain on a long voyage,—or a merchant, and in all these different characters he performs various feats which foreshadow truly what one day he will be. "The child is father to the man," says Wordsworth, giving us to understand what the germ contains.

It was hardly otherwise with the little boy Jesus at that age. His small body, the most perfect that ever was—developed in a fine harmony of proportion, and in an expansion of vigor and pliancy of which His perfect soul was the source. His youthful spirit seemed to be opening up to a conception of life childishly serious. One could have seen Him eagerly busying Himself round about His foster-father, striving to lift heavy loads, carrying them bravely, and trying, but in vain, to handle his carpenter's tools—quite happy when at last He found Himself able to make of two pieces of wood, roughly joined together, a cross of His own height, which He laid on His shoulder and carried to the top of a hillock, in the midst of the young Egyptians, His companions. They, of course, could understand nothing at all of this, and became all at once thoughtful beyond their age, when

Jesus told them that in order to go to heaven, it was necessary henceforth that everyone should carry his own cross, and as for Himself, that He should die upon a cross when He had become a man.

Among these children, there was found one who cried out with beautiful feeling, "I will also die upon a cross; I will die with Thee, Jesus!" A child of good disposition, but spoiled by his parents, he had formed a strong affection for Our Savior. Later on he fell in with bad companions, who corrupted him, and led him into all sorts of crimes, until finally he was condemned to a disgraceful death. Did he then think of this incident of his infancy? In any case he recognized and worshiped his Savior, and merited to receive from His lips the assurance of Paradise.

No doubt it was in this way that Jesus, as a little boy, foreshadowed His future ministry and His great sacrifice.

O Jesus, eight years of age, I bow down before Thee and adore Thee! My God, my true God, my Savior and my Brother! I kiss Thy sacred feet, and rising again upon my knees— ever on my knees—I draw Thee into my arms, and strain Thee to my heart.

Dear Child, dear Child-God, grant that I may ever remain united to Thee, and that I may become wholly like Thee! Work this miracle for the glory of Thy Father, by the virtue of Thy Holy Spirit!

CHAPTER XX

JESUS AT THE AGE OF TWELVE

M Y soul, let us deeply inquire into the mystery of Jesus as a little lad, such as He appears in the incident of His three days' loss, and of His being found again in the Temple, amidst the doctors of the law, both hearing them and asking them questions.

First of all, let us admire this group of three persons:—Jesus, in all the grace of His twelve years; Mary, His Mother, so gentle and so modest; and the humble yet fervent St. Joseph—proceeding with several friends from Nazareth to Jerusalem, chanting psalms in the way, and reciting prayers with intervals of recollected silence.

Behold them at their destination! They give of their poverty to poor beggars, and to the treasury of the Temple; and Jesus amongst the crowd of worshipers passes, all unknown, through that Temple of which He is God. True, Mary and Joseph would worship Him; and I join with them.

Now the Gospel gives us the incident of His disappearance in broad outlines. It is for us to fill in the picture with such details as our devotion can suggest.

First of all, He did it on purpose; knowing quite well what He was doing, willing it both with His Divine and His human will: with full knowledge also of the great sorrow He was about to inflict upon His sweet Mother and His foster-father. For reasons worthy of His wisdom, He stole away from the watchfulness of Mary and Joseph, at the very end of the festival.

It was all the easier for Him to do this, that the devout pilgrims would be leaving Jerusalem in separate bands, first the women, then the men at a distance of half a day; whilst children were allowed to join either the one or the other, indifferently. Thus we see how it happened that Mary and Joseph, each on their part, were persuaded that Jesus was with the other, and how it happened that they could not find out their mistake until after a day's journey, when the two bands reassembled.

What happened to the Divine Boy during the three days that He was lost by Mary and Joseph? Did He spend all this time in the Temple? I do not believe it. I have an idea of my own as to the way in which He spent the remainder of the time. I feel that He most probably employed this time in making a first pilgrimage through the streets of the large city and its immediate surroundings, to all the places which were to be marked twenty-one years later by some incident of His sorrowful Passion.

This would be His first round of the Stations of the Cross. How touching at this tender age! and with what love He did it! Ah! now I understand why He was really unable to take Mary and Joseph into His confidence, and to reveal His secret to them. It would have been too terrible—the very breaking of their hearts.

I take it, too, as extremely probable that the Divine Boy's conference with the doctors of the law, to whom He put questions full of wisdom and penetration, had reference wholly to the coming Messiah, and to His sorrowful Passion.

The Child Jesus no doubt asked, first of all, from one of the doctors, who He thought the Messiah would be. The doctor straightway began to give Him a description as of a terrestrial monarch, more powerful, wealthier and more splendid than Solomon. Giving an interpretation, entirely materialistic, of the things which the prophet had spoken beforehand of the splendors of the spiritual reign of Christ, he assured his youthful questioner that the Messiah would conquer all the enemies of the Jewish people, and would exalt his nation above all the peoples of the earth.

Upon this, Jesus, very gently, and without giving any appearance of desiring to perplex the doctor, said to him: But how do you reconcile the description you have made with that which I have read of Him lately in the synagogue, in the fifty-third chapter of the prophet Isaiah?

"There is no beauty in him nor comeliness; and we have seen

him, and there was no sightliness that we should be desirous of him. He is despised and rejected of men: a man of sorrows and acquainted with grief, and we hid as it were our faces from him. Despised and the most abject of men, surely he hath borne our infirmities and carried our sorrows."

A group of doctors had formed round the two speakers, and they were looking and listening in utter amazement, at the winning gracefulness of the boy and the depth of his remarks.

Just as with the disciples at Emmaus on the evening of His resurrection, Our Lord, beginning at Moses and the Prophets, pointed out that it behooved Christ to suffer and thus to enter into His glory, so the little lad Jesus, by His questions to the doctors, caused all the marks of the Man of Sorrows, one after the other, to rise before their eyes—the Man, such as He Himself would be twenty-one years later.

Perhaps, too, probably quite naturally drawn by the sequence of ideas, may He not have traversed the ages, further back than Moses, and made inquiry as to that which the rabbis had discovered in certain prophetic types of the Messiah? First, Joseph, sold by his brethren and unjustly cast into prison, then made ruler of Egypt, and second in dignity to the King. Then Isaac, carrying the wood of his sacrifice to the mountain top and gently accepting his being offered a bloody victim to the Most High. Then Abel, hated on account of his devotion and the pleasure which God took in his offerings, and cruelly put to death by his brother Cain.

Then it was that Joseph and Mary arrived on the scene.

This very evening more than one doctor of the law returned to his home thoughtful, with a consciousness of supernatural impressions which he had never before experienced, turning over in his mind ideas which up to that time had been entirely unfamiliar to him.

By the hand of this Divine Boy the good seed had been sown in their hearts. What kind of ground was it to find there?

And as for thee, my heart, what sayest thou?

Mary's anxiety and grief had become inconceivable. She feared lest her Son might have fallen into the hands of His enemies. All the terrors of the headlong flight into Egypt came back to her, and her motherly heart showed her in imagination her beautiful Divine Child cruelly put to death, vainly calling His Mother and St. Joseph to His aid, and falling a victim to their neglect and the wickedness of men.

She knew that He was the Lamb of God who would expiate in His own blood the sins of the world. She knew that Isaac on the point of being sacrificed by Abraham was the figure of this dear Son of hers, and that Isaac was nearly at her Son's age when he climbed the mount of his sacrifice. She called to mind the prophecy of the aged Simeon, that a sword of sorrow should pierce through her soul. Ah! that terrible sword! She already felt its sharp point.

"Thy Father and I" ... Mary calls Joseph the father of Jesus as though he were so in reality, in order that the doctors and other people who heard her could perceive nothing of any mystery, and Mary carried this out quite spontaneously, simply and naturally. This proves that Jesus ordinarily gave St. Joseph the name of father, just as He recognized his authority over Himself.

But in this particular instance He illustrates and proclaims clearly His own two natures, His divine nature, that is. His Divine filiation, at the same time as His human nature. Mary is speaking of a human father, the sustainer of the human nature of Jesus Christ; Jesus replies by speaking of His divine Father, with whom He is one, and whose interests He has come to take in hand. *"Did you not know that I must be about My Father's business?"* (Luke 2:49.) As who should say: "O Mary, My sweet Mother, you are speaking of yourself and Joseph, your virginal Spouse, and of the rights of both of you over Me, but before you comes My Eternal Father, and His interests supersede those of your tenderness and solicitude for Me."

Let us notice as we proceed that Jesus at the age of twelve destroys beforehand the argument dear to Loisy and all the modernists, who would have us understand that at this time Our

Lord could not have formed any consciousness of His true self, of His superhuman mission and of the hypostatic union of His human nature with the Godhead, and that He could not have perceived these endowments but by degrees, very slowly, and, as it were, with regret.

Is it possible to display a more explicit knowledge of His own Divinity, and of the great Messianic work laid upon Him than in these forcible words: *"Did you not know that I must be about My Father's business?"* If Mary and Joseph could ignore His divine nature and mission—which was certainly not the case—the Child Jesus at least shows Himself fully conscious of them.

And besides, have we not the famous text of St. Paul in the Epistle to the Hebrews 10:5-7, quoting David's Psalm (39:8) as to this, that the Infant Jesus, in the bosom of His Mother at the first moment of His conception, speaks to His Eternal Father, accepting the entire work of our redemption, in terms He could not have rendered clearer, more all-embracing, more characteristic of thé Man-God, at the close of His life, and at the moment of His death on the cross?

Jesus, sweet child of twelve, Thou art my Teacher, I desire none other! Thou art already the Way, the Truth and the Life. Oh, I will follow, worshipping Thee always, everywhere.

CHAPTER XXI

JESUS FROM SIXTEEN TO
THIRTY YEARS OF AGE

DEAR Lord Jesus Christ, who reignest in glory at the right hand of Thine Eternal Father, and in the midst of Thy Church in the Blessed Sacrament of the Altar, suffer not my devotion to stray into false paths, as for instance, that of an almost entirely natural sentimentality. All the same it is true that Thou hast been a beautiful youth of sixteen years of age, the most lovely that has ever existed. *"Speciosus forma prae filiis hominum"* with all that is most gracious breathing from Thy lips, Thy whole countenance and Thy whole person.

This beautiful youth called Jesus is none other than Thyself, O God, O Word, O Eternal Son of the Father in heaven, "God of God, Light of Light, true God of true God," as we sing in the Nicene Creed.

O Light Divine, mayest Thou render Thyself gentle to the sick eyes of men who could never have borne all Thy brightness!

Thou, O my God, wert this Youth, gracious and strong, more refined than the loveliest of virgins, whose irresistible charms were not those of flesh and blood, but of sanctity and divinity. Gazing once again at Thy attractive form, and recollecting the intolerable splendor of Thy divine essence within the transparent veil of our flesh, taken from the bosom of the purest of virgins, I realize how much Thou hast desired to bind us to Thyself, and to draw us after Thee by the *cords of Adam,* The reason, O Lord Jesus, Divine Word made man, why I wish to contemplate Thee at this lovable age of sixteen, is in order that I may be impregnated with the sweetness of Thy attractions. I want to make with Thee a compact of special friendship, and to be inwardly inebriated with the pure joys which Thou desirest to pour forth from Thy youthful and Divine Heart into mine, which is that of a poor old sinner, who nevertheless bewails and loathes

89

his sins, and renounces them for ever.

At sixteen years of age, I can remember, I became a lover, without being conscious of the fact, without any suspicion of what was happening—a lover, that is, not of women, but of all that then seemed to me most desirable, because great, noble, generous and beautiful; a lover of poetry, eloquence, the beauty of nature, the feasts of the Church, the life of a hermit, virtue wherever I seemed able to find it—finally, and above all, of Thee, O my God—and this, too, after a human fashion, quite naturally, so it seemed to me, by a spontaneous process which did not exclude the supernatural, but which seemed to precede and accompany it, treading in its steps and playing all round it. I can assert that at that age, I had known, in a pure and virginal way, all the transports, the intoxications and the ecstasies of love. By fully recognizing in this love a gift from God, I could not help seeing in it a blossoming of my own nature, fortunately enriched by a Christian education.

But, O God, O Jesus! who shall tell us of the human love, of the ever-springing poetry, of the saintly ecstasies and the holy inebriations of Thy youthful heart? Who will show us the fruits of this garden, of ground like this—human indeed but divine as well—of this young man's heart, united to the Godhead? O the Heart of Jesus at sixteen! I wish to honor this heart aright, as it deserves and desires to be honored. Who will show me the way? You, O Mary, you alone, Mother of beautiful love and Mother of Jesus, you and your holy Spouse St. Joseph.

How did you honor this lovely youth and His Divine Heart? What did He inspire you to do, so as to please Him?

Ah! no doubt He would inspire you to imitate Him, to unite yourself to Him, to share His feelings and His joy in God which comes through the hypostatic union, a joy mingled from time to time, perhaps always, with a painful and vehement sadness because of the sins and the overwhelming misery of man His brother. All this, too, will I do, O Mary, most gentle and loving Mother. With you I shall be gladdened by the mystery of the Incarnation, and the profound joys of the heart of my young

Savior in His hypostatic union with the Deity. With you and Him I will thoroughly mortify myself for my sins and those of the whole world.

JESUS AT TWENTY.

With the exception of Mary, Joseph and the Angels, who will honor, who will worship Thee, O my dear Lord Jesus, at the age of twenty? Who amongst men is aware that Thou art their God, the God of love, the Savior? Who did offer Thee the homage and thanksgivings which were Thy due then, as they are to-day? For although up to that time Thou hadst not shed Thy blood for us, Thou wert willing to shed it: Thou wert ceaselessly mindful of it: Thou didst desire it, oh! so much more keenly than those who desire to go to a wedding banquet. I worship this longing of Thy Sacred Heart. I worship Thee, O Sacred Heart of my Jesus at twenty years of age!

Faber, fabri filius. (Matt, 13:55.) "A Carpenter, a carpenter's son," that, then, is all that men can notice of Thee at this period of Thy life—a man amongst men; a workman; son of a workman; a carpenter. They know not that Creation leaped forth from nothingness at Thy mere word—that Thy hands built the universe, that they molded the temple of our body, so noble, so worthy of being the dwelling-place of a reasonable soul, nay of God Himself—before sin had come to defile both our soul and body. But Thou didst come to retrieve for us this great loss, and Thou didst begin to retrieve it by setting before us the example of a life of humility, hidden, without honor, laborious and painful. What can I do more in order to honor Thee in Thy voluntary abasement than courageously imitate Thee, and set myself to love that which Thou hast sanctified—work by the sweat of my brow? O Jesus, Divine carpenter, I kiss with affection those hands roughened by labor. Would that it had been granted me to wipe away the sweat from Thy sacred brow! Ah! other drops than those of perspiration will soon appear beneath the cruel sharp thorns, dear Lord, dear and gentle Lord Jesus at the age of twenty years! In thirteen more years, it will come to pass. My Love! It displeases Thee not that I speak thus of Thee in anticipation, since Thou, too, dost hold Thyself unceasingly in readiness.

What, then, were the relations of Mary and Joseph with our dear Lord? Doubtless in their hearts they both would worship Him as their true God. They would have desired to do this without ceasing, at all hours, and in public, but He could not allow it. He would gently tell them, as later on He would tell John the Baptist, when he would fain have refused to baptize Him: *Suffer it to be so now, for thus it becometh us to fulfil all justice.* (Matt, 3:15)

JESUS AT THE AGE OF TWENTY-FIVE.

No doubt St. Joseph had been dead some time, and because of this, the young man Jesus, according to Jewish custom, had become the head of the little household at Nazareth.

His gentle Mother, to her unspeakable joy, ranked second after Him, and now more than ever made herself His handmaid, whilst He, the widow's son, the bread-winner, carried on St. Joseph's business. Plough-handles, ox-yokes, country wagons, homely benches and tables— these are what the hands of the Son of God would fashion. He carried these things to His customers, and held out His hand for His hard-won earnings. This money, added to that earned by the Blessed Virgin with her needle, would be divided by them into three portions: one for the Temple, another for the poor, and the third and least, for their ordinary needs.

A young man of twenty-five, if still unmarried, has already looked about him for a companion in life—one who is to be the mother of his children. Frequently neighbors, gossips, and inquisitive persons, have already named, rightly or wrongly, the object of his choice. Good marriages are made—so it is said—in Heaven. Ah! why is it that it is not always these that are realized on earth? But how comes it that with this grand and gentle young man, of refined, nay majestic aspect—there is an exception to the ordinary run of things? His behavior with regard to marriage does not happen to be made the object of the officious attention of his kinsmen and friends. As though by a secret and divine instinct, by an unspoken common agreement, all mention of marriage is excluded from what they say of the young Carpenter. In His presence, trivial chatter ceases; young maidens cast their eyes down, men and women feel uplifted, and carried into a region where there is no longer any question of sex and marriage, but where all live like the Angels of God. They perceive, too, the fitness there is in the fact that this grand and handsome young man should live quite simply with His gentle Mother, who, despite her extraordinary modesty, has the bearing of a queen. No one entertains the idea that they could ever be separated, so perfectly do they seem made for each other, Jesus for Mary and Mary for Jesus.

O my Divine Master, full of gentleness and beauty, it is now that I begin to see in Thee, in Thy very Humanity, in Thy comely, manly countenance, *the whiteness of Eternal Lights the spotless mirror of Gods Majesty, and the image of His goodness.* (Wisd. 7:26.)

I worship Thee. I worship Thee. I worship Thee.

CHAPTER XXII

THE PLACE OF ST. JOSEPH IN THE MYSTERY OF CHRIST

T is Catherine Emmerich, if I mistake not, who says that God called to Himself His faithful servant St. Joseph before the sacred passion of Our Lord, because Joseph was very tender-hearted and could not have endured to see Jesus and Mary go through such a terrible ordeal. Tradition places the event of his death even before Our Lord's entering upon His public life, somewhere between the twentieth and thirtieth year, that is to say at a moment when the mystery of the Incarnation had reached its due development and when the dawn of the mystery of the Redemption by the Cross was not so very far off.

We might call St. Joseph "the Saint of the Incarnation," because God made him its unimpeachable witness and incorruptible guardian, just as we call Gabriel " the Angel of the Incarnation " because he was made the herald of it. At the same time this warrants us to look upon him as our model in the contemplation of this part of the " mystery of Christ," for, indeed, next to our Blessed Lady, no reasonable creature on earth or in heaven, could compare with him in his loving contemplation of Our Lord.

St. Joseph is no doubt a special creation of God's omnipotent love and grace. He was made for the express purpose of bearing a most momentous and delicate part in the historical event of the Incarnation of the Son of God, namely that of shielding the Virgin-mother from all obloquy and of fathering as his own, and rearing, the divine Child. Mary belongs to him as his true wife, and he is completely caught up and enveloped in the sacred history of the humanity of Our Lord, almost up to the time of His public life. He is so near God the Father that he seems the very shadow of His supreme authority over Our Lord and His blessed

Mother. No wonder that he was prefigured by that other Joseph, the illustrious son of Jacob, in the Old Testament.

St. Joseph was a virgin among the virgins. We may well believe that there was no sting of concupiscence of the flesh in him. Not that he had been favored, as Mary, with the privilege of an immaculate conception; but the grace of the Holy Spirit had, no doubt gradually, burnt out of him all remnant of sinful nature and added to the fulness of the seven gifts a special charisma whereby he could fulfil his sublime trust with more than seraphic purity and fervor of love. This we might consider as having been the remote preparation of St. Joseph for the great work of his life.

There took place, moreover, a very mysterious immediate preparation also in the form of a passive purification, the intensity of which we cannot comprehend; I mean the trouble which came upon him when he could not but notice the evident pregnancy of his most sweet and honored bride, Mary, already living under his roof according to Jewish custom, and depending on him for her support and protection.

Their betrothal had been most holy: full of the sweetest grace and mysterious joy. Mary, of course, did not know as yet that she was to be the mother of God; she knew but one great fact, this namely, that since her tenderest infancy, she had, by the special inspiration of the holy Ghost, consecrated her virginity to God. She felt that Joseph was providentially given her to be her comforter and faithful guardian, the strong support on which she might fasten the lily of her ineffable purity. She had begun forthwith to love and honor him as her husband, and he had already experienced that a virtue, an irradiation of sanctity went out of her, and raised him above himself. She reflected in his eyes the very holiness of God: so that not the slightest cloud from the lower regions of the flesh and the senses had come to dim the luster of their immaculate nuptials.

And now conceive the amazement, the cruel pang of sorrow, the inexpressible perplexity of St. Joseph on discovering the pregnancy of Mary, and being unable to find any explanation of it but such as was dishonorable. This was a bitter, bitter discovery; and there was this added sting to it, that in his own eyes, Joseph stood convicted of having been wanting, though he could not see how, in his guardianship of the treasure God had entrusted to him.

In the CANTICLE OF CANTICLES (4:16) the heavenly Bridegroom exclaims: *Arise, O north wind, and come, O south wind: "blow through my garden and let the aromatical spices thereof flow.* The meaning is: Let spiritual joys and adversity alternately blow upon the fervent soul which is to me a garden of delights, for this is the way the perfume of her virtues can best be spread abroad. This is precisely what happened to St. Joseph. By means of the wonderful joys of his betrothal to Mary, of the Angel's message as to her divine motherhood, and of the Nativity of Jesus and alternate tribulations which came down so thick and fast upon him, his virtues and gifts were brought to their highest pitch.

I do not, for my part, suppose that the base and fierce passion of jealousy had the least part in St. Joseph's heart at this crucial moment. His love of Mary was too absolutely spiritual and unselfish for that. His grief was all for God and Mary; deploring that she should seem to have ceased to be what he had thought her, namely a true ark of the covenant built of incorruptible wood and covered inside and out with the refined gold of brightest charity, a choice vessel worthy of the most gracious favors of God. And, then, further, there was this great trouble, which pierced him to the heart; he could no longer continue to dwell with Mary, for fear of making himself, were it but in appearance, a party to the offence against God, by seeming to condone the glaring infidelity to His sacred law of marriage.

What was he to do? He must separate himself from her, and yet he could not bear to make himself her accuser: nay, when he looked at her serene, modest, prayerful deportment, he could not help being convinced that she was not guilty. But, then, what of this state of pregnancy? Truly he was baffled, and during a few days, perhaps weeks, he did not know what course to pursue. At last his mind was made up. One thing he had resolved: there should be no public disparagement of Mary; she should not be made to suffer by any act of his own. To obtain this end there was but one course to pursue, a very hard one indeed for him; to go away privately, deserting his own God-given wife, and thus taking upon himself the obloquy of having seemingly brought her to the state she was in, and of shirking the austere duty of caring for her and her offspring. He would thus call upon his own head all the dishonor, and Mary, he knew, would find at her parents' a safe refuge. She and her babe would be honorably and tenderly taken care of by the aged, saintly and wealthy couple, Joachim and Anna.

All these emotions and irresolutions of St. Joseph one can read between the lines of the sober Gospel statement: *Now the generation of Christ was in this wise: when, as his mother Mary was espoused to Joseph, before they came together she was found with child, of the Holy Ghost. Whereupon Joseph her husband, being a just man and not willing publicly to expose her, was minded to put her away privately.* (Matt, 1:17-19.)

It was then that God, well pleased with the patience and humility and charity of His servant, intervened, sending His angel to reveal to him the mystery of the Incarnation and the part he himself was called to play in it.

Beside this great trouble that we have just related, no sooner was he entrusted with the care of the *Child and its mother,* than tribulations upon tribulations began to fall upon him. He had to set out on his journey to Bethlehem with Mary in a delicate condition. There in the city of David, whose lineal descendant he was, he could not find a lodging for his wife on the point of being a mother, and had to take her out, on the countryside to an abandoned stable. Eight days after, the circumcision of the Child took place, in which He shed, with great suffering, the first drops of His sacred blood, and the compassion of Mary and Joseph for Our Infant Savior could not be expressed, the more so that perhaps they knew already something of the future mystery of our redemption. Thirty-two days later came the Presentation of the Child in the Temple and the dark forebodings of Simeon;

shortly after that and the visit of the Magi, the flight into Egypt, with all its attendant hardships, privations and positive dangers, followed by years of exile amongst a people whose very language they did not know at their coming, and whose religion and customs were abhorrent to them. The return from Egypt was made particularly painful to Mary and Joseph by the hardship it entailed upon the Child Jesus, now too big to be carried in arms and still too young to bear such a long journey which had necessarily to be made partly, if not wholly, on foot. And, then, when Jesus was twelve, there came the greatest of all tribulations: the mysterious hiding away of Our Lord during three days in Jerusalem.

Now all this must have carried to an untold height of intensity the spirit of recollection and of prayer of St. Joseph and made him the ideal contemplative. He contracted the habit of retiring into his soul, and, with deep humility and fervent love, of speaking to God the Father about Jesus and His sweet mother Mary. He would say: "O Lord, it were not too much for all the angelical hierarchies to discharge such a trust and mount guard upon this two-fold treasure; and, lo, Thou hast committed it to my littleness." The sense of his own unworthiness and incapacity had, so to say, scooped out in the depths of his soul abysses of humility into which he plunged headlong. Then God would suddenly illuminate his mind and kindle his heart to such a degree that no Cherub or Seraph could compare with him: and Joseph knew that he was made equal to his wondrous task.

It is piously believed that St. Joseph died of no ordinary illness of the flesh. The burning heat of his ever-growing love of Our Lord had secretly undermined his strength. The time came when he could no longer support the impetuous assaults of his love of God, especially when hearing from the lips of Jesus any prospective details of His sacred Passion. St. Joseph died of Love and of compassion for all that Our Lord was to suffer, and thereby deserves to be considered as more than martyr. He died in the arms and on the bosom of Our Lord, with Mary standing by and wiping the perspiration from his brow and holding his right hand and murmuring sweet words of comfort and farewell till they would meet again in glory.

O blessed death! May my own death be like it!

Then Mary and Jesus Himself fairly broke into sobs and tears at this departure of him who was so dear to them and such a part of their life. It was as though a large part of their very flesh had been ruthlessly torn away. Expressions of sympathy and regret were showered upon them by friends and neighbors; there was quite an outburst of appreciation of the dear departed one. Though St. Joseph had been a man of few words, it was plain that all who had come in contact with him had fallen under the charm of his gentleness and kindness. Mary and Jesus received gratefully these expressions of sympathy and it tempered the keenness of their sorrow.

They kept the memory of Joseph green for a long time by recalling the many incidents of their family life with him, in which his virtues had shone most conspicuously. They also allowed time to do its work, that is gradually to take away the sting of their sorrow, leaving them but the sweet perfume of a dear memory. Thus do Jesus and Mary stand as our models in all our mournings.

CHAPTER XXIII

THE PUBLIC LIFE OF OUR LORD

ASTER, I will follow thee, whithersoever thou shall go (Matt, 8:19). So said this *certain scribe* of the Gospel and so say I also. I will follow Thee lovingly. After all it is only a question of a three years' apostolate through the narrow limits of the two provinces of Judea and Galilee, and I have Thy four blessed Evangelists, Matthew, Mark, Luke and John, for my guides.

I shall follow Thee on the banks of the Jordan, in the desert, on the lake-side, through the cities and hamlets, on the mountains, in the streets and in the temple of Jerusalem; now alone, anon with Thine Apostles, then with the great multitudes. I shall eagerly receive and treasure in my heart Thy words, Thine intimate conversations with Thine Apostles, Thy grand discourses on the Kingdom of heaven. I shall witness Thy miracles of mercy to bodies and souls. I shall observe Thy meekness, Thy modesty, Thy wisdom and prudence, Thy solicitude, Thy patience, Thy love, Thy courage, Thy sovereign mastery over Thyself, over the events of Thy life, over Thine enemies, until the time came for Thee freely to deliver Thyself to them and to allow death violently to wrench Thy sacred soul from Thy poor mangled body on the cross.

How many mighty deeds hast Thou compressed within these three short years! Calling Thine Apostles and undertaking their spiritual education and laying them as the foundations of Thy Church, with Peter as the corner-stone. Preaching the Gospel of the Kingdom; revealing the mystery of the blessed Trinity; proclaiming the great law of the twofold love of God and our neighbor. By the most wonderful series of miracles establishing Thy divine nature and oneness with the Father. Meeting the devil and breaking his power. Meeting Thine enemies, worse than devils, the hypocritical Pharisees, and tearing off the mask

101

of piety with which they covered their malice and perverseness. Instituting Thy Holy Sacrifice of the Mass and Thy seven Sacraments. Giving to Thine Apostles and to their successors to the very end of time, the divine powers necessary to carry on Thy work, till Thou shouldst return in Thy majesty to judge the living and the dead and give to each according to their works. In one word, O my dear Savior! during these three short years, Thou didst establish Thy New Testament and then seal it with Thy very blood. Oh! I will follow Thee through all the incidents of these pregnant years and learn of Thee, and love Thee.

Not by bread alone doth man live, but by every word which proceedeth from the mouth of God.

In these words, O dear Lord, is found, perhaps, the very best description of the purpose of Thy public life. They imply that souls have to be fed as well as bodies, if we want them to thrive; that Thou, Son of the living God, earnest down from heaven upon earth for this very end of feeding the souls of men; that Thy holy Gospel, and around it, the whole order of religion, is a spiritual feast spread before us for our delight; and finally that we ought, in consequence, to be eager to partake of that feast, to feed upon Thy words, nay upon Thy very person, by Holy Communion and by loving contemplation. Didst thou not say: *I am the bread of life; he that cometh to me shall not hunger, and he that believeth in me shall never thirst?* (John 6:35.)—*Eat; this is my body.* (Matt, 26:26.)

One thought should dominate and pervade our contemplation of Thee, O Lord, during Thy life on earth, and more especially during Thy three years of Gospel apostolate, this namely: that by means of Thy sacrament of the Holy Eucharist thou art much nearer to us, much more with us, much more our very own, than was the case in regard to Thy contemporaries and the actual witnesses of Thy life, those who used to press around Thee, to eat with Thee, to touch Thy garments, Thy blessed hands and feet, to kiss Thy lips and receive Thy loving embrace.

By a lively faith and a fervent love, we obtain such an actual enjoyment of Thee, Beloved Lord, as was never vouchsafed to Thy contemporaries, even to the most highly favored. The Apostles themselves were admitted to holy communion but once during Thy lifetime, whilst we can participate in it every day if we like. Ought not this thought to lift up our contemplation of Thee to the highest pitch of rapturous admiration and thankfulness?

When Jesus addressed his third rebuke to the devil, in the temptation in the desert, then *the devil left him,* says the Gospel, *and behold Angels came and ministered to him* (Matt, 4:11). St. Mark puts it in these terms: *He was with beasts, and angels ministered to him* (Mark 1:13). Behold, then, the new Adam in the midst of nature, among beasts which He has created and which come to pay homage to Him. He stroked each of them gently and caressingly. He shared with them the miraculous meat the angels had brought Him from paradise, even as we throw out our crumbs of bread to the birds, and more generous mouthfuls to the dog, our companion.

Our Lord's greatest miracles were wrought, and His sublimest dogmatic and mystical doctrines preached, whilst He was at table with His Apostles and a more or less considerable number of other favored persons. Jesus made of the meals what they should ever be, occasions of the sweetest demonstrations of friendship, benevolence and love. When we sit at table is the time for relaxation and refection and saintly conviviality. There we ought to show the best side of our character. We shall surely do so if we watch Our Lord at table, and sit with Him and receive His teaching and carry it out in our actions. Then, again, we should invite Him to sit with us at our own meals and teach us with what dispositions we ought to partake of them; with what modesty, moderation, purity of intention, Christian cheerfulness, charity to our neighbor, and spirit of thankfulness to God; taking also occasion of what we eat, to raise our minds to the contemplation of the heavenly table, where we shall sit with Abraham, Isaac and Jacob, the Apostles and all the Saints.

The bill of fare of St. John the Baptist in his desert was not a very full or *recherché* one: *Locusts and wild honey* (Matt, 3:4), nothing more, and no doubt he refreshed himself with water from the nearest spring or running brook. There is a marked contrast in this regard between Our Lord and His holy precursor. Jesus never refused the invitations of his fellow-men to eat with them. Whether they were friends as Lazarus, or enemies as Simon the Pharisee, made no difference. *The Son of man came eating and drinking* (Matt, 11:19) He said of Himself.

With some even He invited Himself, as was the case with Zachaeus when He also ate with a number of publicans and poor sinners to the grievous scandal of the haughty hypocritical Pharisees. O my brother, who readest these lines perhaps only in a spirit of curiosity, Jesus is passing by and inviting Hmself to dine with you: happy you, if you come down from your lofty critical attitude and entertain Him cheerfully. Much in the same way and again with most happy results did Jesus, in a way, throw Himself upon the hospitality of the poor Samaritan woman at Jacob's well. Jesus, perhaps, would do the same with you if only you listened to His pleading. He the guest, and you the host! And for the drink of cold water which is all you can afford, He will give you the waters of heavenly consolation, *springing up even unto eternal life.* (John 4:14.) Could you refuse to play the host to so generous a guest? Alas! it is only too true that many do so. Forgive them, O Lord, *they surely know not what they do,* and how great a loss they inflict on their own souls.

Jesus worked His first miracle, at the prayer of his sweet Mother Mary, during the marriagefeast of Cana. He changed water into wine, turning the impending sadness and confusion of His host into joy, and at the same time giving us the first inkling of the mystery of the holy Mass, where bread was to be changed into His body and wine into His blood. A little later on, after He had fed His Apostles and the multitudes with the bread and meat of His marvellous doctrine and had cured all their sick and infirm, He performed the first multiplication of loaves and fishes, and satiated a crowd of more than five thousand persons. He had only five loaves and a few fishes when He blessed them and began to distribute them by the hands of His apostles, but after they had all eaten their fill there remained twelve baskets full of the fragments. Here we have an image and prophecy of the multiplication of His own sacred body in the Holy Eucharist by the hands of His priests, every day, all over the world, and of the Reservation of the Blessed Sacrament.

Our Lord, in the act of performing His miracles, demands of us the tribute of our loving admiration and adoration, as they are wondrous proofs of His omnipotence and of His divine nature. Here there could be ho question of our imitating Him, except in the feelings of tender compassion and love which prompted Him to help all those whom He saw suffering, either in body or in mind. But that to which we ought to apply ourselves most in the contemplation of His miracles is to discover for our own edification their symbolical, spiritual meaning.

We can proceed in this search by means of familiar conversations with our Lord, asking Him whatever questions occur to us upon this subject, and humbly hearkening to His replies, which He will make in the form of some devout impression on our mind or heart or even sensibility: for it is by means of just such impressions that God speaks to us in mystical intercourse, and not by any articulate words, as some erroneously imagine. Whenever real articulate words are pronounced in the hearing of the mystic, then we are out of the common ways of Christian life and in the sphere of the miraculous, or possibly of some counterfeit of the miraculous. Of this it is not my intention to speak here.

Some most touching, most significant incidents took place at several of the banquets where Jesus was invited. How deep in the heart of the whole Christian world has sunk the story of that poor sinful woman who did not hesitate to break in upon the assembled guests at Simon the Leper's house, throw herself upon the blessed feet of the Savior and bathe them with her tears, dry them with her disheveled hair, kiss them and anoint them with perfume! The scorn of the scandalized Pharisee for such a sinner was sharply reprimanded by Our Lord, who also absolved her from her sins and made a saint of her then and there.

When the Apostles bad brought to our Lord some food which they had bought in the city of Sichar, whilst He was busy instructing the woman at the well, Jesus told them: *I have meat to eat which you know not. . . . My meat is to do the will of him that sent me, that I may perfect his work.* (John 4:33-34.)

He never speaks of that other food of His soul, the beatific vision which He enjoyed from the moment of His conception in the womb, all through His life and even at the moments of His bitterest agony during His sacred passion. It seems as though doing the will of His heavenly Father in regard to our salvation was even dearer to Him than the enjoyment of the beatific vision; so strong and great was His love for His brethren whom He had come to rescue from sin and hell.

He spoke of His passion beforehand, and looked forward to it, and longed for it and went forth to meet it as though He were going to a banquet. Not a banquet, O my Jesus, but a very orgy of horrible sufferings will it be. To us also He answers: *My meat is to do the will of him that sent me, that I may perform his work.* And to His Apostles, speaking beforehand of the Last Supper which was to usher in His agony in the Garden and all that followed, He said: *With desire have I desired to eat this Pasch with you before I suffer.* (Luke 22:15.) And then it was that He instituted the two sacraments of Holy Eucharist and Holy Order, and the Holy Sacrifice of the Mass; the three pillars upon which rests securely the whole fabric of His Church.

CHAPTER XXIV

THE SACRED PASSION

*B**EHOLD** the lamb of God, behold him who taketh away* MY *sin.* (John 1:39.)

The true contemplative, instinctively, or rather by an interior motion of the Holy Spirit, always gives to his consideration of the Sacred Passion a distinctly personal turn, applying it all to himself, and bringing to bear upon it his own mind and heart and sensitiveness.

I am a priest. The other day a person came to me with a silver coin which he gave me saying: "Please, Father, will you say a Mass for my intention?" The next day he piously assisted at the Mass. It was his own Mass, all his own, celebrated for him. Now in spirit I walk up to my Lord, as he is just coming out of the room of the Last Supper: I press in His hands not a silver coin, but, ah me! a thing of baser metal, my own sinful heart, and I ask: "Please, dear Lord, wilt Thou celebrate Thy sacred Passion for my benefit? I will assist at it because I know it is mine, all mine own, and I will apply it to the ills of my soul."

There are three acts in the great drama, thus:

1. The terrible beginning, or the three hours' agony in the garden.

2. The terrible progress from the betrayal of Judas to the nailing of Jesus on the cross. Twelve hours: from midnight of Maundy Thursday to midday of Good Friday.

3. The terrible climax, that is to say, the three hours' agony on the cross.

My sins have struck at Almighty God, and the insane blow has recoiled upon me and shattered my being. The mortal offence to the majesty and sanctity of God is atoned for by the sacrifice of the Lamb; and in His blood and in His wounds I find a remedy for my ills.

Take notice, O my soul, that in this grand liturgical function all the incidents of the sacred Passion which go before the crucifixion are so many preliminary ceremonies and as the putting on of the sacerdotal vestments. Only, in the case of Our Lord, instead of His putting on any vestments, it is the reverse which takes place. For this grand liturgical act of His own oblation on the altar of the Cross, our High Priest must put off or rather allow violently to be torn away from Him His own vestments. He must present Himself to His Heavenly Father with no other ornaments than the white alb of His virginal flesh, the purple mantle of His own blood profusely shed all over His sacred person, and the tiara of His crown of thorns. At the supreme moment, one of the bystanders, moved with pity at the confusion of His absolute nakedness, girded His loins with a cloth. Such an alms, at such a moment, will be richly rewarded on the Day of Judgment, when Jesus will say: *I was naked and you covered me.* (Matt, 25:36.)

Now think of the horrible tortures. After all the ill-treatment He has endured during the twelve preceding hours, hear the sinister rattle of these instruments: the enormous nails, the hammer, the pincers. Hear the repeated blows of the hammer, the stifled groans of the victim, the answering cry of anguish of his tenderhearted Mother, Mary, and the jeers of the executioners and the Pharisees. My Lord, was all this barbarous display of wanton cruelty necessary? Thou answeredst: Yes. And I have only to hang my head in deepest confusion and sorrow.

Because my hands have been employed in doing evil actions, the innocent hands of my Savior must be nailed to the cross. My feet have run in the ways of iniquity, therefore must His sacred feet be nailed also. My head I have held erect in proud and rebellious attitude, therefore must His be bowed in pain and shame unspeakable. My whole body has *served unto iniquity,* therefore must the whole sacred flesh of my Savior be torn to shreds by the cruel scourging and then all His wounds be opened again and again by the putting on and taking off of His sacred garments two or three times repeated: so that, at last, as He hung on the Cross, the whole surface of His body looked like that of a man flayed alive.

In very deed is Jesus my victim, my very own victim, of whom I have been, by my sins, the executioner, whom I have cruelly tormented and at last done to death. Ah! my Lord, I DID NOT KNOW WHAT I WAS DOING. (Luke 23:34.) Forgive me and ask our Heavenly Father to forgive me!

I had a friend—a priest—who could not speak of the Sacred Passion or hear about it or think of it (and he did so very often) without being quite overpowered and moved to tears, and who had the gift of communicating his emotion to others. I asked him how he had come by this gift. At first he showed some reluctance to give away his secret, but as I pressed him and implored him, he could see that it was through no idle curiosity, and so he finally yielded. He told me that what had developed in him such a sense of the Sacred Passion, was his having made a two-fold study of it in this wise. He had made out two distinct tables, so to say. The first contained an enumeration of all the incidents of the Sacred Passion in their historical sequence, and opposite to each of these he entered the mention of those sins of his which he thought had most contributed to torment Our Lord on this peculiar occasion. Then in a second table he followed the inverse process, that is to say, he made an enumeration of all his grievous offences against God, from early childhood even up to the time of writing, and he entered opposite to each of these, the peculiar suffering of Our Lord that he thought was the atonement and remedy for them.

I asked him whether the second table was not merely a repetition of the first, so that any one of the two would have served his purpose? He said "Not at all." The first table showed him what pains he had inflicted upon Our Lord and therefore how deeply contrite, and compassionate he ought to be to Him, whilst the second served the purpose of showing him what sovereign remedy he could apply to his sins and therefore how grateful he ought to show himself to the dear Lamb of God. "In the first table," said he, "I have a greater regard to the drama of the Sacred Passion; in the second to the drama of my own wicked life. In both I do find an inexhaustible fountain of tears and contrition."

He went on to say that we must not shrink from facing with Our Lord the horrible and frightful realism of His Sacred Passion. We lose the sense of it too much, through being used to its literature, where it is more or less idealized and enveloped in pious conventional phrases. In truth it was all a display of the most brutal realism. Step by step, from the first stage of His agony in the garden, we wade through a flood of horrors, until at last the climax is reached on the Cross, when all is summed up in this cry of utter desolation: *My God, my God, why hast thou forsaken me?* (Matt. 27:46.).

"Some half-hearted, weak-kneed Christians," he continued, "deprecate our making the sorrowful Passion too hideous and heart-rending a performance as they say. Do they think it was an academical function? Truly the redeemed of Jesus Christ show themselves far too dainty and fastidious. The passion, as it was enacted by the enemies and executioners of Our Lord, was the most atrocious performance that could ever take place against any man; and when we consider that this man was the Son of the living God, the delicate Lamb of God, the marvelous son of the Virgin, the most perfect of men, endowed with the most sensitive organism that could be conceived, there is no limit to the extent to which we may stretch the measure of His sufferings. And these Christians grudge Him their sympathy!"

My friend had to stop at these last words for his feelings of indignation fairly choked him.

I know also a religious who has made it a labor of love to collect all the texts, in either Testament, bearing upon the Passion of Our Lord, and then arrange them in due order, following the sequence of events as it can be made out of the four Gospels.

Thereby he has gained a wonderful impression of the length and width and depth, so to say, of this mystery. Particularly out of the Psalms of David, and out of Isaiah, and the Canticle of Canticles and St. Paul's Epistles, did he gather views of the greatness and winsomeness of Our crucified Lord, which constantly fill him with inexpressible wonder and joy as well as compunction.

He told me that just as the saints of the Old Testament were types or figures of the Divine Victim which was one day to be slain, so also, we of the New Testament, have to be faithful copies of the same Divine Victim. Thus Our Lord bearing His Cross and then nailed on it, is preceded and followed by an immense multitude of loving souls that form around him a guard of honor; such a multitude as stretches out from the beginning of the world even to the end. Whosoever is not with Christ crucified is against Him, so that the history of the world is well summed up in the two cities of the CITY OF GOD of St. Augustine and in the meditation of THE TWO FLAGS of St. Ignatius Loyola.

He told me that at the gate of this new paradise of delights, which is the sacred body of Christ crucified, there are *cherubim and a flaming sword turning every way* (Gen. 3:24), to pierce through and through the loving souls that draw near; a two-edged flaming sword, wounding them, filling them at the same time with inexpressible sorrow and delight, the while they are contemplating now the head of their Lord crowned with thorns, then His dear feet, then His hands, then His side wide open, so that there is an easy access even to His heart all aflame with love.

Upon these words of the Canticle: *My beloved is white and ruddy* (Cant, 5:20), he commented thus: "He is white, oh! so white, so pallid, so very white, on the cross, from having lost nearly all his blood. And he is ruddy from the same cause. There is blood on Him everywhere. On the crown of His head, in His matted locks, all over His face; His beard is soaked with it. Blood on His neck, on His sacred shoulders, all over His chest and back; streams of blood along His thighs and legs. Blood trickling from the middle of His nailed hands, two fountains of it beneath and over His nailed feet.

"My beloved white and ruddy, in His sacrifice of holy Mass which is celebrated in memory of His Sacred Passion: white under the species of bread, ruddy under those of wine. White and ruddy on His throne of glory in heaven: white in His immaculate flesh which He took from the Virgin Mary, ruddy in the splendor of His divine nature which He has from the Father; white in the ineffable sanctity which He has acquired by the exercise of all virtues during His life and still more during His Sacred Passion, for in His passion Our Lord offers to us the most magnificent exercise of all the gifts of the Holy Spirit, particularly the gift of fortitude; ruddy with the glory with which His Father has rewarded Him. *Ought not Christ to have suffered these things and so to enter into his glory?* (Luke 24:26.)

"It seems to me that when Our Blessed Lord entered into paradise on Ascension day, He must have thus addressed the Father: *'Lord, thou didst deliver to me five talents* (Matt. 25:15), that is to say this human heart of Mine wherewith to love Thee and My brethren, all men; these hands with which to serve Thee and them, these feet with which to run in the ways of Thy commandments: *Behold I have gained other five over and above* (Matt. 25:20), namely, these five wounds of Mine, which will endure for ever as a monument of My love and obedience to Thee, Father, and which will incessantly plead to Thee for My brethren.' Here I dare to break in upon my Lord's discourse and say: And behold, sweet Savior, Thou hast gained other five, over and above, namely, my heart which henceforth will be wholly Thine, and these hands and feet of mine which will be employed only to do Thy will." Thus far my friend the religious.

This chapter, already somewhat long, must not close without our singing a paean of joy and victory.

Behold, God is my Savior: I will deal confidently and will not fear. The Lord Jesus *is my strength, and my praise, and he is become my salvation.* (Is. 12:2.)

I have a shield; it is Jesus crucified. I place it before my eyes, between myself and created things, and then their most inflamed and poisonous arrows fall powerless at my feet.

I have a remedy for all my wounds. It is my Jesus crucified. If I have received a petty insult—a slight offence against my self-love— slight but appearing terrible to me, I have only to place on this wound my dear Jesus crucified, and everything at once seems to me to be full of joy and health.

Alas! I receive other wounds; I commit sin. I inflict this evil on my poor soul! The remedy is the same Jesus crucified.

He is my oracle. In all doubts I consult Him, and He gives me a clear Answer. There can be no more hesitation after that! I ask myself how, with such an oracle at hand, a Christian can be unable instantly to find the solution to his greatest difficulties.

He is my best book of meditation. When all others fail me or weary me, this one is always wide open, and causes my soul to be sensible of an appeal so warm that it is impossible for her to feel tired.

He interprets Holy Scripture to me: for this purpose nothing else better or indeed half so good as my Jesus crucified. He throws the clearest light into all the recesses of the Old Testament, and makes for me, not only of Isaiah, but of each of the other sacred Books, a real anticipation of the Gospel.

It is possible at the same time to clothe oneself in Jesus crucified: *Put ye on the Lord Jesus Christ.* (Rom. 13:14.) This is accomplished by covering ourselves with His merits and adorning ourselves with His virtues.

We are nourished with Jesus crucified. *My flesh is meat indeed, and My blood is drink indeed.* (John 6:56.)

Every day my sweetest and dearest occupation, my chief daily action—that which fills my life with glory—is to make, by means of my Mass (or my communion), a solemn commemoration of the sorrowful Passion. *This do in commemoration of me.* (Luke 22:19.) *For as often as you shall eat this bread and drink this chalice you show the death of the Lord until he come.* (1 Cor. 11:26.) I am glad to notice that the devotion to my Lord Jesus crucified and that to his Holy Eucharist are not two different devotions, but one and the same. For what, in reality, is the most Holy Eucharist, but the victim of Calvary, Jesus immolated, Jesus crucified?

The Altar is now the place where we may find Him with His five wounds, which He will keep eternally; but instead of blood they will henceforth shed torrents of grace and rays of glory.

In an ecstasy of joy and gratitude let us repeat with the *thousands and thousands round about his throne in heaven:* THE LAMB THAT WAS SLAIN IS WORTHY TO RECEIVE POWER AND DIVINITY AND WISDOM AND STRENGTH AND HONOR AND GLORY AND BENEDICTION. (Apoc. 5:12.)

CHAPTER XXV

THE SHARE OF THE BLESSED VIRGIN MARY IN THE SACRED PASSION

ER share as being benefitted by the Sacred Passion of her Divine Son, is—I say it with reverence and tenderest love—the lion's share. She is, herself alone, more benefitted by it than all the rest of the redeemed of Jesus Christ. She was redeemed even before the fall by the foreseen merits of her Divine Son, and therefore she was preserved free from the stain and guilt of original sin. And as this privilege was granted her in view of her dignity of future Mother of Christ, she was at the same time and through the same merits, invested with such a sanctity as is second only to that of God Himself. So says the bull of Pius IX in the solemn definition of the dogma of the Immaculate Conception.

The Blessed Virgin Mary had also the lion's share of actual and personal experience in the fellowship with Christ suffering and dying: such a share as no created being, not even herself, could ever have borne without a direct, miraculous intervention of the power of God to sustain her life through it all.

It is God the Father who delivered His own Divine Son to death, and such a death. *He scared not even His own Son, but delivered Him up for us.* (Rom. 8:32.) Now God the Father could not experience any compassion towards Him in His bitter sufferings; because it is impossible for sorrow or pain of any kind to enter into the pure Godhead; but, in order not to fail in this duty of compassion (I am speaking in a human way, of course) God the Father delegated the Blessed Virgin Mary to suffer and be compassionate in His stead. See what a sublime function Mary is discharging!

It therefore fell to the Blessed Virgin, jointly with the heavenly Father, to deliver to death her Son, the Man Christ Jesus, so much dearer to her than her own self. She had, first of all, to give her consent in advance to the Sacred Passion and terrible death of Him who was her life, her all in all. She had to renounce the natural right possessed by every mother of shielding her Son and snatching Him if possible from death; she had to waive even the right of pleading and expostulating for Him with the Father. She had to deliver Him up into the hands of divine justice, to the rigor of its vengeance; to thus deliver Him, not by an act of mere acquiescence, but by a positive giving up, as active and effective and personal as the *Fiat* of the Incarnation. Never has any other mother had to deliver her own son to death in such a way. A father, the only one in the course of all the centuries, Abraham, was ordered by Almighty God to offer his own son in sacrifice; but hardly had he raised his hand on the intended victim when the angel of the Lord intervened. It was a father, not a mother; not such a mother as Mary, not the mother of such a son as Jesus. The Blessed Virgin knew full well that in her case no angel would intervene to stay the hands of the executioners: nevertheless she gave Him up.

Having thus delivered to death Him who was her very life, she does not hesitate to deliver herself together with Him: she opens wide the gates of her soul for the great flood of sorrow of the Sacred Passion to penetrate into her, or rather to overwhelm her in an ocean of bitterness. O *Virgin, daughter of Sion, great as the sea is thy grief.* (Jer. Lament, 2:13.)

> *Sancta Mater, istud agas*
> *Crucifixi fige plagas*
> *Cordi meo validé.* (STABAT MATER.)

> "Rich queen, lend some relief;
> To a heart who by sad right of sin
> Could prove the whole sum (too sure) due to him.
> By all those stings
> Of Love, sweet-bitter things,
> Which these torn hands transcribed on thy true heart;
> O teach mine, too, the art

To study Him so, till we mix
Wounds, and become one crucifix."
(CRASHAW. *Sancta Maria Dolorum.*)

Who plunged in the heart of Mary those seven swords? Alas, I did it, when by my sins I caused the passion and death of her Divine Son. My pride, covetousness, lust, jealousy, gluttony, anger and sloth have been so many swords. They killed the Son and tortured the Mother who was not allowed to die, but was made to suffer beyond all that can be imagined.

O Mary, my Mother: I am sorry!

PART III

MIGHTY SEQUELS TO THE EARTHLY LIFE AND DEATH OF OUR LORD

MIGHTY SEQUELS

CHAPTER XXVI

THE LINK AND THE TRANSITION

BY his wonderful life and sacred passion and death on the Cross, Our Lord laid up an absolutely infinite treasure of merits. Out of this inexhaustible fund there accrued first, to His Sacred Humanity the glory of His Resurrection, of His Ascension, of His Enthronement at the right hand of the Father in heaven, and of His sending down the Holy Ghost upon the beginnings of His Church on the day of Pentecost. Then followed an efflorescence of Him, if we may so speak, into a marvelous multiplicity of presence and life and activities.

Whereas, till then, He had been present, by the bodily presence of His Sacred Humanity in only one spot at a time, namely where He happened to be seen; He is now, in that same Humanity of His, present, living and acting in a multitude of places at the same time. He is on the throne of His glory in heaven, and simultaneously here on earth in millions of places and billions of consecrated particles and fragments of consecrated particles—of His full human and bodily (though non-spacial) presence—wherever the holy sacrifice of the Mass is being offered up, or the consecrated Host kept in the Tabernacle.

Moreover, Jesus is spiritually present and living and acting in His mystical body, the Church of the faithful, wherever found, on earth, in Purgatory and in Heaven; as the head is present and united to its body, infusing life into all its members, giving unity to all its parts and presiding over all their several and varied activities. Particularly is He thus present in His Church on earth, for He said: *Behold I am with you all days to the consummation of the world* (Matt, 28:20), and in each of His living members on earth; and He is actively engaged in the work of making them fruitful unto eternal life; for He said: *I am the vine, you the* branches. *He that abideth in me and I in him, the same beareth much fruit.* (John 15:5.)

All this wonderful multiplicity, and exuberance and efflorescence of presence and life and supernatural activities are rendered possible only by the fact that Jesus is a divine Person; and it is the direct, immediate outcome of the infinite merits of His earthly life, and especially of His Sacred Person and death on the Cross.

We have in both Testaments several prophetic references to this wonderful new phase of the mystery of Our Lord, as well as indications of its strict connection with and dependence on His previous human life and death whilst He was on earth.

Isaiah said: *If he shall lay down his life for sin, he shall see a long-lived seed. . . . Because his soul has laboured, he shall see and be filled. . . . Therefore will I distribute to him very many, and he shall divide the spoils of the strong, because he hath delivered his soul unto death.* (Is. 53:10-12.)

Our Lord Himself said, speaking of His impending passion and of its bearing upon the vocation of the Gentiles: *Amen, amen, I say to you, unless the grain of wheat falling into the ground, die, itself remaineth alone, but if it die, it bringeth forth much fruit,* (John 12:24-25.)

St. Paul says of the Saviour: *Being consummated, he became to all that obey him, the cause of eternal salvation,* (Heb. 5:9.) And again, speaking of God, he says: *Of him are you, in Christ Jesus, who, of God, is made unto us wisdom, and justice, and sanctification and redemption,* (1 Cor. 1:30.)

Isaias again, in his enumeration of the titles that will fit the Messias, says: *A child is born to us and a son is given to us, and the government is upon his shoulders: and his name shall be called Wonderful, Counselor, God the Mighty, the Father of the world to come, the Prince of peace,* (Is. 9:6.)

We now proceed to contemplate Our Lord in this new phase of His life. We shall see Him actively engaged in building up to Himself a mystical body, and bringing forth a new generation all His own, the Christian people, gathered from all the nations of the earth. *The government* is indeed *upon His shoulder* and He is a wise and loving *Counselor* to each of those who belong to Him; and He is emphatically *the Father of the world to come,* since by all His activities He is preparing and bringing about the last stage of the world's history.

This fresh and intensely beautiful unfolding of the mystery of Jesus, runs from the day of Pentecost even till after the end of the present world and the Last Judgement. Only then will our Blessed Lord inaugurate the new era, final for all eternity.

CHAPTER XXVII

THE RESURRECTION OF CHRIST

WITH mere men, however great, or good, or gifted they may have been, death puts an end to all their activities here below. They have finished their task or left it unfinished, as the case may be, but they surely cannot add one more stroke to it For weal or for woe, this is taken quite out of their hands. Not so with Our Lord.

It is quite true that for Him as for every one of us, there was a close to His earthly life. He Himself informs us of this. Before He gave sight to the man born blind, He remarked to His Apostles: *I must work the works of him that sent me, whilst it is day: the night cometh when no man can work* (John 9:4), not even the Son of man. And on the cross, before giving up the ghost He proclaimed: *All is consummated.* (John 19:30.)

So He will never again grow weary, as a pilgrim on earth: and He will suffer no more pain, either in His sacred flesh or in His human soul. He is now entered into His glorified state. *Ought not Christ to have suffered these things, and so to enter into his glory?* (Luke 24:26.) Thus He inquired of the two disciples of Emmaus. But now it remains for Him to reap the reward of His earthly life and death in this glorified state of His, and to unfold the immense benefits accruing from the fulness of merits of this same life and death, to those whom He deigns to call His brethren: *I ascend to my Father and to your Father, to my God and to your God.* (John 20:17.)

Apparently no human eye witnessed the actual event of the resurrection of Our Lord. It is left for our own imaginative faculty to represent to us the actual coming out of the Savior of the world from His sealed sepulcher without removing the huge stone that stopped its entrance. The inspired historians give us not a single word about it. It seems to have been too august an event, as also the visit Our Lord paid first of all to His sweet

125

Mother, the Virgin Mary, for any human writer to attempt to narrate.

Fortunately, the Evangelists are, we may almost say, profuse as well as irrefragable, in their setting forth of the evidence of this mighty event which St. Paul considers as the key-stone of the whole structure of our belief. The chief witness produced is the glorious Christ Himself: appearing, disappearing, entering the room while its doors remain closed; speaking to His friends with His wonted affectionateness and winsomeness, eating with them, offering Himself to be touched, to be handled by them, reproaching the slow to be convinced for their heaviness of heart; bestowing upon them tremendous spiritual powers.

The holy women, and among them conspicuously Mary Magdalen, these are the next witnesses. Then the Apostles. Then the very soldiers who had been set to mount guard over the sepulcher, and had been paid by the princes of the priests and the Pharisees to try to mislead public opinion about the event: finally these worthies themselves, who paid the hush-money, so convinced were they of the truth of the resurrection.

Truly, never did any historical event come in the light of day with more glaring, incontrovertible evidence, for the edification and consolation of all men of good will. But this wonderful four-fold narrative must be read in the Gospel itself if we do not want to lose the aroma of simplicity, candour, human interest and divine condescension which exhales from it.

With Jesus Christ risen from the dead, the mystery of our salvation enters into a new phase.

This great mystery went on developing ever since the angel's Annunciation to Mary, or rather since Mary's Immaculate Conception, or better still, since the promise of Redemption to our first parents; or quite finally, ever since the counsel of the three Divine Persons from the eternal ages, where all was foreseen, fixed, decreed for our creation and our redemption.

Majestically at first, slowly to our thinking, God unfolded His grand design of the world's salvation by His Son Jesus Christ; but towards the end events moved almost precipitately.

Within thirty-three brief years the Son of God was bestowed upon Mary, was made flesh in her chaste bosom, was withdrawn from that white cloud, shown to the world, given to the world. He dwelt among us, one of us, *full of grace and truth* (John 1:14), *conversing with men* (Bar. 3:38), *asking them questions and giving them replies* (Luke 2:46), but most frequently during the first thirty years, instructing us chiefly by His silence, by His humble work and by His obedience to Mary and Joseph. Then in the last three years He shone forth with such an intensity of light by His discourses, miracles and virtues, that all souls of good will in Israel recognized Him, hailed and adored Him as the true Son of God, whilst those with *sore eyes* hated and cursed His light, and desired to quench it wholly and for ever in the blood and mire, in the ignominies and fierce sufferings of His Passion. They could not see that, in thus ministering to their own hatred, they were ministering also to His Love; they could not perceive that in immolating this spotless Lamb they were accomplishing the great sacrifice and all the prophecies, and that they themselves with their own sacrilegious hands were turning over the page in the book of God's great work—they were turning it over to the page of the Resurrection.

But a few days after comes His glorious Ascension. And after ten more days comes the descent of the Holy Ghost upon the Apostles. We may then say that the first volume of God's great works is closed. Another begins from that time, at the descent of the Holy Ghost upon the Apostles: the volume of the life of the Church, or of the life of Jesus Christ in the Church Militant—a volume continuing its story until the end of the world, the Resurrection of the Dead, and the General Judgement. *Christus heri et hodie, ipse et in saecula. Heri, yesterday,* was as far as Pentecost; *hodie, today,* is as far as the end of the world, and they are nothing more than the preliminaries, the preface, so to speak, of the great Poem of the Kingdom of Jesus Christ risen, and finally triumphant in His mystical body, *world without end, in saecula.*

His Resurrection on the third day after His death upon the

cross is the pledge of the supreme triumph yet to come.

Let me read again in the Gospels the account of the Resurrection of my dear Savior, and His various apparitions on this and the following day. On every page of the Gospel narratives, what a honey-comb for the soul, after the milk of Our Lord's preaching, and the generous wine of His dolorous Passion! How we should feed and feast on all this part of the Gospel revelation, and never grow weary of it. *Eat, O friends, and drink, and be inebriated, my dearly beloved.* (Cant, 5:1.)

I rise, then, on the great morning—even I—the third day after the Passion, and humbly— without inquiring whether I am worthy or not—I accompany the holy women who are going to the sepulcher.

They speak only of Him—but with what eloquence, with what flames of love! Ah! He is not dead in those hearts! There, at least, He will live until their last throb.

They follow the way of sorrows without stopping, hastening on, as much as their burden and the nature of the unequal and hilly ground allow them, and they call to mind each detail of His sorrowful progress. Here He fell; there He met His Mother; further on He spoke to themselves, yet a little further, He fell a second and a third time...

Walking up to Calvary, they notice the three crosses, which stood out boldly against the blue of the sky, illumined by the first rays of the rising sun.

They question one another as to how to enter the sepulcher, and how to roll away the great rock, round as a mill-stone, which blocked the entrance.

Here let us leave the account to the sacred historian, or rather to the Holy Spirit. Let us listen in silence, and from the depth of our hearts and with our whole being let us worship.

Let us worship the risen Christ: Let us worship the very prints of His footsteps: *vestigia pedum suorum.* (Is. 60:14.)

OUR LORD'S ASCENSION

T seems likely that Our risen Lord, as the time for His ascension drew near, had the sweet humility to pray for the glory which had been prepared for Him: *Father, the hour is come; glorify Thy Son.* (John 17:1)

The most gentle heart of Mary, notwithstanding the pain of the impending separation, made an echo to this beautiful prayer. She herself also repeated it: "Father, the hour is come; glorify Thy Son, and mine; give to this dear and adorable Son the glory He has so well deserved."

It is thus that these two united in a melody which enchanted the angels and the eternal Father. And we cannot but think also that from the height of heaven, from His sublime throne, the eternal Father replied: *I have already glorified thee,* My dear Son, *and I will glorify thee again.* (John 12:28.) Before Thine Incarnation Thou didst enjoy in My paternal bosom, all My glory, and now that Thou hast assumed human nature, and art bringing it into heaven, it is My will that it should be there invested with the fulness of My divine glory.

The whole of the celestial court kept silence in order to hearken to this wonderful divine concert.

I myself, O my dear heavenly Father, Father of my Lord Jesus Christ, God of everlasting glory—I, too, *dust and ashes as I am,* prostrate, engulfed in my own nothingness, before the throne of Thine infinite majesty, I venture to join my unworthy voice to those of Jesus and Mary, and to entreat Thee for the same end: *Father, the hour is come; glorify Thy divine Son.*

I transport myself in spirit to that time, and I desire and I beg and pray for the Ascension of Our Lord, and all the glory that is to follow it.

The Ascension is the feast of the human body and soul of Jesus, glorified, uplifted, borne onwards and enthroned *where he was before* (John 6:63)—*at the right hand of his Father* (Ps. 109:1) in glory and *set over all the works of his hands.* (Ps. 8:7.)

This statement is soon made, but there was some ceremonial used in the celebration of so great an event, as we may gather from various prophetic passages of Holy Scriptures which refer to it. We can do no better, if we want to have our share of this great joy, than try somehow to reconstitute Our Lord's wonderful progress in his ascent from earth to heaven.

Hardly had Jesus disappeared behind the cloud which hid Him from the eyes of His Apostles, than He put on the crown of gold and precious stones, the flowing robes of purple, that is to say the resplendence of divine sweetness and sanctity and majesty which are His by right, but which mortals on earth could not have borne to gaze upon.

There He is met by the glorious phalanx of the saints He has set free from Limbo, conspicuous among whom are Adam, Abel, Noe, Abraham, Isaac, Moses, David, the Prophets, St. Joseph, St. John the Baptist, the Holy Innocents, and the Good Thief. Oh! how joyously they greet Him and adore Him. Then they fall into ranks, forming a glorious procession, singing the while as they go through space after Him, through the world of stars, getting nearer and nearer to the heavenly Jerusalem.

What do they sing? Of course the praises of their Lord and Captain; in such strains as these: *Thou, O Christ, art beautiful among the sons of men; grace is poured abroad on thy lips: Therefore hath God blessed thee forever.*

Gird thy sword upon thy thigh, thou most mighty. With thy comeliness and thy beauty set out, proceed prosperously and reign. Because of truth, and meekness and justice, thy right hand shall conduct thee wonderfully.

Thy throne, O God, is for ever and ever. The scepter of thy Kingdom is a sceptre of uprightness.

Thou hast loved justice and hated iniquity, therefore hath God, thy God, anointed thee with the oil of gladness above thy fellows.

Myrrh and stacte and cassia perfume thy garments, from the ivory houses. (Ps. 44:3-9.)

So they sing, now in alternate choirs, now in most marvelous Gregorian unison, then again in a most wonderful polyphony. So they sing until for the first time, they catch a glimpse of the City of Light, looming up in the distance, with its high battlements of rubies and topazes, of sapphires and sardonyx, crowded and crowned with innumerable hosts of shining angels, and are awed into silence at the sight. Then, strains of angelic music float down to them, mellowed by the distance, but growing in melodious intensity as they wing their flight still nearer and nearer.

There they are at last, before those marvelous gates of heaven which have been, since the sin of the first Adam, divinely closed, barred and bolted, against the whole human race.

And now takes place on the part of the angels that ceremonious challenge to their King, referred to in Psalm 23 (24). In a burst of holy impatience, the company of saints escorting Our Lord cry out with one voice: *Lift up your gates, O you princes, and be ye lifted up, O eternal gates, and the King of glory shall enter in.*

All the Angels from inside ask with one voice:
Who is the King of glory? The reply is given:
The Lord who is strong and mighty, the Lord mighty in battle. Lift up your gates, ye princes and be ye lifted up, O eternal gates, and the King of glory shall enter in.
Who is this King of glory?
The Lord of hosts, he is the King of glory.

As soon as Jesus, with divine majesty and sweetness, merely touches the wonderful gates, they fly open, revolving on their eternal hinges with a melodious sound, and forthwith the nine choirs of the blessed angels swarm out of heaven, to meet their King and give Him His first welcome.

Then with shouts of joy angels and saints mingle for a few moments in delightful confusion, embracing each other and congratulating each other upon the great event of the reopening of the gates of heaven. Oh, what throngs will pass through them afterwards, as centuries succeed centuries in the Christian era!

But now all those happy children of God form their ranks and tread their way through the golden, resonant streets of the heavenly Jerusalem, and lead our Jesus, their King, up to the foot of the refulgent mountain of the Holy Trinity. They stop there, even as the Israelites in the desert, at the foot of Sinai; but unlike the servile Israelites, not in abject fear, not hiding their faces in the dust, but with faces upturned in an ecstacy of loving adoration, repeating again and again with increasing enthusiasm:

Oh! clap your hands, all ye nations; shout unto God with joy . . . God is ascended with jubilee, and the Lord with the sound of the trumpets. Sing praises to our God, sing ye; sing praises to our King, sing ye. Sing ye wisely: God sitteth on his holy throne. (Ps. 46.)

There is a pause, and then a duet: King David and one of the mighty Cherubim lift up their voices, singing this verse: *This is God, our God unto eternity and for ever and ever; he shall rule us for evermore.* (Ps. 47:15.)

Then a schola of Seraphim, true birds of Paradise, with sweetest voices trill: *Thou hast loved justice and hated iniquity, therefore hath God thy God, anointed thee with the oil of gladness.* (Ps. 64:8.) After which the whole congregation of these happy blessed children of God break forth into this sublime canticle:

The God of gods, the Lord hath spoken, and he hath called the earth . . . God shall come manifestly; our God shall come and not keep silence, A fire shall burn before him, He shall call heaven from above, and the earthy to judge his people.

Gather ye together his saints to him, who set his covenant before sacrifice, and the heavens shall declare his justice: for God is judge,

Again a pause and a silence more impressive than the first and then, from his high throne of glory, in a sweet and mighty voice as of many thunders, at which the very gates of heaven are thrilled and tremble, Jesus lets fall these words:

Hear, O my people and I will speak: O Israel I will testify to thee; I AM GOD, THY GOD.

But this heavenly liturgy is really too grand for us to tell of.

Dear Lord and Savior, mayest thou give us such foretaste of it as we can bear! May we, as little dogs under their master's table, gather some of the crumbs that fall from the feast spread out before Thy blessed ones who are Thy servants and our elder brothers!

CHAPTER XXIX

CHRIST IN GLORY

W E are not left to our own devices to represent to ourselves the life of Our Lord in glory. It is in some way described and celebrated in many prophetical utterances of the Old Testament, particularly in Psalms 2 and 9—then, profusely, in St. Paul's epistles—and finally most magnificently in the Apocalypse.

We are thus given a vivid description of the ineffable glory with which God the Father is rewarding the labors and sufferings Our Lord endured in his Sacred Humanity whilst on earth; of the wonderful praise and homage Jesus is constantly receiving from all the blessed angels and the saints already in paradise; of His taking in hand the government of the whole world and judging in particular judgement the souls of men as they go out of the present life and come to His tribunal in their hundreds of thousands; of His loving care for both the militant and suffering Churches; and of His soon bringing about the consummation of all things.

The fervent Christian cannot wish for anything better than these inspired pages to help him in the loving contemplation of his Lord in glory. We here subjoin them without any comment of our own. The Holy Spirit, if you but listen to Him in the secret of your heart, will comment them for you.

PSALM 2.

Why have the Gentiles raged, and the 'people devised vain things? The Kings of the earth stood up, and the princes met together, against the Lord and against his Christ (saying): Let us break their bonds asunder, and let us cast away their yoke from us.

He that dwelleth in heaven shall laugh at them, and the Lord shall deride them. Then shall he speak to them in his anger, and trouble them in his rage.

But I AM APPOINTED KING BY HIM *over Sion, his holy mountain, preaching his commandment. The Lord hath said to me: Thou art my Son, this day have I begotten thee. Ask of me, and I will give thee the Gentiles for thy inheritance, and the utmost parts of the earth for thy possession. Thou shalt rule them with a rod of iron, and shalt break them in pieces like a potter's vessel.*

PSALM 109.

The Lord said to my Lord: Sit thou at my right hand, until I make thy enemies thy footstool. The Lord will send forth the sceptre of thy power out of Sion: rule thou in the midst of thy enemies.

With thee is the principality in the day of thy strength. In the brightness of the saints, from the womb, before the day-star I begot thee. The Lord hath sworn, and he will not repent: Thou art a priest for ever according to the order of Melchisedech.

The Lord at thy right hand hath broken Kings in the day of his wrath. He shall judge among nations; he shall crush the heads in the land of many, He shall drink of the torrent in the way, therefore shall he lift up the head.

ACTS OF THE APOSTLES.

But he (Stephen) *being full of the Holy Ghost, looking up steadfastly to heaven, saw the glory of God, and Jesus standing on the right hand of God. And he said: Behold I see the heavens opened, and the Son of man standing on the right hand of God.* (Acts 7:55.)

SAINT PAUL.

(Heb. 1:1-3.) *God, who, at sundry times and in divers manners, spoke in times past to the fathers by the prophets, last of all in these days, hath spoken to us by his Son, whom he hath appointed heir of all things, by whom also he made the world. Who being the brightness of his glory, and the figure of his substance, and upholding all things by the word of his power, making purgation of sins,* SITTETH ON THE RIGHT HAND OF THE MAJESTY ON HIGH.

(Heb. 9:11-12.) *Christ being come an high priest of the good things to come, by a greater and more perfect tabernacle not made with hands, that is, not of this creation* (by his divine personality of the eternal Son of the living God): *neither by the blood of goats or of calves, but by his own blood, entered once into the Holies, having obtained* (for us) *eternal redemption. And therefore he is the mediator of the New Testament, For Jesus is not entered into the Holies made with hands, the patterns of the true, but into heaven itself* THAT HE MAY APPEAR NOW IN THE PRESENCE OF GOD FOR US.

(Eph. 1:20-23.) *Setting Him on His right hand in the heavenly places, above all principality and power, and virtue, and dominion, and every name that is named not only in this world but also in that which is to come.* AND HE HATH SUBJECTED ALL THINGS UNDER HIS FEET, AND HATH MADE HIM HEAD OVER ALL THE CHURCH *which is his body and the fulness of him, who is filled all in all.*

THE APOCALYPSE.

(Chap. 1:19-26.)—*I, John, your brother, . . . I was in the spirit on the Lord's day, and I saw seven candlesticks, and in the midst of the seven candlesticks, one like to the Son of man, clothed with a garment down to his feet, and girt about the paps with a golden girdle, His head and his hair were white as white wool and as snow, and his eyes were as a flame of fire, and his feet like unto fine brass, as in a burning furnace, and his voice like the sound of many waters. He had in his right hand seven stars. From his mouth came out a sharp two-edged sword. His face was as the sun shining in his power.*

Chapter 5:1-14.

And I saw, in the right hand of him that sat on the throne, a book, written within and without, sealed with seven seals. And I saw a strong angel, proclaiming with a loud voice: Who is worthy to open the book and to loose the seals thereof? And no man was able, neither in heaven nor on earth nor under the earth, to open the book, nor to look on it. And I wept much, because no man was found worthy to open the book, nor to see it. And one of the ancients said to me: Weep not: behold the lion of the tribe of Juda, the root of David, hath prevailed to open the book and to loose the seven seals thereof.

And I saw: and behold in the midst of the throne and of the four living creatures, and in the midst of the ancients, a Lamb standing, as it were slain, having seven horns and seven eyes which are the seven Spirits of God, sent forth into all the earth. And he came and took the book out of the right hand of him that sat on the throne. And when he had opened the book, the four living creatures and the four-and-twenty ancients fell down before the Lamb, having every one of them harps, and golden vials full of odors, which are the prayers of saints. And they sung a new canticle, saying:

Thou art worthy, O Lord, to take the book and to open the seals thereof: because thou wast slain, and hast redeemed us to God) in thy blood) out of every tribe and tongue and people and nation. And hast made us to our God a kingdom and priests. And we shall reign on the earth.

And I beheld, and I heard the voice of many angels round about the throne, and the living creatures and the ancients (and the number of them was thousands of thousands), saying with a loud voice: The Lamb that was slain is worthy to receive power and dwinity and honour and glory and benediction. And every creature which is in heaven and on the earth and under the earth, and such as are in the sea, and all that are in them, I heard all saying: To him that sitteth on the throne and to the Lamb, benediction and honour and glory and power, tor ever and ever. And the four living creatures said: Amen. And the four-and-twenty ancients fell down on their faces and adored him that liveth for ever and ever.

Chapter 7:9-17.

After this, I saw a great multitude, which no man could number, of all nations and tribes and peoples and tongues, standing before the throne and in sight of the Lamb, clothed with white robes, and palms in their hands. And they cried with a loud voice, *saying; Salvation to our God, who sitteth upon the throne and to the Lamb.*

And all the angels stood round about the throne, and the ancients, and the four living creatures. And they fell down before the throne upon their faces and adored God, saying: Amen. Benediction and glory and wisdom and thanksgiving, honor and power and strength, to our God, for ever and ever. Amen.

And one of the ancients answered and said to me: These that are clothed in white robes, who are they? And whence came they? And I said to him: My Lord, thou knowest. And he said to me: These are they who are come out of great tribulation and have washed their robes and have made them white in the blood of the Lamb. Therefore, they are before the throne of God: and they serve him day and night in his temple. And he that sitteth on the throne shall dwell over them. They shall no more hunger nor thirst: neither shall the sun fall on them, nor any heat. For the Lamb which is in the midst of the throne, shall rule them, and shall lead them to the fountains of the waters of life: and God shall wipe away all tears from their eyes.

Chapter 11:15-17.

The seventh angel sounded the trumpet: and there were great voices in heaven, saying: The kingdom of this world is become our Lord's and his Christ's. And he shall reign for ever and ever. Amen. And the four-and-twenty ancients, who sit on their seats in the sight of God, fell on their faces and adored God, saying: We give thee thanks, O Lord God Almighty, who art and who wast and who art to come; because thou hast taken to thee thy great power, and thou hast reigned.

Chapter 12:10-12.

And I heard a loud voice in heaven, saying: Now is come salvation, and strength, and the Kingdom of our God, and the power of his Christ: because the accuser of our brethren is cast forth, who accused them before our God, day and night. And they overcame him by the blood of the Lamb, and by the word of the testimony, and they loved not their lives unto death. Therefore rejoice, O heavens, and you that dwell therein.

Chapter 14:1-5.

And I beheld: and lo a Lamb stood upon mount Sion, and with him an hundred and forty-four thousand, having his name and the name of his Father written on their foreheads. And I heard a voice from heaven, as the noise of many waters and as the voice of great thunder. And the voice which I heard was as the voice of harpers harping on their harps.

And they sung as it were a new canticle, before the throne and before the four living creatures and the ancients: and no man could say the canticle, but those hundred and forty-four thousand who were purchased from the earth. These are they who were not defiled with women: for they are virgins. These follow the Lamb whithersoever he goeth. These were purchased from among men, the first fruits to God and, to the Lamb. And in their mouth there was found no lie: for they are without spot before the throne of God.

Chapter 19:1-16.

After these things, I heard as it were the voice of much people in heaven, saying: Alleluia, Salvation and glory and power is to our God, For true and just are his judgements, who hath judged the great harlot which corrupted the earth with her fornication, and hath revenged the blood of his servants at her hands, And again they said: Alleluia. And her smoke ascendeth for ever and ever.

And the four and-twenty ancients and the four living creatures fell down and adored God that sitteth upon the throne, saying: Amen. Alleluia. And a voice came out from the throne, saying: Give praise to our God, all ye his servants: and you that fear him, little and great. And I heard as it were the voice of a great multitude, and as the voice of many waters, and as the voice of great thunders, saying: Alleluia: for the Lord our God, the Almighty, hath reigned. Let us be glad and rejoice and give glory to him. For the marriage of the Lamb is come: and his wife hath prepared herself. And it is granted to her that she should clothe herself with fine linen, glittering and white. For the fine linen are the justifications of saints.

And he said to me: Write, Blessed are they that are called to the marriage supper of the Lamb. And he saith to me: These words of God are true. And I fell down before his feet, to adore him. And he saith to me: See thou do it not. I am thy fellow servant and of thy brethren who have the testimony of Jesus. Adore God. For the testimony of Jesus is the spirit of prophecy.

And I saw heaven opened: and behold a white horse. And he that sat upon him was called faithful and true: and with justice doth he judge and fight. And his eyes were as a flame of fire: and on his head were many diadems. And he had a name written, which no man knoweth but himself. And he was clothed with a garment sprinkled with blood. And his name is called: THE WORD OF GOD.

And the armies that are in heaven followed him on white horses, clothed in fine linen, white and clean. And out of his mouth proceedeth a sharp two-edged sword, that with it he may strike the nations. And he shall rule them with a rod of iron: and he treadeth the winepress of the fierceness of the wrath of God the Almighty. And he hath on his garment and on his thigh written: KING OF KINGS AND LORD OF LORDS.

Chapter 20:11-15.

And I saw a great white throne and one sitting upon it, from whose face the earth and heaven fled away: and there was no place found for them. And I saw the dead, great and small, standing in the presence of the throne.

And the books were opened: and another book was opened, which was the book of life, And the dead were fudged by those things which were written in the books according to their works, And the sea gave up the dead that were in it: and death and hell gave up their dead that were in them, And they were fudged, every one according to their works.

And hell and death were cast into the pool of fire, This is the second death. And whosoever was not found written in the book of life was cast into the pool of fire.

Chapter 22.

And he showed me a river of water of life, clear as crystal, proceeding from the throne of God and of the Lamb. In the midst of the street thereof, and on both sides of the river, was the tree of life, bearing twelve fruits, yielding its fruits every month: and the leaves of the tree were for the healing of the nations.

And there shall be no curse any more: but the throne of God and of the Lamb shall be in it, And his servants shall serve him, And they shall see his face: and his name shall be on their foreheads, and night shall be no more. And they shall not need the light of the lamp, nor the light of the sun, because the Lord God shall enlighten them. And they shall reign for ever and ever.

And he said to me. These words are most faithful and true. And the Lord God of the spirits of the prophets sent his angel to show his servant the things which must be done shortly. And: Behold I come quickly. Blessed is he that keepeth the words of the prophecy of this book.

And I, John, who have heard and seen these things. And, after I had heard and seen, I fell down to adore before the feet of the angel who showed me these things. And he said to me: See thou do it not. For I am thy fellow servant, and of thy brethren the prophets and of them that keep the words of the prophecy of this book, Adore God.

And he saith to me: Seal not the words of the prophecy of this book. For the time is at hand. He that hurteth, let him hurt still: and he that is pithy, let him be pithy still: and he that is just, let him be justified still: and he that is holy, let him be sanctified still. Behold, I come quickly: and my reward is with me, to render to every man according to his works. I am Alpha and Omega, the First and the Last, the Beginning and the End. Blessed are they that wash their robes in the blood of the Lamb: that they may have a right to the tree of life and may enter in by the gates into the city. Without are dogs and sorcerers and unchaste and murderers and servers of idol's and every one that loveth and maketh a lie.

I, Jesus, have sent my angel, to testify to you these things in the churches. I am the root and stock of David, the bright and morning star. And, the spirit and the bride say: Come. And he that heareth, let him say: Come. And he that thirsteth, let him come. And he that will, let him take the water of life, freely. For I testify to everyone that heareth the words of the prophecy of this book: If any man shall add to these things, God shall add unto him the plagues written in this book. And if any man shall take away from the words of the book of this prophecy, God shall take away his part out of the book of life, and out of the holy city, and from these things that are written in this book. He that giveth testimony of these things, saith: Surely, I come quickly: Amen. Come, Lord Jesus. The grace of our Lord Jesus Christ be with you all. Amen.

My soul, let us go repeating:
LAUS TIBI DOMINE, REX AETERNAE GLORIAE!

CHAPTER XXX

CHRIST IN THE CHURCH

SO then, Christ Jesus, our Lord risen from the dead is henceforth reigning in heaven, gloriously seated at the right hand of His Father, filling the blessed angels and saints with ineffable bliss, and, together with them all, offering to the majesty of the ever Blessed Trinity the most perfect praise. He is also administering particular judgement (in what mysterious way we know not) to all the souls both living and dead, which are incessantly brought to Him in their thousands and millions, from this earth of ours, where they parted from their bodies, their time of trial being over.

At the same time Christ is also upon earth in the midst of His Militant Church, multiplying His presence and His activities in a wonderful way. The book of Proverbs had prophetically said of Him: *Wisdom hath built herself a house. She hath hewn her out seven pillars, she hath slain her victims, mingled her wine and set forth her table. She hath sent her maids to invite to the tower and to the walls of the city: Whosoever is a little one, let him come to me; and to the unwise she said: Come, eat my bread and drink the wine, which I have mingled for you.* (Prov. 9:1-5.) How transparently clear is the meaning of this prophecy! The *house* is the Church on earth, the *builder* is Christ, who is *the power of God and the wisdom of God.* (1 Cor. 1:24.) The *seven pillars* are the seven sacraments, *hewn out* of the infinite merits of His sacred Passion. *The victims* (in the plural) are so many simultaneous productions of His own flesh and blood on our altars, wherever the holy sacrifice of the Mass is being offered up. The *little ones* are those whose faith is as simple as that of a child. The *unwise* (according to the world) are those who put spiritual things above temporal advantages. The *bread* and *wine* are holy communion.

The Church is the mystical body of Christ, into which He breathed His own life and through which He continues all the various activities of His former life and passion and death whilst He was on earth.

The Church is purely and simply a sprouting out from the open side of Jesus dead on the cross; an extension or continuation of Him, a branching out of His own Sacred Humanity. *I am the vine,* He says, *you the branches: he that adbideth in me and I in him, the same beareth much fruit, for without me you can do nothing.* (John 15:5.) There is an irruption of His own divine life and of the grace of His Sacred Humanity into that group of men, into that little flock (Luke 12:32) of those He calls *His friends.* (John 15:14.) Little, indeed, in comparison with the immense number of men who do not walk with Him. But those who do, Jesus assumes them unto Himself and is fulfilled in them. They are His Church.

All men are Christ's by right. They belong to Him in the most absolute manner. He is their maker. After they had been sold to the devil by the sin of Adam (Rom. 7:14). He bought them *at a great price* (1 Cor. 6:20) paying their ransom with His own most precious blood. By His Incarnation He has become the head of the whole human race. It is the most ardent wish of His heart to win them all over to His love, to make them even now as holy and as happy as it is possible to be on earth, and finally to lead them all as His conquest, His trophy, to His heavenly Father, and make of them all, together with His blessed angels, the Church triumphant, the Bride elect of His love. But it is in the power of men to refuse to avail themselves of such a plentiful redemption: and, unfortunately, being free, too many do so. As we see, it is through no lack of goodwill on the part of Our Lord that He does not assume unto Himself the whole human race.

Before going up to heaven, Jesus said to His Apostles whilst blessing them: *Behold I am with you all days even to the consummation of the world.* (Matt, 28:20.) It may be asked: What kind of presence does Jesus mean in these words? Does He mean His own real bodily, though non-spacial, presence in the Blessed Sacrament? He means this and something more: for His eucharistic presence does not explain all His activities on behalf of the Church. We must understand it as a spiritual presence of love, distinct both from the eucharistic presence under the Sacred Species, and from His divine metaphysical omnipresence which is necessarily implied in all created things, animate or inanimate, good or bad. Jesus is in His Church on earth, with that sort of presence by which the head is united to the body, attends to the welfare of all its parts, keeps them together in one, pours out the stream of life into them and presides over all their operations.

Through His Church Our Lord Jesus Christ continues on earth till the end of the world the mysteries of His own hidden life, of His public apostolate, of His passion and death. In the persons of little Christian children He still waxes strong, full of wisdom and the grace of God is in him ... and he is still subject to his parents. (Luke 2:40-51.) In the persons of pious youths preparing themselves long beforehand for the holy priesthood or a life of virginity in some religious order, He asks wise questions from the doctors of the Law and takes in hand His Father's business. In the persons of the immense majority of His faithful, He earns His bread by the sweat of His brow, by the work of His hands, in the different avocations which divide the world of toilers, adoring and praising His heavenly Father the while. In the persons of apostolic men He continues to be the *Light of the world,* by word of mouth as well as by books full of the spirit of His Gospel.

When the priest preaches, it is Jesus who preaches; so much so that He has said to His apostles and their successors: *He that heareth you heareth me, and he that despiseth you, despiseth me.* (Luke 10:16.) When the priest baptizes it is Jesus who takes away the stain of original sin and fills the soul with grace. The priest absolves, it is Jesus who cleanses the repentant sinner in His own blood. When the priest celebrates holy Mass, Jesus is the principal celebrant as well as the victim of this sacrifice. When the bishop confirms, it is Jesus who pours out the Holy Ghost with the fulness of His gifts into the soul. When the bishop ordains priests, it is Jesus who marks their soul with the indelible sign of His own priesthood and invests them with more than earthly powers. When the Pope governs the Church, names the bishops and assigns their dioceses to them, presides over the whole world's apostolate, renders his decisions *ex cathedra,* convokes, suspends, prorogues, terminates Ecumenical Councils: Christ is with him, doing all these things, assisting him with His own divine light and strength.

Christ it is who does it all through the instrumentality of His faithful servants. He has need of us: (Oh! what divine condescension there is in this!) We lend Him our mind, our will, our hands, our lips for the performance of these supernatural works. All is done in His name, for His sake, with His authority, by the might of His grace, by the virtue which flows from His earthly life and passion, by the application of His infinite merits; by Him, by Him in very deed.

Jesus pursues His life of divine contemplation and divine praise on earth, and His benefactions on souls and bodies in the works of mercy, principally through that admirable multitude and variety of Religious Orders of both sexes, which are the glory of the Church. Finally Our Lord continues His Sacred Passion not only by the sacrifice of the Mass but also in the persons of His martyrs, and of all generous Christians who endure patiently and lovingly the severest trials, and more particularly in the persecutions with which His Church, considered as a corporate body, is incessantly assailed.

To this new dolorous passion, Judases have never been wanting. To speak only of modern times, there have been Voltaire with all his following, then Renan, and now the Modernists. In comparison with Voltaire and Renan, the Judas who betrayed Jesus with a kiss was almost a gentleman: he showed at least some sense of the horror of his crime. As for the Modernists, with all their self-conceit and arrogance, they are only the train-bearers of that honey-tongued caitiff, Renan. Flunkeys of the devil, all of them.

Meanwhile, for the last half-century, Christ in the person of His Vicar upon earth, has been a prisoner in the Vatican, an object of mockery and insult to the rabble of the world.

But in spite of all persecutions, *the stream of the river* of divine grace *maketh the city of God joyful. The Most High hath sanctified his own tabernacle. God is in the midst thereof: it shall not be moved. God will help it in the morning early* (Ps. 46:5-6). The Catholic Church is *from the rising of the sun to the going down thereof, the loveliness of his beauty* (Is. 49:1-2).

Balaam, from the summit of the Phogor, where he could see the camp of the People of God pitched in the desert, exclaims: *How beautiful are thy tabernacles, O Jacob, and thy tents, O Israel! As woody valleys, as watered gardens near the rivers, as tabernacles which the Lord hath pitched, as cedars by the water-side ... God hath brought him out of the land of Egypt. Lying down he hath slept like a lion, and as a lioness whom none shall dare to rouse. He that blesseth thee shall also be blessed, he that curseth thee shall be reckoned among the accursed. ... Israel shall do manfully. ... Who shall live when God shall do these things?* (Num. 24:5-23.) Balaam had begun by speaking of the Israelites, whose camp stretched far and wide at the foot of the mountain, but he ends by singing the glories of the Church of Christ, which he descries through a vista of fifteen centuries yet to come. Well might he utter his wistful query: "Who shall live when God shall do these things?"

This, then, is our privilege. We see the fulfilment of this as well as of all the other prophecies relating to Christ and to His Church upon earth. For well nigh two thousand years, she has been passing through ordeals from without and from within, which no merely human society could have withstood. To-day, in the midst of a decrepit world, of the ruins of revolutions, of crumbling thrones and a tottering social order, the Church of Christ, the Catholic Church, stands as full of vitality as ever, with the same holy sacrifice of the Mass, the same seven Sacraments, the same hierarchy and the same Credo as in the thirteenth century, as in the sixth, as in the first, as on the day of Pentecost.

Christ's doing!

To Him be glory and love for ever!

CHAPTER XXXI

CHRIST IN THE HOLY EUCHARIST

"What is the good thing of him, and what is his beautiful thing but the corn of the elect and wine springing forth virgins?" (Zach, 9:17).

I N the Sacrament of the Holy Eucharist, Our Lord lives a very active, mysterious life, and performs several distinct functions of mighty import. There is first His mystical sacrifice of the Mass; then His giving us His body and blood to be the spiritual food of our souls; finally there is His abiding real presence. We must try and realize all that each of these functions of Our Lord implies; then perhaps we shall be better able to appreciate the extent of His love for us.

St. John the Evangelist introduces his account of the Last Supper with these words: *Jesus having loved his own who were in the World, he loved them unto the end.* (John 13:1.) *Unto the end,* here does not mean only unto the end of His life, but unto the end of instituting so marvelous a sacrament, and securing its permanence till the end of the world, by means of the sacrament of Holy Orders. Our Lord Jesus Christ, in His Holy Eucharist, makes Himself at the same time our oblation to the Father, the food of our hungry soul, the memorial or synthesis of all His other mysteries, and our viaticum when the moment comes for us to pass from this world into that of the blessed spirits.

Let us now consider the activities of Our Lord in the holy sacrifice of the Mass. There is first of all His mystical *birth and oblation* of Himself at each of the two consecrations. Then there is His mystical *immolation and death* as soon as the two elements of the sacrifice are at the same time present separately on the altar, namely: His Flesh under the species of bread, on the one hand; His Blood under the species of wine, on the other. The communion of the priest and of the faithful constitutes the formal *consummation of this sacrifice* of the New Law.

The holy sacrifice of the Mass is first and foremost an extension of the sacrifice of Calvary and an application of its merits to individual persons or particular cases. On Calvary, the main feature of the sacrifice was its being offered up for the expiation of sin, to redeem a guilty world: everything else seems to recede from view before this one great aim, and to give to this sacrifice its formidable aspect: whilst, on the contrary in the sacrifice of the Mass, everything speaks to us of peace and reconciliation. Hence we are able to discern more plainly, in the Mass, the four ends of the sacrifice, which are: adoration of the Divine Majesty; thanksgiving for all benefits received; propitiation for our sins and those of the whole world; and petition for all the temporal and spiritual blessings we stand in need of.

Can we thank Our Lord enough, and admire Him enough, for thus making Himself, in the trembling fingers of His priest, our living prayer, sure to be well received by the Father? Were any man to offer up his whole being, body and soul, intellect and will and senses, the whole tree, root and stock and branch, to the Father, this would constitute an act of adoration, but a very paltry, insignificant one, quite unworthy of the Infinite Majesty. But, thanks to the loving-kindness of Our Lord, we have better than this at our command: we have Himself; and to this Lamb of God we may now add the oblation of our own puny self: it will not be any longer insignificant.

Several other features of the Holy Sacrifice bf the Mass deserve to be noticed.

First its universality. The celebration of Mass is constantly taking place, at every hour of the day and night, all over the world, on many altars at the same time, thus giving a splendid fulfilment to the prophecy of Malachy: *From the rising of the sun even to the going down, my name is great among the Gentiles, and in every place there is sacrifice and there is offered up to my name a clean oblation.* (Mal. 1:11.) To speak in a human way, what activities on the part of Our Lord this reveals to us! None but a divine person could be equal to them. Does not this demonstrate to what an extent the Sacred Humanity of Our Lord comes through the hypostatic union into a share of the infinitude of His Godhead? He is God; He is God in His human body and soul; *In him dwelleth all the fulness of the Godhead corporally.* (Col. 2:9.) That is the all-sufficing explanation of the mystery of His corporal presence and activities in so many places at the same time.

But the wonder becomes still greater when we consider another feature of the life of Our Lord in the holy sacrifice of the Mass; I mean the decided character of intimate intercourse and personal mutual possession between Jesus and the priest who celebrates, as well as between the same Jesus and him who offered the stipendium of the Mass, and again between the same Lord Jesus and each one of those who piously assist at the Mass. Each one of them can say with absolute truth and in the most literal meaning: *My Beloved to me and I to him,* (Cant. 2:16.)

This special character of possession and of intimate intercourse and delightful private friendship is still more palpable in the act of sacramental Communion, which is the natural outcome of Mass. Jesus comes to me, then, as though there were no one else to be loved by Him but my poor self; as though there were in the whole wide world but these two, Jesus and I. He acts upon me and in me with His whole self and He expects me to be responsive to the full extent of my complex nature made up of spirit and flesh. What an endearing familiarity is this! What a loving embrace! What a bridal kiss! And what a heart to heart communion and effusion of love this ought to call forth on our part!

After such a visit of Our Lord to each one of the communicants personally, and knowing as we do that it is His most ardent wish to be so received by every one, no man has a right to say: "Oh! I am a nobody. I am lost in the crowd. God does not care for me, except in a general way." Each one is assured that he is held in particular regard by Our Lord, that he is dearly loved by the Son of God, individually and for his own sake. If Moses could exclaim in the name of his people: *There is not any other nation so great, that hath gods so nigh them as our God is present to all our petitions* (Deut. 4:7), what shall we say on receiving holy communion? But again, what a revelation is thus given of the wonderful activities of our Jesus in His blessed Sacrament! What He does to me, He does at the same time to hundreds and thousands, perhaps millions, of other communicants: so true it is that any number of created beings never could exhaust the powers of a divine person.

In connection with holy communion, there is a last feature of the activities of Our Lord in His Blessed Sacrament which ought to fill us with overflowing tenderness and gratitude: it is His holding Himself in readiness to be carried to the sick and administered as *viaticum* to the dying. So He will come to me at the solemn moment when I am about to pass from this world of shadows and enigmas to the splendid eternal light of the world of the blessed spirits.

Finally, there is the persevering real presence of Our Lord in the Tabernacle, and this reveals new activities on the part of Our Lord and still greater abysses of His loving-kindness in our behalf.

Because Holy Mass lasts but a short half-hour, and Holy Communion but a few entrancing minutes, our dear Emmanuel chooses to recede no farther away from us than behind the little golden door of the tabernacle. There He stands, waiting and watching for every man to draw nigh to Him, and unburden his weary soul, vexed by many temptations. *Come to me,* He says, *all ye that labor and are burdened and I will refresh you,* (Matt, 11:28.) What joy to Him when He sees one of us coming to pay Him a surprise visit of love, be it of ever so short a duration! Some of the saints who received His confidences when they were still on earth, tell us how He decks Himself, in a manner, with the marks we give Him of our loving regard, and shows them forth with a sort of proud ostentation, in the sight of His angels and of His Eternal Father.

One of the Prophets makes Our Lord say of the stigmata of

His Sacred Passion: *With these I was wounded in the house of them that love, me* (Zach, 16:6); now He rings a change on these words, and speaking of the tokens of love He receives from us, He exclaims: *"With these I was adorned in the house of them that love Me."* Thanks be to God, it is no longer in the power of anyone to inflict on Our Lord bodily pain or sadness of heart, because He is no longer in mortal life, a pilgrim like ourselves, but He is now in body and soul *in Patria;* but it is now more than ever in our power to add to the joy of His Heart and to His accidental glory, and therefore He says: *My delights are to be with the children of men* (Prov. 8:31), and He proves it by thus staying day and night in our midst.

Our devotion to the Blessed Sacrament will gain in intensity if we realize that the Jesus who is there on our altars, in our tabernacles, is not a Jesus suffering, but glorified, whom consequently no pain of any kind can touch. Nor is He solitary, but surrounded with millions of adoring angels, if only we could see them. There are not two Jesuses, one enjoying the supremest bliss of heaven, the other suffering in the Blessed Sacrament; there is but one, the Jesus who arose from the dead, ascended into heaven, and sits at the right hand of God the Father Almighty: blissful wherever He multiplies His Sacramental Presence, blissful in all the depths of His Human Soul and Body and Sacred Heart, glorious for evermore; in fact the very King of everlasting glory.

This raises an interesting question. In some revelations of the saints, Our Lord is represented as asking consolation of His friends for the ingratitude of sinners and tepid Christians, as though He were really, even now, a prey to sadness. This must not be understood literally. The best explanation I can discover is that Our Lord has indeed, in very truth, suffered this sadness, at the time of His agony in the Garden, and that He is referring to this fact and not to any present sadness; and furthermore, that any consolation we, who are now living, do offer Him, has been in advance administered to Him in our name by the Angel of the Agony. Thus it is that everything revolves around the great drama of our redemption, and we are made in a manner the contemporaries of it. As I have endeavored to show this at some length in my volume on THE MYSTICAL LIFE, in the three chapters (xii-xiv) on the Pauline doctrine of the *Verbum crucis,* I beg to refer my kind reader to them.

It is of faith that Christ *risen from the dead, dieth now no more, death shall no more have dominion over him. For in that he died to sin, he dieth once: but in that he liveth he liveth unto God* (Rom. 6:9-10), and therefore enjoys a happiness which is absolutely unassailable. We may well return thanks to the heavenly Father that it is so.

St. Thomas in the office of Corpus Christi warns us that in holy communion "a pledge of the glory to come is given us." Is not Jesus therein giving us His own glorified flesh to eat, His own glorified blood to drink? We eat of the glory of heaven, we drink of the glory of heaven. The very substance of the glory of heaven the Lamb of God, who is the very light of the Jerusalem that is above, is given us as the food of our soul. Something of the heavenly glory clings to the priest who is celebrating the Divine Mysteries, spreads to the faithful who assist at them, especially if they receive Holy Communion, and invests also the little altar boy, at times very inattentive and thoughtless, who serves the Mass.

All this of course is discernible only with the eyes of faith.

The contemplative Christian, with a heart all burning with love, exclaims: *Verily thou art a hidden God.* (Is. 45:15.) *Oh! how great is the multitude of thy sweetness, O Lord, which thou hast hidden for those who love thee!* (Ps. 30:20.) *Thou hast prepared a table before me against them that afflict me . . . and my chalice which inebriateth how goodly it is!* (Ps. 22:5.)

CHAPTER XXXII

CHRIST IN ME

N the first years of my missionary life in North America, among the wild tribes of the Indian Territory, now the State of Oklahoma, I was in charge of the Sacred Heart Mission, and my dear parishioners were the Pottowatomie Redskins. In the school, besides their children, I had also some from the neighboring tribes: ranging in age from six to seventeen. Some were Christians already, others were under instruction, and there were also those who became Catholics later in life, thanks to the good seed then implanted in them.

Among these children there was a bright little Chickasaw boy aged seven. I loved to question him because he used to give me rather unexpected replies. One day at catechism, I asked him: "Where is Jesus?" Promptly, with graceful gesture, he pointed to his breast and replied: "He is there in my heart." This he said, not parrot-like, but in a tone of voice which carried with it deep religious feeling; showing that the lesson taught him by the Sister of Mercy, had made on him more than a superficial impression.

Neither the child nor the humble nun could suspect that these few words of his had started in my mind a train of thought. I asked myself: "Is Jesus indeed in that little boy's heart? Is He really there? And how? Then He is also verily in my own heart"; and I, a priest, was startled at the discovery. I had been, by means of that little innocent, brought face to face with a divine fact, the truth of which, until then, I had held only superficially, or as Newman would have expressed it "notionally," that is to say without a sense of its reality.

This happened a long while ago; somewhere between 1882 and 1885. I had entirely forgotten the incident, when, last year, one of my correspondents submitted to me for solution a difficulty which had arisen between her and another lady, a teacher.

The latter had asked a little child: "Where is Jesus?" to which the child had replied: "Jesus is everywhere." The teacher had taken exception at this and corrected the little one, saying: "No, Jesus is not everywhere: it is only God who is everywhere." These two well-meaning people had an argument about it, my friend maintaining that the child's answer, in its naked simplicity, was right, whilst the teacher still held, tooth and nail, that it was wrong.

Of course I had to adjudge that the child was absolutely right. Is not Jesus God and, therefore, everywhere? The teacher, hypnotized so to say, by the sight of the limitations of the Sacred Humanity as such, had failed to realize that the primary fact about Jesus is His Godhead. He is the second person of the Blessed Trinity, one and the same God with the Father and the Holy Ghost, therefore everywhere present. Emphatically, without the shadow of a restriction, we must say that Jesus is everywhere.

Now is this divine person, Jesus, who is the true and consubstantial and coequal Son of God, *everywhere with His human nature?* In other words, are the human soul and the human body of Our Lord everywhere, even as much as His Godhead? To this it is evident that we must give a decided negative. The human soul of Our Blessed Lord and the sacred body it animates cannot be everywhere present. This omnipresence of a created, finite thing, is what is called a metaphysical impossibility, absolute and irreducible.

To procure the real presence of His sacred body and blood and, by concomitance, the presence also of His human soul, in the Blessed Sacrament, in the way He does and in so many places at the same time, Our Lord has to use His divine omnipotence, setting at naught many laws of nature. This could be done, and therefore He did it, His wonderful love for us prompting Him thereto. But nothing further is possible. The attribute of Immensity on which hangs the property of being present everywhere is an exclusive and absolutely incommunicable perfection of the divine nature. The human nature of Our Lord by the fact that it is a thing created is simply incapable of this privilege.

Jesus is not merely the Sacred Humanity. Jesus is the Word, the second person of the Blessed Trinity. True, He is the Word made flesh, but that does not alter the case; the Godhead of the Word exceeds infinitely His Sacred Humanity.

There is but one Word of God, and that Word of God is Our Lord Jesus Christ. There are not two Words, one in the flesh and another out of the flesh. Before the Incarnation took place there was no other Word but the one that was, in the fulness of time, to be made flesh; and since the august event of the Incarnation, there is no other Word than the Word made flesh. Wherever the Word is (and He is everywhere) He is the Word made flesh, the Word that has taken unto Himself a human body and a human soul, though He has not that human body and soul everywhere with Him, as such a thing is impossible.

Nor is this in the least necessary for our consolation.

Through His Godhead which is present everywhere we are in touch with His Sacred Humanity, even at times when we are far from the Blessed Sacrament. Everywhere therefore, and at all times, and under all circumstances we can, with the saintly Carmelite Brother Lawrence, feel very near indeed to Our Lord, and give pleasure to His Sacred human Heart by our acts of love.

Talk of wireless telegraphy! I say it with the utmost reverence: there is between the Sacred Humanity of Our Lord and each one of us, a most wonderful apparatus or medium of transmission of messages, even His own Godhead, present everywhere. Here, at this very moment, in my cell, whilst I am writing these lines, there is God, there is the most Holy Trinity, there is the second Person, the Word. But, is it not the same Word who became man, who assumed a human body and a human soul, nearly two thousand years ago, and who since then has never stood apart from them? The very same. Therefore, wherever this human body and that human soul of His happen to be, the Word who is present here is at the same time hypostatically united with these, and whatever message of adoration and loving sympathy I wish to send to His Sacred Humanity is transmitted in the instant; as on the other hand, whatever influence of grace Our Lord wants to impress me with, is conveyed to me in a moment, by the same medium, straight from his sacred Heart. So that the fact of the Sacred Humanity not being bodily present everywhere does not in the least stand in the way of our perpetual contact and fellowship and intercourse of love with the same Sacred Humanity.

To return to our little Chickasaw boy, he certainly could say with absolute truth, that Jesus was there, in his heart. And it meant more than the metaphysical presence by which Our Lord, in his divine nature, is necessarily everywhere. Besides that sort of presence, He is also in the heart of every one who is free from sin: that is the special presence of love by which the three divine Persons dwell in the Christian. *"If any one love me,"* says Jesus, *"he will keep my word, and my Father will love him, and we will come to him and will make our abode with him,"* (John 14:23.)

But that is not all. Jesus is moreover present in all good Christians by another still more special presence and mode of activity, namely as Head of the Church and therefore of everyone of its living members. *Abide in me and I in you, I am the vine you the branches.* (John 15:4-5.)

In this last capacity of our Head, although Jesus is not in us with His body and blood and human soul, except during a few happy moments which follow Holy Communion, nevertheless He is incessantly pouring into us the influences of the grace which flow from His Sacred Humanity. Thus is Jesus present in me, acting in me, making me all His own, making use of me, for the purposes of His ineffable love.

This was in some sort rendered palpable to me, one day, in the joyful confidences of a young friend of mine. I hastened to put them on record whilst I was still under their charm. We shall call them:

The Youth's Dream.

"Father," he said, "you have no idea how happy I feel just now. Look at me, in my rags: I am rich and I am loved. Loved, tenderly loved, by many of the kindest and grandest people; cherished, desired, sought after, awaited with impatience in order to share their delightful life.

"Oh! what a lovely dream I have had!

"I dreamed that the great God of Heaven was my Father, and that He gave me the sweet name of son; that He took me upon His knees, caressing and embracing me, and pressing me to His heart, and then He set me on my feet, saying: Walk about a little while, and I will give Myself to thee for a reward, with all that belongs to Me. Then Jesus, in the form of a fine youth, took me by the hand, embraced me and said: "Thou art My brother: let us walk together. I have always loved thee: I want to lead thee Myself: thus we shall be sure that thou will not go astray.'

"He then began to talk to me of His sweet Mother Mary, and He told me the most wonderful things about her, and He added, 'I want her to be thy sweet Mother too. Call her Mother, and if at any time thou fearest any danger, cry out to her.' Having said this, Jesus disappeared. Then I immediately began to call out: 'Mary, Mary, mother of Jesus, mother mine!' and the Blessed Virgin hastened to me—oh! so beautiful, so smiling and kind! She imprinted a big kiss on my brow, murmuring as she did so: 'Poor child: have no fear; go forward; we love thee well, and we shall help thee. Behold at thy side the watchful guardian whom thy Heavenly Father, thy Brother Jesus and myself have deputed to keep thee.'

"I looked on my right, and I was quite dazzled. An angel of the Lord stood beside me in shining armor, looking at me with eyes of quite fraternal affection. He too kissed me and said: 'In the Kingdom of Light, of which thou art already a citizen, love is chaste, but it is very tender. There is no such thing there as hardness of heart or indifference. Thou wouldst be astonished were I able to make thee understand how all my brother-angels, and the saints in paradise wish thee well: how they all think of thee, speak of thee, cherish thee, blessing God for thy smallest advance in virtue, and await with impatience the day of thine entrance into heaven, that thou mayest make festival there with us.'

"I replied: 'O my dear guardian angel, can it really be that I am so greatly beloved? Who then has been able to direct thus the glances and the affections of all these dear Saints towards me?' He replied: 'Knowest thou not that all those whom God loves they love too! In thy soul they behold the image of God. In thy soul, in thy body, and in all thy human nature they behold not only the image of our Lord Jesus Christ, but His living member. They behold upon thy forehead the trace of the water of baptism, and of the redeeming blood, and even in thy senses and in thy flesh, the traces of several sacraments; above all of thy Communions. They cannot but love thee, and cherish thee tenderly.'

"At these last words I awoke, and my joy, till then overflowing, changed to a bitter sadness, and I began to weep because my beautiful dream had come to an end. Soon, however, a voice as it were behind me, uttered loudly and distinctly these words: "Foolish one! Dost thou not understand that this is not a dream, but a great reality?' I had heard this voice some moments before in my dream: I recognized its tone and accent—it was that of my guardian angel, and he added, ' Thank God, Our Heavenly Father, humbly and joyfully. Go forward; work; Practice faith, hope and charity and the spirit of prayer; and if at times thy courage appears on the point of giving way, place upon thy heart as a healing balm the recollection of this assurance of affections and of divine favors which visit thee from the height of heaven, coming down from the Father of Lights, through the Hearts of Jesus and Mary, and all the glorious phalanx of Angels and Saints?

"Then I said: 'O my dear Angel! I thank thee, I promise thee that I will be no longer sad; beloved as I am, it seems to me that it would be a sin,' and I began to shout aloud distractedly: 'I am loved! I am loved! I am loved! *Deus charitas est!* Love is in possession: love triumphs: love in God rejoices!'"

Thus far my young friend. This was a dream, a natural dream and nothing more. Certainly it was no vision and no revelation, but a real dream. What does it prove? This: that when one lives the supernatural life and allows it to have full sway, it even gets hold of the subconscious activities of our inferior powers and weaves itself beautifully into their ephemeral products. Several other examples, as striking as this one, have come under my observation.

***

What Jesus wants to do with me, and is actually engaged in carrying out, is no small undertaking. He wants to express Himself in me, through me, through my own idiosyncrasies. He takes me just as he finds me, a wretched sinner, wretched in body, wretched in mind, wretched in all the debilitated powers of my soul, and behold, He sets about to heal me, making me one with Himself, making me do His own works upon earth. *I must work the works of him that sent me, whilst it is day, the night cometh, when no man can work.* (John 9:4.) I must whilst I am here below, even as He did, praise the Divine Majesty of our heavenly Father, show filial love to Mary, love my brethren, go about doing good, take up my cross, climb my own little Calvary, suffer whatever there is to endure in union with Him in His Sacred Passion and for the dear intentions of His Sacred Heart. Here is divine life; here is divine fruitfulness: now that is what Jesus is achieving in His poor servant, if only I put no obstacle in the way.

As St. Paul expresses it, every individual Christian who is in earnest, can and ought to say: *"I live now, not I, but Christ liveth in me."* (Gal. 2:20.)

CHAPTER XXXIII

MY BLESSINGS UPON THE DEAR CHRIST

DARE to call Him " my Jesus," for is He not mine, and am I not His? He said to His Apostles at the Last Supper after He had given them communion with His own Flesh and Blood, *Remain in me, and I in you* (John 15:4), and the spouse in the divine Canticle cries out in the exuberance of her heart's joy, *My well-beloved is mine and I am his.* (Cant, 2:16.) Then I dare, in my turn, to speak of Him as being wholly mine, and I say:

Blessed for ever be my Jesus!

Blessed for ever be the Father of my Jesus with whom He is one and the same God!

Blessed for ever be the Holy Spirit of my Jesus, who is also Himself one and the same God with Jesus and His Divine Father!

Glory be to the Father, by the Son, in the Holy Spirit of love; glory! glory for ever!

Blessed for ever be the most sacred humanity of my Jesus! His Body, His Soul, His Heart, His Precious Blood: may they be blessed for ever!

Blessed for ever be the incomparable and most sweet, Immaculate Virgin Mother of my Jesus.

Blessed be the chaste womb that conceived, carried and ushered into the world my Jesus, the true Son of God!

And blessed be the virgin paps that gave Him suck. Blessed, blessed for ever!

Blessed for ever be the foster-father of my Jesus, the humble and all-glorious St. Joseph.

Blessed for ever be the most holy Forerunner of my Jesus, virgin, martyr, more than prophet, John the Baptist, *the friend of the Bridegroom!*

Blessed be all the mysteries of my Jesus!

Blessed be all the actions of my Jesus whilst He lived on

earth, *full of grace and truth* (John 1:14), all His affections, all His wishes, all His words, all His miracles, all His fatigues, all His sufferings, all His humiliations, all His secret joys. May they all be blessed for ever!

Blessed be the holy Apostles of my Jesus, especially John the well-beloved, and Peter upon whom He founded His Church; and Paul, whom He called from the height of His glorious heaven to come after Him!

Blessed be all the holy ancestors of my Jesus, and the holy people of God in the Old Testament!

Blessed be all the angels of my Jesus, in their dazzling holiness and their admirable hierarchy, and in their service of love which they render to the Lord God; and blessed be most specially the guardian angel which my Jesus has chosen for me, and to whom He has entrusted me!

Blessed be all the Saints in the paradise of my Jesus!

Blessed be the Holy Souls in Purgatory, sorrowful spouses of my Jesus! I entreat Him to admit them as quickly as possible to the nuptial chamber of His glory. May He be blessed in His rigorous justice with regard to them, and in the unspeakable joy which He holds in store for them!

Blessed be each true servant of my Jesus who upon earth fights the good fight, beneath the banner of the cross, and for love of Him!

Blessed be the Holy Church of my Jesus on earth, the Church Catholic, Apostolic, Roman.

Blessed be my Jesus in the most Holy Sacrifice of the Mass, celebrated unceasingly throughout the world by Catholic priests!

Blessed be my Jesus in the most Holy Sacrament of the altar, in every place where He deigns to reside beneath the sacred species, in order to put to the proof our faith and our love, to nourish our souls, and to cheer us in our exile. May He be blessed, exalted and passionately adored!

> *Lauda Sion Salvatorem,*
> *Lauda ducem et pastorem,*
> *In hymnis et canticis.*
> *Quantum potes tantum aude.*
> *Quia major omni laude,*
> *Nec laudare sufficis!*

Blessed be my Jesus in the other sacraments which His Heart full of love has instituted so as to provide for all our spiritual needs during our pilgrimage here below!

Blessed be my Jesus in the glory of Paradise, enthroned at the right hand of His Eternal Father, having Mary on His right, *in vestitu deaurato,* surrounded by the shining cohorts of the nine choirs of blessed angels and all the orders of the Saints; my Jesus who at the same time, in the very heart of these splendours, deigns to think of me, and to love me! O tender Jesus, my brother and Bridegroom of my soul, when wilt Thou call me to the abode of perfect charity? Meanwhile I shall not cease to praise and bless Thee.

Blessed be the Heart of my Jesus in glory, ever burning with intensest love for us!

Blessed be the five wounds of my Jesus which He displays before His eternal Father to soothe His righteous ire against the sins of the world!

Blessed be the adorable brow of my Jesus which will eternally show the marks of the cruel thorns with which He was crowned, and His most gentle countenance, which was shamed by blows and covered with spittle, but whose beauty now fills with its splendors the whole of the heavenly Jerusalem! *Lucerna ejus est Agnus.* (Apoc. 21:23.)

Blessed be the most gentle eyes of my Savior Jesus, which wept over Jerusalem, and over all sinners—especially over me, the worst of all! Would I had been allowed to wipe away those tears, O my Love, and to behold Thee rejoicing in our good works and wholly cheered by them.

Blessed be the lips of my Jesus, which have uttered words so full of pity, which call me by name and which address me with smiles so alluring and so encouraging!—I can no longer resist Thee, Conqueror of my soul. Each one of Thy sweet smiles is an arrow which pierces me through and through. Would that by them I could die! Delightsome death!

Blessed be my Jesus in all His mysteries, past, present and yet to come! *Benedictus et superexaltatus et gloriosus in saecula!* (Dan. 3:52.) Worthy to be praised and glorified and exalted above all for ever!

CHAPTER XXXIV

THE CHRIST OF THE PRAYER OF SIMPLICITY

WHEN the fervent Christian has for many years explored the vast field of the contemplation of Jesus, undertaking separately each of His mysteries as they come in their turn throughout the liturgical year, doing this over and over again and each time going deeper and deeper into them, a time comes at last when his soul will be enabled, by a special grace of God, to view her Beloved at one glance as it were, and to Practice in His regard the Prayer of Simplicity.

In this one glance the mystic takes a comprehensive and simplified view of Our Lord, and lives on it. He is able to put into the one word *Jesus* all that the Saints put into it; all that we feel a St. Catherine of Siena put into it, for instance, when she used to write at the end of each of her letters: "Jesus! dear Jesus!"

Whoever conceives the noble ambition of reaching such a state of contemplation, ought before anything else, ardently and unceasingly to pray for it. In the second place, he ought to make attempts at it; not that he should pretend to reach it by his own efforts: he knows full well he cannot do that; but he wishes thereby to prepare himself for it, so that Our Lord, seeing his ardent desire, may be graciously pleased to grant it.

Let, therefore, the enamored contemplative make to himself in the secret of his heart a small picture of his Lord and Love, which he will carry in his mind and at which he will be gazing rapturously whenever he is disengaged from creatures.

Thus we see an earthly lover do in regard to the idol of his heart. If he be a rich man he will have a tiny image of that person engraved or painted in enamel and set in a locket of precious metal and rare workmanship and carry it everywhere with him, held by a chain round his neck. When alone, he will be looking at it incessantly, covering it with burning kisses and fondly telling it of his love. If his condition be too poor to allow of this, what of it? Is not love the most wonderful limner and engraver? He will then make in imagination his own drawing of the object of his affections, paint it with more than earthly colors, enshrine it in the locket of his own heart of hearts and never be done contemplating it there and holding sweet converse with it.

Let then the contemplative frame and paint for himself a picture of his Beloved, small enough for him easily to carry about in his mind at all times, and yet accurate enough to give him a full consciousness of the diverse elements which go to make the infinite loveliness of Our Lord.

All the mysteries of Jesus come under one or the other of these four heads:

1. That He is our very *God.*

2. That He makes himself our true *Brother* by flesh and blood and the affections of a human heart.

3. That He is our *Hostia pacifica* as well as Our High Priest, on Calvary, on our altars and on the altar of heaven.

4. That He is our heavenly *Bridegroom* in time and eternity.

We have these four aspects of Our Lord presented to us in the Apostles' Creed, which we recite every day. That Jesus Christ is God is expressed in the words: "I believe in God . . . and in Jesus Christ, His only Son Our Lord." That He is our Brother is set forth in these terms: "Who was conceived by the Holy Ghost, born of the Virgin Mary." That He is our Priest and oblation, in these: "Who suffered under Pontius Pilate, was crucified, dead and buried." Finally that He is our glorious heavenly Spouse is shown in these last words: "The third day He rose again from the dead, He ascended into heaven, sitteth at the right hand of God the Father Almighty, from thence He shall come to judge the living and the dead."

In these few lines of the Apostles' Creed we have the whole adorable person of Christ finely drawn for us; with a sketch of His wonder fill career, starting from the height of heaven to return even to the highest throne therein—all so simply put that the ignorant, the uneducated, the very young are not debarred from the privilege of learning it by heart, carrying it about so to say everywhere with them, and making it, if they wish, the constant object of their loving contemplation.

This compendious manner of looking at our Blessed Lord may even derive some encouragement and corroboration from Holy Scripture. We have all read of the grand and marvelous vision that was given first to Ezechiel, the Prophet, on the banks of the river Chobar; and then, centuries after, to St. John the Evangelist, in the Island of Patmos. They respectively and at a great distance of time saw four living winged creatures in the midst of a whirlwind and a great cloud of fire: *"One with the face of a lion, another with the face of a man, a third resembling an ox and the fourth with the countenance of an eagle. Their wings were joined to one another and they went together straight forward whither the impulse of the spirit was for them to go."* (Ezech. 1:10-12.)

All Christian antiquity is agreed that these four symbolical creatures are types of the four Evangelists and a clear prophecy of Him about whom they speak. But what I wish here to point out is how admirably it answers our present purpose of paving the way for us to the Prayer of Simplicity. We perceive in the lion the image of the irresistible strength of the Divinity of Christ; and in the figure of the Man, the mystery of His Incarnation, and in the figure of the Ox, which is the beast of sacrifice, an allusion to the mystery of our Redemption and Sanctification by His death on the Cross and His symbolical death on our altars, and finally in the Eagle, swooping down to his quarry and soaring on high with it in his talons, the image of His conquering love, which will not rest until He has carried us bodily into Paradise, there to make us share in the feast of His eternal Nuptials.

God, Brother, Oblation, Bridegroom: these four aspects of Our Lord and Love we must link together in the memory of our hearts, so that whichever of His mysteries we may happen at any time to be contemplating, these four aspects of Him present themselves at the same time, claim our attention and admiration and inspire the ardent ejaculations that we will surely be prompted to produce.

This manner of lovingly contemplating Our Lord, besides paving the way to the Prayer of Simplicity, has a wonderful effect on the person of the Christian who practices it. It makes him reproduce in himself the features of His divine Master as shown in the vision of Ezechiel and St. John. He becomes figuratively, a Lion, a Man, an Ox and an Eagle.

The Lion is the king of beasts. Its bearing is noble; its strength irresistible; its very roar carries dismay into the hearts of its enemies. The mystic shows himself a lion by subduing all the mean passions of the flesh and the spirit; covetousness, lust, pride, anger, and by overcoming the world and the devil.

He becomes a Man after the image of Jesus; that is to say a new man, a regenerate man, a man fully grown in Christ, gentle and strong, meek and humble, loving and merciful, a very son of God, not of Belial; carrying everywhere and spreading around him the sweet perfume of his evident brotherhood with Jesus Christ.

Is that all? It is already much, but it is not all. He becomes so to speak a beast of sacrifice: ready, willing, eager to suffer, to shed his very blood if called upon to do so, to give his life for the honor of God and the good of the brethren; uniting himself with his whole heart and soul to the sacrifice of the divine Victim on Calvary and on our altars; partaking eagerly of the flesh and the blood of Our Lord in the Holy Eucharist, that he may at the same time imbibe His fortitude in life and death; that he may, if need be, endure the most cruel privations and tortures, even as the martyrs, even as his Beloved Lord.

One more trait of resemblance to his divine Master is realized in him. He becomes an eagle. Even as Jesus kept the gaze of His human soul unflinchingly fixed upon the blazing Sun of the divine Essence; in like manner does our contemplative soar high above all petty concerns of temporal life and keep the gaze of his soul steadily fixed upon the Sacred Humanity of his Lord, that blazing Sun of Justice whose mysteries are like so many sunbeams which spread the divine splendor far and wide.

When the aspirant to the Prayer of Simplicity has by the grace of God become thus mortified, transfigured, sacrificed and ecstatic, Our Lord grants him the object of his ardent desire. The four previous considerations of the mysteries of Jesus are finally bound for him together into one, which is of infinite sweetness. Then does the mystic exclaim in the transport of his joy: *A bundle of myrrh is my Beloved to me: He shall abide between my breasts.* (Cant, 1:12.)

CHAPTER XXXV

THE WHOLE CHRIST

IT is no novelty to speak of the *Whole Christ.* This expression carries with it the best interpretation of some particularly characteristic passages of St Paul.

It is St. Augustine who first directed my attention to this aspect of Our Lord. I here subjoin a certain number of texts which I collected from various works of his, at a time when I had no intention of writing and publishing books. As my aim then was solely to minister to my own edification, I neglected to mark down chapter and verse and even the titles of the works whence I extracted them: hence I must beg my kind reader either to look them up for himself or accept them on trust.

Christus tribus modis dicitur in Scripturis: ut Deus, ut Deus et homo, ut caput et corpus. Christ is spoken of in the Scriptures under three different aspects: as God, as God made man, as head and body.

Totum quod annuntiatur de Christo, caput et corpus est.—Whatsoever is predicted of Christ is head and body.

Christus et membra ejus unus est Christus.— Christ and His members form one only Christ.

Ipsa caro Christi caput Ecclesiae est.—The very flesh of Christ is the head of the Church.

Adjuncta ejus carni Ecclesia fit Christus totus, caput et corpus.—Join the Church to the flesh of Christ and you have the whole Christ, head and body.

Christus et Ecclesìe caput et corpus, unus homo est, unus Christus.—Christ and His Church, the head with the body, that is one man, one only Christ.

Christi substantia populus ejus.—The Christian people is Christ's very substance.

Christus totus in corpore et in capite.—The whole Christ is equally found in the body and in the head.

Christus in membris suis.—Christ is in His members.

Voluit esse nobiscum unus qui est cum Patre unus.—He chose to be one with us even as He is one with the Father.

Non dedignatus est assumere nos in se.—He has deigned to assume us in Himself.

Christus solet in se membrorum suorum transferre personam.—Christ is wont to transfer into His own self the persons of His members.

Christus ex nobis omnibus tanquam membris unum corpus sibi facit.—Christ is building to Himself a body made up of all of us as His members.

Non solum Christiani sed Christus facti sumus. —Not only are we made Christians, but we are made Christ.

CHRISTUS TOTUS *haereditatem Patris accepturus est, nondum accepit.*—It is the "Whole Christ" that shall receive the Father's heritage: He has not as yet received it.

We may, in a limited sense, apply to Our Lord the epithet of the whole Christ, even now, inasmuch as He has already a mystical body, made up of the Church Triumphant, the Church Suffering and the Church Militant, such as they are at present This is already a view of Our Lord extremely sweet and consoling; and it is well for us to contemplate Him in that light. It will serve moreover to put in full relief the dogma of the Communion of Saints.

The ancient philosopher Pythagoras pretended to be listening to the music of the heavenly spheres. Much more truly is it given us to listen, if we will, to the harmony of the Church Militant, Suffering and Triumphant. It will give us the last word on that grand IN CHRISTO, so much emphasized and celebrated by St. Paul, and beautifully commented upon in the books of Abbot Vonier, especially in his PERSONALITY OF CHRIST, chapter xvi.

The Communion of Saints implies the following divine facts: 1. Union of all the members, wherever situated, into one body; 2. Reciprocal love of all the members; 3. Mutual communication of their spiritual goods; 4. Union of all to the head which is Christ; 5. Identification of each of them with Christ.

These two together, Jesus and the Christian, form one Christ in two persons. They are indeed two distinct persons, and yet they form one and the same Christ, without either of the two losing his own personality. This is very felicitously expressed in the famous words of St. Paul: *I live now not* 7, *but Christ liveth in me,* (Gal. 2:20.) These words are often wrongly quoted as meaning the intensity of the love of St. Paul for Christ. In reality that is not their meaning, as anyone may see for himself by reading attentively the context, from, let us say, verse 16 to verse 21. All this passage, and verse 20 along with the rest, is purely and simply the theological statement of a divine fact, which applies to every Christian in the state of grace.

Now as this marvelous union and identification with Christ takes place in all the brethren, they are therefore all one in Christ, all one with Christ, all one with the others, all one Christ together. My brother is not only Christ's *(Christi),* but Christ *(Christus).* All my brethren in heaven, in purgatory, and here on earth, not only are Christ's, but they are, one and all, Christ in very deed. When I do any kindness to my brother on earth, Christ is the recipient of this. When I offer Mass or some prayer for the Holy Souls, it is Christ to whom I afford relief in their persons. When I honor the dear Saints in Paradise, it is Christ whom I am praising in them. Now I understand better the full import of these words of the Supreme Judge at the end of the world, addressing Himself to the elect: *I was hungry and you gave me to drink; I was a stranger and you took me in; naked and you covered me; sick and you visited me; I was in prison and you came to me,* (Matt, 25:35-36.)

Grand doctrine this, which ought to break down the last resistance of my perverse and corrupt nature to the love of my neighbor, so peremptorily enforced throughout the New Testament. Meanwhile let us not omit to notice in all this intercommunion of the threefold Church of all the Saints, the activities of Our Lord, the wonderful activities by which He binds us all together in one, drawing us all to Himself, making us all one with Himself.

We were all one all together in Adam before ever we were born, and that is why we have all sinned in Adam (Mary alone excepted), and we have all lapsed and been lost in Adam. Now it is required that we should all become one in Christ, in order that we may be saved. Whosoever separates himself from Christ damns himself.

It may not be amiss to make here one more observation about the Communion of Saints. It seems to me that it is in our intercourse with the Blessed Virgin Mary and the other saints that the words of St. Paul: *Our conversation is in heaven* (Phil, 2:20), find their literal fulfilment and verification. For, in order to converse with Our Lord, the mystic has only to visit Him in His Blessed Sacrament; and in order to converse with the Most Holy Trinity or any of the Three Divine Persons in particular, he has only to retire into his own heart. So that it is really devotion to the dear Saints which compels us, in a way, to break into Paradise.

This is a very precious aspect of devotion to the Saints. God is indeed with us and we are with God and in God; but the dear Saints are no more with us; they are in heaven. If I want to have converse with any of them, I must, by faith, in spirit, go right up there and enter right in. It is true that I do not thereby leave the earth of my pilgrimage, and yet it is equally true that I am for the time being, admitted to their blessed company, in their abode which is paradise. I am successful to the extent, at any rate, of obtaining a hearing, whatever answer they, in their charity, in the light of God, may see fit to vouchsafe me.

The same holds good also in regard to our having converse with the Holy Souls. We must go right in; we must by faith and in spirit go down into Purgatory. I would suggest as one of the best possible practices of piety, that besides praying for the Holy Souls, we make it our business thus to visit them in their fiery prison. Besides procuring them additional solace, it would have the most salutary effect upon the whole tenor of our own Christian life. If I mistake not, this is true mysticism.

Now to return to our concept of the "whole Christ." After

what we have just said about the limited sense in which the expression applies at present to Our Lord, it follows that the whole Christ in His final integrity will be fulfilled only at the end of the world, after the general Resurrection and at the conclusion of the Last Judgement. Then will the Lord Jesus, the Lamb of God, the Heavenly Bridegroom have with Him His Bride, the Church of the elect, blessed angels and risen saints, in their full number, each crowned with the glory of all the good works he did whilst in life, and their after-effects during the time that elapsed till the end of the world; arrayed in the order of the final hierarchy, which is based upon no other consideration than the degree of love of God each one will have attained. Then as Our Lord has warned us beforehand, some of the last will be first. Some humble lay brothers, some ignorant goodwives who did not shine in the least during their lives, will, on account of the intensity of their charity, be raised above priests, doctors, abbots, bishops, popes even, and placed in the highest choir among the resplendent Seraphim.

The Lord Jesus under this aspect is still unfulfilled, still in the making, as it were, and it is our privilege, whilst on earth, to take a hand, if we will, in the mighty work of His being brought to completion.

Adam needed Eve; the New Adam wants an Eve worthy of Himself. *The Lamb of God* wants for *His wife* (to use the expression of the Apocalypse) *the New Jerusalem,* that is to say the full congregation of the elect, *coming down out of heaven from God, prepared as a bride adorned for her husband.* (Apoc. 21:2.)

CHAPTER XXXVI

OF THE FINAL UNFOLDING OF THE MYSTERY OF CHRIST

E may distinguish in the unfolding of the mystery of Christ four successive eras or periods. The first began at that very beginning of all things created, which is recorded in the first verses of the Bible: *In the beginning God created heaven and earth; and the earth was void, and darkness was upon the face of the deep; and the spirit of God moved over the waters; and God said: Be light made.* (Gen. 1:1-2.) An era in which, through the six mysterious days, all things are being made ready for the coming of the first human couple upon the scene of the world. Adam and Eve are the ancestors of Christ and they adumbrate Him already.

The second period then began with the creation of the first Adam. It extends through the antediluvian and patriarchal ages and the whole history of the Hebrew race as the people of God, *to whom is made the Promise* (Gal. 3:16), even unto the actual coming upon the scene of the world of the second Adam, better than the first. This is Our Lord Jesus Christ who comes now to repair the great damage done by the disobedience of our first parents. Mighty events take place during this period, such as the corruption of all mankind, the great Flood, the propagation of the race all over the world, the spreading of idolatry among the Gentiles, the rise and fall of mighty empires, the foundation of Rome and its conquest of the world. The misery and degradation of the whole human race proclaim loudly how much it is in need of a Savior.

The third period extends from the birth of Our Lord, through all the centuries past and yet to come of the Christian era, to what Jesus calls the *Regeneration* (Matt, 19:28), or rebirth. Then all men having been raised from the dust, the Son of Man shall come with divine majesty and infinite power to judge the living and the dead and to render to every one according to his works. This era is characterized by the wonderful process of the vocation of the Gentiles, and the formation of the Church of the elect, which, when entirely fulfilled, is to be the immaculate, all-beautiful bride of the Lamb of God.

Now these three first periods, taken altogether, are but the preparation for the fourth and final and eternal one, which is called enigmatically by Isaiah *the World to come* and more clearly and joyfully by St. John in the Apocalypse *the Nuptials of the Lamb.*

This last era will be inaugurated at the moment when, having sent the reprobates to their doom, Our Blessed Lord will pronounce these words pregnant with mysterious, blissful meaning: *Behold I make all things new.* (Apoc. 21:5.)

Then shall we see the last unfolding of the *mystery of Christ:* and we shall be in it, a part of it, if we have been to the very end faithful, living members of His Church. But no words of man could give the slightest inkling of what it will be like.

EPILOGUE

Reader, we are at the end of our journey.

This, then, is the way of the loving contemplation of Our Lord. The fervent Christian in his pious, prayerful meditation of the mysteries of the life of Christ, as they present themselves one after the other in the sacred liturgy, draws near to the heart of his Savior, nay boldly penetrates right into it, for the lance of the soldier has made this an easy task. From the Sacred Heart he passes into the very Soul of Jesus and delightfully loses himself for a while In its all but infinite depths. But he soon finds therein a golden door, at which he has no sooner knocked than it opens of itself and admits him into the sanctuary of the divine nature of Our Lord, the Godhead of the Word.

Speechless, swooning for very excess of joy, turned into a tiny spark of intensest fire of love, this happy mortal discovers that he is now, with the Second Person of the Blessed Trinity, in the ineffably sweet company of the Father and the Holy Ghost. He can now truly begin to live that *life hid with Christ in God* (Coloss, 3:3), of which St. Paul speaks. He can now proceed to the obscure and yet most illuminating and comforting contemplation of the Divine Essence of the Most Holy Trinity. This matter will be the burden of our next treatise.

And now, before we close this volume, and as a fitting conclusion to it, O my soul, let us sing a hymn to the Lord Jesus Christ. Let us sing to Him, with the whole Church Militant, Suffering and Triumphant:

Tu Rex gloriae, Christe. *Tu Patris sempiternus es Filius.* *Tu ad liberandum suscepturus hominem, non horruisti Virginis*	Thou, O Christ, art the King of glory. Thou art the eternal Son of the Father. In order to save us, thou hast not disdained to take our human nature in the Virgin's womb.

uterum. *Tu devicto mortis aculeo, aperuisti credentibus regna coelorum.* *Tu ad dexteram Dei sedes, in gloria Patris.* *Judex crederis esse venturus.*	Thou hast broken the goad of death and opened the kingdom of heaven to those who have faith. Thou art seated at the right hand of God, in the glory of the Father. We firmly believe in thy next coming as Judge. (Extract from the *Te Deum.*)
Tu solus sanctus. *Tu solus Dominus.* *Tu solus Altissimus,* JESU CHRISTE. CUM SANCTO SPIRITU, IN GLORIA DEI PATRIS. AMEN.	Thou alone art holy. Thou alone art the Lord. Thou alone art the Most High, O Christ Jesus, with the Holy Spirit, in the glory of the Father. Amen. (Extract from the *Gloria in Excelsis.*)

THE END

The Immaculate Conception
—Esteban Murillo

BOOK VI

MYSTICAL INITIATION:
THE CANTICLE OF CANTICLES

PREFACE

N order to convey from the beginning some idea of what the reader may expect to find in this new treatise, I should have given it a lengthy sub-title, something in this wise:

MYSTICAL INITIATION—"BY MEANS OF THE FIVE FIRST CHAPTERS OF THE CANTICLE OF CANTICLES, ABRIDGED, PARAPHRASED, AND COMMENTED ON FOR THE LITTLE ONES OF THE FLOCK OF CHRIST."

This of course was inadvisable; a short, pregnant title being always preferred both by publishers and readers.

It has always struck me that the Sacred Liturgy does not hesitate to put under the eyes of all the faithful, indiscriminately, diverse passages of the CANTICLE OF CANTICLES; and I have had occasion to observe how sincerely and deeply pious souls have their feelings stirred by these. Now and again persons under my spiritual direction have begged to be allowed to read and meditate upon this, the most mysterious book of Holy Scripture, for their own edification.

Following in this regard the traditional discipline of the Church and the rules of prudence, I have thought fit to grant this permission to a restricted number only. But the question soon arose in my mind, whether it were not possible to bring this, the most mystical and consoling of all the sacred books, within the reach of everyone, by eliminating here and there a certain number of verses.

It is to be noted that, according to the teaching of the Fathers of the Church, the Canticle of Canticles is susceptible of a threefold interpretation: the first applying exclusively to the Blessed Virgin Mary in her relation to her Divine Son, who is at the same time the heavenly Spouse of her soul; the second, applying to the Church, who, as the corporate aggregation of all the children of light, is the perfect Bride of the Son of God; the third, finally, applying to the individual Christian soul, who brings into her relations with Our Lord a most fervent love. Now the verses of the Canticle of Canticles which it is not advisable, on account of the infirmities of our present condition, to propose to every one as a subject for study and meditation, are precisely those which have a direct reference either to the Blessed Virgin or to Holy Church; so that it were, in my opinion, quite possible, if we leave aside those particular verses, to establish a running text of this most precious book, in some measure abridged, to which no one could take objection, and which would still retain a rich fund of devout exegesis for the edification and comfort of all the faithful. This is precisely the end I have had in view in the following pages. Still, diffident of myself, I submitted this idea to the judgement of theologians as pious as competent, and received from them the warmest approbation and encouragement.

I had not the intention at first of bringing out this work so soon; but it ripened and came to full maturity more quickly than I had anticipated; thanks particularly to the intense labor which the preparation and composition of my preceding volume THE MYSTERY OF JESUS entailed upon me.

This is indeed its proper place in the series of my treatises on Catholic Traditional Mysticism; for it is, as its elder brother, a book on the love of Jesus. Whilst THE MYSTERY OF JESUS states the broad principles concerning the contemplation of Our Lord, the present treatise applies those principles to the individual soul. In fact, it is to be considered as a companion volume to THE MYSTERY OF JESUS.

Mindful of the warning of Our Lord (Matt, 7:6) *not to give that which it holy to dogs, neither cast our pearls before swine, lest perchance they trample them under their feet and turning upon us they tear us,* I protest I have written this little book in the presence of God, in the fear and in the love of His Divine Majesty, and therefore nor for the scurrilous or the foul-minded, whoever or whatever they may happen to be; but only for the clean of heart. Only *the clean of heart will see God* through its pages.

PART I
THE CHILD-BRIDE

MYSTICAL INITIATION

CHAPTER I

THE CANTICLE OF CANTICLES: ITS DIVISION AND INTERPRETATION

SUMMARY.—An allegory by which is declared the love of God for each individual soul. Three parts corresponding io the three stages of the spiritual life. One comprehensive rule of interpretation.

THE Canticle of Canticles is the sweetest of all the books of Holy Scripture, inasmuch as it makes to each individual soul an application of the whole love of God, such as it shines forth in the other parts of the Holy Bible, and particularly in the Gospels. It moreover has this peculiarity, that it initiates one, in the most persuasive manner, into the art of taking one's delights in Jesus alone.

Under an allegory, which blends together things rural with kingly pomp and splendor, we are presented, in the persons of the bride and bridegroom, with a lively image of the reciprocal love which ought to hold sway during this present life, between the Christian soul and her heavenly Spouse, Our Lord.

Each verse, each separate sentence, nay even each word of this wonderfully inspired composition, hides some heavenly mystery which it is extremely sweet to investigate and to discover by the interior light of the Holy Spirit.

At first sight, it would seem as though from the very first word to the last there was in the Canticle of Canticles a complete absence of method, of logical sequence, of that systematization which is so dear to the hearts of certain dry-as-dust professors or writers of manuals. It is in very deed, if one may use such an expression, a veritable explosion of love. The incidents seem tumultuously to press upon one another like the waters of a rich spring, and to overflow on all sides without any conventional symmetry, .but with a liveliness that is a delight to the eyes, the ears, the mind of the beholder. Origen calls this book: "Jubilus amoris divini: The joyful canticle of divine love." Does love measure its movements by rule and compass, or submit to the slow process of logic?

Yet on close inspection we discover some ground for dividing the Canticle of Canticles into three parts, corresponding to the three stages of the spiritual life, to wit: the Purgative, the Illuminative, and the Unitive Way. It is easy to find in the first two chapters, the picture of the beginnings of a life of love. The Christian soul is then as yet but a child: she is led principally by the sweets of a sensible devotion and has yet to get rid of a good many imperfections. This is the first relay. In the second (chapters 3-5) the soul waxes strong, full of wisdom, and the grace of God is in her. She makes great progress in the knowledge and love of her divine Spouse, at the same time as she is made to pass through severe trials. In the last three chapters (6-8) the soul waxes strong, full of wisdom, and has come to the full maturity of love: the Divine Word, her Bridegroom, wants her all to Himself, and will not let her turn for a single moment to any one else, and He lifts her up to heights of charity which seem to us well nigh incommensurable.

We must understand that every Christian soul, without any distinction of age, or sex, or condition is the bride of the Son of God made man, Our Lord Jesus Christ. She came into the supernatural world through the sacrament of Baptism, she grows tn adult age in Jesus Christ by living the life of grace, that is to say, by the fervent use of the sacraments, by meditation on the Holy Scriptures, especially the Gospel, and by practicing the virtues proper to her state of life. Finally she becomes the *wedded wife of the Lamb,* as soon as she enters finally into the ways of purely supernatural life. Then does Our Lord deal with her most lovingly and intimately; then does He make her feel the joys of her union with Him: then does He Himself take His delights in her.

Whosoever you are who take this little book in hand, I

recommend you to read it slowly, thoughtfully, with great simplicity, and praying the while. Keep your soul open to the illuminations and secret impressions of the Holy Spirit; and when the mood comes upon you of breaking into transports of love for your virgin Spouse, the Lord Jesus Christ, the Word of God and your sweet Savior, allow it full sway.

I even wish you would, first of all, and before anything else, read the sacred text, such as I have prepared it for you in Chapters III and XXVII of this volume, endeavoring to find out by yourself one, or more than one, of the several mystical, that is to say spiritual, meanings of it. One does not need to be very learned for that. With your knowledge of the Catechism and of the Holy Gospel, and your own personal experiences, however limited they may have been, of the ways of God, it must be possible to you to discover, were it but on the surface of the sacred text, some pious meaning.

One rule of interpretation will suffice, an extremely simple rule, this namely: always to read a spiritual, supernatural and evangelical meaning into the material representations and lively expressions of conjugal human love which the Holy Spirit has judged good to place under our eyes, in order to make us understand some small part of the excess of the love of the Son of God for us, and the wonderful familiarity which He wants us to bring into our relations with Him.

As a rule we are not daring enough to believe in the fullness of the love of Jesus for each one of us personally, individually. Nor do we dare freely to allow ourselves to use expressions of tender affection, such as this dear heavenly Spouse has a right to expect and positively longs to receive from us. When He is looking for a loving embrace we content ourselves with presenting Him with a cold, stiff reverence: when He wishes to press us tenderly upon His heart, we offer Him ceremonious adoration at a distance. Ah! what a different lesson the Canticle of Canticles teaches us!

Before proceeding to our paraphrase of the sacred text it is advisable that we should present some preliminary theological notions. We will do so in the next chapter.

CHAPTER II

ONE WORD, WHISPERED IN THE EAR OF THE BRIDE

SUMMARY.—How much the Word of God has loved us from all eternity. How He began loving us with His human Heart at the very moment of His Incarnation. How He has loved us throughout all His earthly life and Sacred Passion, and since He is seated in glory at thy right hand of His Father. What He wants to do with us.

O LITTLE soul of good will, if it is thy wish to learn how to lisp the syllables of divine love, listen first of all to what I have to tell thee.

Jesus, the Son of God and Our Lord, has loved thee first, He has loved thee personally, for thine own individual sake, from all eternity. He has loved thee with an ineffable, incomprehensible love, which moved Him, together with His heavenly Father and His Holy Spirit, to decree thy creation which was to take place in due time, making thee into His own image and likeness, raising thee to the supernatural order of grace as a preparation to that of glory which is to follow: in short, wishing to impart to thee a share of His own divine sanctity and of His own divine bliss—in part whilst thou art yet here below, to the full of thy capacity when thou wilt be in heaven.

And now, listen! for this is a deep mystery and a most affecting one, though so often passed over in silence by those who deem themselves *masters in Israel* (John 3:10); listen! At the precise moment of His Incarnation, Our blessed Lord received in His created mind the infused knowledge of everything that it was necessary for Him to know in His capacity of Redeemer of the world. A full and dear perception was given Him of everything connected with His work as Savior of all men. From that moment forth He knew them all and every one of them in particular; as well those who had lived from the time of Adam until then, as those who were yet to come, century after century, to the very end of all time.

Therefore thou must realize that, from the very first moment of His Incarnation, Our Lord has known thee with His human mind and loved thee with His human heart, although thou wert not yet in existence. He called thee by thy name, chose thee and marked thee for His own, and forthwith began to love thee, thee I say, personally, individually, with a singular and exclusive love, with a love humano-divine, quite distinct from the purely divine love with which He has loved thee from all eternity.

True, even such a marvelous supplement, the humano-divine love of the heart of Jesus for thee, added on to the purely divine love of the Eternal Word, cannot swell its sum total, since divine love is in itself infinite; but it is a fresh demonstration, and a very moving one, of this infinite love.

Why do we call "humano-divine" this special love of the heart of Jesus for thee? Because it is at the same time human and divine. On the one hand it is truly human, being the love of a human heart, the love that comes from the heart of the *Son of Man,* and from His whole human nature, for thee. And, on the other hand, this same human love is at the same time divine on two accounts: first because although human, the heart of Jesus belongs to a divine person, the second of the Blessed Trinity; then, because from that very fact that it belongs to the Person of the Word, that same human heart has, so to say, behind it, the full infinitude of the pure divine love of the Word; it is the created organ or instrument and the most expressive symbolical representation of the love of the Word of God, nay, of the whole Blessed Trinity, for us men.

Since the first moment of His life on earth, through all the incidents of His sacred passion, and afterwards in glory, Jesus has not ceased a single instant to think of thee, to love thee, to carry thee about in His heart, during all the time that elapsed before thou earnest into the world. And when at last thou wert born; when above all, thou wert baptized, Jesus began in earnest to play the game of love with thee.

Understand, O my dear Christian, man of good will, meek and humble—understand that this lover of thy soul is none other than thy very God. He wants to take hold of thee, body and soul, and make thee wholly supernatural. He longs to see thee lay down as thy wager in this divine venture, in this game of love, the whole man of thee, body, soul, intellect, sensibility, will; the whole tree, root and branch and leaf and fruit.

Having raised thee, His rational creature, to the dignity of His spouse, He now wants to communicate Himself to thee in an ineffable manner, and to take hold of thee from within: but, of course, with thy consent; only with thy consent.

I entreat thee, allow Him so to love thee. And as for thee, do thou make return to the love of Jesus with all the energies of thy being both natural and supernatural, even as does the bride of the Canticle of Canticles, as thou shaft presently see.

CHAPTER III

ABRIDGED TEXT OF THE FIRST TWO CHAPTERS OF THE CANTICLE

SUMMARY.—The Spouse speaking to herself, then to her companions, finally to her Heavenly Bridegroom. Reply of the Beloved and passionate dialogue which ensues.

NOTE.—The sacred text set in italics: I wish I could have written it in letters of gold, on most precious illumined vellum, with a pen forged by some Seraph and dipped in the flames which burn on the Altar of Paradise.

What is written in common type is no part of the sacred text, but interwoven with it, merely to help the reader to grasp the literal meaning of the Hebrew phrase, which would remain obscure if it were translated word for word.

CHAPTER I OF THE CANTICLE OF CANTICLES

THE BRIDE, speaking to herself, says outright:
"Let him kiss me, with the kiss of his mouth."
Then turning to her Beloved, she adds:
"Thy name is as *oil poured out.*
"Therefore young maidens have loved thee.
"Draw me.
"will run after thee to the odor of thy ointments."

Now addressing her maiden companions, she says:
"The King hath brought me into his storerooms"

Then she turns again to her divine Bridegroom and exclaims:
"We will be glad and rejoice in thee."
"The righteous love thee."

Again, to her attendants:
" O ye daughters of Jerusalem," listen: I have a secret to

impart to you.

"*I am black, but beautiful.*"
(Black) "*as the tents of Cedar*"
(Beautiful) "*as the curtains of Solomon*"
Pray: "*Do not consider that I am brown,*
Because the sun hath altered my complexion.
The sons of my mother have fought against me.
They have made me the keeper in the vineyards;
My own vineyard I have not kept."

To her Bridegroom:

"*O thou whom my soul loveth*
Show me where thou feedest.
Where thou liest in the mid-day,
Lest I begin to wander after the flocks of thy companions."

THE BRIDEGROOM replies:

If thou knowest not where I feed and lie in the mid-day,
"*We will run after thee to the odor of thy ointments.*"
Now addressing her maiden companions, she says:

"*The King hath brought me into his store- rooms.*"

Then she turns again to her divine Bridegroom and exclaims:

"*We will be glad and rejoice in thee.*"
"*The righteous love thee.*"

Again, to her attendants:

"*O ye daughters of Jerusalem*" listen: I have a secret to impart to you.

" I am black, but beautiful."
(Black) "*as the tents of Cedar,*"
(Beautiful) "*as the curtains of Solomon.*"
Pray: "*Do not consider that I am brown,*
Because the sun hath altered my complexion.
The sons of my mother have fought against me.
They have made me the keeper in the vineyards;
My own vineyard I have not kept."

To her Bridegroom:

"O thou whom my soul loveth
Show me where thou feedest.
Where thou liest in the mid-day.
Lest I begin to wander after the flocks of thy companions."

THE BRIDEGROOM replies:

"If thou knowest not where I feed and lie in the mid-day,
O fairest among women,
Go forth,
And follow after the steps of the flocks.
And feed thy kids beside the tents of the shepherds."
"O my lave,
To my company of horsemen, in Pharaohs chariots, have I
compared thee.
Thy cheeks are beautiful as the turtledove's. Thy neck as
jewels.
We will make thee chains of gold, inlaid with silver."

THE BRIDE, calling to mind one of her dearest remembrances:

"While the King was at his repose My spikenard sent forth its
perfume.
A bundle of myrrh is *my beloved to me. . . .*
A cluster of Cyprus is *my love to me*
In the vineyards of Engaddi."

JESUS, to the soul freshly baptized or made white in the
sacrament of penance:
"Behold: thou art fair, O my love.
Behold, thou art fair.
Thy eyes are as those of doves."

THE SOUL in the transport of her admiration:

"Behold, thou art fair, my beloved, And comely.
Our bed is flowery.
The beams of our houses are of cedar,
Our rafters of cypress trees."

CHAPTER II OF THE CANTICLE OF CANTICLES

JESUS, the heavenly Bridegroom, speaking to Himself, or else addressing His angels and saints in paradise, exclaims:

"I am the flower of the field and the lily of the valleys.
As the lily among thorns, so is my love among the daughters."

THE ENAMORED SOUL:

"As the apple-tree among the trees of the wood,
So is my beloved among the sons of men.
I sat down tender his shadow, whom I desired,
And his fruit was sweet to my palate.
He brought me into the cellar of wine,
He set in order charity in me.
Stay me up with flowers,
Compass me about with apples,
Because I languish with love.
His left hand is under my head,
And his right hand shall embrace me."

JESUS addressing Himself to all His servants both in heaven and on earth:

"O ye daughters of Jerusalem,
I adjure you,
By the roes and the harts of the fields,
That you stir not up
Nor make the beloved to awake,
Till she please."

THE SOUL, in the midst of the ecstatic sleep of divine contemplation, exclaims:

"The voice of my beloved!
Behold he cometh, leaping upon the mountains.
Skipping over the hills."
" My beloved is a roe, or a young hart. Behold he standeth behind our wall, Looking through the windows, Looking through the lattices.
Behold my beloved speaketh to me."

JESUS to the fervent soul:

"Arise, make haste and come,
My love, my dove, my beautiful one.
For winter is now past,
The rain is aver and gone.
The flowers have appeared in our land,
The time of pruning is come,
The voice of the turtle is heard in our land;
The fig-tree hath put forth her green figs,
The vines in flower yield their sweet smell.
My love, my beautiful one, arise and come!
My dove in the clifts of the rock,
In the hollow place of the wall,
Show me thy face,
Let thy voice sound in my ears,
For thy voice is sweet, and thy face comely."

Now THE BRIDE makes this recommendation to her companions: unless it be Our Lord Himself speaking to the spiritual directors of the Bride:

"Catch us the little foxes that destroy the vine:
For our vineyard hath flourished."

Then musingly to herself, THE BRIDE says very sweetly:

"My beloved, who feedeth among the lilies,
Is to me, and I to him,
Till the day breaks and the shadows retire."

Nevertheless He hides himself at times. Then she cries out:

"Return, my beloved, Be like to a roe, or to a young hart
Upon the mountains of Bether."

CHAPTER IV

LET HIM KISS ME WITH THE KISS OF HIS MOUTH, (1:1.)

SUMMARY.—These words reveal to us how God wishes to be loved of us and in what manner our own heart craves to love God. They indicate also the starting point of the Bride in the career of the spiritual life and whereto she aspires. Certain things she does not ask for.

HE musician of genius stands revealed at one touch of his bow on the violin; so with the Canticle of Canticles: its very first words betray the flaming spirit of love divine which inspires it.

These first words cast a vivid light upon the deep enigma we are to ourselves. They reveal that we are made for love, for love divine. To love and be loved is the craving of our heart, a craving that no created object can appease. Now God is love, all love, love in three persons, a shoreless and bottomless ocean of love. *Deus carinas est.* (1 John 4:16.) As for Jesus, He is *love made man.* In his turn, the fervent Christian, by the virtue of the sacraments, to which he gives their full effect in himself, is *man made love.* Shall we then wonder that the Holy Spirit should put on his lips this strange request:

"Ah! let God kiss me with the kiss of his mouth!"

Moved thereto by grace, the soul, whether she be still quite innocent or a convert from a life of sin, begins thus to beg and plead for the divine endearments. She is not ashamed to request the Son of God, from the throne of His infinite majesty, lovingly to look down upon her and stoop down to her very level, whilst she is still on earth and laden with imperfections, and embrace and kiss her, and let her be familiar with Him, in the same way as human lovers are with one another.

The amazing thing is that the Son of God, in the splendor of

His glory at the right hand of His Father, surrounded with millions of angels and saints, does not disdain to listen to and tenderly receive, the sighs of love of this little soul in exile, and to grant her bold request. See what takes place at the Communion rail. Is not Holy Communion a kiss of the mouth of the Son of God, a kiss on the lips of that lowly one?

The first kiss of God was impressed on that soul at her Baptism, and divine love made it so burning that it left a mark which can never be erased. Now the fervent soul wishes ever to receive fresh impressions of the divine sweetness, and therefore she keeps repeating: "Oh! let him kiss me with the kiss of his mouth." Longing for actual graces, longing for Holy Communion, longing for divine contemplation, longing for the vision face to face and the joys of paradise; all these are expressed in that short ejaculation.

God has nothing so much at heart as to impart to us all his goods: only we must wish for them and beg for them.

By these words: "Let him kiss me with the kiss of his mouth," the bride shows what is her starting-point in the race for sanctity and where she aspires to reach. She is already firmly established in the state of grace and in fervor; and she aims at the more perfect union which is obtained by the practice of mental prayer, in that act of divine contemplation which is properly "Mystical Theology." That is what she longs to obtain. Shall we mention also the things that she does not wish for herself? These are the extraordinary and miraculous favors, such as ecstasies, raptures, visions, revelations.

Just as we ought ardently to wish and prepare ourselves for the mystical union which is brought about by mental prayer and the use of the sacraments, so must we also guard against desiring the miraculous gifts.

Following on the footsteps of Origen, St. Gregory the Great, St. Bernard, St. Thomas Aquinas, St. John of the Cross, St. Francis de Sales, and our contemporary writer, Father Arounder, O.P., I interpret the Canticle of Canticles as treating of the ordinary mystical union, towards which every one may tend, and to which all our efforts ought to be directed.

A petition like this: "Let him kiss me with the kiss of his mouth," abruptly proffered, seemingly without rhyme or reason, shows forth what a fire of love is already burning within that little soul. In this wise does a volcano emit violent and unexpected jets of flames.

Thus, at the outset, the Canticle of Canticles declares how God wishes to be loved of us, and the way in which our own heart craves to love God and be loved by Him. Let us follow the lead of the Child-Bride; let us make for the Lover of our soul; let us go repeating: "Yes, let him kiss me; oh! let him kiss me with the kiss of his mouth."

CHAPTER V

THE NAME AND SURNAMES OF THE BRIDEGROOM

SUMMARY.—Thy name is as oil poured out. How the name of Jesus has spread itself in the world and done good io it. The surname of Christ and other appellations.

HAT is the name of this dear Bridegroom of our soul? It is Jesus.

Jesus! JESUS! two short syllables, but the sound of which have shaken the world to its very foundations. *In omnem terram exivit sonus eorum: Their sound hath gone forth into all the earth.* (Ps. 18:5.)

This name of Jesus, brought from heaven by the Archangel Gabriel, is the culminating point of the history of the world: we date events according as they took place before or after the solemn moment when it was for the first time pronounced on this earth.

Note how the name of Jesus spread all over the world, percolated through every century, entered as an *oil of gladness* into every heart of good will.

When she proclaimed that the name of Jesus was as oil poured out, did the little bride perceive that she was giving him also His surname? Christ means the man upon whom the consecrating oil has been poured out; the anointed of the Lord.

Our Jesus is indeed the Lord's anointed. Anointed as King since he is *King of kings* (Apoc 19:16)—*immortal King of ages* (1 Tim. 1:17.) *The Lord to whom my Lord said: Sit thou at my right hand* (Ps. 109:1)— *and of whose Kingdom there shall be no end.* (Luke 1:23.)

Anointed as prophet, He that is not only *propheta magnus* (Luc. 12:6), the greatest of all prophets, but the center around which all prophecies are converging; the supreme object of them all.

Anointed with priestly unction, since *The Lord hath sworn it and will not repent: Thou art a priest for ever, according to the order of Melchisedech.* (Ps. 109:4.)—*And Christ did not glorify himself that he might be made a high priest, but he that said unto him: Thou art my Son, this day have I begotten thee.* (Heb. 5:5.) —And *Christ being come an high priest of the good things to come, by a greater and more perfect tabernacle not made with hands, that is, not of this creation; neither by the blood of goats or of calves, but by his own blood, entered once into the Holies, having obtained eternal redemption.* (Heb. 9:11-12).—*For it was fitting that we should have such a high priest, holy, innocent, undefiled, separated from sinners, and made higher than the heavens.* (Heb. 7:26.)

This, then, is his name: Jesus, and this his surname: CHRIST. Jesus Christ: oh! what oil poured out upon the gaping wounds of the human race! and how quickly and thoroughly it would heal them, if only the unfortunate men would allow this good Samaritan Jesus to attend to them! Peter, at the gate of the Temple which was called Beautiful, said to the man lame from his mother's womb: *Silver end gold I have none, but what I have I give thee: in the name of Jesus Christ of Nazareth, arise and walk: and he leaping up stood, and walked and went in with them into the temple, praising God.* (Acts 3:6-8.)

Another way in which the name of Jesus spreads like oil and penetrates through all the regions of the mind and the avenues of the heart, is by means of the beautiful multiplicity of its other surnames. Here are a few:

The Lord. (passim in the whole New Testament)
The Holy One. (Luke 1:35.)
The Holy of Holies. (Ps. 109:3.)
The desired of all stations. (Agg. 2:8.)
The Promised One. (John 4:25.)
The Word. (John 1:1-15.)
The Word made-flesh, (ibid.")
The Only Son in his Father's bosom. (John 1:18.)
Alpha and Omega. (Apoc. 1:8.)

Emmanuel, that is to say: God with us. (Is. 7:14.)

He that is Wonderful. (Is. 9:6.)

Angel of the great counsel. (Is. 9:6.)

Father of the world to come. (Is. 9:6.)

Son of David, of Abraham, of Man, Son of the Virgin. (Is. 7, 4; Matt, 1:23; Luke 1:27.)

The New Adam. (1 Cor. 15:45.)

The Good Shepherd. (Eccl. 18:13. Is. 40:11; Jer 21:10. Ezech. 24:12-23, 24. John 10:11-16.)

Good Master. (Mark 10:17.)

Prince of Pastors. (Pet. 5:4.)

Prince of Peace. (Is. 9:6.)

Greater than Solomon. (Matt, 12:42.)

The Light of the world. (John 1:9, 8:12.)

The Living Bread which came down from heaven. (John 6:41-51.)

Lamb of God. (John 1:29. Apoc. 5:12.)

Savior. (2 Kings 22:2. Job 13:16. Ps. 24:5. Is. 12:2. Jer. 14:8. Osee 13:4. Zech, 9:9. Luke 2:11. John 4:42. 1 Tim. 4:10. Acts 5:31.)

Mediator between God and man. (1 Tim. 2:5)

The first begotten of the dead. (Apoc. 1:5.)

The Resurrection and the life. (John 11:25.) *Our Pasch.* (1 Cor. 5:7.)

Our advocate with the Father. (1 John 2:1.)

Judge of the living and the dead. (Act. 10:42.)

The Bridegroom. (Ps. 18:6. Cant, *passim.* Osee 2:19-20. Matt, 9:15, 25:6. Apoc. 21:9.)

O Christian soul, do not read the above as a dry land meaningless nomenclature. Do not pass lightly by these various appellations of the one object of thy love, the Lord Jesus. Learn to see and taste, by prayerful meditation, how sweet is each one of these surnames. It will even do thee good to look up the references in the Bible: it may serve to introduce thee to a working knowledge and appreciation of this Book of books.

JESUS: most enchanting and tremendous of all names, on hearing which let *every knee bow, of those that are in heaven, on earth or under the earth, and every tongue confess that the Lord Jesus Christ is in the glory of God the Father.* (Philip, 2:10-11)

Oh! how the fervent Christian delights in repeating incessantly that blessed name of the Lover of his soul I and how he grieves to hear it bandied about in blasphemy by men and women and even little children, as is so often the case nowadays! Then he applies himself fervently to make amends and offer condign reparations to his Lord and love.

CHAPTER VI

YOUNG MAIDENS LOVE THEE (1:2.)

SUMMARY.—Who are the young maidens. What is theirs already and what they lack. Some specimens. What our Lord proposes to them at the outset.

OUNG MAIDENS.
Who are they? In the Canticle of Canticles, in the mind of Our Lord and of His Church, they are those little souls who are beginners in the spiritual life, just starting in the race-course of the love of God. Such are, first of all, the little Christian children and the youths of both sexes who have been properly brought up, instructed in the catechism and preserved from contamination; then. those persons who have just received a special vocation, as for instance the Apostles of Our Lord, when He called upon them to follow Him; or again whosoever is called to a more perfect life and has only just begun it, as is the case With novices of various religious orders, or young men aspiring to the holy priesthood; finally all fresh converts either from heresy, or infidelity, or from a sinful life or from a tepid one: in one word, all those who, once and for all, have really broken with the previous sinful past, but are not as yet far advanced on the way of spiritual perfection.

Such are the little souls, *adolescentulae,* of whom the Bride speaks in this verse, and one of whom she humbly reckons herself to be.

These little souls already love Our Lord with tender affection. Jesus knows it; but He is pleased to hear His child-bride telling Him so. At times, He will inspire her, by the grace of His Holy Spirit, with prayers like the following: "O dear Lord, allow me to offer to Thee, together with my own heart, also the love and adoration of my sisters, of my brethren, of all who are in this Church, around thy altar: all this do I offer to Thee. Young maidens love Thee! Little souls love Thee!"

The Apostles, whilst their divine Master was with them: see how full of real good-will they were, and full also, at the same time, of great imperfections. Though admitted to such a familiar intercourse with Our Lord and favored with such intermittent flashes of spiritual illumination, yet they were but beginners. They were of the number of little souls.

The poor Samaritan woman at the well of Jacob, good-natured Nicodemus, Zacheus the publican, the woman caught in adultery and brought for Our Lord to condemn, but whom he sent away absolved, Magdalen after He had exorcized from her seven devils, all these were only little souls; little for the time being, but who were to grow and wax strong. The racecourse to the goal of Christian perfection stretched out its endless path before them, and by the grace of God, they did not hesitate to enter upon it with all their heart.

The Royal Magi, no doubt, dated their first steps in the career of Christian sanctity from the happy moment when they were privileged to offer to the little infant Jesus gold, frankincense and myrrh, together with their own loving hearts. Oh! how they then began to love Him!

Even the good thief on the cross, sprinkled .with the dew of the blood of Jesus at his side, suddenly was turned into a little soul, very pure, very meek and humble, very loving. And. Jesus made him, then and there, run the whole race of sanctity in the short space of three hours; when it takes others thirty, sixty, ninety years, and perhaps some purgatory in the end, to do it.

All the prodigals who with sincere repentance turn back to their heavenly Father and begin a new life, are of the number of little souls, for whom we are writing this commentary on the Canticle.

St. Paul struck down as by lightning on the road to Damascus, found himself turned, at the voice of Our Lord, into a little soul quite meek and humble, and began forthwith to love Him who had revealed Himself in such dazzling brightness.

Our Lord teaches the mystical doctrine in all its sublimity

even to little souls, and whilst they are yet only quite at the beginning. His discourse during the night to Nicodemus (John 3:1-22), to the Samaritan woman at the well (John 4:1-31), to His Apostles, to the crowds; the very first sentences of His sermon on the Mountain (Matt, 5:3-13): are they not so many examples in point? He sets it before us in his first public utterances, the Beatitudes, which are the very highest goal and crowning attainment in the practice of the mystical life.

Should not this consideration suffice to show the reasonableness of the thesis we are setting forth in our treatises on Catholic traditional Mysticism, to wit that all men, without exception, are called to the fullness of the life of love, and that the words "Mystical life" mean nothing else but such a life?

CHAPTER VII

DRAW ME. (1:3.)

SUMMARY.—What God says by the prophet Osee of the cords of Adam. Humble avowal the child-bride makes of her weakness. What part the will plays in the business of love.

THE soul says to God and Our Lord: *Draw me,* because unless His prevenient grace first of all draws us out of our. apathetic mood, and sets us walking, then running and, in the end, flying, in the ways of his commandments, we are not able to follow Christ. But, through the grace of the sacraments, when we give it its full play, not only are we able to follow-our Lord, but we do so with the eagerness of true love.

"Draw me, drag me along, do me violence if need be, but I must go out of myself, out of the narrow mansion of my self-love, out of all the toils of created things. Cost what may, I want to be set free and to follow after Thee, my dear Lord?'

Six hundred years before the Christian era God said by the mouth of the prophet Osee (11:1-4) "*Israel was a child and I loved him . . . and I was like a foster-father to Ephraim. I carried them in my arms.* Now it happened that by their own fault *they knew not that I healed them. But I will draw them with the cords of Adam, with the bands of love;* I will make myself man, their very own brother by flesh and blood; I will be a sacrificial lamb, giving myself up, for their love, to the most cruel death; I will give them my flesh to eat and my blood to drink during the days of their pilgrimage on earth; I will be the lover and husband of their souls during time and for all eternity. Be these the cords with which I shall draw them. We shall see whether they will withstand."

Now in saying: *Draw me*—the converted soul takes the part of God, falls in with His designs, surrenders to His love and mercy, and entreats Him to make her all His own.

Two things are implied in that short prayer: first an avowal by the soul of her own inability to do anything supernatural, unless the grace of God moves her to it; then a firm resolve of the will to co-operate with grace. It is as though she said: "It is true, my Lord, that without Thy help I can do nothing th the way of love: neither begin, nor keep up, nor persevere to the end. Alas! I have but too much experienced my own weakness. But, O my heavenly Spouse, dear Lord Jesus, do Thou take me in hand, 'draw Thou me' I beg of Thee; for I am ready to co-operate. It is my will."

Hereupon let us examine the part played by the will in the business of love.

It were an error to persuade oneself that in love one has only to let oneself be, as though the inclination once being there, one had only delightfully to follow, and things would of themselves go smoothly, without any hindrance. Not so indeed, no. Whether it be question of human love or divine love; of that which is purely natural or that which is supernatural, some vigorous exercise of the will is required.

To love, deeply to love, as those do who plight their faith to one another before marriage; as it is their duty to continue to love after they are married, is not an affair in which only the senses and the emotional part of man are concerned. The will has something to say in the matter. One must will to love. One must will to keep it up. Or else it is not serious; not solid and firm. To will to love, to look upon it as a duty, not an amusement, brings into the mutual relation of the lovers dignity and nobleness. One must not enter upon the adventure of love, unless it be in view of the honorable and far-reaching ends of marriage such as God has instituted it, binding the two together into one for their whole life.

When once therefore the lovers have lawfully entered upon this way of life, they must take the means to make it lasting; the will must assert itself; one must love because in duty bound; one must continue to love, whatever may afterwards betide; one must carry on the will to love. Assuredly that is no child's play, nor an amusement of a few passing hours, nor a few days' or weeks' adventure, where the emotions of the senses, the cravings of an undisciplined heart and the tricks of a wild imagination run riot for a while and then die out suddenly. The foundations of an enduring love must be firm and unshakable.

Now what we say of human love is equally true, nay much more so, when it is a question of our love of God. A courageous and persevering exercise of the will is required thereto. An act of the will is called for at the outset; acts of the will are necessary ail along the path; one must constantly stir one's will to love God; or else after a while, one will simply cease to love.

There comes a moment in the spiritual life, when the novelty of it wears away; when the sensible impressions of grace recur only at ever widening intervals. God, nevertheless, has lost nothing of His rights over our affections: He remains the same, as worthy of love as He ever was; and the bond between Him and our soul is not broken. Now is the time for our will to assert itself. The bride redoubles her supplications to the heavenly Spouse, to the effect that He should draw her after Him, out of her natural sluggishness.

Draw me. Draw me always. Do not permit, O my God, that I should ever henceforth falter in that beautiful path of love. Oh! do not permit that I should again betray Thee! Do thou strengthen my will. I want to love Thee, I will it, I want to will it, do Thou see to it that I keep on willing and that I do so more and more vehemently, energetically. *Domine custodi hanc voluntatem,* (1 Paral, 29:19.) Lord, preserve in me this will, inviolate to the end. Do not cease one single moment to draw me after Thee.

So it is clear that our queen-faculty, the will, is paramount in the act of love as well as in the act of spiritual faith. Neither faith nor love can be imposed from outside on a man, without that man giving in and co-operating. One must will to believe, one must will to love. Whosoever erases thus to will, turns traitor both to God and to self: he murders faith, he kills love; he is guilty of his own spiritual death: and that is the greatest of all misfortunes.

Whosoever is desirous of preserving in himself the life of faith, the life of love, let him take up arms against his own natural fickleness.

In the same way, whosoever wishes to remain faithful, to divine love must sedulously keep ward and watch around his own fickle heart. The soul who has engaged herself with the heavenly Spouse could not be allowed to take herself back again after a while, on the pretext that she had not realized to what extent she would miss the passionate love of things created. "This dealing with creatures is so entrancing! My heart goes out to them. I cannot, cannot help it. I am simply overcome. What shall I do? Surely under these circumstances I am not expected to be held down by obligations which have become irksome, unbearable? Who will blame me for breaking an engagement which would prevent my tasting and enjoying such sweets?"

Unfortunate one! What have you done? Why have you slackened the austere bonds of love? Why have you put away helmet and breastplate and sword and ceased to mount guard around the citadel of your heart? Only disaster could be expected from such a course.

Therefore, O you who wish to safeguard your treasure, *watch and fray*. Force yourself to will; you must make your own this business of loving God; you must enter into it with a will, and remain all along actively engaged in its performance: then you will not in vain sigh out to the heavenly Bridegroom: Draw me, Draw me!

CHAPTER VIII

WE WILL RUN. (CANT. 1:3.)

SUMMARY.—That we are never isolated, either in the good or in the evil we do. We ought to hurry, for time is short. The two feet or wings of a fervent soul.

FTER saying: *Draw me,* the child-bride adds these words: *We will run.* She does not say: "I shall" but "We will"; thereby proclaiming an important spiritual fact, namely that one is never quite alone or isolated, in the paths of virtue, or (if so be) in those of vice. There is always someone or several to bear us company. We always draw someone along with us by the compelling virtue of example.

Still more true is this when it is a question of Superiors of religious communities, ecclesiastical superiors, fathers and mothers in regard to their household, priests, and in general all those in authority of whatever kind. If these allow themselves to be drawn by the sweet bonds of divine love, all those clustered about them will spontaneously follow suit, and tread the paths of virtue. If on the contrary they become slack and tepid, all those who hang on to them will experience a proportionate diminution of fervor.

Whosoever passionately loves Our Lord, will be drawn by Him, and never lose a moment, for Jesus never lags on the way to perfection. From the very beginning He points out to us the distant goal, sublime, impossible of attainment He says: *Be ye perfect as also your heavenly Father is perfect* (Matt 5:48); thus opening out before us an interminable racecourse. He does not want us to set any limit to our ambition for personal holiness. He gives us a start, then urges us on and draws us after Him, giving encouragement by word of mouth and gesture. How could one help running, under those conditions? Ceaseless progress on the way of perfection without ever coming to a stop and saying:

"There, that is enough," such is the law of the spiritual life during our pilgrimage on earth, as we have already pointed out in a preceding volume. (Cf. THE MYSTICAL LIFE, Ch. III.)

We are obliged to press on, because we have no time to lose, life being so short. As soon as death intervenes, one cannot gain any more merit or grow in the love of God. One's final degree of perfection is attained and will remain unchangeable for evermore. Our Lord states this unequivocally, and shows that this law held good even for Himself. He said (John 9:4): *I must work the works of him that sent me whilst it is day; the night cometh when no mon can work.* Obviously the day of which He there spoke was the time of His life on earth, and the night was the hour of His death. But how shall we run?" By means of divine contemplation and saintly action alternately or sometimes simultaneously practiced, as I have described them already in my treatise on THE MYSTICAL LIFE and in that on DIVINE CONTEMPLATION FOR ALL. Contemplation, Saintly action, these are the feet or the wings with which a Christian soul may walk or run or even fly in the footsteps of her Beloved.

CHAPTER IX

THE ODOR OF THE OINTMENTS OF THE BELOVED

SUMMARY.—The ointments here spoken of are the infinite perfections of the Divine Word and the mysteries of His Sacred Humanity. That a mystic is known by his taste for divine things, whilst a non-mystic by his taste for earthly things.

THE ointments of Jesus, what are they?

They are on the one hand the infinite perfections of His divine nature, and on the other, the sweet mysteries of His Sacred Humanity. These two sorts of ointments, mixed together in the person of Our Lord, spread their perfume all through the heavenly Jerusalem and the suffering Church of Purgatory and the whole militant Church; but, here below, only fervent souls perceive their sweet odor; and this is precisely the test by which they may be known as genuine mystics.

It is possible once to have been a mystic and after a while to have ceased so to be. One may think oneself a mystic and be, figuratively speaking, thousands of miles away from it. And also one may be a mystic and of the finest quality, unknown to oneself. It is important to give such a definition or description of a mystic that no mistake un be made about it; so that, you for instance, my dear reader, may find for yourself whether you are one or not.

Well, here it is: the mystic is simply a Christian who has a relish for God and divine things; whilst the non-mystic is any man, whether Christian or not, who relishes only earthly things. This twofold test is pointed out in the celebrated exhortation of St. Paul to the Colossians (3:1-3) *If you be risen with Christ, seek the things that are above, where Christ is sitting at the right hand of God; mind the things that are above, not the things that are upon the earth, for you are dead and your life is hid with Christ in*

225

God.

Yes, in the mystic, the relish for God and heavenly things is paramount, gets the mastery, rules supreme in spite of all its deadly enemies, the old Adam in him, the world and the devils.

With the non-mystic, in spite of his Baptism and the other sacraments he may have received, the government of his life is left in the hands of self-love with its thousand subtle trickeries and its disordered appetite for things created; to this extent that, even if he be in the state of grace, he makes but scanty use of the marvelous resources this state of grace brings him. His mind and heart are filled with delight in things created. The love of this world speaks so loud if him that God un hardly be heard. Self-seeking creeps into all his acts, spoiling even the holiest, causing them to lose much of their spiritual fragrance and of their meritoriousness.

In Catholic, traditional mysticism, which is the only orthodox one, the beginning of the process is relish for God: *O taste and see that the Lord is sweet,* exclaims the Psalmist (33:9). God forestalls us with the blessings of sweetness; He it is who acts upon our soul and at times even upon our senses. *By the Lord tins has been done.* (Matt, 21:42.) *My heart and my flesh have rejoiced in the living God.* (Ps. 83:2.)

The mystic takes his delight in God. He never tires of His company. He dearly loves to converse with Him, either speaking to Him or hearkening. Much as he likes this sort of conversation, there is yet something more entrancing to him: it is when he can, in the presence of God or before the Blessed Sacrament, hold himself speechless, motionless, doing nothing but love, love, simply love—let his heart go out in silent, burning love.

The mystic becomes a child again, a wee child, playing in the presence of God, playing with God, playing the great game of love. There is a marvelous playfulness in the manifestations of the human love of two affianced or of two married persons, also of parents with their little ones and of these with their fond parents. In the same way there is a marvelous, holy playfulness in the effusions of piety of the mystic, in the way he basks in the sunshine of God, and reciprocally in the communications of His very self which the loving God imparts to his darling child. We see this in the Canticle of Canticles. What a divine playfulness and liveliness in those dialogues, throughout all this little love-drama! It is a veritable enchantment. No wonder we hear the child-bride cry out: *We will run after thee to the odor of thy ointments.* No wonder she is eager to give herself up either to mental prayer or to the practice of any good work, as the Spirit of God may move her.

CHAPTER X

KINGLY DIGNITY OF OUR LORD

SUMMARY.—That Jesus is King, proved by the Scriptures. To get at the right idea of the transcending quality of the Kingship of Jesus we must consider in Him the divine nature.

OUR Beloved is King, a most magnificent King; and the fervent Christian soul is raised by Him to share His honors as well as His love.

Zacharias the prophet exclaims: *O daughter of Sion,* that is to say: O city of Jerusalem, O Church of Christ, O little soul full of love: *Rejoice greatly, shout for joy. Behold thy King will come to thee, the Just and Savior: he is poor and riding upon an ass.* (Zach, 9:9.) In the Annunciation, the Archangel Gabriel told the Blessed Virgin Mary: *Behold, thou shall conceive in thy womb and shalt bring forth a son, and thou shalt call his name Jesus. He shall be great, and the .Lord God shall give unto him the throne of David his father, and he shall reign in the house of Jacob for ever, and of His Kingdom there shall be no end.* (Luke 1:31-33.)

The simple-hearted Wise Men from the east came to Jerusalem asking: *Where is he that is born King of the Jews? for we have seen his star in the east and we are come to adore him.* (Matt. 2:2-3.) A few days after the raising of Lazarus to life again *a great multitude . . . when they had heard that Jesus was coming to Jerusalem, look branches of palm-trees, and went forth to meet him, and cried: Hosanna, blessed is he that cometh in the name of the Lord, the King of Israel.* (John 12:12-13.)

Even in the midst of the ignominies of His sacred Passion, the kingly dignity of Our Lord is proclaimed. Pilate asks Him: *Art thou a King then? Jesus* answered: *Thou sayest that I am a King;* and in consequence the Roman governor, writes out the title of the cross thus: *Jesus of Nazareth, the King of the Jews,* and maintains this reading in spite of the furious expostulations of priests and Pharisees (Matt. 27; John 19:22).

Now to pass from this earth to the heavenly region. Psalm 23 (24) helps us somewhat to picture to ourselves the enthusiastic welcome that was given to this *King of Glory* who is also *the King of virtues,* at His coming into his heavenly Kingdom on Ascension day.

Finally, Psalm 2 shows to us Our Lord throned in the highest heaven at the right hand of God the Father, whilst-our faith discerns Him seated at the same time, with unspeakable meekness, on the throne of His love in the sacrament of Holy Eucharist.

O Christian soul, art thou pleased at last? are thou well satisfied? art thou happy? Behold, He that is taking thee for His own well beloved little bride. He is God, He is the Divine Word. Is such a bridegroom comely enough? and noble and pleasing enough in thy sight?

It is the Godhead we must take into consideration in the person of Our Lord even more than his human nature. Both natures, the divine and the human, are indissolubly united in Him. Even human nature in Jesus is divine inasmuch as it has no other personality than that of the divine Word, and inasmuch as His flesh has been conceived by the operation of the Holy Ghost, who caused it to germinate or spring forth from the most pure blood of the Immaculate Virgin Mary. It cannot be but that a work of which the Holy Spirit is the immediate author be divine. It is a perfect individual human nature, the most perfect human nature that can ever be thought of, since it has in the most absolute perfection all that is required to the making of a man; and at the same time it is truly divine on account of its immediate author, who is a divine person, the Holy Ghost, and of its mode of production, which transcends all the potentialities of created nature, and finally on account, as we have already said, of its mode of existence in the hypostatic union with the Divine Word.

So, therefore, the flesh of Our Lord is human flesh, born of human flesh; and it is at the same time divine, because produced by the Holy Spirit and united in person with the Son of God. The most holy soul of Jesus is a human soul, perfectly and fully human, because it is the soul which informs and animates that human body of Our Savior; and it is at the same time divine in quality and dignity, for the same reasons-that its body of flesh is divine. Flesh and soul in Jesus are one and the same person with the Divine Word, and the Divine Word is one and the same God with the Father and the Holy Spirit. That is why Jesus could say reproachfully to one of His Apostles: What, *so long a time have I been with you, and have you not known me? Philip, he that seeth me seeth the Father also. How sayest thou, show us the Father?* (John 14:9.)

It was as though He had said: "Stop seeing in Me only a man, or considering my human nature as the main thing in Me: take notice above all of this paramount fact that I am God. I reach out infinitely beyond My human nature; through the transparent veil of My humanity you must discern the splendor of My divine nature. You ought to see in Me, as Peter eloquently proclaimed, *The Son of the Living God.* (Matt 16:16.) Whenever you have dealings with Me, it is with God, not with man, you are having dealings, although My sacred Humanity most assuredly enters into this loving intercourse and is the very sign and sacrament of My love for you."

Our Lord had this same truth in mind when He gently rebuked the youth who called Him *Good Master,* but who, in so doing, did not look beyond the manhood of Christ. *Jesus said to him: Why callest thou me good? None is good but one,* that is *God.* (Mark 10:18.) By these words Our Lord does-not deny that He is good, but affirms that He is God, and that this is the primal fact about Him which is to be taken into consideration.

Precisely because the sacred flesh of Our Lord is so truly divine in its quality and dignity, it is able to enjoy the unique privilege of being present at the same time both in heaven and on earth; on our altars, in our tabernacles, in all the consecrated hosts or fragments of consecrated hosts.

Such then (now to return to our starting-point) such is the

absolutely transcending kingly dignity of Our Lord. As God, obviously, He is King; and moreover He is also King in His character of the Man-God; King of angels and men and of all things; King from all eternity and unto all eternity, King of kings, overflowing with magnificence and justice and meekness; a King *whose government* or mark of authority *is upon his shoulder* (Is. 9:6), and *of whose Kingdom there shall be no end* (Luke 1:33).

O little soul, behold Him that cometh to thee with such loving tenderness: thy Bridegroom! The wife of an earthly king is aware that her husband's kingly power will soon cease and that this will be the end of the supreme honors she is receiving on all hands. It is not so with thee, O little soul, enamored of the King of heaven and wholly given up to His good pleasure: thou art assured that of His Kingdom there will ,be no end and that thou, His lowly bride, wilt be the well-beloved of His heart throughout all eternity.

CHAPTER XI

THE STORE-ROOMS OF KING JESUS

SUMMARY.— That these store-rooms are the sacraments which impress a character on the soul. How splendid is the fulness of Christian life even at its beginning. Why is it that people overlook this fact? The Jansenistic thesis. Intense joy of converts. Holy priesthood and religious life.

Y these words: *The King hath brought me into* his store-rooms, the child-bride celebrates her joy at being a Christian.

What may well be the store-rooms of so opulent a King, except vast secret recesses, crowded with casks replete with the most generous wines and choicest liquors, and perhaps with treasures which He wishes to keep hidden from the vulgar gaze? The store-rooms here mentioned are the mysterious receptacles of the most precious and overflowing graces, such as the sacraments which can be received but once, because they impress on the soul an indelible character, thus giving her a right to a marvelous series of special graces, and giving her access, according to her needs, to the other sacraments and to all the treasures of Holy Church.

In the divine plan, Christian life is designed to begin with a magnificent completeness. In the ancient discipline which prevailed during the first centuries of the Christian era; following upon a more or less protracted period of catechumenal instructions, three sacraments were conferred upon the neophyte on the same day or within a few days: that of Baptism, which made him a child of God; that of Confirmation, which brought to him a supplement of vital strength, making him spiritually an adult, a perfectly equipped Christian and a soldier of Jesus Christ; finally that of the Holy Eucharist, in which he was made to feed upon the very flesh of Our Lord, upon God himself who is the bread of the angels in heaven. In the present discipline of the Church, converts from heresy or Judaism or infidelity, may receive Baptism (under condition if need be), Penance and Holy Eucharist, all on the same day; and they are exhorted to present themselves to the Bishop for Confirmation at the earliest date possible. As for children who are baptized before the age of reason, in some countries, as for instance in Spain, they are confirmed whilst still in infancy; and whether confirmed or not, they are now admitted, thanks to the decrees of Pope Pius *X* concerning Holy Communion, to the sacraments of Penance and of Holy Eucharist as soon as they reach years of discernment, that is to say at the age of seven or eight.

It is from such heights and with such a fulness of grace that God wants the new-comer to start in the race-course of Christian life for the conquest of perfect love and personal sanctity.

Unfortunately we have well nigh lost sight of the fact that such is indeed the divine plan in the economy of the supernatural order. We are accustomed to the sight of sin upon a grand scale as it is in the surrounding world, also to the sight of the tepidity and crass ignorance of the things of God which large numbers of Christians display on all sides; and we are but too much aware, by sad experience, of our own cowardice and treachery: now all these causes work together to dim before our eyes the genuine notion of Christian life. One would fain persuade oneself that it were rash to aspire to love God with one's whole heart, even from the beginning, and all along, and to be tenderly loved by Him. And yet, did He not positively and peremptorily say, speaking to all and to each of us without any distinction: *Thou shalt love the Lord thy God with thy whole heart, and with thy whole soul, and with thy whole mind?* (Matt. 22:37.) *With thy whole strength* (Mark 12:30; Luke 10:27)? Thus shalt thou love God under penalty of falling beneath Thy Christian vocation. It is to all Christians in the persons of the Corinthians that St. Paul says: *See your vocation, brethren* (1 Cor. 1:26), and addresses this exhortation: *I beseech you that you walk worthy of the vocation in which you are called* (Eph; 4:1).

But, it may perhaps be asked, from the fact that ordinarily, at least now, such as are beginning to live the true spiritual life are converts from a life of tepidity and neglect, or still worse from a life of downright grievous sinfulness, have we not to make certain reservations? This was a proposition dear to the hearts of Jansenists. Most energetically has the Church condemned it.

Such then are the store-rooms of our beloved King: the sacraments which can be received but once, and give us free access to all the resources which God has accumulated in the hands of Holy Church for our personal sanctification.

Nothing can picture the entrancing joy of a sincere convert, when at last the grace is given him from God, to open his eyes to the wonders of his Baptism and of his Confirmation; when he is brought into these store-rooms of the great King, to take stock of their rich contents, and without hindrance to slake his thirst at those overflowing reservoirs of sweet things: Holy Scripture, the Sacraments of Penance and the Eucharist, the liturgical cycle all round the holy sacrifice of Mass, the lives of the Saints and the History of the Church. He becomes inebriated with delights.

What cries of joy were raised by a Silvio Pellico, a Louis Veuillot, a Paul Févai and, nearer still to us, a Psichari or a Charles de Foucauld, to name but a few among those that are now no more with us—upon the happy event of their return to the practice of Christian life! Nay, what exuberant joy, though perchance outwardly unexpressed, springs forth from the heart of any Christian who, once for all, turns to the passionate love of the Lord Jesus! With what delight does he not *drink at the Savior's fountains!* (Is. 12:3.)

Baptism therefore is a first store-room of our dear King of Love. And contiguous to it is that other store-room, the sacrament of Confirmation, to which Baptism is even as a door of entrance. Therein one is made a perfect Christian, and is put in possession of the fulness of the seven gifts of the Holy Ghost. Moreover there is nothing to stay him from laying hands on the treasures of the Beatitudes and of the Fruits of the Holy Spirit.

But if our Christian happen to be raised to the priestly dignity, there is quite another storeroom thrown open before him with the key of the sacrament of Holy Orders. What additional, most precious and costly treasures are not the daily celebration of the Holy Sacrifice of Mass, the grand official prayer of the Breviary, the incessant study and meditation of Holy Scripture in order that he may be able to thrive on them and feed the souls of his brethren with them?

Or is he perhaps one of those who have heard, in the secret of their heart, the divine call to religious life, and who in consequence have left all things to follow Christ in a higher state of sanctity? Then, by the very fact of his religious profession, he has been brought into that store- room of the King, where are heaped up enormous quantities of the diamonds and precious pearls of the evangelical counsels of Poverty, Chastity and Obedience. *Numquid ingressus es thesauros nivis?* asks God of holy Job: *Hast thou entered into the store-houses of the snow?* (Job. 38:22.) These are indeed the true store-houses of the virgin, immaculate snow, our religious vows, especially that of chastity, faithfully observed. Alone the King holds the keys of these marvelous storehouses and brings into them whomsoever He pleases: THE KING, namely our beloved Lord Jesus.

CHAPTER XII

OUR JOY IN THE LORD JESUS

SUMMARY.—The mystery of our indwelling in Jesus. Our Lord's two bodies, the one physical the other mystical. Communion of Saints and joy that flows therefrom.

E will be glad and rejoice in thee. (1:3.) How could it ever be otherwise? In the midst of such a plenty of the good things of God as we have just described, it were a sin to allow sadness or discouragement to overcome us.

Note this short expression: *In thee.*

Evidently the bride has learned well the lesson Our Lord read to us at the Last Supper when He said, with such insistence: *Abide in me ... Abide in my love ... that my joy may be in you, and your joy may be filled* (John 15:4-11).

Not only do all good things come to us through the hands of Our Lord, through the merits of His sacred passion and death, but we enjoy them only in our union with Him even or *the branch to the vine.* We abide in Him. Through, this indwelling of ours in Him are we enabled to live the supernatural life.

Thus this brief word *In thee* reveals to us an immense, a very far-reaching mystery, that of the actual indwelling of every Christian in Jesus Christ. St. Paul is never tired of bringing forward this doctrine by his repetition of the familiar expression IN CHRISTO. It is, all in one, the doctrine of the mystical body of Christ and that of the Communion of Saints. Here is a Person, the only one in the whole world who has to Himself two organic bodies. This divine Person, the Word, not only took unto Himself a body of flesh in the womb of the Virgin Mary, but it is His wish vitally to unite unto Himself the whole human race. Jesus has really two distinct bodies: the one physical or natural, animated by His own human soul in the way that other human bodies are animated by their own souls; the other mystical, made up of the assembly of all men of good will wherever found, either on earth, or in purgatory, or in heaven, together with all the blessed angels. *Now therefore, says St. Paul, you are no more strangers and foreigners, but you are fellow- citizens with the Saints, and the domestics of God; built upon the foundation of the apostles and prophets, Jesus Christ himself being the corner-stone: in whom all the building framed together groweth up into an habitation of God in the Spirit.* (Eph. 2:19-22.) We all belong to Jesus Christ, we are all the demesne of Jesus Christ, His property, nay we are all in Him, a part of Him, His very members, living His supernatural and divine life.

We will be glad and rejoice in thee.

How entrancing is the sweetness, how irrepressible are the transports of the spiritual joy one finds in Jesus! a joy which the world knows not, which carnal men cannot understand and must perforce gainsay. But we know it; we have tasted it; we give testimony about it and we proclaim that it absolutely transcends all sensual delights, all intellectual enjoyments within the limits of the purely natural order, all the raptures which can be procured by the sciences, the liberal arts, human glory, the company of the most cultured and friendly persons, or the most pleasing habitation, or all these goods put together. And we know that if during the days of our earthly pilgrimage our joy in Jesus has its hours of eclipse, the time is near at hand when this same joy will be granted us without measure and without any intermittence.

Such is not the case with the worshipers of the world. Whatever they may do in order to amuse themselves and divert their minds from an unpleasant remembrance of solemn truths, they are sad at heart with an incurable sadness, because nothing can take the place of the love of Jesus. Even though unconsciously, their soul wears mourning for the absence of this love.

O Lord Jesus, my heavenly Spouse, there is no true joy but in Thee. Be Thou blessed for ever!

CHAPTER XIII

THE RIGHTEOUS LOVE THEE

SUMMARY.—Who those are that do not love Jesus. How few the truly righteous are, even among those who profess a devout life. What a glorious company that is of the lovers of Jesus.

THE righteous.

With that one little word, with one light, touch of the hand, what a burning condemnation is inflicted on all who do not love Jesus: THEY LACK RIGHTEOUSNESS!

And also what a. revelation of the secret of the lamentable weakness of those who commit sin: it is simply that THEY HAVE NO LOVE FOR JESUS!

Unhappy men: they do not love Jesus! Then indeed nothing that they do ought to be a matter of surprise: they are capable of any heavy fall, any spiritual misadventure, any disaster, any moral and material catastrophe.

Ah! my brethren, my dear fellow-men, whosoever you may be, give me leave earnestly to beseech you: do, love Jesus. Love Jesus and all things will work together for your happiness, even though material ill-success should seem to dog your footsteps. You will at least secure for yourselves that great boon, righteousness; you will stand erect in that fearless moral attitude which strikes terror into the hearts of the enemies of your soul. O Lord Jesus, the righteous love Thee! and it is precisely because they love Thee that they are righteous.

O Thou the Bridegroom of my soul, dear Lord Jesus in the Holy Eucharist: how well advised are those who love Thee tenderly, passionately, who give to Thee alone and exclusively the most substantial part of their affections! But who are those? They are the just, the righteous, the souls that know no double dealing, keep no shameful secret, hold nothing back, make no compromise, obey no mean motive, drive no hard bargain in the matter of loving God. Shall I dare to say it? such souls are few and far between, even among the crowd of so-called pious people. O my brother, do you wish to taste the sweetness of Jesus in the Blessed Sacrament, to enjoy the extreme familiarity of this most holy Bridegroom in the sacrament of His love? Be candid and simple-hearted as a little child. Cultivate this splendid and dazzling righteousness which is found only in the little ones and such as strive to become like them.

The righteous love thee.

See how true this is. The blessed angels— how righteous they are! they never committed the smallest sin; and now, how they do love Jesus! With what eagerness they make themselves the servants of His Incarnation and of His bride the Church, and of the souls He redeemed by His death on the Cross! See again the true servants of God on earth, the mystics; I mean those who endeavor to live the life of grace to the full extent of its resources. And see the holy souls in purgatory; how they have not any longer the least attachment to sin, and how they love the holy will of Jesus, though His hand is so heavy upon them. Indeed they love Jesus more than themselves. Finally, see the glorious inhabitants of paradise, all the orders of the saints in their bright array: oh! how do they love their Lord!

But what shall we say of the love of our great Queen, the Blessed Virgin Mary, for her divine Son? she the most immaculate, the most righteous among the righteous, she the most resplendent in holiness among all other creatures!

Finally, above the love that Mary bears to Jesus, there is the ineffable love and complacency with which the Father and the Holy Spirit look upon Our Lord. Indeed we are in glorious company, when we dedicate ourselves to the passionate love of Jesus.

CHAPTER XIV

I AM BLACK BUT BEAUTIFUL, O YE DAUGHTERS OF JERUSALEM

SUMMARY.—The daughters of Jerusalem here alluded to are the angels and the saints. Comparing herself to them as they are in the splendor of glory, she finds herself black with all the imperfections and miseries of the present life; nevertheless she cannot but see and proclaim the beauty of her own state of grace.

UNDER the figure of the earthly city of Jerusalem, which was the capital of the Kingdom of Juda, the Canticle alludes one after the other to two spiritual cities of Jerusalem, the one heavenly, which is the Triumphant Church of the angels and saints, the other the Militant Church which is still on this earth. In this verse the bride is speaking to the angels and saints: but wherever, in the sequel, we shall hear the Bridegroom addressing Himself to the daughters of Jerusalem, as in chapters 2, 3, and 7, He is speaking to members of the Militant Church.

Though at present they are so sharply distinguished from each other, these two spiritual Jerusalems are really but one in Christ and through the Communion of saints: one only *City of the living God,* spreading out wherever true servants of God, in heaven, on earth and in purgatory itself, are to be found. (Heb. 12:22.)

Therefore the daughters of Jerusalem to whom the bride is speaking, are all the blessed inhabitants of paradise, angels and saints. Is it not a great wonder to see how the Canticle of Canticles leads us to a literal fulfilment of the word of St. Paul such as it sounds in the translation: *Our conversation is in heaven.* (Phil, 3:20); for whenever the fervent soul is not actually conversing with her Well-Beloved, then she is speaking with His servants, angels and saints. If perchance she talks with men and inferior creatures, she does it under compulsion, and even then it is of her own Beloved she wants to talk.

As for the angels, besides those who never leave paradise, because their special functions are all about the throne of God, there are also, in dose proximity to us, first of all our own guardian angel and all the guardian angels of the persons among whom we live, and also the adoring angels around the Blessed Sacrament, in the Churches where we worship. All these angels we are able to greet lovingly and to venerate; we may beg their kind assistance, congratulate them upon their holiness and bliss, unite our feeble prayers to their sublime acts of adoration, confide to them our pious desires, our sorrows, our hopes, and rest quite assured of the interest they take in all these things, because of the great love they bear us in God. Moreover there are hosts of angels, occasionally flying together through space, alighting and camping here and there around us, in order to check the insolence of the devils and to perform other duties which God entrusts them with. *Castra Dei sunt haec,* exclaimed Jacob when he saw legions of angels meeting him at his return from Haran: *These are the camps of God.* (Gen. 32:2.) Now the true contemplative has the eyes of his soul open to these splendid realities invisible to bodily senses; he lives in the company of these pure spirits and holds converse with them; he looks upon them as his very best friends, his helpers; he does not hesitate to pour out all the secrets of his heart into their tenderly sympathetic bosoms. The genuinely spiritual man prefers such an intercourse to any conversation with men. Is not that right? People seeing him solicitous to avoid whatever would disturb his holy recollection, accuse him of being a savage. He does not mind. Does he not live with a grand and noble company—the angels of God?

In comparison with them and ail the blessed inhabitants of heaven, the Christian soul, in her present condition of a pilgrim, walking by the dim light of faith, assailed by hosts of enemies, vexed with all sorts of tribulations, sees herself as quite black; and yet it is the will of the Holy Ghost that she should also realize her native dignity, both natural and supernatural; I mean the nobility of her nature, the excellency of her gifts of grace, the really great things that God has done to her and the greater gifts He wants to grant her in the future. She therefore humbly acknowledges her frailty and defects, which are the consequences of sin, and yet does not lose sight of the beauty with which God invests her inwardly by His grace. Thereby she keeps herself at a safe distance both from discouragement and presumption.

I confess, she says, that I am indeed very plain and black, black with the soot of all my past sins, deformed with all my present defects which are legion. Alas! when compared with you, O blessed angels and saints, I am an ugly little monster, a concentrated evil: such am I in my own self: yes, an evil thing, purulent, contagious, capable of infecting and poisoning the whole world and its inhabitants, capable of causing their death if they could see me in all the honor and malignity of my sins. And now, to think that my dear Lord has not been discouraged by this! and that He still wants to come to me! Now I can understand the heroic fortitude of some saints who, during their life on earth, did not shrink from kissing the lepers' sores. They seemed to say: My dear Lord Jesus Christ has not shrunk from handling me, full of sores as I was, and washing me in His most precious blood, and kissing me and straining me to His heart, at a time when my soul was a million times more nauseous and revolting than these poor suffering members of His: how, then, should I not consider it an honor and a privilege to be permitted to give Him back love for love in the persons of the poor and the afflicted?

But gently! Enough, more than enough has been said in this strain. What will the fastidious Christians of our own days say to this? How small, O my Jesus, is the number of those who now can bear only to picture to themselves or to hear related what Thy saints of either sex, persons of high rank, princes, kings and queens, have heroically and joyfully done for Thy love!

I am black but beautiful.

Black *as the tents of Cedar,* Genesis in chapter 25, verse 13, informs us that Cedar was the second son of Ismael and the father of the tribes of Arabia Petrza. It is as though she said: I am black as the tents of the Arabs of the desert, which are rudely made of skins and coarse cloth, without any adornment, besprinkled with innumerable weather-stains of which no one takes any notice, because these tents have to be pitched every night, folded again in haste in the morning, carried away on the backs of camels, handled without any precaution, and stretched out under all the inclemencies of the seasons.

And yet beautiful *as the curtains of Solomon,* which undoubtedly were made of the most precious materials, adorned with silver and gold, jewels and diamonds and priceless gems and pearls, and embroidered by the most skillful hands. "Yes. I repeat it, O blessed angels! though I am black with many involuntary imperfections and ignorances and sins of frailty, yet am I conscious of being beautiful. It were, on my part, a silly affectation and a real ingratitude to pretend I do not know it, since it is all God's doing in His poor handmaid and to Him alone the glory is due.

I am beautiful first of all in the divine image and likeness which is in me, and which even original sin has not blotted out. Beautiful moreover with the foundations and beginnings of sanctity, which my Jesus has already laid down in me, through the efficacy of His grace. Beautiful with all that the sacraments have already wrought in me: as well those sacraments which can be received but once, namely Baptism, Confirmation (and if so be, Holy Orders), as those which I have received hundreds, nay thousands of times, such as Penance and Holy Eucharist. Beautiful with the merits of curbing my unruly passions, performing many works of mercy corporal and spiritual, doing all my actions with purity of intention and fervent love, with sincerest devotedness to the interests of God, with tender solicitude towards the poor, the sinners, the little ones, those in sorrow and distress of any kind. Beautiful finally, on account of the indignities with which I am treated: lashes of the tongue, calumnies, unfair dealings, downright acts of wickedness. These bring to me a likeness, be it ever so faint and far off, to my dear Savior, Jesus crucified.

It is evident that the fervent soul, illumined by the light of faith, does not admit the hopeless and heart-breaking doctrine of Luther, Calvin and Jansenius about the total and totally irremediable depravity of our nature as a consequence of original sin.

Black but beautiful.

Has not our dear Lord said of Himself, speaking. by the mouth of the prophet, at the time of His sacred passion: *I am a worm and no man, the reproach of men and the outcast of the people. All they that saw me have laughed me to scorn: they have spoken with the lips and wagged the head.* (Ps. 21:7, 8.) But was He not, even at that very time, God, the Holy One, the splendor of the Father, the flower of the most Holy Trinity, endowed with an infinite loveliness? O Christian soul, who art made somewhat to resemble Him, how worthy of envy is thy lot!

CHAPTER XV

TRIBULATIONS AND CARES OF
A LOVING SOUL
(Verses 5, 6 and 7 of Ch. I of the Canticle.)

SUMMARY.—Some consequences of original sin; the acts of uncharitableness of devout persons, persecutions of the worldlings, disturbing cares with which those of her household try to take the little bride away from the thought of God. She turns to Jesus, the good Shepherd, for consolation.

THE fifth verse is only a development of what she said in the preceding one. The bride continues her discourse to the daughters of Jerusalem thus: *Take no notice of my being so brown, it is the sun that has altered my complexion.*

The scorching heat of the sun's rays are a very apt figure of all the tribulations of the present life which, in a very short time strip the soul of all its outward graces of spiritual childhood and of the superficial charms of spiritual youth.

The scorching rays of the sun of the justice of God, incensed against the sin of our first parents, have caused me to forfeit in their persons all the privileges of primitive innocence which they had received and were to transmit to their posterity. Although Baptism supervened and blotted out the stain of original sin, from my soul, so that I became in Christ the child of God and truly beautiful, nevertheless it has not abolished for the time of the present life certain consequences of this terrible accident of our nature at its origin: I mean a decided inclination to evil, a blindness of the mind, the motion of unruly passions, the being liable to all sorts of accidents, illnesses, infirmities, with the perspective of death at an uncertain date; in one word, all sorts of miseries. All these evils are the common lot of both sinners and saints.

247

The sons of my mother have fought against me.

As if all the evils already enumerated were not enough, instead of helping one another to bear their burdens, as St. Paul (Gal. 6:2) exhorts us to do, it happens too often that even persons who make a profession of piety, turn violently against each other, whilst the worldlings all together "with one accord league themselves against whomsoever they see endeavoring to lead a life of union with God, and they persecute him. That is why the oracle of the Holy Ghost gives this warning: *Son, when thou contest to the service of God, stand in justice and in fear, and prepare thy soul for temptation.* (Eccl. 2:7.)

They have made me keeper in the vineyards: my own vineyard I have not kept.

In order to draw a pious soul away from the search after God in contemplation; in order to prevent one from entering the religious state or holy priesthood, parents and relatives sometimes conspire to overwhelm such a one with all sorts of distracting cares, frivolous occupations, dangerous pleasures, until he is not even left free to attend to himself. Hence this complaint of the bride of the Canticle: *My own vineyard I have not kept.* Added to this cause for anguish there is also this, that a loving and generous soul is always chiding herself for the least want of fidelity to grace. Keeping our own vineyard means keeping watch over our senses, our imagination and all the powers of our soul, as we are going to see in the sequel.

Literature, science, the arts, politics, trade, the pursuit of wealth, the enjoyment of life, worldly success: these are the vineyards where they want to see me toil from morning till night, till the day of my death. But now I am quite resolved to leave to them all these vanities; I want to turn exclusively to Thee, O my only Love, my beloved Bridegroom. O Lord Jesus, do Thou teach me, direct me, tell me where Thou takest Thy repose, where fervent souls take their delights in Thee in the midday. *Show me, O thou whom my soul loveth, where thou feedest, where thou liest in the midday, lest I begin to wander after the flocks of thy companions.*

Jesus is here compared to a shepherd: did He not say, *I am the Good Shepherd?* (John 10:11.) But He is now resting from his heavy work, and. the loving soul, like a faithful bride, wants to keep Him company, seat herself at His feet with Magdalen, and listen to Him, adoring Him With her whole heart in silent love.

O thou whom my soul loveth.

Happy the Christian who, in spite of all his shortcomings in the spiritual life, can give himself this testimony that at least he loves Our Lord and loves Him tenderly. The great misfortune of a tepid and negligent Christian is precisely this, that he has no tender affection for Our Lord. All that Jesus has done, and endured for his own personal sake makes not the least impression upon him, evokes not in him the faintest spontaneous movement of gratitude.

Show me where thou feedest, where thou liest in the midday.

The midday for Our blessed Lord is the present time, I mean the space of time extending from the day of His glorious Ascension to the last day of the present state of the world, when He will come with great majesty to judge the living and the dead. He is, in a way, taking some repose after having accomplished the heavy work of our redemption by His dolorous passion and death on the cross; and, moreover, because He does not show Himself any longer in His bodily appearance among men as He did during His earthly life.

Where, therefore, ought we now to look for Him, that we may contemplate Him? Where? Well, first of all at the right hand of the Father in heaven, where He sits in glory surrounded by all the blessed. Besides this trysting place, we may also meet Him in His sacrament of the Holy Eucharist. We are always sure to find Him there, busy feeding His sheep, feeding them with His flesh and blood, and feeding Himself, so to say, with the delights He takes in their love. Ah! let us hasten, we too, and feed Jesus; let us raise to His sacred lips what causes Him an inexpressible joy, I mean the vessel of a pure heart, overflowing with love, and exhaling the sweet perfume of the most delicate virtues.

Lest I begin to wander after the flocks of thy companions.

In His character of God made man, Our Lord has for companions the rest of men. The flocks of these companions of His are the vanities and follies of this wicked world. Unless one is very careful to follow Christ, there is danger of wandering and losing oneself after the flocks of His companions.

Jesus is the great Shepherd of souls, the only good One. He alone is the true Leader of men, who can save them. But, alas! there are many false Christs, many false leaders, many false shepherds, tricked out *in the clothing of sheep whilst inwardly they are ravening wolves.* (Matt, 7:15.) Many have the audacity to tell their fellow-men, "Follow me," and they secure a hearing for a time. Journalists, writers, poets, philosophers, heterodox preachers, modernists of every grade, charlatans, demagogues: whither do they lead their flocks? They lead them to perdition. Blind men who rashly undertake the task of leading other blind men: they will fall one upon the other over the edge of the precipice. My God! I do not want to follow such leaders.

O thou fairest among women!

Here at last is Jesus Himself coming upon the scene. What is He going to say? Touched by the fervent appeals of His little bride, His first word is one of praise to her, and of such praise as must thrill her with joy: for it tells so plainly how greatly Jesus is pleased with her.

O thou fairest among women—that is to say fairest among all creatures of this visible universe. St. Francis de Sales says: "Man is the perfection of the universe; the light of reason is the perfection of man; love is the perfection of reason, and charity is the perfection of love (*Treatise on the Love of God,* book x, ch. 1). There we have, beautifully set down in their proper order and sequence, all the titles of nobility of the Christian, which bear out Our Lord in His proclaiming the fervent soul as *the fairest* of all creatures in this visible world of ours. Human nature is indeed the supreme perfection of the visible world; now, what constitutes the loftiness of our human nature is that it has a soul in the image and likeness of God, that is to say spiritual, intelligent, inexterminable; moreover, what is most entrancingly beautiful about this image of God, is its power of freely clinging to God through love, as to its highest good; finally this sublime faculty of loving God is enhanced in the Christian by the gift of supernatural charity. No sooner has a man been baptized, no sooner has a poor sinner recovered the State of grace, than Our Lord descries in his soul a beauty so great that He cannot restrain Himself for joy. He proclaims how well pleased He is with it: He cries out, *O thou fairest among women,* fairest among all the creatures of this visible universe!

If thou thyself know not.

If thou know not where I feed my flock, where I lie in the midday. Such is the meaning of the Hebrew phrase, which is translated wrongly because too literally, where Our Lord is made to reply: "If thou know not thyself."

Go forth:

Go out of the house of thine own self-love, deny thyself in accordance with the gospel prescription: *If any man will come after me, let him deny himself and take up his cross and follow me.* (Matt, 16:24.) Even, if need be, that is to say if thou hast a religious or priestly and apostolical vocation, *go forth* like Abraham *out of thy country, and from thy kindred, and out of thy father's house.* (Gen. 12:1.)—*Hearken, O daughter, and see and incline thy ear, and forget thy people and thy father's house, and the King shall greatly desire thy beauty.* (Ps. 44:11-12.) Go forth in perfect disengagement from all things created, in perfect abnegation of all passing and sensual affections.

Follow after the steps of the flocks.

That is to say: consider attentively the wonderful course of nature, and the foot-prints, so to say, which inferior creatures leave behind them as they hasten to accomplish the will of God: these will lead thee up to God, to Myself.

Thus Our Lord teaches His bride to begin her ascent to God by the contemplation of this visible universe, by the good use of created things, by the well-ordered handling of her own powers.

Again: *Follow after the steps of the flocks* may be taken to mean: Walk in the footsteps of the blessed angels and the saints, imitate their virtues, listen to their teaching. They will lead thee up to Me.

Feed thy kids beside the tents of the shepherds.

Thy kids are thy senses, thy imagination, thy memory, thy intellect and thy free will; all the subtle powers of both thy body and thy soul, which it is thy duty to govern, as a shepherd his flock, and to lead into fertile and salubrious grazing grounds.

The tents of the shepherds here represent the holy Catholic Church on earth, as it has spread itself all over the world. Therein are found splendid grazing grounds, namely the Seven Sacraments, the Holy Sacrifice of the Mass, *the words of eternal life* (John 6:69), the examples of the saints, and finally the Beloved Himself. Therein does He take His midday rest, until the end of the present world, for He said: *Behold I am with you all days, even to the consummation of the world.* (Matt, 28:20.)

The shepherds are: first of all, the Pope, vicar of Christ, to whom Jesus has entrusted the care of the whole flock of the faithful, saying to him in the person of Peter: *Feed my lambs, feed my sheep* (John 21:17); then the bishops, successors of the Apostles, to whom Our Lord gave the command: *Teach ye all nations ... to observe all things whatsoever I have commanded you.* (Matt, 28:20.) Finally the priests, who have the care of souls, and all the spiritual writers approved by the Church. We must be careful never to stray from their doctrinal teaching.

CHAPTER XVI

JESUS EXTOLS THE CHARMS OF HIS LITTLE BRIDE
(Verses 8, 9, and 10 of Ch. 1 of Canticle.)

SUMMARY.—The mystical chariot. The bride's cheeks and neck. The God-given chains of gold inlaid with silver.

MY love.

In thus familiarly addressing his little bride, does not Our Lord show with what ineffable tenderness He cherishes her? We cannot entertain the shadow of a doubt about His sincerity: such are therefore the genuine feelings of His Sacred Heart.

But oh! what a wonder is this, that He who has for Himself the whole heavenly court of the blessed angels and saints, the incomparable love of His sweet mother Mary, the infinite enjoyment of His Heavenly Father and the infinite sweetness of the Holy Spirit, should still condescend to beg for the love of such a poor and lowly handmaid as I am, and wish to take me for His bride! And now His amazing love for his little bride is carried to this excess that He must Himself need to celebrate her praises. He says:

O my love, to my company of horsemen, in Pharaoh's chariots, have I likened thee.

How glorious must have been King Solomon's cavalry, with the chariots given him as a present by the Egyptian Pharaoh! But our Solomon is Jesus, the King of heaven: how much more resplendent and glorious must not be the squadrons of His nine choirs of blessed angels, to whom must be added all the orders of the Saints, who have come forth out of the Egypt of this sinful world, and are, so to say, kept under the cart-sheds of Paradise? Our Lord in the transports of His love for a pure and fervent soul does not hesitate to declare that her charms attract Him as

253

irresistibly as those of the blessed inhabitants of the heavenly Jerusalem: and He shows the genuineness of His feelings towards her by His most sweet condescension. "O my love," says He, "by the admirably disciplined vigor of all thy movements and the swiftness of thy course towards such sublime objects as those of divine contemplation and the performance of all sorts of good works, I find thee comparable to the most noble and spirited coursers which draw my chariots in paradise, when I *ascend upon the cherubim and fly upon the wings of the wind."* (Ps. 17:11.)

Certain chariots of antiquity were drawn by four horses yoked together in one front-line. These were called a *quadriga;* their pace was more a sort of flying than running: it called on the part of the driver for great coolness, dexterity-and firmness of grip to avoid upsetting. Now the mystic, that God-bearer or Christophoros, is likened by the heavenly Bridegroom to Solomon's quadriga, drawing, on His triumphal car, Him who is his only love. The four symbolical horses are 1° the flesh of the mystic. St. Paul tells us: *Glorify end bear God in your bodies* (1 Cor. 6:20), 2° his imaginative faculty, 3° his memory, 4° finally his intellect. His queen-faculty, the will, is the driver; it is through its exertion that God is thus, freely and with a holy enthusiasm, carried in state in the very midst of a hostile world. This feat wins the admiration, almost the envy, of the inhabitants of the heavenly Jerusalem; for they cannot any longer gain merits, whilst this little soul does not take a single step forward, without giving greater glory to God, increasing her own capacity to love Him throughout all eternity and heaping up to herself a treasure of merits.

Thy cheeks are beautiful as the turtledove's.

We must read into these words a purely spiritual meaning, for Jesus is not an earthly lover, but a heavenly one. He is not sensitive to the charms which come from flesh and blood, but only to such as are produced in the soul by the grace of the Holy Ghost. We have therefore to attribute to the cheeks of the bride a symbolical meaning. Here is the one I propose.

Let us see in the cheeks of the bride, figuratively, the first two theological virtues, faith and hope: full, firm, healthy and beautiful. Indeed how firm and lively and bright is the simple faith of the servant of God, in whatever condition he may happen to be: the faith of the coal heaver, the faith of the Breton peasant, the faith of many a young Catholic student, the faith of the holy priest, of the monk and of the nun, the faith of a St Thomas Aquinas, of a Bernard of Clairvaux, of an Augustine of Hippo; the faith of a Simon Peter, who with firm assurance said to Our Lord: *Thou art Christ, the Son of the living God.* (Matt. 16:16.) This elicited from Jesus a magnificent reply: *Blessed art thou Simon Bar-Jona: because flesh and blood hath not revealed it to thee, but my Father who is in heaven; and I say to thee that thou art Peter* (a rock), *and upon this rock I will build my church, and the gates of hell shall not prevail against it: and I will give to thee the keys of the Kingdom of heaven; and whatsoever thou shalt bind upon earth it shall be bound also in heaven, and whatsoever thou shalt loose on earth it shall be loosed also in heaven.* (Matt. 16:17-19.) Again, how very firm, lively, luminous and unconquerable is the virtue of hope, of every true servant of God. His trust in the loving mercy of God and in the infinite merits of the Savior is simply absolute. In many Psalms, but most particularly in the one hundred and seventeenth, David gives the most varied and wonderful expression to his hope in the Lord. Then see how Saint Peter presents a fine demonstration of his unshakable trust in our Lord. After he had had the great misfortune of thrice denying his divine Master, at the crow of the cock he came to his senses again, and full of repentance he wept bitterly; then on Easter morning we see him as eager as St John to find Jesus dead or alive: so absolute a trust had he in His mercy. All the poor sinners of the world, after even the most lamentable falls, were they even repeated hundreds and thousands of times, have in Peter a most encouraging example of sorrow for sin and of the virtue of hope. Indeed the mercies of Our Lord are inexhaustible: as a matter of fact they are infinite. The worst of sinners has still the power of giving great joy to Our Lord, by his return to Him. The Prodigal has no sooner confessed his sin with tears of repentance than his heavenly Father gives him the kiss of peace and reconciliation, gives him back the white robe of innocence, and proclaims him as much a member of the heavenly family as if nothing had happened.

After Jesus has sung the praise of the faith and hope of His bride, it is only natural that He should proceed to celebrate her charity. He does it under this graceful image: *Thy neck,* he says, is beautiful *as jewels.* Just as the neck is the support of the head, thus is charity the support of everything that is noble in a Christian. Charity is at the .same time the pivot upon which turn all the manifestations of his supernatural life, as well those which have God directly for their object as those whose object is the love of one's neighbor. Just, therefore, as the suppleness and flexibility of the neck allows a man to raise his eyes to heaven or cast them down upon his fellow pilgrims and all inferior creatures, and to look cither closely or at a distance, to the right or to the left, just so does charity, the third and noblest of the theological virtues, render a Christian capable of ail sorts of good works, and make him gain innumerable and most varied merits which adorn him as so many jewels of great price.

There is yet another meaning, perhaps even more mystical, to read into the words: *Thy cheeks are beautiful as the turtledove's.* We may look upon them as a delicate way which Our Lord has of praising the chastity of all persons consecrated to Him by the practice of the Evangelical Counsels. What constitutes the exquisite loveliness of the cheeks of such a bride of Christ, is that those cheeks will not be offered to the kisses of an earthly husband and of children born of an earthly marriage: because for the love of Jesus, who is the only object of her affections, this little bride deprives herself of the most pure and legitimate, though inferior, pleasures of family life. Body and soul, she dedicates herself wholly to Him alone: and it is such a free renunciation of all joy in the creature which confers on her a supreme touch of loveliness in the eyes of her heavenly Bridegroom. In heaven, the virgins of either sex form the escort and guard of honor of the divine Lamb. (Apoc. 14:4.) It is their exclusive privilege to follow Him whithersoever He goes, singing the while a canticle which no one else can repeat.

We will make thee chains of gold, inlaid with silver.

We, that is to say the three divine Persons of the Blessed Trinity. If it be the heavenly Bridegroom who speaks these words, we must understand that He does it not only in His own name, but also in the name of the other two divine Persons. But it seems more natural to suppose that the three divine Persons together speak these words: *We will make thee chains of gold,* just as at the dawn of the history of the world, the Father, the Son and the Holy Ghost deliberated and said together: *Let us make man to our image and likeness* (Gen. 1:26); that is to say: Let us give man that which is the very foundation of his nobility and goodness, to wit, a spiritual nature, intelligent and free. Now that it is a question of adorning the Christian soul] more and more, the three divine Persons work together to this end.

Although this is the first place in the Canticle of Canticles where a direct allusion to the Blessed Trinity is made, we must, however, take it for granted that, in the mind of the inspired writer, the thought of the three divine Persons is never absent a single moment, on account of the nature of the heavenly Bridegroom. Is He not the Word? the Word of the Father? the Word who, conjointly with the Father, eternally produces the Holy Spirit? We must, in our thought, in our contemplation, in our effusions of love, never fail to keep Our Lord united to His divine Father and His Holy Spirit, since He is in reality inseparable from either, being one and the same God with them.

Is it not precisely in order to introduce us into the circle of the divine life of the Blessed Trinity that Jesus comes to us? Is it not with this object in view that the Father and the Son communicate to us their Holy Spirit? Is it not for this very end that the Holy Spirit comes down to take up His dwelling in the very center of our being, in the most secret part of our soul? Hence whosoever, in the transports of his piety, does not raise his eyes and affections still higher than the Sacred Humanity of Our Lord, nay, beyond the divine personality of the Word, even to the most Holy Trinity, has not yet so much as begun to understand what it is to love Jesus.

Let us never lose sight of what follows upon the fact of the divine nature of our heavenly Bridegroom. This great dogma of the divinity of Our Lord enables us to apprehend the mystery of the three divine Persons in their relations with the fervent soul: it shows us how indeed the whole love of God comes to her, the whole Blessed Trinity enters within her through our Lord Jesus Christ, *per Dominum nostrum Jesum Christum,* that is to say, by the very fact of her nuptial union with Christ. Thy heavenly Bridegroom, O Christian soul, is given thee by the Father, and it is His Holy Spirit who consecrates thee to Him, rendering thee not unworthy of His chaste embraces.

We will make thee chains of gold.

What are those chains of gold but the moral infused virtues, summed up in the four cardinal ones of Prudence, Justice, Temperance and Fortitude? They hold together as the links of a collar, they always accompany the theological virtue of Charity and set its beauty even as a gold chain on a neck as white as ivory. Now just as the brightness of gold shines the more for being inlaid with silver, so the Christian's moral infused virtues receive greater luster from their being accompanied with the corresponding natural and acquired virtues, which are inferior to the infused ones as silver is to gold.

In the just man, who according to the Apostle *lives by faith* (Heb. 10:38) the natural acquired virtues are inseparable from the supernatural infused ones: that is why the three divine Persons say: *We will make thee chains of gold inlaid with silver.*

CHAPTER XVII

OF THE VIRTUE OF COMPUNCTION
(Verses 11, 12 and 13 of c. 1 of Canticle.)

SUMMARY.—That a fervent soul does not cease to grieve for her past sins though forgiven; and yet Our Lard is grateful to her for having procured Him an occasion of exercising His mercy. How a season of tears can be procured; and of the delights to be found, in the contemplation of Jesus crucified.

HILE the King was at his repose my spikenard sent forth its perfume.

From a shepherd, as He was represented to us in the preceding verses, behold our Jesus is become a King again; King of angels and men, immortal King of ages: He lies in state on His bed of repose, in the glory of paradise.

We have already noted that the midday repose of King Jesus extends from the time of His Ascension even to the end of the world, when He will come to judge the living and the dead. He seems to be asleep. He does not appear to intervene any longer in the events of history; the bride, however, is well aware that He has His eyes upon her and that the delicate perfume of her virtues, especially of her humility and compunction, mounts up to His very throne.

My spikenard sent forth its perfume.

Spikenard is a precious ointment much used in the East. The fervent soul makes it the image of her sorrow for past sins. She keeps green her repentance for having ever offended the divine Majesty, perhaps grievously, perhaps repeatedly, possibly hundreds or even thousands of times. She is well aware that God in his ineffable mercy has forgiven them as soon as absolution supervened; but as for herself she will never, to her last breath, forgive herself, the horrible misfortune she has had of wounding Divine Love. Now this spirit of holy compunction greatly pleases Our Lord. It is as the smell of the perfume of great price which

Mary Magdalen once poured out together with her tears upon the feet of the Savior, and at another time over His sacred head, whilst He was at table; the sweet odor of which has filled the house of Holy Church.

Understand who can, but it is true that Jesus loves His little bride even on account of the sins He has had to forgive her. He is quite grateful for the occasion she thus gave Him to exercise His mercy. Our Jesus is really too good, beyond all limits of discretion: but that is His nature and I am not ashamed to be benefitted by it. But how marvelous this is! In heaven Our Lord will draw His glory from every one. of His elect: from those who will have persevered in innocence, precisely because they will have led immaculate, irreprehensible lives (O blessed ones!) and then also, from those miserable sinners, of whom I am one, who will have offended Him grievously and often; precisely for this reason that they will have given Him the joy of making a display of the magnificence of His mercies. Therefore, never ought any past sin, provided it has been duly absolved, to stand in the way of our giving free rein to the transports of our love of Jesus, or damp our familiar intercourse with Him and our absolute trust in His mercy.

O dear Lord Jesus, King of Love: neither earth nor heaven, neither the blessed angels nor all the saints together with Thy most sweet Virgin Mother Mary, neither time nor eternity, will ever praise Thee enough in my estimation for that immense charity of Thine. Happily, Thou art to Thyself Thine own praise, wholly sufficient O my Beloved, I offer Thyself to Thyself. I offer to Thee Thy five Wounds which Thou didst receive when Thou wert atoning for my most vile sins. To this precious offering allow me to join that of my sincere repentance.

O my dear reader, you who are perusing these lines: perhaps there is just one thing wanting for you thoroughly to enter into the spirit of the Canticle of Canticles, namely, a season of tear-shedding. You should make a sorrowful review of all the guilty past, with or without a general confession, according as your spiritual director may advise. But I would have you shed tears, real, burning tears of shame and sorrow, springing up from a broken heart, deliciously shed over your holy crucifix, in the secret of your chamber. It is evident that before one should dare to request, as does the bride of the Canticle in her very first words, the ecstatic joy of the kiss of the lips of Our Lord, it is proper that the novice in the spiritual life should first of all spend some time in kissing His sacred feet with Mary Magdalen, shedding over them copious tears. Such is, at any rate, the advice of St. Bernard.

It is because he ignored or neglected this first exercise of a lively and persevering repentance for his sins, that many a beginner in the career of sanctity, who seemed ever so promising, has pitifully failed in the end.

A bundle of myrrh is my beloved to me.

This compunction is excited in the loving soul, especially by the contemplation of the sorrowful passion of Our Lord *Jesus Christ and Him crucified,* (1 Cor. 2:2.) Such is the bundle of myrrh, of a holy and purifying bitterness, which she wears constantly upon her heart. As though she said: Jesus crucified wilt ever be the object of all my deliberate thoughts and of my burning affections.

A cluster of kofer my love is to me in the vineyards of Engaddi.

Such is the translation given by the learned. The kofer, they say, is a shrub whose flowers bloom in clusters and exhale the perfume of mignonette. As the kofer or kennet of the Arabians is unknown to me, I own I much prefer to see in this text the symbolism of a cluster of grapes. Engaddi was famous in those days for its vineyards.

Not only is Jesus crucified a bundle of myrrh, and the most efficacious means of constantly compelling my tears and groans of genuine, heartfelt sorrow over my past sins, but He is moreover, immediately after the essence of the Most Holy Trinity, the sweetest, the most delectable object of contemplation which may engross the attention of a fervent Christian. Yes, the contemplation of the sorrowful Passion and of the ineffable love of my Savior quenches my thirst even as a. lovely bunch of grapes that of a thirsty traveler. Indeed, is there anywhere a man who could feed upon this bunch of grapes, that is to say who could sedulously apply his mind to the consideration of the Sacred Passion of Our Lord in all its details, without finding his thirst for love fully allayed?

O man, thou reasonable creature, who hast also been endowed with an exquisite sensitiveness, thy heart cannot do without love of some kind: now what more noble and delightful object for thee to love could there ever be than the Lord Jesus Christ, the Son of God and thy very own brother, suffering and dying for thee on the cross? Then again, thou art longing to feel that someone cares for thee; then plunge thyself in the deep waters of thy Savior's Passion, in the crimson tidal wave of His sacred blood. Bear in mind that it is all for thee, for thee personally and individually, for thy sake, for thy love even as though thou wert the only one He cared for, that He has endured all these humiliating and atrocious torments. He would indeed be hard to please, the man, whosoever he might be, who, attentively meditating upon these great truths, would not feel that he has indeed therein full scope for loving and being loved.

When we are thus well pleased with the Sacred Humanity of our dear Savior, we are imitating our heavenly Father Himself. We will do well to meditate upon these words of St. Francis de Sales in his treatise on the Love of God (Book ii, ch. 5.) "Generally, people plant vineyards only in view of the grapes they will produce; therefore the grapes are the first things desired and intended, although leaves and flowers are produced before them. In the same way our great Savior was the first object of the divine will in the eternal plan which divine providence wrought for the production of all creatures: it was in view of this desirable fruit that God planted the vineyard of the universe: then He ordered the succession of many generations, which, like so many leaves and flowers, were to go before and prepare and foretell the production of this marvelous cluster of grapes which the holy bride celebrates in the Canticles, the juice of which inebriates God and men."

CHAPTER XVIII

MUTUAL BENEVOLENCE OF THE BRIDEGROOM AND THE BRIDE
(Verses 14, 15 and 16 of Ch. I of the Canticle.)

SUMMARY.—When speaking of His child-bride, Jesus takes His wishes for realities. The cross is the nuptial couch whereon the Divine Word will espouse her. All things are in common between these two lovers. What is meant by their houses and, the rafters of cypress trees.

O N hearing the expressions of the passionate love of His child-bride, Jesus is touched to the heart. In an outburst of tender emotion He exclaims: *Behold, thou art fair, my love, behold thou art fair; thy eyes are as those of doves.*

In these words of praise which Our Lord bestows upon his child-bride, who is as yet but on the threshold of the race-course of sanctity, we must understand that He takes His wishes as already accomplished facts. This little soul—let us say it is our own—is, alas! as yet very far indeed from perfection, but the all-consuming charity of our divine Lover makes Him see her already in that degree of perfection to which He intends to lead her. No sooner has a soul begun fervently to love Jesus than He finds in her an irresistible attractiveness. Here is some consolation for those who might be tempted with discouragement at sight of their present miseries and shortcomings.

The eyes of the bride which are *as those of doves,* are the first two theological virtues of faith, and hope, by which she keeps the glance of her soul firmly set upon the adorable person and all the mysteries of her Well-Beloved. From such an assiduous contemplation of Our Lord, the eyes of the soul take to themselves a brightness and liveliness which makes them very beautiful. Nevertheless, on hearing herself thus praised by her divine Spouse, the bride promptly rejoins:

263

Behold, thou art fair, my beloved, and comely.

As who would say; Ah! my dear Lord Jesus, do not, I beg of Thee, give me such high praise. Thou alone, O my love, Thou alone deservest to be praised for Thine infinite loveliness. *Tu solus sanctus, tu solus Dominus, tu solus Altissimus.* Alone art Thou holy, alone art Thou the Lord, alone art Thou the Most High, with the Holy Spirit, in the Father's glory!

Our bed is flourishing.

The couch whereon the Word of God, our Bridegroom, espouses the fervent soul, is none other than His cross. This couch He chose for Himself, ostentatiously to lie thereon as upon a couch of state, strewn with flowers. On this couch, His cross, He expects me to lavish upon Him the passionate tokens of my love and to unite myself to Him. It is when on the Cross that Our Lord wins all the hearts which have not the hardness of flint; there it is that he accomplishes His mystical espousal with the Christian soul who is not afraid to embrace mortification, to accept pain from all hands: from God, from men, from self; to inflict on herself voluntary penances. It is related in Exodus (4:26) that when Sephora, the wife of Moses, found herself obliged hastily to circumcise her boy with her own hands, she exclaimed: O Moses, *a bloodstained spouse art thou to me!* With much more reason may the loving soul give this title to Our Lord:

Sponsus sanguinum; A blood-stained spouse!

This does not prevent her from proclaiming: *Our bed is strewn with flowers;* with roses, and lilies, and violets and laburnums, and hyacinths and bunches of lilac ... that is to say with the flowers of all virtues: charity, self-abnegation, humility, purity, simplicity. Every drop of the sacred blood of Jesus and every thorn of mortification of the generous Christian are changed, on the nuptial couch of the Cross, into flowers whose lovely colors will never fade, and whose delicate perfume keeps for ever spreading far and wide and rising upwards to the very throne of God.

And now consider the amazing audacity of love. The bride

begins to talk as though all the goods of the heavenly Spouse were also her very own. What splendid assurance sounds in these words: *The beams of our houses are of cedar, our rafters of cypress-trees.* So vivid» is her faith, so firm her hope; her charity so full-hearted and irrevocable, that henceforth all goods are held in common between her and her Beloved. Whatever she may call her own, whatever she is in herself, she has abandoned into His hands, never to claim it back; and as He, on His part, gives Himself up so entirely and with such tender affection to her, it is no presumption on the part of the child-bride to consider all the goods of her Beloved as her own as well. They live together under the marital regimen of holding all they have in common.

Now what can those houses be which she mentions, and of which the beams are of cedar and the rafters of cypress-trees? These are, first of all, the Church Militant, with its indestructible hierarchy composed of the Pope, Bishops and Priests; then, within the Church, if the bride happen to be a religious, the Order or pious Institute to which she belongs and which is made firm and solid by the approbation of the Holy See; finally, and above all, the heavenly Jerusalem whereat the fervent Christian burns with desire to arrive one day, and wherein he already lives in spirit. The perfection of charity which is the rule there and the unfailing enjoyment of the beatific vision both of Our Lord's Sacred Humanity and of the Most Holy Trinity, are aptly figured by the incorruptible and perfumed woods of the cedar and the cypress-tree.

O Christian soul, who art the conscious and willing and loving bride of the Lord Jesus, take pleasure in repeating these words of the Canticle: *The beams of our houses are of cedar, our rafters of cypress-trees.* Let it be thy delight to meditate on the splendid history of the Holy Catholic Church, and on the glories of thy own religious Institute; but most of all on the gorgeousness of the heavenly Jerusalem, where thy Beloved will share with thee all His treasures, and where thou shalt love Him perfectly.

CHAPTER XIX

FLOWER OF THE FIELD, LILY OF THE VALLEYS

(Verses 1 and 2 of c. 2 of Canticle.)

SUMMARY.—The blessed Host compared to the Easter-daisy. Of what valleys Jesus is the lily.

I T is not clear, for there is nothing to indicate it, whether it is the Bridegroom or His child-bride who speaks these words: *I am the flower of the field, and the lily of the valley.* They suit both equally well, though in a different way. Therefore we may apply them first to Our Lord, and then to the fervent soul. We can even imagine that both the Bridegroom and the bride, one after the other, made these words their own. We may suppose without an undue stretch of probabilities, that this phrase was thus twice repeated, in the original Hebrew text, and that in the course of time some ignorant or blundering copyist, failing to perceive the meaning of such a repetition, simply suppressed it. We should then have in the first three verses of the second chapter of Canticle a short, , but very lively, dialogue in this wise:

JESUS: *I am the flower of the field and the lily of the valleys.*

THE FERVENT SOUL: Nay, my Love: is it not rather *I who am the flower of the field and the lily of the valleys?*

JESUS: Indeed *as the lily among thorns, so is my love among the daughters.*

THE CHILD-BRIDE: And *as the apple-tree among the trees of the woods, so is my beloved among the sons of men.*

It is worthy of remark that on the one hand many interpreters place these words: *I am the flower of the field* on the lips of the Bride, whilst on the other hand the sacred liturgy, in many passages, makes an apt application of them to Our Lord.

How is it possible for Our Lord to describe. Himself under such a lowly figure as that of the daisy? a graceful flower, it is true, but one which does not seem to suit the sovereign Majesty!

Let us see. The modest daisy, with its heart of gold and white coronal of petals, seems a smile of God fallen upon our earth, to rejoice the hearts of the little ones. It offers itself to any hand that wants to pluck it, be it the hand of the wayfarer, of the mendicant, or of the little child. Now is it not a fact that our Jesus has made Himself, in the Holy Eucharist, as much at hand to everyone as this flower of the field? The Blessed Host is to be found everywhere in the whole world, in all the churches of our towns and villages, and even in the rude log cabins or huts of reeds which serve as chapels in the forests of the New World or in the heart of Africa. Then also, the Vicar of Christ, our Holy Father the Pope, invites, nay urges, every Christian without any discrimination of age or social condition, provided only they be in a state of grace and approach with a pure intention, to cull this heavenly flower every morning, if they like, in order to sweeten with its ineffable perfume their day's drudgery.

The blessed host is circular and flat and light, even as a daisy whose golden heart should be veiled with white. As much as the Easter daisy by the wayside, Jesus is silent in the Holy Eucharist There are those who cull it reverently with ardent love and lay it on their heart of hearts: 'tis a minority. By far the larger number pass Him by in utter indifference, unseeing or not deeming Him worthy a moment's attention. And, alas! there are those who are not afraid rudely to pluck this heavenly flower, to bruise it, to throw it in the mud, to trample upon it. I ask: "O my dearest Lord, why art Thou exposing Thy sweet divine Majesty to such indignities?" He replies: "My child, 'tis for love, all for love. That I might be enabled to come to thee and to every one who will receive Me in his heart with joy, I had to run this risk. A flower in the field in very truth; this is what I am."

I propose yet another interpretation of these words: *Flower of the field.*

Jesus being the Divine Word is, so to say, the very flower of the Divine Essence; a flower which without intervention of any husbandman, has from all eternity sprung and bloomed in the vast verdant field of the infinite perfections of the Heavenly

Father. The Holy Spirit is the sweet perfume emanating both from this marvelous flower, the Son of God, and from the field which spontaneously produces it, namely the Heavenly Father.

Lily of the valleys.

We may first of all understand as the valleys of which Jesus is the lily, the two blessed-eternities, that *a parte ante,* as the theologians call it, and that *a parte, post.* The first is eternity as we conceive it in God before He created anything; an eternity in which, according to our way of speaking, God lived with Himself, perfectly self-sufficing, having no need of any one or anything whatsoever outside His own Divine Essence, enjoying an infinite bliss in the inviolate Trinity of His Persons. Jesus, in His character of the Word or the Son of the Father, is the lily of that first valley. Then He is also the lily of that other valley, the eternity *a parte post,* in which He deigns to associate with His own sanctity and bliss, the creatures He has made to His own image and likeness, angels first, and then men. Now in either of these two eternities, Jesus, because He is the splendor of the Father, first as the pure Divine Word, then as the Word made flesh, is a fragrant lily, whose ineffable beauty is a charm to the eyes of the contemplative and loving, soul.

We may also liken the two Testaments to two fertile valleys where Jesus is equally to be found; in the Old, He is under cover of the promises, prophetic figures and theophanies, that is to say, divine apparitions to the prophets. In the New Testament we meet Him in His own adorable Person and the union of His two natures. And He is indeed a lily, this Son of the Virgin, who is God; a lily of incomparable majesty, of dazzling whiteness, rejoicing heaven and earth with the penetrating sweetness of His perfume.

Finally we may also see in the valleys where Jesus flourishes as a lily, first the human individual nature of the Virgin Mary, which on the scale of creation is inferior to the angels; then the deep valley of her humility; a humility so profound that all her ineffable privileges of an immaculate conception, absolute sinlessness, positive sanctity so great that it is second only to that of God, and divine motherhood itself, could not raise her in her own estimation above the rank of a handmaid. *Behold,* she said to the Archangel Gabriel, *the handmaid of the Lord.* (Luke 1:38.) Then in her *Magnificat,* her retort to the praises bestowed upon her by St. Elizabeth is: *He* (the Lord) *hath regarded the lowliness of his handmaid.* (Luke 1:48.) Jesus is the lily which sprung up just where those two valleys meet.

Finally let us note that under those two charming images of the *flower of the field and the lily of the valleys,* Our Lord describes once more to us His two natures, the human and the divine. His own divine nature which He has from the Eternal Father whose Son He is; and His own human nature which He took in the chaste womb of the blessed Virgin Mary, His sweet Mother.

As the lily among thorns, so is my love among the daughters.

A fervent soul whose love of Jesus is genuine, and who for His dear sake keeps herself unspotted, is in the midst of a tepid, negligent and sinful souls, even as a lily among thorns.

CHAPTER XX

IN THE SHADE OF
THE APPLE-TREE

(Verses 3 and 4 of c. 2 of Canticle)

SUMMARY.—How refreshing and delightful is the contemplation of Jesus. That the Wine-cellar of Jesus is His Sacred Heart.

S the apple-tree among the trees of the wood, so is my beloved among the sons. The trees of the forest or crab-stocks, produce only bitter fruits, unfit for the nourishment or refreshment of man. So is the case with men in comparison with Our Divine Lord. Of themselves, and unless they be grafted upon Jesus Christ, they produce only bitter fruits. He alone is the healthy food and refreshment of souls.

From the sole point of view of nature, it is a noble thing for a man to carry within himself some grand idea and, so to say, live upon it. So does a man of genius, whether he be a poet, an historian, a philosopher or an artist. He can afford to despise the sordid preoccupations of other men and have nothing to do with them; he finds within himself a fount of entrancing joys, worthy of the elevation of his mind and of the exquisite sensitiveness of his heart But when the idea with which a man lives and upon which he feeds in the secret of his heart is God, the living and life-giving Idea, who is at the same time the grandest and also the very sweetest of realities, and when this Idea-Reality presents Itself to us as does the Divine Word, clad in the garment of our human nature, living and suffering, dying for us and loving us as never did any other man live and suffer and love and die; oh! then how the fervent contemplative is entranced, and inebriated and satiated with ineffable delights!

That is why the bride, after having likened Our Lord to an

apple-tree, adds: *I sat down under His shade, whom I desired, and His fruit was sweet to my palate.* This the bride does, whenever she seeks, in the peaceful contemplation of her Beloved, some relief from the burning and parching ardors of the active life. Yes, I shall proclaim it to His praise, I have found in the contemplation of the mysteries of my Savior, ever fresh and inexpressible delights. Just as when after choosing, by sight and touch of the hand, the best fruits hanging on an apple-tree, we carry them to our mouth to taste them and enjoy their sweetness, just in the same way do we taste and enjoy in the depth of our soul the life-giving truths which our mind has culled in the course of holy reading and meditation.

He brought me into His cellar of wine.

The cellar of wine of Our Lord is His Sacred Passion. Oh what generous wine is all the blood He has shed for us with such prodigality, and which He offers every day to all who want to drink it, in the blessed sacrament of the Holy Eucharist! *Drink ye all of this, for this is My blood.* (Matt. 26:27-28.) Again, the wine-cellar is His most Sacred Heart, which is the very head-spring of His precious blood. The lance of the soldier has opened for everyone a free entrance to it.

Communion of some sort is in very deed the law which prevails all over nature, whether animate or inanimate. Any tree, any plant, which ceases to absorb the life-giving juices extracted from mother earth, promptly dies. Any animal which happens to be deprived of its proper nutriment wastes away and dies. In the case of man, this natural law of his living and feeding upon the things that are inferior to him, serves to ennoble, and in a way to deify, the whole material universe; because when we absorb some food, we change it into our very self, into our own substance. Then we eat at Holy Communion, the Blessed Host, that *Living Bread* which is the very flesh and blood of our Lord; only, to our unspeakable joy, it happens that instead of our changing this divine food into our own substance, it, on the contrary, changes us, into Christ, makes us a part of Him—His living branches.

CHAPTER XXI

THE ORDER OF CHARITY
(4th verse of Ch. 2 of Canticle.)

SUMMARY.—In what this order consists, and how it expands the heart of man. The evil of an unlawful passion. An answer to the objection of worldlings when they say that whosoever has not experienced love as they understand it, is ignorant of real life.

E set in order charity in me. That is to say: He has set charity supreme in me; He has set my affections in order; He has subjected them all to the control and command of divine love.

The order of charity is that I should first of all love God for His own sake, above all things; and that I should love all other persons and things only in reference to Him, for His sake, and in Him: first of all myself, then my parents, teachers, benefactors both spiritual and temporal, the poor, the afflicted, the sick, not forgetting my enemies, and finally all men. So much for those on earth. But our spirit of faith must make us rise higher still and extend our charitable compassion to all the holy souls in Purgatory, nay, it ought to take us up into the eternal dwellings of Paradise, and cause us joyfully to share the bliss of the angels and saints. Thus is expanded the heart of good will where Jesus has put everything in order.

May we take the liberty of briefly touching here upon the subject of unlawful passion? For it is a lamentable fact that anything may happen and does happen on this earth of ours. Not only does an almost infinite number of Christians refuse to enter into the plan of divine Love in their behalf, but it may even happen, sometimes, that persons who have freely consecrated themselves to God will suddenly fall, to the great scandal of all who witness it. Still, whenever such a mishap occurs, we should bear in mind that, as our Lord warns us, along with the *wise virgins* of the parable, there were also the *foolish ones.* Jesus did not think it beneath Him to notice this peculiar feature in the history of His future Church (Matt, 25:1-11).

One of these unfortunate beings will give as an excuse: "But I feel such a craving for loving and being loved!" which being translated into plain language should read thus: "Alas! during a more or less protracted period, I have ceased to *watch and pray* and be on my guard; and now I find myself so goaded on by carnal lusts that I do not know how to overcome them." This would be a truer statement of facts. Poor silly creature! loved indeed you are, infinitely, divinely; and as for loving, who stays you from, so doing? A race-course of love is wide open and stretches out before you to an infinite extent. But that is not any longer what she wants. There was a time when Jesus was to her the all-sufficing Love, but that time is past. *Hear, O ye heavens, and give ear, O earth,* and ye angels and saints of paradise, listen and be amazed: This person, one day, gave herself to God and God gave. Himself to her, and now she wants to go back on this stupendous exchange! God does not any longer please her.

God does not please her!
Ah! the trouble is that God offers no delight to the senses. God does not bestow coarse endearments. Now this person has, rather late in life, discovered that this is precisely the kind of thing she wants; that is what she calls loving and being loved. That Jesus died for her on the Cross, that He gives Himself to be her food in Holy Communion, that He vouchsafed to become her Bridegroom and promises her special, highly coveted, privileges in His paradise of glory: all that counts for nothing; one does not feel that one is being loved wonderfully. But to receive on both cheeks and give back with interest the sort of kisses that fond parents bestow upon their darlings, ah! that is the thing I this indeed is loving and being loved!

Great simpletons! What a sorry figure you cut! Why, then, did you ever enter religion? or why did you ever present yourself for Holy Orders and become priests? One asks: Is it perchance that, they were mistaken as to their vocation? No, no! Do not you believe it. Most of the time such is not the case. All went well in the beginning. We can but repeat with St. Paul: *O senseless Galatians, who hath bewitched you? You did run well: who hath hindered you that you should cease to obey the truth?* (Gal. 3; 1:7.) All went well in the beginning, but there came a time when they lent a pleased ear to the persistent rigmarole of the tempter, and they would covet what was not good for them; they ceased to be faithful to their plighted love. It is the history of our first parents over again; over again, the history of the traitor Apostle, Judas.

Worldlings show themselves astounded, nay scandalized, when we tell them that the love of God is above and subdues and sanctifies all other loves; and that, in the case of persons consecrated to God, it supplants and takes the place of the natural love of those who *marry and are given in marriage.* This they cannot take, they cannot believe it. They look upon us priests, nuns or monks, as either so many blind persons or 60 many fools. Above all they consider us as suffering a great privation, and they pity us, as though our life were loveless and empty. For them love is solely and exclusively sexual concupiscence—an affair of the senses. To love God, to love Him with a bridal love wholly spiritual, to wed Him and be wedded to Him, seems to them as chimerical, as impossible as to catch the moon with one's teeth. Hardly do they discern in such expressions anything beyond some figures of speech, some bold rhetorical tropes which ought not to be taken literally. And I really give them up as hopeless.

But whether they can see it or not, it remains true that God wants to be so loved, I mean supremely and with nuptial love, by every Christian soul, even here below, even though they be engaged in legitimate human wedlock; and that moreover God calls a certain number of souls to the service of His altar and to divers religious orders, to be His exclusively and to make of Him alone, even during the present life,, their All-in-all. Blessed are those chosen and called to such a life; blessed indeed, if only they be faithful!

Here is the way this kingly Lover proceeds. He sets a regular siege to the heart of the Christian, generally early in life; and when He has conquered and so to say captured all his affections, He pledges His faith to him and unites him to Himself by a mystical betrothal; and soon after, if He should find him generously responsive to His love, He adorns his soul with the jewels of the most precious virtues, and celebrates His marriage with that soul and lives with her as the husband with his wife. I repeat it: we shall never get people who appreciate only the things of flesh and blood to understand this: *The sensual man perceiveth not these things that are of the Spirit of God; for it is foolishness to him and he cannot understand.* (1 Cor. 2:14.) Well, all we can say is that the Canticle of Canticles was never written for such Christians, supposing that they can still be called Christians; nor is it for such as they that it has been inserted by the Church into the canon of Holy Scriptures, and woven into the web of the sacred liturgy.

I have been told sometimes with a considerable amount of scornful reproach fulness: Oh you, monk, you have never loved; you cannot know what it is like. You were in your teens when you entered the cloister; during your whole life you have scorned woman's love; something is wanting to you. You know not what love is, you have not really lived to the full extent and meaning of the word. My answer is:

I beg your pardon, but I must contradict you.

If I may be allowed to give testimony in my own behalf, I am conscious of having lived really and fully and intensely. I think I can say that I have lived a very great deal. For one thing, I have loved and loved much. I have loved certainly more than if I had fallen in love with a perfect woman and made her my wife and had of her all earthly happiness and many beautiful children; yes I have loved even more than would have then been the case. Does that surprise you, my friend? Then it is you yourself who do not understand what love is.

You stumble upon this narrow and indigent notion of a purely human love and cannot get away from it Let me assure you that there is another kind of love, which takes hold of the heart and the senses, to say nothing of the purely spiritual part of our being, far more forcibly than anything created could ever do. *My heart and my flesh have rejoiced in the Irving God,* sings David. (Ps. 83:3.) Is there need of proving this? Is not this truth brighter than the noonday sun? True, its very brightness only serves to dazzle the bat's eyes and owl's eyes of worldlings. O you, who are wise according to the world, stay where you arc, in your own wisdom, and in your darkness. It were cruelty to try to enlighten you; because in a vivid light causes intolerable pain to sore eyes. But at least do not try to force the *children of light* themselves, against their will, to become like you, bats and owls of darkness. *We are the children of the light: Filii lucis* (1 Thess. 5:5)

Besides, do you really think that an elderly priest is quite ignorant of what purely natural love is? For him to be so, it were necessary that he should have passed through life with his eyes and ears stopped. During half a century of priestly activity have I not met lovers by the score, and observed them before and during and after the thunderbolt of what you call *la grande passion?* Have I not had to read from time to time in your newspapers horrid details of domestic tragedies? Out of a stern sense of duty and to my intense disgust, I have been obliged to read some of the day's most famous novels where adultery is celebrated on the lyric mode, where marriage as God instituted it is derided, where divorce is perched as from the house-tops and the free love of dogs without a master or of monkeys in the equatorial forests is held up as the ideal. Besides all this, in my capacity of spiritual father, I have received confidences which have opened my eyes upon the miseries which beset human love even of the purest and most legitimate kind.

In very truth, I ask myself sometimes, whether an aged priest does not know more on this subject than all the lovers in the world. For it is not the man who is caught as a fish in the meshes of human love, who has the better knowledge of it all; he, poor man, does not understand anything beyond the fact that he is no more master of himself. But the man who sees the whole thing from outside, who is a calm, dispassionate and disinterested spectator, whose lucidity of vision is enhanced by the help of a special grace for the guidance of others, this is the man who understands and can say: I know all about it.

No indeed, I am not ignorant of what human love is. I could, if I chose, write a novel. And without wishing in the least to disparage human love—for I think highly of it, whenever it does not stray from the right path—I am so far from finding myself an object of self pity because, for the love of God, I have deprived myself of the sweets of woman's love, that I have caught myself congratulating myself and saying: "Well, well; we have had a lucky escape!" I cannot enough thank Our Lord that He has been pleased to take all the room in my heart, leaving none for other affections; *Ordinavit in me caritatem.* May He be blessed for ever!

CHAPTER XXII

LOVE LANGUORS
(Verses 5, 6, 7, 8, of Ch. 2 of Canticle.)

SUMMARY.—Flowers and fruits. The left hand and the right of the Bridegroom. The soul asleep. How Jesus protects her repose. How even in her sleep she hears His voice.

TAY me up with flowers, compass me about with apples, because I languish with love.

Let us begin with the last words—*I languish with love*—that is to say I am consumed with passionate desire; and He whom I so fondly, ardently love, hides from me His sweet countenance. Hence these sighs, which I cannot restrain.

It were only right that ail Christians should, from a full heart, incessantly heave sighs of love of God during their exile here below. They should be seen wandering here and there at random, with no other end in view than to give utterance to their pent-up feelings, as though wounded and incapable of stopping the bleeding, and as who could only grow weaker and weaker. If such be not the case with us, if we have not yet received full tilt in our heart the piercing arrow of divine love, it is because we have not as yet entered into the ways of divine contemplation. If, on the other hand, like the bride of the Canticle, we are languishing with love, then we shall exclaim with her—*Stay me up with flowers.*

In his *Treatise on The Love of God,* Book V, Ch. 9, St. Francis de Sales discerns in these words and those which follow, a pressing invitation addressed by the bride to all creatures to join her in the praise of God. Let me refer readers to this chapter. Let them read it attentively: they will find themselves deeply edified by it; and if perchance they should feel inclined to read and reread, not only chapter 9, but the whole Book V, or still better the whole treatise, it will be to «their advantage; for there goes out of it a pure flame of divine love.

St. Francis de Sales is an eminent philosopher and theologian, a genuine poet in prose, a master writer and a quaint and charming story-teller; above all he is a mystic among mystics. He is the writer on the spiritual life whom I would most warmly recommend, because he is so nearly akin to our modern mentality. But, O my God, what confusion is it not for me, wretch, to dare to be writing on this sacred Epithalamium of divine love, the Canticle of Canticles, after such geniuses as St. Francis de Sales, St. John of the Cross, St. Teresa, St. Thomas Aquinas, St. Gregory the Great, to name but these few! My only excuse is that having read and reread the works of these saints and having imbued myself with the Holy Scriptures, there is perhaps tome hope that, in spite of all, my readers will still find in these pages, which I write with a trembling hand, some faint echo of their noble teachings. This much by way of parenthesis. Now let us take up the thread of our paraphrase.

Stay me up with flowers.

The flowers of pious sentiments and of holy discourses. Sentiments, discourses, be they ever so holy, are still but flowers; pleasing to the eye and to the sense of smell, figuratively speaking; stimulating to the soul, up to a certain degree, but which can bear no comparison with the ripe and luscious fruits of good works. That is why these words are added:

Compass me about with apples.

Compass me about and load me with ap abundance of the fruits of good works; show me something for me to do for the dear love of Christ; either to comfort the sorrowing, or to visit the sick and those in prison, or teach the ignorant, or form little children to the practice of virtue, or serve "our lords" the poor, as they were styled in the ages of faith. This will be to me some relief; it will help me bear the pain of my exile far from Him who has wounded my heart. But what do I say? Is *He* really so very far, *whom my soul loveth?* No; only I am blind, and although I have not as yet the joy of seeing His blessed countenance, I am conscious of His dear presence near me and I feel His fond embrace.

His left hand is under my head.

She means that Our Lord most tenderly intervenes, lest «he should hurt herself against the hard surface of the things of this world. The left hand of our heavenly Bridegroom in this symbolical discourse, is His sacred Humanity.

And his right hand shall embrace me.

The right hand or rather the right arm of Our Lord with which He embraces the soul of good will, means His Divinity. Yes, the glory of His divine nature envelopes, embraces and presses upon His loving heart, all those who allow Him to have His way with them. Shall we be surprised then, if the bride should fall in a sweet repose in the shelter of His arms and upon His bosom, as did St. John during the Last Supper? How different is such a trance from the heavy stertorous lethargy of a sinner, surfeited with the pleasures of the world! And yet, this same sinner could also have been, if he had but consented thereto, a loving and greatly loved soul; he too could have tasted the sweet repose and the ecstatic joy of divine contemplation.

A man who is asleep does not take any notice of what is going on around him, nor does he seek for any information about it. This is the case also for the Christian, whether he be asleep with the sleep of charity or with that of sin. The deep slumber, the kind of lethargy of the sinner, during which he may pass suddenly to the sleep of death and of death eternal, excites a feeling of pity in the bosom of the true servants of God; they try in every way to wake up the imprudent man. Alas! too often it is all in vain. On the other hand, worldlings and tepid Christians try also to awaken the fervent soul out of the sleep of divine contemplation, because they do not understand it. The spiritual director himself and the Superior in religion, unless they also be adepts of mental prayer and experienced in the secrets of mystical life, will be found as anxious as any one else to draw that soul out of her state of supernatural repose, and violently to pull her back, against her own will, to the threshold of the spiritual life. On seeing which, the Bridegroom takes her defense. He exclaims:

I adjure you, O ye daughters of Jerusalem, by the roes and the harts of the fields, that you stir not up, nor make the beloved awake, till she please.

Daughters of Jerusalem.

Already we have noticed that there are two distinct cities of Jerusalem, figured in Holy Writ under the symbolism of the capital city of the People of God in the Old Testament: there is first the heavenly Jerusalem, where dwells the true People of God, which is made up of the blessed angels and the saints; then, the earthly Jerusalem of the Militant Church, at present made up of a medley of saints and sinners. In this verse Our Lord speaks to the daughters of this earthly Jerusalem, that is to say to Christians, who are yet in their earthly pilgrim state here below, and among whom the bride is living.

So eagerly does He wish to save her from their importunate, ill-advised interference, that He uses the most emphatic form of entreaty: *I adjure you.* As an adjuration is always made in the name of something sacred, capable of commanding attention and winning respect, we are to understand by the roes and the harts of the fields—*"per capreas cervosque camporum"* aeternitatis—the blessed angels and the dear saints in glory, whom the little bride is endeavoring to emulate. Jesus does this honor to His beloved elect in paradise, to swear by them, to adjure by them. In their name does He entreat and dissuade those on earth, who would inconsiderately draw the fervent soul from divine contemplation.

"Allow her," He says, "to lay her head on My bosom, as did John the Beloved, during the Last Supper; or quietly to sit at My feet, as did Mary Magdalen in the house of Lazarus, and enjoy our secret intercourse and mutual outpourings of love."

Thus did Our Lord sharply rebuke the Pharisee who, at table with Him, would have liked nothing better than to see Him repel with contempt the sinful woman who was actually recovering both purity of soul and peace of mind in the kiss of His feet. He scolded also Martha, though a friend of His, when she would have torn away her sister Mary from the Savior's converse, in order to make her share in the bustle of preparing for Him a sumptuous repast. Even a third time did Jesus intervene in behalf of happy Magdalen, when Judas the miser accused her of undue prodigality, because she. had poured out a perfume of great price on the head of the divine Master. In the same way, some Christians who are low-minded and heavy of heart would fain awaken the fervent soul from her ecstatic sleep, and force upon her the vulgar cares of an almost exclusively material nature, as though the very highest of realities of a spiritual life were mere illusions.

The voice of the Beloved.

Even in her sleep the fervent soul hears His voice. She hears it, first of all, speaking to her through the divinely inspired books of the Old and the New Testaments; and more particularly through the Holy Gospels, the Apocalypse and the Canticle of Canticles. Then through the liturgical cycle of the feasts, entwined with the lowly splendors of the pageant of the seasons all the year round. Then again through the official authoritative teaching of Holy Church in the person of Pope, Bishops and priests, to whom Our Lord has said: *Whosoever heareth you, heareth me.* (Luke 10:16.) Finally through the legitimate commands of parents, masters, State or Church officials, religious Superiors; through the sound of the bell calling to the Divine Office or to some regular exercise; through the providential course of events, whether they bring her joy, or on the contrary sorrow.

But where the mystic bride hears more particularly the voice of her Beloved, is in her visits to the Blessed Sacrament From the Sacred Host shut up in our tabernacles, there goes out a powerful cry, a loud clamor of love, which is only perceived with the heart, not with the ears of sense. Above all, during holy Mass, at the moment of consecration, the soul hears the voice of her Beloved at the same time as the vibrations of the bell, sounded by the little altar boy. That is the moment when Jesus, taking full possession of the person of His priest, uses his lips as His own instruments and makes them utter in His own name and with His own divine omnipotence, these amazing words: *This is my body . . . This is my blood . . . Eat . . . Drink.* (Matt, 26:26-27.) Then it is that the bride can well cry out: *The voice of my beloved!* She is right. Could anyone else utter such omnipotent words of love?

Finally the bride hears His sweet voice in the depth of her own heart. He is pleased to keep tryst with her, in that intimate sanctuary, away from the profane gaze of creatures. There He speaks to her " without sound of words " as the author of *The Following of Christ* so well describes in his 1st book, ch. iii and in his 3rd book chapter ii.

CHAPTER XXIII

THE BRIDEGROOM LOOKING THROUGH THE LATTICES
(Verses 8-15 of ch. 2 of Canticle.)

SUMMARY.—What the mountains and hills art which Jesus passes over in order to come to us. Of the wall behind which He stands and the windows and lattices through which He is looking at us. What He says.

EHOLD he cometh, leaping upon the mountains, skipping over the hills.

We know by these words that the bride heard from afar, during her sleep, the voice of her Beloved, so great is the strength of her feelings towards Him. Now she is wide awake; she looks to the far horizon, hemmed in by mountain ranges and hills; she descries Him bounding and leaping over all obstacles to come to her, with the alertness of the roe-buck.

In order to come to me, as He does in Holy Communion, my heavenly Spouse, the Divine Word, has had to overcome formidable barriers which stood in His way, as so many mountain- ranges and hills. He did it with the greatest ease.

The mountain ranges represent, on the one hand, the pure nothingness that we are of ourselves, then our present condition of a fallen race, finally the enormous and forbidding accumulation of our own personal sins.

In order to come to us as He does in Holy Eucharist, Our Lord had moreover to overcome other less formidable obstacles, though very real ones, which stood in His way as so many hills; I mean the natural laws which govern spirit and matter, substance and accident, time and space. Hence this exclamation of the bride.

My beloved is like a roe or a young hart.

Graceful images which aptly represent the ease and haste

with which, in the eagerness of His love, the Word *of* God overcame every obstacle, one after the other.

Behold He standeth behind our wall.

The wall means our common human nature, which the divine Word took in the chaste bosom of the Blessed Virgin Mary and united hypostatically to Himself. Behind the man Christ, *Homo Christus Jesus,* as says St. Paul, and forming with Him one and the same person, is to be found the true Son of God, consubstantial, co-eternal with the Father. Now what are those windows and lattices, through which He looks at us as one who is separated from us, though very near?

Looking through the windows.

This means that since His Incarnation and human birth, Our Lord makes use of His senses even as we do. Our eyes, our ears and the other senses are as so many windows through which our soul looks, in order to get into touch with the exterior world, and know what it is like, and in order to carry on the life of relation with our fellow-men. With His human eyes, so full of the sweetest compassion for us His brethren, with those eyes which were so often moistened with tears as we see in the Gospel, it is the Divine Word, the Bridegroom, who is looking at us. With the lips of His Sacred Humanity it is the Word of God who speaks to men in the language that is familiar to them.

Looking through the lattices.

These lattices are, to our Lord in the Blessed Sacrament, the sacred, species, that is to say the material appearances of bread and wine. Behind these species stands the heavenly Bridegroom, in His bodily presence as the Word made flesh, the same who has been immolated on the Cross. Through these lattices, behind which He is held captive, He casts upon us glances of intense desire and love. He is asking Himself: "Will they come to visit Me? Will they have some good words from the heart to address to Me, who so ardently love them? Are they going to unite themselves to My sacrifice, by assisting with devotion at the celebration of Mass? Are they going to bestow upon Me the kiss of their fervent communion?"

Behold, my beloved speaketh to me.

Jesus speaks to each of us, individually, personally, privately, in the secret of our heart. But all do not listen, or their unmortified passions raise such a din, that His meek voice cannot possibly be heard of them. Only a soul that is recollected within herself and very attentive, can perceive the faint sound of His voice. But what is it He says? Oh! such words as fill the soul with an inexpressible joy. He tells her:

Arise, make haste, my love, my dove, my beautiful one, and come.

Oh, the lovely behest and command. How it shows the eagerness of Our Lord to enjoy the endearments of His little bride? and what enthusiastic response it elicits on her part!

Arise, come—come to Me in Holy Communion! After this command of His loving heart, shall we at last understand that whenever it is in our power to receive Him, but we fail to do so under some flimsy excuse, not only do we deprive ourselves of an inestimable benefit, but we moreover deprive Him of something He dearly loves and ardently wishes for. What folly is this!

But, my Lord, how can you possibly bestow such tender appellations and praises upon so vile and wretched a being as I know myself to be? Does, perchance, love make you also blind as it does poor human lovers? Ah! well, no indeed, it is not that It is perfectly true that a soul in a state of grace, even though she be still full of the imperfections of a beginner, is already beautiful in the eyes of God and deserving of His most tender love. In those that are born again (through Baptism) there is nothing displeasing to God (*Council of Trent*).

For, winter is now fast, the rain is over and tone.

By the word *winter* we must especially understand the moral consequences of original sin; and by *the rain*, the consequences of tepidity, that is to say the manifold, more or less grievous offences, which fall upon a soul like the showers of rain or hail-storms and cause it considerable damages.

Oh, my dear reader, I hope such is the case with you; and that winter is now past and the rain is now over and gone, that is to say that you are once for all done with tepidity and above all with mortal sin. If this were not so, what a shame! what a misfortune! What! you would have dared to take up this book, which is for the pure only; you would have been reading it with a profane curiosity, very likely with the secret, though unavowed, hope of finding therein something with which to gratify the pruriency of your thoughts, some excuse for indulging in lascivious imaginations. In that case let me say it again: What a shame! how horrible! how abominable! Make haste to renounce sin for good and forever, or to put away this book which is not written for you and which is your emphatic condemnation! Just as whosoever eats and drinks unworthily the Holy Eucharist, eats and drinks his own condemnation and turns into a violent poison the very thing which, in the mind of Our Lord, was to be to the soul the food of eternal life; just in the same manner, within due proportion, whosoever dares to drink at the cup of the Canticle of Canticles with impure lips and a putrid heart, offends God grievously and does to his own self an inexpressible injury.

> *The flowers have appeared in our land.*
> The flowers of holy desires and courageous resolutions.

> *The time of pruning is come.*

Of this pruning does Our Lord speak in the Gospel, when He says: *I am the vine . . . you the branches. . . . My Father is the husbandman. Every branch in me which beareth not fruit, he will take away; and every one that beareth fruit he will purge it, that it may bring forth more fruit* (John 15).

As we advance in the Canticle of Canticles we shall see more and more how the Holy Ghost joins together the freshness, poetry, beauty and sublimity of nature, with the mutual praise of the Bridegroom and the bride; precisely because nature has been created for the sake of man, above all for *the man Christ Jesus* and for His beloved ones.

The voice of the turtle is heard in our land.

The turtle-dove is the emblem of simplicity and love. All its cooings are for its mate. It is a most sweet sound of love. Happy the human dove whose every sigh is for Jesus alone! With what delight does Our Lord listen to the cooing of His dear little dove! No danger that He will ever find monotonous or tiresome this voice of love, which sounds above the din of the forest of earthly things.

Our land.

We must not let pass unnoticed this little word, twice repeated in the same verse, and which we shall meet again and again. *Our land* means a certain region held in common by both the Bridegroom and the bride. What can this be, but the body and soul of the mystic? They surely belong to the mystic, since they are his very own body and soul; and they also belong to Jesus, since the mystic gives them up to Him as a free gift and will never claim them back again. It is their demesne which they hold and enjoy in common; they are joint owners.

But what a joy to hear my beloved Master speak of poor me in this strain: *Our land!* Well said, my Lord! I am yours, I belong to you entirely, I am one of your goods and chattels. And on the other hand you are Mine, you are My garden of delights. Thus to hold all things in common, is not this, as we have already seen, the law. of love and the condition of our divine marriage?

The fig tree has put forth her green figs.

That is to say, fervent love has now produced its first fruits; a multitude of good works show themselves on all sides in the daily life of our mystic.

The vines in flower yield their sweet smell.

The vines are the four cardinal virtues of Prudence, Justice, Temperance and Fortitude. They yield their sweet smell as soon as the fig tree of charity begins to put forth her green figs.

My dove—in the clifts of the rock, in the hollow places of the wall.

Often has this passage been explained as signifying the wounds in the hands and feet of Our dear Lord, and the deep hollow place of His sacred side, dug out by the lance of the soldier, where the mystical dove likes to take cover. This is certainly a pious interpretation from which, at certain moments, the fervent Christian is able to derive much comfort. However, from the point of view of the literal and dogmatic interpretation of this book of the Canticle of Canticles, we must acknowledge that it is only an accommodative meaning and not a strictly mystical one, for this last must of necessity rest upon the logical sequence of ideas in the text. Now, if we take into consideration the fact that, in this passage, it is the Bridegroom who addresses these words to His bride, and that He is actually separated from her by a wall and lattices, it is more to the point to interpret it as follows:

The rock is the Church, the Holy Catholic Church Militant on earth, which has been founded by Our Lord Himself upon the firm authority of St Peter and his successors. Genuine mystical life is only found in the clift of that rock, that is to say within the precincts of the Catholic Church. As for the hollow places in the wall, they mean the lowly employments and hidden life, where a mystical soul finds her delights, the more so that they are a help to divine contemplation. The humbler your place and office in your community, the better for you, if you only know how to appreciate it. "Love to be unnoticed and held for naught," says the author of *The Following of Christ.*

Show me thy face, let thy voice sound in my ears.

The bride complies with these tenderly proffered requests of Our Lord, and causes Him joy by her spirit of internal recollection and by mental prayer. The more she withdraws herself from intercourse with the creatures, the more also does she show her face to the Beloved, and the more does her voice become melodious and sonorous in His ears.

For thy voice is sweet.

The voice of adoration, in the divine praise of the psalmody by day and night, and in the outpourings of love from a burning heart. Sweet to Jesus is such a sound. Sweet also to men is the voice of the bride, because she is meek and humble after the pattern of her Beloved, full of gentleness to all men of any rank or profession, but above all, to those who are in trouble. Not only does she speak kind words, but she does it sweetly. By an effort of charity, she, of set purpose, modulates the very sound of her voice in accordance with her feelings of sympathy and compassion, so that it does one good merely to hear it. In the intercourse of our daily life, a gentle voice charms everyone and softens and wins even the most rebellious hearts.

And thy face is comely.

The face is the mirror of the soul. When all is well ordered inside, there shows itself on the face a beautiful expression of peace which cannot deceive. See the candid expression of the face in little children. But here it is a question of the face of the soul, not of the body. As for us, we have no direct perception of the natural comeliness of the human soul, made to the image and likeness of God; still less can we form any idea of its supernatural beauty, when, through the efficacy of the Sacraments, it is raised to the dignity of the state of grace. God alone can appreciate to the full the comeliness of such a soul; as for ourselves let us at least make an act of faith in this regard, upon the testimony of the Heavenly Bridegroom. "O Christian," exclaims one of the Fathers of the Church, "become conscious of thine own dignity."

Within a soul in the state of grace, Our Lord descries not only her virtues and the merits of her good works, but moreover the marks left by the Sacraments. There are, first of all, the indelible characters of Baptism, Confirmation, Holy Orders; then the marks left at each fresh reception of the Sacraments of Penance and Holy Eucharist. They are as so many strokes of the chisel or of the brush of the Divine Artist, incessantly adding new charms on the face of a well disposed soul.

Let us once for all understand that, by the very fact of her Baptism, the Christian soul has become the bride of our Lord Jesus Christ, and that the Son of God has conceived towards her the tender affection of a husband. She may have had the misfortune of straying away from Him by sin; she has not ceased to be His. She may have been unfaithful, an adulteress (Oh great pity!) she has not ceased to be His wedded wife; and He, on His part, has not ceased for a single moment from ardently longing after her return to Him, and calling after her, and promising her that all would be forgiven and forgotten. No sooner has she returned to Him than He gives her tenderly the kiss of peace.

Winter it now past.

Here is a delightful word of St. Francis de Sales, which may help us to comprehend the ways of God in regard to beginners. "There are," he says, " souls who, having recently been delivered from the thraldom of sin and having quite made up their mind to apply themselves to the love of God, are nevertheless still novices, apprentices, without much firmness or strength; so that they have a liking for divine sweetness, but they mix it up with so many other different affections, that their love of God must be considered as being as yet in its infancy. They love Our Lord, and together with Him a large number of things superfluous, vain and dangerous. Just as a phoenix, recently born again out of its own ashes, is only covered as yet but with small weak feathers and soft down, by the help of which it cannot be said to fly but only to skip; in much the same way these tender young souls, freshly born again out of the ashes of their penance, are as yet unable to raise themselves aloft and wing their flight in the high regions of divine love, being prevented from so doing by the multitude of their evil inclinations, and vicious habits which past sins have left behind them. They are nevertheless living birds, animated and feathered by divine love of the genuine kind; otherwise they would never have abandoned sin; but their love of God is still weakly and inexperienced; and as it is surrounded with a quantity of other loves, it cannot produce as much fruit as it would if it were in total and exclusive possession of the heart." (*Love of God,* Book X, Ch. iv.)

CHAPTER XXIV

THE LITTLE FOXES THAT DESTROY
THE VINE
(Verse 15 of Ch. 2 of Canticle)

SUMMARY.—Those little foxes are our daily imperfections against which a relentless war has to be waged. Why we must be careful not io outrun our present grace.

ATCH US the little foxes that destroy the vines.

Those little foxes are our defects and customary imperfections. If they already do so much havoc whilst yet small, what will it not be if we allow them to grow? They destroy the vineyard of our soul, diminishing its sightliness and value and production; endangering the vintage of eternal merits.

In the soul which is being led forward by the Spirit of God to a perfect union with His divine Goodness, there remain but small defects and imperfections; it is impossible for anyone whilst here below to be quite free from such. Nevertheless, be these ever so small, they still do a great deal of damage in the soul. Therefore one must pursue them, trap them, exterminate them without any mercy. They are not the same in every man, nor are they the same in the same man at diverse periods of his life. They change and metamorphose themselves, according to the age, environments, temper, occupations and employments of the subject.

The defects in which devout persons may fall in the beginning of the spiritual life are analyzed with great subtlety by St. John of the Cross in *The Dark Night of the Soul,* Book I, Chapters iii to vii. Let it suffice here to put our readers on their guard against spiritual pride, spiritual jealousy, secret self-seeking even in the things of God, intemperance of the tongue, the eyes, the other senses, and in human friendships.

These defects are described as small foxes, because, although she cannot prevent them from being born, a faithful soul will never allow them to grow to any size. The danger is only that whilst they are so small, they may be allowed to pass unobserved. Catch hold of them and crush them against the stone by the contemplation of Jesus crucified.

Our vineyard hath flourished.

It is Jesus who speaks thus, and it is of His little bride that He speaks thus. He and she are now one and the Same vine, so closely and vitally are they united. *I am the vine, you the branches.* He tells His apostles at the Last Supper. *As the branch cannot bear fruit of itself, unless it abide in the vine, so neither can you unless you abide in me* (John 15:4-5). But oh! how pleasing it must be to the little bride, to hear herself spoken of by the Beloved as *our vineyard;* the vineyard which belongs to us both! A pure and fervent soul by right belongs to God, because it is He that made her what she is; and yet she belongs also to herself in strict justice, since God gave her into the hands of her own counsel, freely to dispose of herself as she lists. This vineyard is the vineyard of Jesus, since He planted it and infused into it His own divine life, the sap of grace; and it is the bride's vineyard, since it is the bride herself and since she puts no obstacle in the way of grace and cooperates with all her might with its operations in her. Hence the fruits of this vineyard when they ripen will be the joint property of the two.

Please, note that it is only question of one who is a beginner; that is why Jesus does not as yet speak of the fruits, but only of their promise in the flowers. The loving soul who is as yet but a beginner, produces first the flowers of holy, desires and generous resolutions; the fruits will come in due time. One must not try to steal a march upon God by reaching out beyond one's actual gifts of grace and setting at naught the laws which regulate the ordinary process of supernatural life. Let us be humble, patient, and let us go forward one step at a time. We shall be doing very well indeed, if we only never stop on the road to perfection; thus shall we please God. Do not little children please their parents and everybody, even though they are not as yet capable of doing any work? That will come in due time.

When Jesus says: *Our vint yard hath flourished,* and speaks of the little foxes, it is as though He said, "O soul of goodwill, I am fully aware that there are in thee the happy beginnings of every virtue—but for that very reason I want thee to be very much on thy guard against thy smallest enemies, for it is only in appearance that they are contemptible."

CHAPTER XXV

REPLY OF THE BRIDE TO JESUS
(Verses 16 and 17 of Ch. 2 of the Canticle)

SUMMARY.—The holy exercise of the presence of God superseded by that of enjoying God. How this exercise is disengaged from all that ir sensuous. Conclusion of this first Part.

N hearing the tender appeal of her Beloved, who said to her: *Show me thy face: let thy voice sound in my ears,* the bride seems at first to fall into a sweet reverie of self-communing. Speaking to herself, she says: *My beloved to me and I to him, who feedeth among the lilies.* Then, all at once, she turns towards Him and exclaims with deep emotion: *Return, O my beloved. Till the day break and the shadows retire, be like to a roe or to a young hart upon the mountains of Bether.*

My beloved to me and I to Him.

These words of the bride are verified in her divine contemplation, in her persevering union with Him even in the midst of the bustle of her active life, but more especially at the happy moments of Holy Communion.

For the true mystic, the holy exercise of the presence of God is soon superseded by another much more precious exercise, namely that of enjoying God. The august reality of the natural presence of God everywhere almost sinks into insignificance in the eyes of the fervent Christian, in comparison to this other reality of the supernatural presence of God in his heart, the presence by way of love.

The Archangel Gabriel, in the opening sentence of his message to the Blessed Virgin Mary, says with unmistakable emphasis: *The Lord is with thee,* thereby proclaiming that God was already present with the presence of love in Mary, and that, on her part, this admirable Virgin was actively holding herself united to His infinite Goodness. Must it not be so even with us, though of course in a lesser degree? *Behold,* says Our Lord in the Apocalypse, *I stand ai the gate and knock. If any man shall hear my voice and open to me the door, I will come in to him, and will sup with him and he with me* (Apoc. 3:20). And in St. John's Gospel: *If any one love me, he will keep my word, and my Father will love him, and we will come to him, and will make our abode with him* (John 14:23).

My beloved to me and I to him.

To me; yes, even to me, does Jesus give and surrender His sweet divine self. He makes Himself my guest, my solitary friend, the dweller in my heart.

And I to Him.

On my part, I give and dedicate and surrender my own self wholly to Him. I deliver into His blessed hands my entire being, body and soul; I transfer to Him all my rights; freely and willingly do I abandon to Him the only thing that is truly mine, namely, my poor self. Therefore, O creatures, ye come too late; do not beg for my affections; do not try to wrest my heart from Jesus, who alone is worthy to have it in His possession. Do not proffer to me your deceitful charms and empty consolations. I have something better. I have my Jesus, who loves and wants to be loved with a chaste affection, *who heedeth among the lilies.*

See how chaste, pure, modest, *verecundus* is our loving Lord in His Blessed Sacrament. He does not so much as show to us His blessed, virginal countenance. We can neither see His face nor feel Him with our hands, nor embrace Him and kiss Him and strain Him to our breast. Although He be therein present in His two natures of God and man, what we descry with our bodily eyes is not His dear self but only the species of bread and wine; under which commonplace appearances He does riot solicit either the caress of the hand nor that of the lips. Moreover a strict ceremonial stands in the way of any familiar dealing with Him.

Therefore I repeat, how very holy and virginal and above the senses and heavenly is our intercourse of love with Jesus in Holy

Communion. It is an intercourse with Him who *heedeth among the lilies.* Nevertheless, when all has been said, it remains that my dear Lord give Himself wholly to me and take hold of my whole being. And I, on my part, though such an unspeakable wretch, I want to give up into His hands ail that I am, without restriction or division and without any return, and that is why I bid an eternal adieu to all things created.

Therefore, O my brothers and sisters, wayfarers with me upon this land of our pilgrimage, I am quite resolved neither to love you nor allow you to love me after a purely natural manner. I do not want anyone to give himself to me, nor do I want anyone to filch any part of my affections. Of course I shall never cease tenderly to love you in the Lord, for did He not say: *This is my commandment that you love one another* as *I have loved you?* (John 15:12) but then it is not you, for what there is of yourselves, I am loving, but Him in you; that is to say, ail that there is of Him in you, together with ail the divine possibilities of which He deposited the germs in you. I will joyfully, and with humble gratitude, accept such kind services and tokens of good will as you may be pleased to bestow upon me; and I for my part, will greatly honor you and serve you with all my heart, for His dear love. Thus far will I go, but not a step farther.

The mystic is never less alone than when alone, for then he is all to his Beloved and his Beloved is wholly to him. The presence and above alt the conversation of other men only serve to hinder the embraces and heart-to-heart effusions of these two lovers.

Here, then, O my Lord Jesus, my dear heavenly Spouse, here am I; body and soul, the work of Thy blessed hands, Thine by every right: although love has thrown in the shade and superseded all the other rights save that which arises from our divine marriage. All I ask for, henceforth, is only this: first Thine own glory; and secondly that Thou shouldst find Thy delights in me. Yes, Thy glory above all things and before all things, in such a way that without any regard to my being in existence, Thou, my Lord, Thou alone be praised, loved and exalted by every creature, world without end. And then, since as a matter of fact I do exist, since Thou hast made me for Thyself, I ardently desire that Thou shouldst now render me worthy of Thyself, so that it be possible for Thee to take Thy delights in me.

Ah! my Lord, Thou art but very ill served in me and by me. Thou hast the worst of the bargain; this is just what the world calls a bad business. Thou to me, and in exchange the vile wretch that I am, to Thee! This is an incredible adventure! *My beloved to me and I to Him, who feedeth among the lilies.*

It is upon such sentiments of humility, gratitude and burning love that the end of the first stage of the spiritual life is reached. The bride ceases to be a child: she feels her wings. Opening eyes of wonderment upon the immense azure fields and free spaces of divine love, she is all a-tremble with emotion and ready to take her flight.

PART II
THE YOUNG BRIDE GROWING
INTO THE FULNESS OF HER
CHARMS

CHAPTER XXVI

CHARACTERISTICS OF THE SECOND STAGE OF THE SPIRITUAL LIFE

SUMMARY.—The soul now seeks her Beloved not for His gifts but for Himself. How rich and dramatic a life she is living. What we mean by ecstatic love.

IN the first two chapters of the Canticle of Canticles which we have just paraphrased, the bride was in her spiritual childhood: quite small, graceful, innocent, fond of receiving endearments and sweets; at the same time full of the imperfections of that age, incapable of performing heavy work or sustaining any grievous trial. That soul was thinking principally of herself: not any longer, as of yore, in a way displeasing to God, but in a saintly way, seeing herself by the light of Our Lord, by the light of His Holy Gospel and of His Holy Eucharist. She was enamored with the charms of her Heavenly Bridegroom, much more for the sweet comforts they afforded her, than for the sake of Him. Yet, Our Lord did not, for all that, find fault with her, just as good parents do not find fault with their little darlings for being fond of caresses, smiles and all sorts of sweetmeats.

What characterizes the pages of the Canticle we are how going to paraphrase and interpret, is the anxious search after the Beloved, in the midst of the most trying vexations. It comprises three chapters of the sacred text (3-5) and corresponds to the phase of the spiritual life known as the Illuminative Way.

In it the soul is more vividly enlightened and touched with a more efficacious grace; she goes beyond the limits of spiritual infancy and leaves them far behind. Henceforth she anxiously seeks after her Beloved, not for His gifts but for Him; her only pain being to discover her manifold miseries. She attributes to her unworthiness the fact that Jesus often withdraws from her the sight of His loveliness or the feeling of His presence. She feels keenly that she has not yet come of age in Jesus Christ and become nubile to Him, which is the object of her most ardent wishes. She is most generous, and no trial whatever, either from outside or from within, is able to discourage her.

The three chapters of the Canticle of Canticles which form this second part of our little treatise, place this fresh aspect of the mystical life under our eyes in a most dramatic fashion. It would seem at first sight that for the ecstatic love of our Lord, to which it serves as a practical introduction, nothing else should be required except God and the soul, but indeed it is not so. The dramatic action of the Canticle develops itself in the midst of the most varied and enchanting scenery. Besides the fields, vineyards, trees, flowers, perfumes of nature or made by the skill of man; besides the hills and mountains, the roes and harts, the doves, the lambs with their dams as in the preceding pages, we have now moreover dens of lions, mountains haunted by leopards, choirs of angels and troops of young maidens; then the city with its guards by day and night and all sorts of incidents which happen. Why all this? It is in order to give us to understand that the bride, if she wants to live her life of divine love, has need, not only of Jesus, her Lord and Bridegroom, but also of His sweet Mother, the blessed Virgin Mary, of the blessed angels, of the dear saints of paradise, of the holy souls in Purgatory, and finally of the whole Militant Church with her hierarchy, her holy sacrifice of the Mass and the treasure of the word of God and the seven sacraments, which. have been entrusted to her keeping and ministration. By God's ordinance, the loving soul, in her present condition, has need of the whole creation, animate and inanimate, and of all these persons and of all these things, to help her to live in the midst of the flames of divine love, to give her some relief from the intensity of her feelings, so that she may take breath; otherwise she would simply be crushed to death under the weight of the love of God and of the mysteries of Jesus, contemplated in too exclusive, sustained and protracted a manner.

Besides, although the mystical life essentially consists in the intercourse of the loving soul with the loving God in the secret of her heart, nevertheless it cannot be confined within such a narrow place: it must needs break out into all sorts of saintly activities, and, as we shall see, into downright apostolate.

Thus understood, mystical life is assuredly the richest, the fullest, the most opulent, the most marvelously vast and spacious and comprehensive, which a man could possibly live; and yet, at the same time, it is a wonderfully simplified life, since it refers and subdues everything to the sole object of his ardent love, the Lord Christ.

When I speak of the ecstatic love of Jesus, I do not mean thereby such a love as would impel one to have or wish to have ecstasies, private revelations or other miraculous things: but such a love as will make one go out *(ex stare)* of himself, wholly to pass into Jesus and dwell in Him. Such a love does not leave the beaten paths of Christian piety, but it does, in these lowly paths, demean itself with most extraordinary purity of intention and fervor of love.

The chapters of this second part are conspicuously fewer in number and more lengthy than in the first, for the reason that herein we meet with incidents which it would not do to curtail or cut into pieces, as such a process would infallibly detract from their beauty and high significance.

CHAPTER XXVII

CHAPTERS 3 TO 5 OF THE CANTICLE

SUMMARY.—What happened just before the bridal procession. How Jesus celebrates the charms of His wedded bride. Her mysterious tribulations. She describes her Beloved.

HE BRIDE, speaking no doubt to some of her companions, relates to them the first adventure she met with in her new life. She says:

In my bed, by night, I sought him whom my soul loveth: I sought him and found him not. Then I said: I will rise and will go about the city. In the streets and the broad ways I will seek him whom my soul loveth.

I sought him and found him not. The watchmen who kept the city found me. I asked them: *Have you seen him whom my soul loveth?*

When I had a little passed by them, I found him whom my soul loveth: I held him and I will not let him go. I will bring him into my mother's house, and into the chamber of her that bore me.

Having said this, the bride falls into the sleep of divine contemplation, so that her Beloved, speaking to her companions, repeats a second time this entreaty, which we have already heard in chapter ii of the Canticle.

The Bridegroom.

I adjure you, O daughters of Jerusalem, by the roes and the harts of the fields, that you stir not up, nor awake my beloved, till she please.

Now the angels, on witnessing the rapid progress of the youthful bride in the career of the love of God, ask one another:

Who is she that goeth up by the desert, as a pillar of smoke of aromatical apices, of myrrh, and frankincense, and of all the powders of the perfumer?

308 MYSTICAL THEOLOGY: A LAYMAN'S GUIDE II

They wonder at the happy lot which has fallen to this puny child of earth. They remark:

Behold threescore valiant ones of the most valiant of Israel, surround the bed of Solomon, all holding swords end most expert in war: every man's sword on his thigh, because of fears in the night.

They add: *King Solomon hath made him a litter of the wood of Libanus: the pillars thereof he made of silver, the seat of gold, the going up of purple, the midst he covered with charity for the daughters of Jerusalem:*

Then addressing themselves to the maiden friends of the bride the angels conclude:

Go forth, ye daughters of Sion, and see King Solomon in the diadem, wherewith his mother crowned him in the day of his espousal and in the day of the joy of his heart.

The heavenly BRIDEGROOM now lavishes magnificent praises on the ever growing charms of His youthful bride. He exclaims:

How beautiful art thou, my love, how beautiful art thou!

Thy eyes art dove's eyes, besides what is hid within. Thy hair is as flocks of goats which come up from mount Galaad, Thy teeth as flocks of sheep, that are shorn, which come up from the washing, all with twins, and there is none barren among them: thy lips are as a scarlet lace, and thy speech is sweet. Thy cheeks are as a piece of pomegranate, besides that which lieth hid within. Thy neck, as the Tower of David, which is build with bulwarks. A thousand bucklers hang upon it, all the armor of valiant men.

Reddening with the blushes of sincerest humility on hearing her heavenly Bridegroom praise her so highly, the fervent soul interrupts Him with these words of self-abasement.

Till the day break and the shadows retire, I will go to the mountain of myrrh and to the hill of frankincense

But the heavenly Bridegroom begins again with renewed feelings of tenderness:

Thou art all fair, O my love, and there is not a spot in thee.

Come from Libanus, my spouse,
Come from Libanus:
Front the top of Amana,
From the top of Sanir and Hermon,
From the dens of the lions,
From the mountains of the leopards, Come: thou shall be
crowned.
Thou hast wounded my heart,
My sister and spouse,
Thou hast wounded my heart
With one glance of thy eyes.
With one hair of thy neck.
Thy lips, my spouse, are as a dropping honeycomb.
Honey and milk are under thy tongue;
The smell of thy garments is as that of frankincense.
My sister and spouse is a garden enclosed.
A fountain sealed up:
The fountain of gardens,
The well of living waters,
Which run impetuously from Libanus.
Thy plants are a paradise of pomegranates with the fruits of the
orchard: Cyprus with spikenard, and saffron; sweet cane and
cinnamon, with all the trees of Libanus; myrrh and aloes with all
the chief perfumes.
Arise, O north wind, and come:
O south wind, blow through my garden:
Let the aromatical spices thereof flow.

Then there follows a lively little dialogue between the
enamored soul and the heavenly Bridegroom.

THE BRIDE: *Let my beloved come into his garden and eat the*
fruits of his apple-trees.

JESUS: *I am come into my garden. O my sister and spouse: I*
have gathered my myrrh with my aromatical spices; I have eaten
the honeycomb with my honey; I have drunk my wine with my
milk. And now, turning to the other two Persons of the Most

Holy Trinity He adds: *Eat, in your turn, O friends, and drink, and be inebriated, my dearly beloved,*

THE BRIDE: *I sleep and my heart watcheth. The voice of my beloved knocking!*

JESUS: *Open to me, my tester, my love, my dove, my undefiled: for my head is full of dew, and my locks of the drops of the nights.*

THE BRIDE: *I have put off my garment, how shall I put it on? I have washed my feet, how shall I defile them?*

Hereupon there follows the narrative of the second adventure of the young bride, given by herself in a most feeling manner. Thus:

My beloved put his hand through the keyhole and my bowels were moved at his touch. I arose up to open to my beloved. My hands dropped with myrrh and my fingers were full of the choicest myrrh, which the hand of Jesus had spread over the key-hole. *I opened the bolt of my door to my beloved, but he had turned aside and was gone. My soul melted when he spoke. I sought him and found him not, I called and he did not answer me. The keepers that go about the city found me: they struck me and wounded me. The keepers of the walls took away my veil from me.*

The bride concludes her narrative with this entreaty which she addresses to the blessed angels and saints of paradise: *I adjure you, O daughters of Jerusalem, if you find my beloved, that you tell him that I languish with love.*

Then they ask her with tender compassion:

What manner of one is thy beloved of the beloved, O thou most beautiful among women; what manner of one is thy beloved of the beloved, that thou hast so adjured us?

THE BRIDE: *My beloved is white and ruddy, chosen out of thousands. His head is as the finest gold, his locks as branches of palm trees, black as a raven. His eyes as doves upon brooks of water, which are washed with milk and rest beside the plentiful streams. His cheeks are as beds of aromatical spices set by the perfumers. His lips are as lilies dropping choice myrrh. His hands are turned and as of gold, full of hyacinths. His belly is of ivory, set with sapphires. His legs as pillars of marble, that are set upon bases of gold. His form as of Libanus, excellent as the cedars. His throat most sweet, and he is all lovely. Such is my beloved, and he is my friend, O ye daughters of Jerusalem.*

Whereupon all the blessed angels and saints ask again in a chorus:

Whither is thy beloved gone, O thou most beautiful among women? Whither is thy beloved turned aside, and we will seek him with thee?

CHAPTER XXVIII

ABOUT HOLY EXERCISES
(Verses 1 to 5 of ch. 3 of Canticle)

SUMMARY—Holy exercises are required in the beginning, and in the progress and to the very end of the spiritual life, Their great variety. Magdalen at the tomb of Jesus, and the soul seeking after her beloved. What happens then.

N my bed by night I sought him whom my soul loveth; I sought him and found him not.

Let us take these words first in their natural, literal meaning.

Even on her bed of rest, and during night, when people are wont to sleep, the loving soul applies herself to the search after God, to divine contemplation. It is even at such moments that she experiences the greatest spiritual delights, in the hush of creatures around her and the quietude of her own faculties. Our Lord spent whole nights in prayer after dong days of apostolic labor. *Erat pernoctans in oratione Dei.* (Luke, 6:12.) David practiced the exercise of holy compunction on his couch of rest. He says (in Ps. 6:7) *Every night I will wash my bed, I will water my couch with my tears;* and he exhorts us to do the same: The wicked *things you say in your hearts, during the day time, be sorry for upon your beds.* (Ps. 4:5.)

Then, we may consider the bride's bed to mean her condition in the present life, as long as it pleases God to keep her in it. On this bed she sweetly abandons herself to the sleep of implicit trust in God: an austere and narrow bed it is, on which nevertheless one sleeps soundly, looking forward to the awakening of the life to come, which will soon and so happily surprise us in the middle of the night, *media nocte,* as Our Lord tells us in the parable of the Virgins. On that bed one yearns to enjoy already the delights of intimate union with the Beloved: one seeks after Him, but perchance one finds Him not.

Those nights here spoken of by the bride are the three kinds of obscure nights which St. John of the Cross has so carefully described in the ASCENT OF MOUNT CARMEL: the night of the senses, the night of the spirit, and finally the Great Dark Cloud of the Divine Essence, in regard to which the eyes of the soul are as those of an owl in regard to the sun in the firmament. Through these nights the loving soul seeks after her Beloved and finds Him not: then she cries out:

I will rise and will go about the city, in the streets and the broad ways I will seek him whom my soul loveth.

Evidently the loving soul has no sympathy for the errors of the Quietists, who would fain reduce the spiritual man to have no personal initiative He should, they say, annihilate all his powers and hold himself absolutely passive in regard to good or evil, even as a dead body. The bride of the Canticle is well aware that spiritual exercises are necessary in order to enter into the interior life, that they are necessary if one is to progress in it, that they are necessary for anyone, who wishes to persevere in it unto the end and attain the goal of perfection. At no stage of the career of sanctity may the soul stand absolutely passive, or imagine that she could do so with impunity. Hence it is that such a multitude of books of spiritual exercises have been inspired by the grace of God and written by so many holy and learned personages, such as, for instance: the INSINUATIONES DIVINÆ PIETATIS of St Gertrude, the SPIRITUAL EXERCISES of Abbot Cisneros of Montserrat, the most renowned BOOK OF THE SPIRITUAL EXERCISES of St Ignatius Loyola, who has been lately proclaimed by the Holy See the very Patron of all who Practice spiritual exercises in any shape or form; the less known and yet really wonderful books on this subject, which the famous Capuchin Father Joseph, who was surnamed "L'Eminence Grise," the confessor of Richelieu, composed for the Benedictine Nuns of Calvary. Such again as the volumes of THE LITURGICAL YEAR of Dom Guéranger.

Yet the liturgical year itself of Holy Church, what is it from end to end, but a succession of varied exercises of piety in regard to each mystery of our Redemption, as they follow each other in the cycle of the year? Then the admirable variety of private devotions produced from time to time under the inspiration of the Holy Spirit, *who breatheth where He wills* (John 3:8), and when He wills, and nowadays preached and practiced all at the same time with the sanction of Holy Church: what are they but so many spiritual exercises calculated to keep alive the piety of all souls of good will?

It is the fashion with a certain class of halfhearted Christians to speak lightly of this multitude of devotions. Yet they have their reason. It is a sign of fervor for a soul to have had at a certain period of her career a large number of private devotions. This, of course, does not last. As she progresses in her spiritual life, she will shed them one by one and the tendency will be for her to simplify more and more her interior life: meanwhile these private devotions help her to keep warm and to strike, out of the dull stone of her heart, sparks of divine love. That is why the bride of the Canticle sets out in search of her Beloved, by means of holy exercises. But, spite of all her endeavors, He does not as yet show Himself to her. This wrenches from her the painful avowal:

I sought him and I found him not.

With the purpose of putting to the test the loyalty of that soul, Our Lord hides Himself from her for a while. Thereby her love for Him is bound to break out, if it be genuine. The half-hearted Christian, weak and negligent, takes occasion of such a trial in order to slacken his pious exercises and turn to what comfort he may find in creatures; on the contrary, whosoever is fervent, will give himself no repose until he has found again Him whom his soul loves above all things. Thus Mary and Joseph, as soon as they had noticed the disappearance of Jesus, on their return from Jerusalem. Thus again the inconsolable Mary Magdalen, on the morning of the Resurrection, when Jesus, under the figure of the gardener, asked her: *Woman, why weepest thou? Whom sickest thou?* She answered Him incoherently: *Sir, if thou hast taken him hence, tell me where thou hast laid him, and*

I will take him away. (John 20:15.)

But, poor Mary Magdalen, really, realty, in the intensity of thy grief, thou knowest not what thou sayest. Canst thou believe thou couldst carry all alone in thy arms, as though it were a baby, the dead body of a full grown man? But love will hear no reasoning. It goes straight ahead without so much as a glance at impossibilities. Then is Jesus satisfied. Then does He speak only one word, but oh! in what a tone of voice, so loving, so moving! At once the heart of the illustrious penitent is overwhelmed with joy; she throws herself at His blessed feet exclaiming: *Rabboni! my good Master!* and she would fain devour them with kisses.

Very much in the same way did things fall out with the bride of the Canticle. Hear what she has to relate:

The watchmen who kept the city found me: and I asked them: *Have you seen him whom my soul loveth? When I had a little passed by them, I found him whom my soul loveth: I held him and I will not let him go.*

This meeting of hers with the watchmen of the city and her asking of them: "Have you seen Hi who my soul loveth?" signifies that in her distress the fervent soul manifests to her spiritual directors the painful state of dryness and helplessness she finds herself in, so that they may wisely counsel her what to do. Very often, no sooner has the fervent soul performed that act of humility than Jesus begins again to show Himself to her.

Entrancing moment this—when Jesus after having submitted His youthful bride to her first severe trial, allows her to *hold Him* and strain Him to her heart; and begins Himself to console her tenderly wiping the tears from her eyes! Then does she give free rein to the expression of her wild, impetuous joy, holy and supernatural. Then truly, like Mary Magdalen, is she out of herself, not knowing what she says. Hear her exclaim:

I will not let him go, till I bring him into my mother's house and into the chamber of her that bore me.

Indeed it is proper that the nuptial procession, which we shall soon see marching past, should start from the house of the happy bride, that is to say from her parents' dwelling.

The loving soul speaks but of her mother, because she has no other parent, no father, here below. She has only a mother who is a virgin: I mean the most Holy Virgin Mary whose house is the Church. The Catholic Church is indeed the only Church which has constantly loved Mary; loved her tenderly, honored and glorified her: whilst the dissentient sects have vehemently protested against this worship of hyperdulia, or highest reverence, paid to the sweet Mother of God, as well as against the simple worship of dulia, that is to say of deep reverence, which we render to the saints who are all inferior to Mary: as though such a worship either of dulia or hyperdulia could in any way detract from the worship of latria, that is ter say of absolute adoration, which is due to God alone.

After so many emotions, the bride needs some rest. Jesus puts her to sleep in an ecstasy of joyful contemplation. Then we hear Him repeat to the maiden-companions of the bride the touching admonition which we have already met with a first time in chapter 2:7, of the Canticle: *I adjure you, O daughters of Jerusalem by the roes and the harts of the field, that you stir not up, nor awake my beloved till she please.*

CHAPTER XXIX

THE NUPTIAL PROCESSION
(Verses 6 to 11 of Ch. 3 of Canticle.)

SUMMARY.—What the angels admire in it: first the bride, then the nuptial couch, the cross, borne in great pomp, finally the Bridegroom with His retinue. The diadem of our King and of His little bride.

HAT follows is sung or declaimed by some angelic choir. They narrate the splendors of the nuptial procession.

Three objects more particularly rouse their admiration: first of all the bride herself decked in most gorgeous raiment, which enhances her personal charms, as she gracefully walks, surrounded by her maiden attendants; then the nuptial couch, that is to say the Cross, borne aloft in triumph and duly escorted; finally the heavenly Bridegroom, wearing on His head the kingly diadem and surrounded, no doubt, with a fitting guard of honor.

The angels then first ask one another:

Who is she that goeth up by the desert, as a pillar of smoke of aromatical spices, of myrrh and frankincense, and of all the powders of the perfumer?

Let us here notice a fact which I have already pointed out in my previous treatises: this namely, that when the blessed angels witness the generous and notable progress of a fervent Christian in the path of divine love, they talk of it among themselves with admiration and do not stint their praises of him.

Who it she?

That is to say: How very sweet and beautiful, she is! How far has her proficiency in all virtues exceeded our expectations I and how much has it graced her with fresh charms! She has become a compound of all the virtues mixed together as a light pillar of smoke of aromatical spices. *Myrrh* is the first named, because sorrow for her past sins and the tears of compunction have been the very first manifestations of her love of Jesus; *frankincense* follows, which represents the acts of the most fervent adoration: finally the acts of all the cardinal, theological, priestly and religious virtues put together, are alluded to under the expression: *all the powders of the perfumer.*

The *perfumer* (pigmentarius) is the Holy Spirit. By the exercise of the Seven Gifts He fills the soul of good will with innumerable merits as with a sweet-scented powder. Then, small wonder is it that she should exhale and spread around a sweet perfume.

But now, behold, there comes into view *the bed of Solomon;* borne in great pomp. I mean the Cross of Our Lord Jesus Christ The narrow couch, *lectulus,* of Jesus, the true Solomon, the true *King of peace,* was first of all the bosom of the immaculate Virgin, then the poor crib of Bethlehem, finally the rugged cross, and now it is first the ciborium in the tabernacle, then my own heart, a very narrow couch, this last; far too small indeed and unworthy of the Divine Majesty. But, O my Love, is it impossible then to enlarge its dimensions? Art not Thou the omnipotent God? Thy love was at ease and found its delights during nine months in the most pure tabernacle of the virgin flesh of Mary, Thy sweet Mother. It was also at ease in the crib of the poor stable. There it is that it chose to receive the visit of its first courtiers, the angels, and then the poor shepherds and a little later the three Wise men from the east. It still finds itself at ease within the narrow precincts of the tabernacle and the ciborium. Alas! is it only in the wretched abode of my heart that Thou wilt feel straitened? O my King, for Thy honor's sake, let us enlarge this narrow heart of mine; let us make it spacious and powerful in love. Cannot we achieve this, Thou on the one hand, by the effort of Thine infinite charity, and I on the other hand, by giving my full consent and hearty co-operation to Thy grace?

Now let us turn again our attention to the royal couch, which *threescore valiant ones of the most valiant of Israel surround.*

Threescore. This is a mystical expression to mean an indefinite number of worshipers. Century after century all the fervent souls, the world over, have vied with each other in their eagerness to press around the crib of Bethlehem, the Cross on Calvary, and the lowly Tabernacle in our Churches, just as, by command of the Most High, millions of blessed angels mounted guard invisibly around the sweet maiden of Nazareth, who had become the mother of God without ceasing to be a virgin; as also legions of good angels crowd around our altars during the holy sacrifice of the Mass, and around our tabernacles by day and night, and around every Christian who has just received Holy Communion; in order to pay reverence to King Jesus in his living and breathing tabernacle of flesh, on His narrow bed of state, a human heart!

Those *threescore valiant ones of the most valiant of Israel, holding swords and most expert in war,* who are they? They are the Fathers and Doctors of the Church, who with jealous care watch, over the purity of faith and morale They are also the blessed angels who are sent out to protect us.

The most valiant choirs angelical who invisibly press around our tabernacles, have given proof of their courage in the great battle which they had to fight, in the heaven of their trial, against the rebel archangel and his battalions. They now continue the same fight, only the stage where it is fought is different: it is our earth, and the things at Stake are the souls of men. Here again the blessed angels would be sure to conquer, were it not that we, whose interests tremble in the balance, are sometimes perverse enough to play the traitor. Their multitude is beyond al] imagining. One day Marie Fustelle had a vision of the adoring angels around the Blessed Sacrament. So prodigious was their multitude that she never would have thought it possible for such a number of created beings to exist anywhere; and yet it was only a fraction of one of the nine choirs of angels, that of the Virtues.

Every man's sword upon his thigh, because of fears in the night.
The blessed angels employ themselves with great solicitude

and joy in mounting guard around the fervent soul, who has made of her heart a throne to Jesus in the center of all her affections. For that wayfarer is still in the night of the present life and many enemies are lurking in the surrounding darkness.

King Solomon hath made him a litter of the wood of Libanus: the pillars thereof he made of silver, the seat of gold, the going up of purple: the midst he covered with charity for the daughters of Jerusalem.

In these mysterious accents do the angels celebrate the mystery of the Incarnation, without which that of Redemption by the cross would never have been possible, nor, consequently, that of grace and glory for the. predestinate.

King Solomon here means the Divine Word who is the splendor and wisdom of God the Father. *He made for Himself a litter* when, by the operation of the Holy Ghost, He fashioned His own sacred Humanity out of an incorruptible wood, namely, the immaculate flesh of the Blessed Virgin Mary. It is upon this litter, His sacred Humanity, that henceforth the Holy of Holies will be moved and carried from place to place, through the desert of the present life, even as of old He was carried upon the Ark of the Covenant, from camp to camp, in the desert, with the People of God.

The pillars made of silver are the sacred members and the various organ of the body of Our Lord. The *seat of gold* is the adorable breast of Our Savior; the *going up of purple* is an allusion to the various sheddings of His most precious blood. Finally *the midst which He covered with charity for the daughters of Jerusalem,* designates the tender loving affections of His Sacred Heart, which cover up and at the same time manifest the immense treasures of His divine mercy towards all men of whom He became the true brother by the Incarnation.

Go forth, ye daughters of Sion, and see King Solomon in the diadem wherewith his mother- crowned him in the day of his espousals, and in the day of the joy of his heart.

In such gorgeous, magnificent language, do the blessed angels invite all men to contemplate the joy of Our Lord when it is given Him to meet with a fervent soul. Only, if we want to enjoy such a marvelous sight, we have first to *go forth* out of the house of our self-love and of the vanities of the world. Then it shall be given us to see. Then perhaps also will it be given us to become enamored of the loveliness of King Solomon and to unite ourselves to Him in the sweetest bonds of a spiritual marriage.

In the diadem wherewith his mother crowned him.

What diadem! Oh! simply, a crown of thorns. He is King and He is a Bridegroom: on both these accounts does it behoove Him to wear a crown. Here, then, it is: a whole bush of long, cruel, sharp-pointed thorns which pierce deeply into His sacred head and inflict on Him the most excruciating pains: a twofold crown, first of mockery and shame, because He had proclaimed Himself King; then of sorrow and unutterable suffering, in order to express the greatness of his love as Bridegroom of our souls. And it is His mother, His mother, say we, not the Virgin Mary, but the Synagogue, which so treated Him.

On becoming His bride, O my soul, thou becamest at the same time also a queen: does it not behoove thee, then, also to wear a crown? What sort of a crown? Assuredly one of the same kind as that of thy Beloved. I must not wish for any other. Gold and precious stones are vile things compared with the thorns which the blood of my Savior has imbued. Come then, thou crown of thorns of heroic mortification and crown of thorns of humiliations, either voluntary or received in spite of myself: yes, come and encircle my brow, make my head bend down meekly, lovingly, and may at last my heavenly Bridegroom have the joy of finding me a bride of whom he will not have to be ashamed before His Heavenly Father.

In the day of his espousals and in the day of the joy of his heart.

That is to say on the day of His espousals with the fervent soul. It looks as though the Word of God had become man and suffered His dreadful passion, just for the sake of giving Himself to that lowly bride; just as though there were no one else for Him to love on earth; so absolutely exclusive and personal and inflamed is His love for her.

And in the Day of the joy of his heart.
Here is the first revelation of the Sacred Heart of Jesus and of His immense love for us. Let us be amazed and prostrate ourselves and adore!

CHAPTER XXX

WITHIN THE BRIDAL CHAMBER

SUMMARY.—Why the Holy Ghost reveals to us the love of God in terms of human love. Of the sanctity of Matrimony, and that it is a kind of revelation. That God gives to Himself due praise for the beauty of the human form divine. What is to be understood by the eyes, the hair, the teeth, the lips, the cheek, the neck of the bride.

HE Bridegroom and His bride have now arrived in the nuptial chamber. With John the Baptist, as friends of the Bridegroom, let us stand guard at the door and *hear with joy the voice of the Bridegroom* (John 3:29) whilst He pours out a passionate encomium of the mystic charms of His youthful bride. With utmost tenderness He exclaims:

How beautiful art thou, my love, how beautiful art thou!

Whosoever would fain persuade himself that it were a kind of profanation to speak of the divine love in terms of human love, let him read attentively this fourth chapter of the Canticle of Canticles and hundreds of similar passages both in the Prophets of the Old Testament and in all the books of the New. No better proof can be wished for that human marriage has been instituted by God, among other reasons, precisely in order to offer to men an image and a foretaste of divine love and in order to serve as a natural introduction to it. Such was indeed the mutual love of Adam and Eve innocent. Such were the chaste loves of the holy Patriarchs as also now the loves of truly Christian husbands and wives.

In the Canticle of Canticles God gives to Himself, by the mouth of the Holy Spirit, the praise which is due Him for having endowed the body of both man and woman with beauty. It is the master-piece of His hands,, a masterpiece which sin has been able to defile, but without robbing it of the native nobility it has from its Creator; a master-piece which puts on a fresh splendor, wholly supernatural, in the Sacred Humanity of Our Lord Jesus Christ and in the immaculate flesh of the Blessed Virgin Mary; and in the bodies of all the fervent Christians who adorn themselves with the incomparable jewel of virginal purity, or with that of the virtue of continence and of conjugal chastity, or with that of an austere penance for past transgressions. *And God saw all the things that he had made and they were very good.* (Gen. 1:31.)

From that exalted point of view, it is allowable to us also to cast admiring glances upon this master-piece of God's creative hands, not indeed to take in it either a feeling of vain complacency or a forbidden pleasure, but in order to praise God who with so much wisdom and love made us what we are. Praise God for the wonderful mystery of our creation, by which He made us naturally inferior to the angels, it is true, but superior to the beasts, in such wise that we find associated in our human nature the functions and excellencies of both the pure spirits and the beasts. Praise God above all for having called us to the supernatural state, to the divine life even here below, and to the glory of the future resurrection. In one word: praise God and return thanks to him for the mystery of the Incarnation and for the way in which it is extended even into each one of us.

Thy eyes are dove's eyes.

They have the meekness and simplicity of the dove.

Besides what is hid within.

Indeed meekness and simplicity are the signs of many other virtues, hidden in the secret of the heart

Thy hair is as flocks of goals, which come up from mount Galaad.

Let us not be disconcerted by these comparisons of a quite oriental richness. They contain an edifying meaning, in a true servant of God, good thoughts spring up thick and dose together as the hair upon his head; and they all spring up towards the Beloved, by skips and jumps, with the irrepressible boldness of goats on the mountain-side.

Thy teeth are as flocks of sheep, *that are shorn, which come up*

from the washing, all with twins and there is none that is barren among them.

The teeth here signify the holy desires of the soul. In the bride of Our Lord Jesus Christ, holy desires must be as strong as teeth, in order to seize hold of their proper food and grind it and assimilate it. They must be *like flocks* of sheep, *that are shorn, which come up from the washing,* that is to say they must be of a dazzling whiteness. *All with twins and there is none that is barren among them:* these desires must be efficient, not sterile; they must bring forth those twins, the love of God and the love of our neighbor.

Thy lips are as a scarlet lace.

On account of the burning sighs of love which those lips never cease to utter to the Heavenly Bridegroom, and so to weave as a garland or as. a scarlet lace.

And thy speech is sweet.

Sweet is the speech of the fervent Christian, because ever charitable, sympathetic, compassionate; ever redolent of chaste affection, sincerity, humility.

Thy cheeks are each as a piece of pomegranate, besides that which Heth hid within.

Thy maidenly modesty shows itself in the promptness with which, on the least provocation, thy cheeks become suffused with a lovely redness; and this is a token of the virgin purity of thy most secret affections.

Thy neck is as the tower of David which is built with bulwarks: a thousand bucklers hang upon it, all the armor of valiant men.

The *neck,* firm and upright, is the emblem of a delicate and right conscience which will not permit either sin or vain scruples to come near it. The *thousand bucklers* which *hang upon it* are the various considerations of the truths of faith on which a good Christian is ruminating day and night, and which afford him great security. The *valiant men* here alluded to, are the saints who have left us such beautiful examples of rightly ordered consciences.

On hearing her Beloved make of herself such a splendid

encomium, the bride begins to fear the temptation of vain glory. As an opportune remedy she now brings forward the bitter remembrance of her past sins and the consideration of the ineffable sanctity of God; and this prompts her to exclaim: *till the day breaks end the shadows retire, I will go to the mountain of myrrh, and to the hill of frankincense;* as though she said: During all the rest of my life here below I shall not cease to go to the mountain of Calvary where my love is hanging on the Cross, and to the foot of bur altars upon which He offers Himself anew to the Divine Majesty, and where He is kept day and night in the ciborium shut up in the tabernacle. It is, as a matter of fact, in these two places that the love of Our dear Heavenly Bridegroom shows itself the more: therefore there also is it, that we shall be the more able to learn its burning lessons; there must we Practice its exercises, *till the day* of the beatific vision *break* and the shadows of earthly life *retire.*

On the mountain of myrrh, that is to say on Calvary, the bride of Jesus will deplore her sins and all the sins of the world: she will strip herself of all disorderly or even purely natural affections: she will gladly crucify herself with Jesus, her *blood-stained spouse.* (Exod. 4:26.) On the hill of frankincense, that is to say at the foot of the altar, she will, in a spirit of ecstatic adoration, give free rein to her demonstrations of the most tender and the most ardent love.

On the *mountain of myrrh,* that is to say on Calvary, Jesus, the Divine Word and our Bridegroom, seems to display with an affectation of magnificence the purple robe of His Sacred Humanity, flayed alive, so to say, and bleeding from head to foot; with the gaping wound in His side and His transpierced Heart, making an irresistible appeal to the hearts of all His brethren of good will, for a return of their love.

On the hill of frankincense, that is to say on our altars, as He hides His Sacred Humanity, He seems to be wishing that we should pay greater attention to His divine nature by which He is one and the same God with His Heavenly Father and the Holy Ghost.

This then is the way for me to go in my mental prayer from Calvary to the tabernacle, and again from the foot of the altar to the mount of crucifixion: contemplating with transports of. love and gratitude the Sacred Humanity of my Savior, in order to be led up to the contemplation of His divine Essence, and to rise thence to the contemplation of the mystery of the most Holy Trinity, which is the summit of *the hill of incense,* all dazzling with wondrous light, and fragrant with the most exquisite perfume. As I could not possibly stay long in so sublime a contemplation, when I perceive that fatigue and distractions are beginning to assail me, I shall humbly return to the meditation of the sufferings and humiliations which my Savior endured in His Sacred Humanity *an the day of His espousals* with me, which was also *the day of the joy of His heart.*

There are not wanting interpreters who attribute these words: *till the day break . . . I will go to the mountain of myrrh,* etc., to the Heavenly Bridegroom. It is only fair to own that these words do indeed admirably express the whole-hearted love with which Our Lord went up to Calvary, in order to atone for our sins, and with which He renews every day in so many places His immolation on our altars. As for these words: *till the day break,* they put magnificently into relief the perpetuity of the Sacrifice of the Mass which is to be carried on even to the end of the world, to the day of resurrection and general judgement, to the last advent of the *Son of Man,* as He loves to call Himself.

CHAPTER XXXI

THE WEDDED WIFE OF THE LAMB
(Canticle 4:7, to 5:1)

SUMMARY.—Jesus gives lo the soul the coveted name of wife, and adds to it that of His sister. Lions and leopards. Thou shall be crowned. Fresh encomium of the faithful soul. North wind and south wind. The most Holy Trinity and the honeycomb.

NOW that the youthful bride has been admitted to the nuptial bed of a complete self-abnegation, to the stripping herself of all things created and to a perfect self-surrender in the arms and upon the heart of her Jesus Crucified, she looks, in the eyes of her Divine Lover and Spouse, as having at last reached the fulness of her supernatural charms. This makes Him exclaim: *Thou art all fair, O my love, and there is not a spot in thee.*

Now this is literally and absolutely true of the Christian newly-made by Holy Baptism, whether he be an infant or an adult; true also of any Christian who has just gained for himself a plenary indulgence; true also of every fervent Christian who has made, either in confession or out of it, an act of perfect contrition, or again an act of perfect charity. This last case is precisely that of the bride of the Canticle at this juncture, and Jesus therefore proclaims that she is all fair and without any blemish, and He immediately proceeds to bestow upon her the supreme title which she ardently coveted, a title in which are summed up all the endearing appellations which have hitherto been used by Him: that of Spouse or Wife. He says:

Come from Libanus, my spouse, come from Libanus, come.

This is the first time He pronounces this sweet name of *spouse,* and He Himself seems so taken up with the enchanting sweetness of it, that He is going to repeat it thrice in a short space of time, as though to taste and enjoy its sweetness, or to accustom Himself to it and engrave it deep upon His own loving

Heart. But oh! what a music it must be to the ears of the privileged soul! Listen!

> *Come, my spouse;*
> *Come from Libanus,*
> *From the top of Amana,*
> *From the top of Sanir and Hermon,*
> *From the dens of the lions,*
> *From the mountains of the leopards:*
> *Come: thou shall be crowned.*

The diverse places mentioned in this verse are emblems of the sublime states of contemplation to which this soul is raised from time to time. As for the dens of lions and the mountains of leopards, they give us to understand that the Christian, as long as he is here below, does not fear to encounter the enemies of God and of his own soul. Strong in the grace of his Baptism, which he keeps ever springing up and flowing over the face of his soul, armed from head to foot with the seven Gifts of the Holy Ghost whose fulness he received on the day of his Confirmation, fed with his daily or at least frequent ration of Eucharistic Bread, periodically renewing his vigor in the healing bath of the Sacrament of Penance, this good Christian is not afraid to venture into the midst of sinners, wherever his state or profession or some providential disposition calls upon him to do so as a matter of duty, in order to Practice the good works of a saintly active life, and, if occasion offers, even to exercise some apostolate.

> *Come; thou shall be crowned.*

The bride had previously by the words: *till the day break,* alluded to the future day of her death, which will also be, so at least she hopes, that of her entering into glory, Now Jesus assures her that He is looking forward with a sort of holy impatience to that same day of her death, when it will be possible for Him to crown her. It is as though He were saying:

"Bear in mind, O Christian soul, My spouse, that I am throned in glory in the highest heaven, and am preparing for thee a throne worthy of My love, and a bright crown set, as with so many jewels, with the merits of thy good works. Turn thine eyes often towards the heaven of glory; look forward to that crown; stir thyself to renewed efforts to make it still richer and more beautifully adorned, for My sake, in order to enhance thereby My own (accidental) glory and bliss. To this end be never tired to pass constantly, during the days of thy pilgrimage on earth, from divine contemplation to saintly action and from action to contemplation.

Jesus pronounces His tender invitation with an insistence which makes her heart leap for joy: *Come . . . come, my spouse . . . come: Thou shall be crowned.* And on their part, the blessed angels and saints, vying with each other, echo the words of their King and sing out in chorus: *Come, come,* O thou our beloved sister: *come; thou shall be crowned.*

Jesus adds:

Thou hast wounded my heart;
My sister—spouse,
Thou hast wounded my heart,
With one glance *of thy eyes,*
And with one hair of thy neck.

Again what a melody for the loving soul! How good it must be to hear Jesus singing such music in one's hearing! In the. past, O my beloved Lord, I have had the misfortune, the dreadful misfortune, which I shall lament to my dying day, the horrible misfortune of wounding Thy Sacred Heart with my sins: ah! but henceforth this will never be again. Now I see Thy dear loving Heart stirred with glad emotion at the sight of my firm resolve and puny efforts to give Thee pleasure. Oh what an encouragement! What a consolation!

With one glance of thy eyes,

And with one hair of thy neck.

That is to say with thy smallest prayers and the most lowly of thy actions, when these are made, as is the case with every true mystic, in utmost purity of intention and fervor of love.

Thy lips, my spouse, are as a dropping honeycomb; honey and milk are under thy tongue.

Under, these poetical figures, Our Lord wants to give us to understand the delights He finds in our dealings with Him, above all, in our Holy Communions.

The smell of thy garments is as the smell of frankincense.

So it is indeed, figuratively speaking, whenever the loving soul consumes herself in acts of adoration of the Divine Majesty: and this she is attentive to do continually, day and night.

My sister, my spouse!

As though the name of sister by itself, or only that of spouse, were not enough to express the extent of His tender affection, Our Lord unites them together so as to throw us into transports of joy. In His Incarnation, the Son of God, the Word Eternal, made Himself really and truly my brother by flesh and blood and the affections of a human heart, and now behold, by the grace of His sacraments, He unites me to Himself in the mystical bonds of a divine marriage. The Christian soul is at the same time both the sister and the spouse of her Lord.

My sister-spouse is a garden enclosed, a fountain sealed up.

A garden indeed, since within a fervent soul spring up, bloom and pullulate the flowers of holy desires and the trees of virtues whose fruits are her many acts meritorious unto eternal life. No one save the Beloved is admitted within the precincts of this garden.

And o *fountain sealed up.* That is to say, so guarded, so protected that neither the beasts of the field nor the passers-by are permitted to contaminate it or ruffle its surface by drinking of it. No evil passion and no creature merely as such, has any part in the pure affections of this Christian's heart: they are all jealously guarded for Jesus alone.

O soul who hast been endowed with manifold and wonderful graces, and who art ambitious of advancing rapidly on the austere path of sanctity, mayest thou never more give leave to thine own heart to love anyone but in the Lord Jesus Christ! Then wilt thou be to Him a fountain sealed up, a fountain of living waters, fresh and sweet, springing up towards heaven, and Jesus will slake His thirst therein with intense delight.

Thy plants are a paradise of pomegranates, with the fruits of the orchards. Cyprus with spikenard and saffron, sweet cane and cinnamon, with all the trees of Libanus, myrrh and aloes with all the chief perfumes. The fountain of gardens is in thee, the well of living waters, which run with a strong stream from Libanus.

Under the poetical figures of the two first sentences, the Heavenly Bridegroom gives, with a marked complacency, the detail of all that He finds beautiful and winning in that holy soul, and He adds: "Now I will proclaim the two-fold cause of her marvelous fertility: first, there, is in her the *fountain of gardens,* which is none other than My Holy Spirit with His Gifts, Fruits and Beatitudes, and secondly, she holds within herself *the well of living waters which run with a strong stream from Libanus.* Those living waters are the delightful and refreshing mysteries of the two natures in Christ, which the contemplative soul is never tired of drinking in. *Libanus* stands here for the lofty personality of the Word of God.

Now the Divine Goodness closes this episode of a supernatural idyll with this characteristic adjuration:

A rise, O north wind, and come, O south wind: blow through my garden, and let the aromatical spices thereof flow.

In other words: Let periods of dryness or desolation in that soul of good will, who is to me a garden of delights, alternate with periods of spiritual peace and joy; these contrary winds in shaking the branches of the trees and blowing over shrubs and flower-beds, load themselves with their fragrance and spread far and wide their perfumes. Whenever a soul is really dead to self and does not live any longer but for the Heavenly Bridegroom, it is indifferent to her whether she encounter joy or pain, as long as she is doing His holy will. This serves to show the exquisite quality of her every virtue: their perfume spreads far and wide, giving great comfort and edification throughout the Church of God.

At this point of her spiritual life, the enamored soul is consumed with her insatiable desire of Holy Communion. See what a graceful turn she gives to the expression of her holy desires: *Let my beloved come into his garden, and eat the fruits of His apple-trees.* If this is not poetry, I wonder where we shall ever find it. All true lovers are poets when they speak of their love to him who is the object of it.

And after this fervent Christian has received Holy Communion, Jesus tells him in the secret of his heart: *I am come into my garden. O my sister and spouse, I have gathered my myrrh with my aromatical spices; I have eaten the honeycomb with my honey; I have drunk my wine with my milk..*

We shall do well to note the particular insistence with which our Lord in this verse employs the possessive pronoun, in order to express the sense of delight with which He dwells within a soul so admirably fenced in and cultivated: He says *my* myrrh, *my* aromatical spices, *my* honey, *my* milk. Well said, dear Lord! for indeed everything within that soul is Thine own.

And now suddenly the divine Word-made-man turns towards the other two Persons of the Most Holy Trinity and invites Them to take Their share of the delights He finds in that little soul. He says to the Heavenly Father and the Holy Spirit: *Eat, O friends, and drink, and be inebriated, my dearly beloved.* Mysterious words well worth our closest attention.

Assuredly, if we isolate such a sentence from its context, it may lend itself to a great variety of accommodative or conventional meanings. When, however, instead of so isolating it, we are careful to view it, in its proper place, in the sequel of the Canticle, we are compelled to see in it a speech of Our Lord directed, not to the blessed angels nor to the saints or the earthly companions of His spouse, but to the other two Divine Persons: so that we have therein, under a transparent veil, a certain revelation of the Most Holy Trinity.

He that is speaking is Our Lord, the Divine Word; and His invitation, as it is couched, can be extended but to the Heavenly Father and the Holy Spirit, because only Divine Persons could enter within a human soul, to take their delights in her virtues. An angel, pure spirit as he is, is incapable of such a privilege being conferred upon him, either naturally, or supernaturally, or miraculously. To enter within a spirit is possible only to God; every individual angel and also every human soul is open to God alone and shut to all creatures. These can. come into touch with another spirit but externally, and derive some enjoyment of it only from the outside.

On the other hand, there is in St. John's Gospel the Scriptural reference for this—Our Lord: *If any one love me, my Father will love him, and we will come to him, and will make our abode with him.* (John 14:23.) Who are meant by this *we,* if not the same three Divine Persons who, on the sixth day of Creation, held counsel together and said: *Let us make man to our image and likeness?* (Gen. 1:26.)

This act of entering in within spiritual substances, which is proper to God alone, is a very mysterious operation which ought to fill us with inexpressible joy, when it is brought about, as in the case of the bride of the Canticles, by means of the Divine presence of love, that is to say by a special effect of Divine Love. It is in this sense again that Our Lord says in the Apocalypse (3:20), *Behold I stand at the gate and knock: if any man shall hear my voice and open to me the door, I will come in to him, and will sup with him and he with me.* At the same time as the three Divine Persons of the adorable Trinity take together Their delight in that soul of good will, they also impart to her a certain obscure feeling and consciousness that such a divine fact is taking place within her.

Here then is an intimate dealing with God, not of course, such as we would have ever dared to ask for, but such as alone can give satisfaction to the inmost cravings of our heart. I am God's little friend; the friend of each one of the Persons of the Most Holy Trinity. Each one of these Divine Persons is my intimate friend, my loving guest, all to myself, in the sanctuary of my soul. My God is wholly mine and I, puny thing, am wholly His. O ye human loves, O ye friendships with creatures, where are you when compared with such a love?

Therefore under the graceful and familiar invitation of the Heavenly Bridegroom to His Divine Father and His Holy Spirit, there is concealed an allusion to a mystical experience of the soul which defies description. This fervent soul is become "God's honey" and God in His turn is become "her honey" as St. Augustine assures us. The Most Holy Trinity is the honeycomb infinitely sweet which this soul is permitted to take hold of, blindly and joyfully, and to feed upon.

As to the assertion of Our Lord that He has eaten *the honeycomb with His honey*, it means that the loving God takes His delights, not only in the soul of the mystic, but also in the frail body of flesh in which she is lodged as the honey in the comb, a body purified, sanctified, deified, together with the soul, by means of the sacraments.

Wonderful mystery of the Divine Love! Let us adore it in silence.

CHAPTER XXXII

THE GREAT TRIALS OF WEDDED LIFE
WITH JESUS
(Canticle, 5:2 - 8)

SUMMARY.—A word about angelical contemplation. Jesus knocks at the door: the wedded soul delaying to open to Him, He turns aside and goes away. Adventures of the soul in quest of her Beloved. How the daughters of Jerusalem soothe her pain and inferior creatures help her in her search after God.

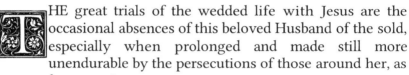

HE great trials of the wedded life with Jesus are the occasional absences of this beloved Husband of the sold, especially when prolonged and made still more unendurable by the persecutions of those around her, as we are about to witness.

Left by herself in a rustic dwelling, in the midst of her garden which she was trying to tend and render very beautiful for His sake, the spouse of the Canticle has been thinking the whole day long about her Beloved. When she retired at night and went to sleep, her mind and imagination were full of His picture and her heart overflowing with tender and burning affections for Him, to such a degree that she dreamt of Him and kept talking to Him in her sleep.

With absolute truth she could say: *I sleep, but my heart watcheth.* So true was this that even in her sleep she perceived the sound of His voice. Then she exclaimed: *The voice of my beloved: He is knocking at my door!* and instantly she found herself wide awake.

One degree further and we should have been face to face with that marvelous phenomenon, rare even among the saints, known to mystical theologians under the name of "angelical contemplation," a contemplation which is not interrupted even by sleep. Yes, it has happened to some servants of God, whilst yet on earth, to perform certain sublime operations of the soul without any participation of any bodily organ, even as though they were already in the region of the spirits. Sleep, which was wont to suspend for them the organic functions of the life of relation with the exterior world, had no effect on their soul, so that they could keep up even then their contemplation, their converse with the Beloved, all their secret intercourse of love with God; they could also receive, either straight from Him, or through the intervention of the angels, His divine communications.

We know this to have been the case with St. Joseph, at the three different times when the Gospel relates that he was made aware of the secrets of God and received His directions. (Matt, 1:20-24; 2:13-15; 2:19-21.) There is nothing to prevent us from holding that it was so with St. Joseph habitually, as also with his most holy spouse, the Blessed Virgin Mary, as it was also most undoubtedly the case with Our Lord during all His earthly life.

Our bride of the Canticle, now promoted to the dignity of *wife of the Lamb—to* use the vocabulary of the Apocalypse—is just one degree below this sublime mode of contemplation, called angelic. She is no sooner awakened than she hears Her Divine Lover pleading from outside for admittance. He says:

Open to me, my sister, my love, my dove, my undefiled: for my head is full of dew, and my locks of the drops of the nights.

Upon which words St. Francis de Sales comments in this wise: "It cannot be expressed, O my Theotimus, how ardently Our Savior desires to enter into the dwelling of our soul by means of this kind of love," which he calls one of sorrowful complacency. "Now what is this dew and what are those drops of the nights but the sorrows and torments of His Passion?" *(Treatise on the Love of God.* Book V, ch. v.)

We ask again: What is this dew and what are. those drops of the night, but the repulses which this Divine Lover of souls meets with, when He knocks at the door of the hearts in which He desires to take shelter? Kept in the cold by those wretches, He turns to the faithful soul for comfort.

Happy soul! Only she must not, under any excuse whatever, put Him off, keep Him waiting outside, hesitate to admit Him instantly within. She must receive Him at His own chosen moment, without any regard to her own convenience. It seems the little bride of the Canticle had yet to learn this lesson by her own experience. Let us hear the candid account of how things went in her behalf.

From the bed of her repose she answered to her Beloved: *I have put of my garment, how shall I put it on? I have washed my feet, how shall I defile them?*—that is to say: "Until now, dear Lord Jesus, I have made use of a certain ceremonial with Thee: I have accustomed, myself to certain devout practices to which I cling; allow me first to perform these; then will I turn wholly to Thee in the most absolute surrender."

But Jesus would not be put off. In spite of her silly objections, He makes an effort to gain, admittance without a moment's delay. She relates the incident with great feeling, thus:

My beloved fut his hand through the hole in the door, by which one may work the wooden latch inside; and at the noise He made, *my bowels were moved.*

Oh what saintly emotions are experienced at the near approach of the Heavenly Bridegroom! They thrill not only the spirit but the flesh as well. This it is which prompted David to exclaim: *My heart and my flesh have rejoiced in the living God.* (Ps. 83:3.) The joy of the superior part of the soul overflows and communicates itself to the inferior faculties and spreads even into the senses. It is only fair that it should be so. The fervent Christian holds himself united to Jesus by every fibre of his whole being, as on His own part Our Lord lays hands upon every component part of this human being, in order to purify it all and transform it into the *new man* which He Himself is.

Let us now see what happened. The bride continues her narrative.

I arose to open to my beloved: my hands dropped with myrrh, and my fingers were full of the choicest myrrh; I opened the bolt of my door to my beloved, but he had turned aside and was gone. My soul melted when He spoke. I sought Him and found Him not; I called and He did not answer me.

As Jesus had passed His hand through the hole in the rustic door, He had smeared the wooden bolt and latch with the myrrh, the choicest myrrh of His sacred blood trickling from His wounds: that is to say, in order to prepare His little spouse for the ordeal of His sudden departure, He had left the sweet perfume of His recent passage there. No wonder then that as the bride took hold of the bolt and latch, she found her fingers all dripping with the myrrh left there by the touch of the hands of Jesus— that is to say she found herself quite penetrated with the remembrance of His sorrowful Passion.

Many are the souls who fail into the same mistake as the spouse of the Canticle, losing their time in secondary considerations, at the very moment when their Beloved is knocking at the door of their heart for immediate admittance. Instead of instantly jumping out of the bed of their self-complacency in many special devotions, and rushing unadorned, unceremoniously, without any formal preparation, in the state of the mystical nudity of pure love, they allow themselves to get caught into the webs of a formal, complicated and narrow piety and thus keep at bay, on the other side of the door, Him who so graciously comes to visit them.

He does His best to gain admittance. He tries with His own hand to work the secret spring of the human will which is as the latch of the door. He spreads the sweet odor of His near presence, but He fails to effect an entrance, because the spouse who should have co-operated with Him was busy with her private devotions and raising chimerical difficulties. Then what happens is this: when at last she comes to the door and throws it open, the moment of special grace is passed: the Beloved is no more there and her disappointment is unspeakable.

O thou, therefore, who art espoused to the. King of Heaven, whosoever thou mayest be, let me give thee this advice; whenever the inspiration of divine grace visits thee, put aside thy accustomed exercises of devotion, books, rosaries, pictures, vocal prayers, pious practices of any description. Set them aside. Allow thyself to be caught up and impetuously carried away by the Holy Ghost wherever He lists; He will throw thee in the arms and upon the loving heart of thy Heavenly Bridegroom. All the rest does not matter at such a moment. All the rest are only means, whilst the Lord Himself is the end. When He is pleased to suppress all intermediaries and to present His dear Self to thee in an immediate manner, He will brook no delay; do not thou therefore oppose to Him the walls and doors and wooden bolts of thy accustomed exercises of piety.

It remains now for us to listen to the delightfully dramatic account of the youthful wedded wife, in her search after the Beloved; and as we do so, we may note also how the interest of this marvelous idyll, so perfectly natural in its very supernatural ness, grips our hearts and waxes more and more poignant.

The keepers that go around the city found me; they struck me and wounded me; the keepers of the wall took away my veil from me.

We have already seen these guards in the second chapter, verse 5, of Canticle: but then the bride had no complaint to proffer against them, whilst now they handle her rather roughly, they strike her and wound her and take away her veil. The meaning of all this is that the loving sou], now aware of how wrong it was for her not to have opened at once to Jesus, went and accused herself of this fault to her Superiors or to her Spiritual Director. This time, far from consoling her in her distress, they have spoken severely to her; they have torn or violently wrenched from her the veil of self-love, in which, unconsciously perhaps, she had been wrapping herself up. However, so great, so ardent and sincere is her love of Jesus, that she loses not a single moment in self-pity or futile complaint. She turns to the blessed angels and saints of paradise and addresses them in these touching words:

I adjure you, O daughters of Jerusalem, if you find my beloved, that you tell him that I languish with love.

Is not this charming? as also charming is the method which

our heavenly friends take, in order to soften the grief of their little sister still on the earth of her pilgrimage: they make her speak of her Divine Lover; they ask:

What manner of one it thy beloved of the beloved, O thou most beautiful among women? What manner of one is thy beloved of the beloved, that thou hast so adjured us?

And after she has described to them her beloved, as we shall see in our next chapter, the choir of heavenly friends give her this reply full of feeling:

Whither is thy beloved gone, O thou most beautiful among women? Whither is thy beloved turned aside, and we will seek him with thee?

Can sympathy manifest itself in more sincere, artless accents F Such are the feelings which the blessed sons of light, who dwell in the Heavenly Jerusalem, entertain towards us, their brethren, who in obscure faith and in the midst of manifold obstacles grope our way in search of God.

To the choirs of the blessed angels and the dear saints, the chorus of inferior creatures join themselves, if only we will hearken to them. They too seem to address us this query, *O thou most beautiful one, whither is thy beloved turned aside and we will seek him with thee?*

These inferior creatures cannot, by themselves and for their own account, set out in search of God, and attain Him, but only through us and with us. Does not the star of the three Kings seem to say: "Let us go together and seek Him: nay, it is I who will point Him out to you?" So do all inferior creatures, whether animate or inanimate. Each of them has its own way of leading us up to God, provided we listen to them and receive their testimony. They are all saying: "We wilt seek thy Beloved, with thee and for thee, faithfully and disinterestedly; for we, who are inferior creatures, can lay no claim to His divine love: this is thine own exclusive privilege, O thou human nature, who art most beautiful among us all: *pulcherrima mulierum.*"

It cannot be doubted that if the beasts, the plants, the stars and all other creatures could only speak, they would express their admiration of an intelligent and free being, who is self-determining, whose glance of the eyes is so imperial, whose voice can be in turn so soft or so terrible, whose hands possess such cunning, whose brow is so majestic, whose heart is so deep, whose mind is so acute, who, to sum it all up in one word, is so divinely beautiful. See how the dog, for example, bestirs. himself around his master, and at a sign or a word from him, eagerly springs forward to do his behest. The horse, the ox, the camel, the elephant hold their strength and their marvelous instinct at his service. Although they do not understand what they are bidden to do or why, they seem to say: "Thou O man, and our master, thou knowest; that is enough for us; art thou not constituted King over all nature?"

Even the mighty waters, even light, even lightning, allow themselves to be tamed by the hand of man, yoked to his triumphal car. And whenever, instead of bidding them to draw him nearer to God, he forces them to serve sin, by ministering to his evil passions, these creatures groan and protest in their own way. *For we know,* says St. Paul, *that every creature groaneth and travaileth in pain even till now.* (Rom. 8:22.) *For the expectation of the creature waiteth for the revelation of the sons of God. For the creature was made subject to vanity, not willingly, hut by reason of him that made it subject in hope: because the creature also itself shall be delivered from the servitude of corruption, into the liberty of the glory of the children of God.* (Rom. 8:19-21.) So the inferior creatures are groaning and, so to say, blindly reaching out for the grand revelation of the children of God, when absolutely every part and parcel of Nature, having been purified, will henceforward be used only unto the glory of its Creator.

In the meanwhile they unite their voices to those of the blessed angels and saints of paradise, saying to the soul of good will: *We will seek* thy Beloved *with thee.*

CHAPTER XXXIII

THE LITTLE SPOUSE MAKES A DESCRIPTION OF HER BELOVED
(Canticle. 5:10-17.)

SUMMARY.—How the Bridegroom is white and ruddy. His head. His locks, His eyes. His cheeks, His lips, His hands, His breast, His throat. He is all lovely and he is my friend.

ET us now retrace our steps and see what kind of an answer the spouse of the Canticle made to her heavenly friends when they pressed her to describe to them her Beloved.

I have already interpreted this lovely page of the Canticle in my little treatise on THE MYSTERY OF JESUS (Part I, ch. x, towards the end). I might be content to refer my reader to this; however as he may not have the volume at hand, and as, on the other hand, the present treatise would not be complete without this passage, I beg to reproduce here my paraphrase of it, not, however, without adding to it a great deal.

My beloved is white and ruddy.

Jesus is ruddy by the splendor of His Divine nature; He is *white* by the immaculate flesh which He took in the most chaste womb of His Virgin Mother. *White* again by the ineffable innocency of His human life. He could ask the Jews: *Which of you shall convince me of sin?* (John 8:46) without any of them being able to give him a reply; and He is *ruddy* by all the blood which He shed for our redemption. *White* again in His Blessed Sacrament under the species of bread, *ruddy* under those of wine.

Chosen out of thousands.

Not only out of thousands or ten thousands, but out of the millions of millions of blessed angels and holy men: chosen out of them all, preferred above them all. And why? Ah! because in this *Betrothal of the beloved* we discern two natures, the divine and the human united together, and so marvelously knit into one Person that they make our Jesus to stand as the most absolutely and supremely lovable object in the world.

His head is as the finest gold.

The head of our Lord is His divine nature. *Caput Christi Deus; the head of Christ is God,* says St. Paul. (1 Cor. 11:3.) It is as though the spouse exclaimed: "The first thing to be noted about Him is that He is God. In the words of the Nicene Creed: "*I believe in God . . . and in Jesus Christ His only Son, begotten of the Father before all times: God of God; light of light, true God of true God.*" Can anyone describe to us the splendor of His beauty more dazzling than the finest gold, the intense brightness of sanctity with which His Father begets Him eternally? O ye creatures, can you believe that He is my lover, my Bridegroom, my Husband, and that He vouchsafes to stoop to my lowliness, to kiss me and embrace me and unite me to Him?

In commenting on the Canticle of Canticles, one ought never, for a single moment, lose sight of the great fact that our Beloved is the Divine Word, the second Person of the Most Holy Trinity, the Son of God. True, He is the *W ord-made-flesh, "the Son of Man"* as He loves to call Himself, the Man-God: but the one feature of His theandric complex being, which ought at first to arrest our attention, is His Godhead.

As for the physical head of His Human body, can anything be found in the whole range of the created universe, more noble, comely and attractive? Every feature of His dear countenance is breathing out meekness and the most burning charity.

His locks are as graceful *as branches of palm trees, black as a raven.*

Here allusion is made to the divine perfections which are found in Our Lord, coequal to those of His Divine Father; and which also are black, that is to say obscure and impenetrable to the eyes of human understanding, especially whilst man is here below. Still, although we cannot pretend to understand the infinite perfections of Our Lord, we are permitted to celebrate them and to declare that they are absolutely incomparable. The spouse makes use for this purpose of a charming image, that of the green palms as they shoot forth from their parent-tree and fall around it with magnificently graceful curves. On the other hand each one of the locks and of the hair of the adorable head of Jesus, imbued with the blood of His sacred Passion, is to us a token of salvation and as a palm of victory, similar to that of the martyrs and confessors who are already in the glory of paradise.

His eyes are as doves upon brooks of water, which are white as though they were *washed in milk, and sit beside the plentiful streams.*

The eyes are the mirror of the soul: therefore, oh! what modesty, what purity, what simplicity, what candour, what meekness and tenderness, what compassion, must the eyes of our Divine Master have reflected, during His earthly life! And now that He is seated in glory, must it not be so still?

During the whole space of His sacred life and still more so during His Sacred Passion, the eyes of Our Lord shed many tears over the great evil of sin and over the misfortune of those who commit it—tears full of bitterness for Him who was shedding them, whilst they are full of sweetness for us who by their merits have obtained the grace of our conversion.

His cheeks are as beds of aromatical spices set by the perfumers.

Rows of aromatical flowers in a garden are set in straight lines parallel to each other. The spouse here asseverates that the blood which trickled from the brow of Jesus under the cruel prick of each thorn of His crown of derision, gave to his cheeks the checkered appearance of a bed of flowers, and that each tiny drop of this blood is infinitely more precious than the most sweet-scented aromatic, since it has virtue enough to heal a thousand worlds.

Hit lips are as lilies dropping choice myrrh.

The very choicest myrrh is assuredly the reparation for the sins of the world, offered to God by Him who is without sin. Our own sorrow for sin, as we are the offenders, and still so wretched, our own expiations and reparations offered to the Divine Majesty are but myrrh of a very inferior quality. In order for it to exhale a sweet perfume and be acceptable to God, it must be mixed with that of superior quality: that is to say with the infinite merits and satisfactions which Jesus offers up to His Divine Father.

From the lips of our Savior crucified have dropped the seven supreme words of His, which, as so many drops of choicest myrrh, have found their way to the very depths of all Christian hearts. No sooner was this meek Lamb of God raised aloft on the atrocious instrument of torture, the cross, than He proffered His first supplication to the Father in behalf of His tormentors. *Father,* He exclaimed, *forgive them, for they know not what they do.* (Luke 23:34.)

His hands beautifully molded, are as of gold, full of hyacinths.

There is no doubt but that the hands of Our Lord, viewed from a purely artistic standpoint, were the most beautiful that ever were: after them, those of His sweet Virgin-Mother Mary: hands which had been molded, so to say, with infinite care and complacency by God Himself, on account of the sublime tasks they were to perform and the works of mercy they were to sow broadcast in the world.

The spouse says that the hands of Jesus are of gold, because of the refulgence they shed in blessing and caressing little children, giving sight to the blind, touching and healing lepers, taking dead people by the hand and raising them to life again, multiplying the five barley-loaves and small fishes to the point of feeding more than five thousand people, blessing the bread and wine and transforming them into His very body and blood.

But oh! never did these adorable hands perform a greater wonder than when they meekly surrendered themselves to be nailed to the wood and slowly torn by the weight of the sacred body of the Lord. Then it was that they became filled as with so many precious hyacinths, by the clots of blood which stopped in their wounds and clustered around the ghastly nails. My God, how we should love and venerate these dear hands of our Savior dying on the cross!

His belly is as of ivory, set with sapphires.

The immaculate whiteness of the flesh of Our Savior was gleaming on the cross and was enhanced by the purple marks of the cruel flagellation which had not spared a single spot in His body. *From the sole of the foot unto the top of the head,* said Isaiah (1:6) *there is no soundness therein: wounds and bruises and swelling sores: they are not bound up nor dressed, nor fomented with oil.* Those bruises were as so many sapphires set in the ivory whiteness of His flesh.

Besides its dazzling whiteness, the characteristic properties of ivory are its hardness and incorruptibility. It had been predicted of this sacred body of Our Lord, centuries before He came into the world, that *not a bone of Him would be broken.* (Exodus 12:46; John 19:36) —and *that He should not be given to see corruption.* (Ps. 15:10). Is there anything less incorruptible than the soft parts of the human flesh, contained within the cavities of the breast and of the stomach.? Yet, although our Jesus will be made to taste, in every part of His sacred body, inside and out, the bitterness of all sorts of torments and of death itself, neither will His bones be broken, nor will any part of His sacred flesh see corruption.

His legs as pillars bf marble that are set upon bases of gold.

Noble pillars which support the most beautiful temple that has ever been built for the honor of the Divine Majesty, namely the sacred body of Christ. The sanctuary, of this temple is the sacred breast of Our Lord, and its *Holy of Holies,* His most Sacred Heart, wherein we can easily gain access, since the lance of the soldier has pierced it through and through. There must we often repair, if we wish to thaw the ice of our own miserable hearts and he set all aglow with love. *I am come to cast fire on the earth, says Our Lord, and what will I but that it be kindled?* (Luke 12:49.)

Pillars of marble *that are set upon bases of gold.*

Gold is even more precious than marble. In telling us that the feet of the Beloved are of gold, the spouse intends to direct our attention to the horrible pains they endured on the cross when the whole weight of the body of the Savior was pressing upon the ghastly wounds which the nails had made in piercing them through and through.

O my poor Jesus, my dear Lord, how terrible are Thy sufferings! and all for me. I crave Thy forgiveness. It is I indeed who caused these particular sufferings of Thine, by the guilty alacrity with which my own feet have carried me to seek after mine own will, or after created things, nay after sin.

The statue of the dream of Nabuchodonosor (Dan. 2:31-33) had a head of gold, but its feet were part of iron and part of clay: Our Beloved has not only the head but also His hands and His feet of finest gold, because, according to the forcible expression of St. Paul: *In him dwelleth all the fulness of the Godhead corporally.* (Coloss, 2:9.)

No indeed, the feet of my Savior are not of clay. And not His statue, but His living Self, stands erect in the midst of the human race, which He transcends wholly with His surpassing greatness, setting, century after century, all the combined forces of sin and hell at defiance, until the time when His heavenly Father will make *His enemies His footstool.* (Ps. 109:1) We shall witness this great triumph of His on the Day of the Last Judgement

His form as of Libanus, excellent as the cedars.

Indeed what more noble, majestic aspect could be imagined than that of the Lord during the succeeding periods of His earthly life, especially during His Sacred Passion, and now on His throne in the glory of heaven?

Was there ever a more elegant and shapely torso than that of the New Adam, stripped, and drawn out or bent double for the scourging? Or again—and then it was draped—bent double under the weight of the cross and its beam? And the most beautiful arms, are not they those of my Jesus, extended on the cross? They will not fold again: they are nailed, so that poor sinners, to the end of the world, may ever throw themselves upon His loving, merciful, gentle Heart.

I am lost in admiration before the transcendent, majestic figure of Moses (Exod. 17:10-12) interceding for his people,., praying with arms extended, supported on the right hand and on the left by two faithful servants; but my admiration knows no limits when I contemplate Him of whom Moses was only a prophetic figure, and I adore Him, feelingly, enthusiastically. In order that His extended arms should not relax, He willed that they be nailed to the cross. Nailed! dost thou hear, O my soul! nailed I say; nailed! Great heavens! what an atrocious torment!

True, my Lord is not any longer hanging on the cross, He will suffer now no more; He is now seated in the ineffable repose of His glory: on which account I return endless thinks to His Eternal Father: but then He never ceases to apply to us the merits of His sufferings and death on the Cross. Even now it is still as though He were actually suffering and dying; I can, therefore, do no better than transport myself in spirit with the Spouse of the Canticle, to the time when, being nailed upright and arms extended on the Cross, my Jesus was offering His sweet Self and suffering unspeakable agonies for me.

How comely Thou art, O my dear Lord Jesus crucified! How worthy of all love! Ah! let me break my heart as a poor vessel of sweetly perfumed ointment and pour out its contents upon Thy sacred feet!

His throat most sweet.

His throat, considered as the organ of His speech. How sweet to hear Him utter all these words of mercy and compassion that are related in the four Gospels: among them all, those which are His last will and testament to Mary and to each one of us: *Behold thy Son—Behold thy mother!* (John 19:26, 27). Oh! thanks, my dearest Lord, everlasting thanks be to Thee!

And He is all lovely.

The spouse sums up in one word all the transcending excellences of her Beloved. In the person of my Lord, even during His earthly life, there were already found in absolute perfection the human natural order, the angelical natural order, the supernatural order both of grace and of the beatific vision, the divine order. In very deed He is *all lovely.*

In his book entitled JESUS INTIME, Mgr. Sauvé warns us

against losing sight, to the great detriment of our faith and love, of most of the splendid treasures of divine glory, and bliss, and science, and grace that are hidden in Our Lord. This is a timely admonition. We are but too prone to make to ourselves a representation of Him so narrow and paltry that it will be incapable of nourishing our souls. Not so the little spouse of the Canticle. She embraces her Beloved in the totality of His being and of His perfections and she proclaims Him all lovely and delectable. Is not the Heavenly Father *well pleased in Him?* (Matt, 17:5.) Is He not all lovely in the eyes of His sweet Mother Mary the Virgin? All lovely also in the eyes of the nine choirs of the blessed angels and of alt the saints and just in heaven, in purgatory and here on earth? How, then, were it possible that I, the least and last of all, should not also find Him all lovely and sweet and delectable?

Such is my beloved, and he is my friend, O ye daughters of Jerusalem.

In these concluding words of the spouse there is a very human, and very feminine, note of legitimate pride in the possession of such a friend. It is well for the Christian to testify to his appreciation of the immense honor done Him by Our Lord, when He comes so lovingly and familiarly to Him as He does in Holy Communion, and in the intimate intercourse of mental prayer.

Arrived at the summit of the second stage of the spiritual life, or the Illuminative Way, the spouse has not a shadow of human respect left in her. She boldly proclaims to all who will listen, whether angel or demon or man, that she is desperately enamored of the Son of God, and that she will know no other joy during the remainder of her pilgrimage here below, than that of His divine embraces. Her mystical initiation is now perfect.

End
of the Sixth Treatise.

BOOK VII

THE BURNING BUSH

The Heavenly and Earthly Trinities
—Esteban Murillo

PREFACE

SUMMARY.—Why the contemplation of the Most Holy Trinity is here called ecstatical. That ecstasy may be either active or passive. The purpose of the present treatise. Its division.

IN order not to begin this new treatise—the seventh in the series of my books on mysticism—with a misunderstanding, we must first of all state in what sense the contemplation of the Most Holy Trinity is here called ecstatical.

There are two sorts of ecstasies, an active one and a purely passive one. Passive ecstasy is that which is caused by the intensity of the supernatural impressions which a fervent soul receives at times: it is' only of this sort of ecstasy that most spiritual writers speak. Yet there is also another kind which might well be called the *active one;* it is that which consists in a spontaneous movement of the soul, in its endeavor to quit self and all created things, in order to apply herself to God alone. It is in this latter sense that we speak here of ecstatical contemplation.

The contemplation of the Most Holy Trinity must perforce be ecstatical first of all in that manner; only later may the fervent soul hope to experience the purely passive ecstasy if God be pleased to grant it. However, we do not at present take this eventuality into consideration.

The purpose of this new treatise is not to restate, after so many others, the metaphysical proof of God, or scientifically to expound His infinite perfections. My ordinary readers have no need of such a demonstration. More modest—some perhaps would say, more exalted—is my ambition, I simply aim at leading them up to the contemplation of God in whom they already believe with their whole heart; so that they may find their joy in Him, that they may learn how to play with Him *as most dear children* (Eph. 5:1) the beautiful game of reciprocal love, that they may break out into praise of His Divine Goodness and Majesty.

It were therefore a mistake to seek in the following pages anything else but what I have intended to present to my readers —namely, a practical introduction to the art of dealing lovingly with God in the secret of one's own heart. I am following up the general plan outlined in chapters v and vi of my second volume *(The Mystical Life).* We are still, as in volumes iv, v, and vi, busy about the first function of the mystical life, which is Divine contemplation; we are now to treat of its supreme object—namely, the Most Holy Trinity.

Already in a previous volume we have had occasion to speak at some length of the respective activities, so to say, of each of the three Divine Persons in regard to the mystic *(cf. The Mystical Life,* chs. viii, ix, x, xv, xvi). In the present work we place ourselves at a different point of view —namely, that of the contemplative activity of the fervent Christian himself in regard to the great mystery.

Throughout all this treatise the reader will do well to remember what has been said in chapter xx of *The Mystical Life,* as to each man being supremely alone with God alone. In the light of this principle many of the following pages, which might otherwise remain unintelligible, will be, we trust, quite clear.

With his whole heart and soul, with his whole being, ought the contemplative to approach the Mystery of the Divine Essence, and he must be ready to pay the price of so noble an objective: to strain his every power of soul and body in a mighty, long-sustained, and yet at the same time very pleasing effort, bearing successively upon diverse points of the vast field of knowledge.

This is, perhaps, the most halting and uncouth of al) the books I have thus far written, though it is the one which made the greatest demand upon my energies and the one which I wrote with greatest enthusiasm and care and fervor of love.

No wonder it should seem incoherent and its chapters a succession of abortive attempts —no wonder, indeed, when we take into consideration the sublimity of the subject and the vileness of the writer. All I can say in excuse of my rashness in attempting such a high theme is that I had to do it under penalty of leaving my series of treatises incomplete. May the good and loving God forgive me and help my readers! It is in His power to make even such a wretched instrument as this book of mine, the means of drawing them nearer to Him. At least, amidst all its shortcomings, it has one redeeming feature—namely, this, that as in my book on *The Mystery of Jesus,* in this one also I have drawn largely from the fountains of living waters of the Holy Scriptures, and copiously poured them out all over the surface of my little garden; so that even so barren a plot of ground may yet be found to flourish and exhale a sweet odor and bear some fruit unto eternal life both for my dear readers and for me.

The treatise is divided into three books, thus:

Book I.—God in Himself.
Book II.—God in His Works.
Book III.—God in the Heart of the Mystic.

This may not be the order that would recommend itself to certain minds. Perhaps some would prefer that we should begin in a first book with the testimony of God in our heart, then proceed in a second book to read the glorious Name of God written in flaming letters all over the magnificent scroll of the universe; and finally rise to the consideration of God in Himself, in the ineffable Trinity of His Persons. Such would indeed be the logical order to follow, were we bent upon writing a theoretical or academic treatise on God. But quite different is our purpose.

We take the fact of the existence of God and that of the revelation of the Trinity of His Persons as granted. At the very outset, we fasten our gaze exclusively upon God in Himself, in the unity and unicity of His Divine Essence splendidly blooming out into the Trinity of His Persons; and we would even wish, were this possible, to do nothing else but lovingly to contemplate him thus. But, as we are as yet but pilgrims on earth, we soon grow tired of this sublime exercise and have perforce to turn to a less exhausting process, that of contemplating the same Triune God in the mirror of the works of His Hands at large and, at last, more particularly in His dim but so sweet revelation of Himself in our own heart.

PART I

GOD IN HIMSELF

THE BURNING BUSH

CHAPTER I

WHAT THE ANCHORITE SAID

SUMMARY.—*The priest a Magister in Israel in the art of communing with God. Meeting God officially. Also unofficially, in the secret of one's heart. Something wrong in his method of mental prayer. How to set about it. Tell God what is uppermost in your heart. What followed upon the attempt. Praise of the heart over the mind: it is the real master of the spiritual life. The finest of fine arts.*

PRIEST well-known for his zeal and piety comes one day to an old anchorite, and, without any preamble, humbly proffers his request:

"Please, Father, do teach me the art of communing with God."

"What," replied the old anchorite, "is it for me to give you lessons in that art? Are you not a *Magister in Israel?* With your daily Mass and Divine Office you are constantly, one might almost say day and night, in touch with the Divine Majesty, communing with God, treating with Him of the affairs of the world."

THE PRIEST. "True. But that is my official meeting with God, in the name of the Church and of the whole Christian people, and what I have to say is, to use a familiar expression, cut and dried and set down for me. I try, indeed, to discharge this duty faithfully and devoutly, but I wish moreover to do something else; to commune with God unofficially, in the secret of my own heart, sweetly and familiarly and spontaneously, after the manner described in certain recent books; or, to be perhaps a little more precise, after the manner set down in the Introit of to-day's Mass. (This happened to be the Tuesday of the second week of Lent.) The Introit is taken from Ps. 26:8 and is as follows: "*My heart hath spoken to Thee; my face hath sought Thee; Thy face, O Lord, will I seek.'"*

THE ANCHORITE. "What about daily mental prayer? Are you faithful to it?"

THE PRIEST. "Yes; but that is precisely where the trouble comes in. I make a it a practice every evening carefully to prepare the points of the morrow's meditation. Then in the morning, I consider these points as attentively as I can, but when it comes to producing affections, somehow I find it impossible to press anything out of my heart, and I have an impression that something is wrong in my method, though I could not tell what it is."

"I see," said THE ANCHORITE thoughtfully. "I see. Well, the remedy is not far to seek.

"Suppose now, that instead of meeting God first with your mind and only afterwards with your heart, you reverse the process, and begin by pressing your heart into service; it will make all the difference in the world."

THE PRIEST *(eagerly).* "Will it indeed? How good! Now, please tell me how to set about it? What shall I say to God to begin with?"

THE ANCHORITE. "My friend, do you mean that I should dictate to you your first words? This were too ridiculous. Simply tell the loving God who is here, and is intently listening to you, whatever is uppermost in your heart. Speak! I am not going to say another word until you have done it."

After a few seconds of embarrassed silence the good priest, raising his eyes upwards and, perhaps, unconsciously joining his hands, slowly and deliberately spoke these words in an undertone:

"My God! Thou art my God. I confess Thou art the sovereign Lord of all and my very own loving Father. To Thee I am indebted for all I have and am, but it seems to me as though I had never yet returned Thee thanks for all this.

"Thanks, then, O my God! hearty thanks to Thine Infinite Goodness. Oh! how good Thou art! how sweet! how lovely! and how beautiful must Thou be! Oh! when shall I see Thy countenance? Then shall I be happy. *Satiabor cum apparuerit gloria tua. . .* (Ps. 16:15).

Which having said, or rather sighed out, the dear man colored up deeply and his face became radiant.

In the meanwhile the anchorite had been taking down in shorthand that effusion as it was artlessly poured out of the fervid heart. He now translated the cryptic signs into ordinary writing and showed them to the good priest, who was simply amazed at what he had been saying, and stammered out: *Eructavit cor meum verbum bonum* (Ps. 40:2), "Verily, my heart hath uttered a good word."

THE ANCHORITE. "Yes; that is just it, my friend. Well, now you see, you had it in yourself to begin communing with God, speaking to Him heart to heart. You have done it; you have made a beginning; what remains now for you to do is simply to carry on. Try and discover your own feelings when you advert to the presence of God who is always at hand, then express them in as direct, simple and candid a way as you possibly can. Allow your heart to ' have its say. Let flow freely the tender filial feelings which press upwards towards Him who so prodigiously loves you, and who, independently of your personal debt of gratitude to Him, so richly deserves to be loved for His own sake. That is the way to commune with God."

After a pause THE ANCHORITE continued:

"In the beginning this novel exercise may seem somewhat awkward: it does not seem natural thus to hearken to the promptings of one's own heart in preference to the thoughts of one's mind. But this is a wrong impression due mainly to the fact of our having been spoiled by too bookish an education. If you persevere you will soon grow so used to it that it will become as a second nature, and this will make you very happy. The heart takes much for granted. It suppresses a great deal of the slow plodding of the mind. It has wings, the wings of a carrier pigeon, and flies straight as an arrow, home to its love.

"Moreover, it is a fact that the mind is curious, inclined to pride, easily puffed up, secretly self-seeking, unbending and harsh, whilst the heart, under pressure of Divine grace, is the real master of the spiritual life.

"Are you surprised to hear me say that the heart, not the brain, is the real master of the spiritual life? Yes, the heart is, under God, the prime mover in the business of communing with God—the heart, not the intellect. The heart is tender, disinterested, indefatigable; a revealer and an initiator, both charming and captivating. Yes, charmed, indeed, and Captivated by his own heart will a Christian be, if he only knows how to make it speak and will hearken to what it tells. But this is a small thing why, the Christian heart even charms and captivates God Himself. God cares not at all for the discourses of your mind, whilst He does lovingly incline His ear to catch the faintest sounds of love and praise which proceed from the true Christian heart. Only a moment ago, your heart produced the first little syllables of love, and you were entranced at the sweetness of the melody. Now, when it is so good only to begin, what will it be to go on, to unravel the melody as it will sing itself out? How sweet to pour it all out in the ears of the good and loving God, thus communing with Him not with your brains, but with your affections.

"Is not this the finest of fine arts? Little by little you will become proficient in it.

"But what am I saying—little by little?

Promptly, impetuously, will the Holy Spirit lift your soul above itself, above your ordinary purely human practice of faith and hope, lift you up on the wings of Understanding and Wisdom—those two sublimest gifts—causing you to travel in an instant an infinite space, to find your rest in the very bosom of God."

So spake THE ANCHORITE.

CHAPTER II

A FIRST IDEA OF GOD WITH WHICH
TO BEGIN

SUMMARY.—The most real, simple, entrancing being. We cannot grasp the extent of the wonder. How man on earth views the loveliness of God. Effusions. Have we succeeded in our attempt at forming an idea of God?

GOD! God! Oh, what is God?

We know—at least in theory, even if we do not let it influence us in the practice of our life—we know that God is the most real, noble, beautiful, magnificent, and majestic being, and at the same time the most simple, familiar, affable; the nearest to each one of us, the most inclined towards us; the most communicative, sweet, charming, alluring, entrancing; the most loving, tender, and affectionate: infinitely above everything else that is so, in the realm of nature, or of grace, or of glory.

Let us suppose that all the rays of beauty and of goodness which are scattered in this visible universe and in the world of souls and of pure spirits could be united and, so to say, fused into one single created being, and that the beauty and goodness of this one single being could be intensified one hundred millionfold, and this again multiplied by one hundred million, we should have what we could consider as an object of very dazzling splendor indeed; and yet, compared with the Divine loveliness, the beauty and goodness of that extraordinary being would be less than a drop of water compared with the ocean. Do we need to demonstrate this? Is it not self-evident? God is the Absolute, the Infinite, the *I am who am* (Exod. 3:14), whilst all that exists outside Him is but a shadow of being. Multiply a shadow as many million times as you will, it but remains what it is, a pure shadow, unworthy to enter into parallel with the substance which casts it. Our Lord one day told St. Catherine of Siena: "I am who am and thou art who is not."

God in His own sweet Self is a shoreless and bottomless ocean of life and light and sanctity.

Do we understand this, O my soul? Of course not: or rather let us say that we perfectly understand that it must be so, but we cannot grasp the extent of the wonder.

O my Lord God, most Holy; Thou the One, the Strong, the absolutely Good, the All-lovely; help Thy poor servant somehow to represent to himself and to picture to his brethren a glimpse of the ineffable splendor of Thy Divine Essence, of the sweetness of Thy sanctity, of the gracious condescension of Thy sovereign heart, which wants to be loved of me, even of me, of little me!

Suppose a man had never been able to look up to the sun because of some cruel infirmity which held him bent double, but that he could see the image of the sun reflected in a tiny dewdrop at the top of a blade of grass. Could such a man flatter himself that he possessed a just idea of the splendor of the sun? Now that represents very nearly the situation of those on earth in regard to God. They view the loveliness of God, not in itself, but only as it is reflected in that dewdrop of the material universe: *"Ecce gentes quasi stilla situlae "* says the prophet (Isa. 40:15). *Behold the Gentiles are as a drop of a bucket,* which has been dipped in the fountain.

O splendor of God, which to me seems so refulgent already when only seen through the tiny glass of our universe, can it be that I am destined soon, steadily and fearlessly to gaze upon the luminous orb of Thy Divine Essence, even as the eagle looks fixedly at the sun? Thou art my Sun, and on the day of the Beatific Vision, Thou wilt grant me to see Thee face to face without being consumed or dazzled into blindness.

Meanwhile, it is Thy sovereign pleasure that I should contemplate Thee alternately, first in the marvels of this visible world, which is the work of Thy hands, and then, as often as I may, in the Dark Cloud, that is to say, in Thy very Self without the interposition of any created image, by the exercise of faith and ardent love, whenever Thou vouchsafest to help Thy poor servant by special grace. And whilst I am as yet unable to see Thee unveiled, this at least is granted me, to feel the warm rays of Thy Divine Goodness enveloping me on every side.

O my God and my all, I do desire thus to contemplate Thee during the remaining years of my pilgrimage here below, to spend the rest of my life seeking after Thee, striving to lay hold of Thee, humbly making love to Thee and enjoying Thee as much as Thou wilt be pleased to grant me.

My soul, what have we done? We have tried to express God, to give some idea of Him; have we succeeded? We have been stammering only.

Whatever we can say of God (and precisely because we can say it) is unworthy of Him. Would even angelic speech, that of the cherub or seraph, be equal to the task of telling us what God is? No! This is His glory, that alone His own Divine Word, an infinite Person, expresses Him worthily.

Let us hold our peace and adore.

CHAPTER III

GOD'S DESCRIPTION OF HIMSELF

SUMMARY.—The vision of the Burning Bush. God speaks to us also from the burning bush of Creation. The one only God in three Persons. Never separate these two ideas, God and Trinity; read them one into the other. "I am who am" tells the infinite intensity of God's inner life. The reply to infidel philosophers. Effusion of admiration and love.

NOW *Moses fed the sheep of Jethro, his father-in-law, the priest of Madian: and he drove the flock to the inner part of the desert, and came to the mountain of God, Horeb. And the Lord appeared to him in a flame of fire out of the midst of a bush, and he saw that the bush was on fire and was not burnt. And Moses said: I will go and see this great sight, why the bush is not burnt. And when the Lord saw that he went forward to see, He called to him out of the midst of the bush, and said: Moses, Moses. And he answered: Here I am. And He said: Come not nigh hither, put off the shoes from thy feet, for the place whereon thou standest is holy ground. And He said: I am the God of your fathers, the God of Abraham, the God of Isaac, and the God of Jacob. I am who am"* (Exod. 3:1-6 and 14).

The Lord God speaks to every soul of good will from the burning bush of creation. Here by the word creation we must understand not only this material universe, but at the same time the world of grace and that of glory—a bush that is ever burning and never consumed. Now what does the Lord God tell us? First of all He warns us how we ought to stand on the holy ground of Divine ecstatic contemplation—with what purity of intention, detachment from all things created, and feelings of reverent awe and love. All this is inculcated in the words: "Put off the shoes from thy feet."

Then the Lord God goes on to reveal Himself to the mystic, as the one only God in three Divine Persons: "I am the God of

Abraham, the God of Isaac, the God of Jacob. I am who am." And just as Moses, prostrate on the ground, hid his face and durst not look at God, though he heard Him and spoke to Him, so also the contemplative, prostrate on his own nothingness dares not look at the Divine Essence, nay cannot do so, but he nevertheless hears what God tells him of His own Divine Self, and is filled with joy at this wonderful revelation.

God is the Blessed Trinity of the Father, the Son, and the Holy Ghost. We must never separate, nay we must be careful ever to keep joined together in our mind these two ideas, God and the Trinity: we must see these two ideas one into the other. There is no other God than the Blessed Trinity of the Father, the Son, and the Holy Ghost. The Trinity of Persons is not something secondary in God, superadded from outside to the Divine Essence; the Trinity is God, the three Divine Persons are the one only God. God is essentially these three distinct Persons, the Father, the Son, and the Holy Ghost. To be God is to be the Father, the Son, and the Holy Ghost.

When God tells us magnificently *I am who am* (Exod. 3:14), He reveals to us the infinite intensity of His Divine Life. True, when we glance into the abyss of light which this definition of God by Himself gives, our purblind intellect cannot as yet, without Divine assistance, discern therein the Trinity of Persons. But this Divine assistance has been granted to us. We have been told distinctly, in many scriptural passages, that God has a Son; and in the fulness of time this Son of God was made man and lived among men and was seen by them *full of grace and truth* (John 1:14), and has left shining and imperishable monuments of His passage here upon earth. It has also been revealed to us that there is in God yet another mode of production and procession, distinct from that of generation, and that it results in a third Person, the Holy Spirit. Thus are we made to understand all that is implied in this declaration *I am who am.* We realize that God is a Trinity of Persons and that whenever we name God, we name the Blessed Trinity, we must think of the Blessed Trinity, we must believe in and confess and adore the Most Holy Trinity of the Father, the Son, and the Holy Spirit.

O my God, with what joy do I render to Thee this homage! I believe in Thee, O Most Holy Trinity; to Thee do I submit my feeble understanding; gladly do I embrace this revelation of Thyself by Thyself to us under the veil of faith, pending the time not so very far distant, when, as I firmly hope from Thine ineffable Goodness, I shall receive the fulness of Thy revelation in the splendors of the Beatific Vision.

Infidel philosophers would like to reduce Thee, O my God, to a mere abstract idea, a vain word without meaning, a vague and impersonal thing: and behold, Thou revealest Thyself as being not only personal as we see that we ourselves are, but thrice Personal. Thou, O Lord God, subsistest in three distinct hypostases: so opulent, so magnificent is Thy being! Thou art more personal than we can possibly conceive or realize. This fact has to be revealed to us, and even when thus revealed, we can as yet take hold of it but by faith. But, O my God, how sweet it is for us to know that Thou vouchsafest to draw near each one of us, with Thy whole Divine Self, with Thy three Divine Persons.

In vain does the poor sinner, in his blindness, draw back and withdraw himself from Thee, turn his back on Thee, enjoying Thy benefactions and denying that they come from Thee, O Most Holy Trinity. It remains true, nevertheless, that our dealings with Thee, O my God, must, on our own part, be personal, most intimate and loving, whilst Thine own dealings with each one of us are three times personal, because Thou art one God in three distinct Persons, the Father, the Son, and the Holy Ghost.

To Thee be glory for ever.

CHAPTER IV

HOW TO PROCEED IN THIS CONTEMPLATION

SUMMARY.—The process devised by some in order to arrive at a pure concept of the Divine Essence. The Church does not teach the method of abstraction nor Holy Scripture either. The child's notion of God, the right one, to which philosopher and theologian finally return. Simplicity of little children. The way we recommend: A lively method, based upon the very nature of the Divine Essence. Circumincession. The blending of notions which our contemplation of the Blessed Trinity demands, until the experience of "mystical theology" supervenes.

LEARNED and saintly personages have devised a certain process by which the soul may, with the grace of God, arrive at the pure concept of the Divine Essence. Such, among others, are first the pseudo- Areopagite, then the author of the treatise *De adhaerendo Deo,* long attributed to Blessed Albertus Magnus; then again the anonymous author of *The Cloud of Unknowing* whom Father Baker follows in his *Sancta Sophia.*

It is not for me to find fault with them in this matter: at times I have used their books and found profit in so doing. However, we must all admit that nowhere does Holy Church teach her children the method of abstraction; far otherwise, as anyone familiar with the whole range of the sacred liturgy may convince himself. St. Augustine, though himself one of the mightiest philosophical geniuses the world ever produced, does not hesitate to call our attention to the fact that very seldom does Holy Writ bring forward or express the Divine properties in the abstract. "Quae propriè de Deo dicuntur, quaeque in nulla creatura inveniuntur, raro ponit Scriptura divina" *(De Trinitate,* 1,2).

Our first concept of God is a very formless and obscure one, as of something indefinite, something, indeed, infinitely grand,

and good, and beautiful, but without any distinct shape, so to say. The mind of the child, in thinking of God, cannot catch at anything: for him God is God, simply that and nothing else. When the learned Christian has gone the round of all philosophical and theological speculations about the Supreme Being, he comes back to this, the child's notion of God, and finds it to be the very best. He exclaims: "O my God, what art Thou? Thou art God and all is said, O God, my God!" The more he clings to this obscure, formless idea the nearer is he to the truth. It is in this contemplation, if ever, that we must return to the simplicity of little children, allowing ourselves to be led thereto much more by love than by understanding, confessing freely that, so far as understanding is concerned, we are unable to do aught but stammer with the prophet: *A, a, a, Domine Deus, Ecce nescio loqui quia puer ego sum: Ah, ah, ah, Lord God, behold, I cannot speak, for I am but a child* (Jer. 1:6), and relinquishing the task of discoursing for that of loving and being loved, kissing and being kissed. *Let Him kiss me with the kiss of His mouth,* exclaims the little bride at the very beginning of the Canticle of Canticles.

Now, here is the way I would have you, my dear reader, proceed in this contemplation.

Address yourself successively and separately to each of the three Divine Persons: adore that Person for His own sake, and yet be careful to adore in that Person, at the same time, each one of the other two; thus you will derive the special benefit of a distinct knowledge and love of each of the three Divine Persons, and thereby gain an increased realization of the supereminent unity of the Divine Essence. Thus you will enter deeper and deeper into the mystery of the life of God in Himself, and of our relations with each Divine Person. I mean it in this wise.

Address yourself to the first Person of the Most Holy Trinity, the Father. Bring to remembrance all that you know which constitutes Him the very first Person as we describe it in a subsequent chapter ©. VIII). Praise Him for this, and then go one step further and consider that He has in Himself eternally His Divine Son and His Holy Spirit of love, and adore them in Him.

Proceed in the same manner in your contemplation of the second Person, the Son.

First apply your mind and heart to the appreciation of what constitutes Him, the second Person, and what special excellencies shine in Him in consequence; and then, as the second step in this process of contemplation, notice that He has ever with Him His Divine Father and His Holy Ghost; adore them in Him.

Follow the same mode of contemplation in behalf of the Holy Spirit. Consider what constitutes Him, the third Person, and characterizes Him as such, and how, indeed, He is inseparable from the Father and the Son; adore Him for His own sake and adore Them in Him.

This is not an artificial method, but a lively mode of procedure based upon the very nature of the Divine Essence as revealed to us in the *deposit of faith.* One cannot long Practice it without entering somewhat, even during one's pilgrim days, *into the joy of the Lord,* into the secret of His Divine operations, into light unspeakable.

The presence of the other two Persons in each separate Person is a very beautiful property of the Divine Essence, which we must never cease to admire, and reverence, and praise.

It is called *Circumincession,* but we need not mind the learned word, as long as we apprehend the Divine reality it serves to express in human language.

In this contemplation of the Blessed Trinity there must therefore be found a blending in our mind of the abstract theological notions and catechetical formulas, together with what we can of our own conjecture and express about God, from our notions of things created: until it shall please Him, of His own gracious Goodness, to vouchsafe to us the ineffable soul-experience of " mystical theology."

The Blessed Three in One, this is the refulgent Dark Cloud impenetrable, gazing upon which the soul exclaims: "O God! O my All in All! O fire of Love!" but soon, silent, motionless, she concentrates all her energy upon the act of loving.

CHAPTER V

WHEN, WHERE, AND HOW

SUMMARY.—Two distinct answers to be given to this set of questions. In this chapter we give the first answer, to this effect—namely, Whenever, Wherever, and However you feel inclined. The spirit of prayer is free. Examples as to the special worship of each of the three Divine Persons. Some beautiful practices in regard to the Holy Spirit.

O you, O my dear reader, now ask when, where, and how to apply the principles enunciated in the preceding chapter? The reply to this query is twofold. In this chapter we give our first answer.

Adore more particularly any one of the three Divine Persons, either the Father, or the Son, or the Holy Spirit, for His own sake, whenever and wherever and howsoever you happen to feel inclined to do so. The spirit of prayer, the spirit of adoration and of fervent outpourings of love, knows no limits of time and place, no etiquette or ceremonious observance, obeys no set rules, breathes out when and where and how it listeth.[2] No one knows beforehand when it will arise or where it will lead. No matter. The only important thing is that you should be ready to welcome it as soon as you feel its presence and that you should follow it.

Thus, at times you will be suddenly stirred with filial emotions of love and gratitude to God the Father, or feel yourself led into the entrancing contemplation of His abysmal Sanctity. At once yield to these precious feelings, give vent to them, give them voice, follow eagerly the train of thoughts and of burning affections which may arise in consequence. Follow after, follow after, panting, breathless, self-forgetting, lost to all things created. You will come out of these ecstatic moments with deeper knowledge both of God the Father and in Him of the

---

[2] *Editor's note*: where it wills, from the middle english *liste*.

379

other two Persons. Not, of course, knowledge that you could put into words, but experimental knowledge, "mystical theology" proper.

Or, is it the second Person of the Blessed Trinity, the Word, who, quite unaccountably, happens to captivate and sweetly to compel your loving attention, either as He is from all eternity in the bosom of the Father, or again in some of the delightful mysteries of His sacred Humanity?

Then, of course, contemplate Him, eagerly feed your soul with the sweets of His blessed countenance.

As I have already consecrated a whole volume, my fifth, *The Mystery of Jesus* to show how this ought to be done, there is no need of my insisting on the point further than to say that you will grow thereby in the special, personal, distinct knowledge of the second Person of the Blessed Trinity, and, of course, through Him, of His Divine Father and of His Holy Spirit.

Finally, let us suppose that this time—anywheresoever and anywhensoever—it is the Holy Spirit who happens mysteriously to win your loving attention and concentrate it upon Himself personally and for His own sake. Do, then, gaze with all the eagerness of an inflamed soul upon this wonderful third Person of the Blessed Trinity. Talk to Him and hearken to Him, and allow your heart to overflow with joy at the sweetness of this meeting. You will come out of it all aglow with experimental knowledge of this Holy Spirit of love, and, of course, also with deeper appreciation of the two first Persons who produce such a marvelous third Person and give Him to you as Their gift.

A beautiful practice, if rather uncommon, and one which may require some delicate discernment, is that of worshiping the Holy Ghost, first in the persons of little baptized children, then in the persons of those adult Christians who lead transparently blameless and fervent lives. Church history relates how the glorious martyr, St. Leonides, was wont during the night reverently to uncover the breast of his youthful son, Origen, whilst he was asleep, and to kiss it as the living, breathing temple of the Holy Spirit. This was genuine mysticism, as much even as the loving kiss given to the lepers by some saints. Only a real mystic could do such an act, and in the right spirit.

Whenever a beautiful act of virtue is performed under our eyes, we ought at once to trace it to its prime author, the Holy Ghost, and if the act be an heroic one, such as, for instance, setting human respect at naught, forgiving some cruel or even slight injury, but which one keenly resents, bearing in a spirit of faith some great reverse of fortune or loss of dear ones, performing some act of charity against which human nature cannot but revolt, then we ought to discern in this a manifest intervention of the Holy Spirit, and take occasion of it to break forth into rapturous praise of the third Person of the Blessed Trinity.

In my long life of priest and missionary, I have witnessed quite a large number of such manifestations of the Holy Spirit, and it is to me a matter of regret that I did not set them down in writing at the time. They would make fine and edifying reading. One ought to be on the lookout for such occasional flashes, so to say, of the inner fire of the Holy Spirit, burning in the souls of really fervent Christians. Such a habit would serve to offset the pernicious effects which the scandals of the world, in the midst of which we move, have upon us, and about which we are perhaps quite unconcerned. I said "fervent Christians." Only with such can we venture to adore the Holy Ghost in them. With the tepid, unedifying, frivolous, and careless, one is never sure whether they are actually in a state of grace. As I have shown in my third volume, *Mysticism. True and False,* it is the misfortune of the tepid Christian to have occasional lapses into mortal sin.

This, then, is my first answer to the questions: When, Where, and How, one may apply oneself to the special worship of each one of the Divine Persons. The answer which I am going to give in the next chapter is the very antithesis of whenever and wherever and however, for it points to set times and circumstances when one is called upon to give particular attention respectively to each one of the Divine Persons.

CHAPTER VI

A SECOND ANSWER TO THE SAME QUERY

SUMMARY.—This comes as a complement to the first answer. We are to pay special attention to God the Father at Mass; for then He fills the Church with His unspeakable Majesty. Also when out of doors, contemplating natural scenery by day or night. To the second Person, when out of Mass, visiting the Blessed Sacrament. *Dominus est.* The eyes of faith discerning Him in the Sacred Host. To the Holy Ghost, when at private prayers and through the day's occupations.

HERE, then, is now the second answer. It comes not as an alternative or a contradiction, but as a complement to the previous one.

First, when are we called upon to pay particular attention to God the Father? I say when we are assisting at the Holy Sacrifice of Mass. This may perhaps surprise unenlightened piety, but a moment's reflection ought to suffice to satisfy anyone as to the soundness of this view. For, indeed, to whom is this sacrifice offered? Is it not to God the Father? The three Divine Persons are there, because they are never separated, but in this solemn act, by the very nature of the function, you are invited to visualize first and foremost God the Father. He it is who at this moment fills the Church with His unspeakable, infinite majesty. To make you realize this fact more vividly you have only to read the Canon of the Mass, especially that part which follows the Consecration down to the Agnus Dei. Then also observe how almost all the Collects, Secrets, and Post communions of the Masses the year round are addressed to God the Father. Of course, it may help your piety to think of the millions of blessed angels surrounding the altar at that moment and in silent adoration of the Divine Victim upon it. Still more so, to think of the dear Lord Jesus Himself, there present in flesh and blood, mystically renewing the sacrifice He once offered on

Calvary. But, I ask it in all earnestness, were it not a great mistake to forget, to lose sight of, or perhaps, ignore entirely, the principal personage—namely, God the Father, who is at that very moment reconciling to Himself the guilty world, through the blood of His Divine Son, receiving the adorations, thanksgivings, propitiatory prayers and demands of His Divine Son in our behalf?

And yet how many Christians are scarcely conscious of this?

In spite of the progress of the liturgical movement, people are not yet used to reading their Mass-book aright, or to drawing from it for their piety the most obvious lessons. Then, also, as ail the rest of the Divine Office by day and night, recited by priests and chanted in choir by monks and nuns, is a prolongation of the Holy Sacrifice of Mass, it is also addressed directly to the first Person of the Blessed Trinity, God the Father—through His Divine Son, of course, in the unity of the Holy Spirit— but first and foremost to God the Father, thus putting us in touch with Him.

We may also most appropriately pay special attention to God the Father and give Him our loving praise, when we happen to be out of doors contemplating the beauties of nature, since the work of creation is, by appropriation, attributed to Him. We ought to look upon the firmament, by day and night, as the most wonderful visible temple built by the Father Himself through the wisdom of the Son by the power of His Holy Spirit— a temple which the Father does indeed fill with the splendor of His infinite Majesty. *Pleni sunt coeli et terra majestatis gloriae tuae.*

We shall have occasion in the sequel of this work to come back upon this consideration. Let this at present suffice as to the proper set time and occasions when it is natural and incumbent upon us to pay special attention to God the Father.

And now, when are we called upon and expected to hold personal intercourse with, and pay special attention to, the second Person of the Blessed Trinity, God the Son? I answer: When, outside the time of the Mass, we are visiting the Blessed Sacrament. Then, indeed, is the time for us to turn all our speech to Him as to *the Son of the Living God,* who eternally proceeds from the Father by way of generation; who is one and the same God with the Father and who, in that oneness, produces with Him, by way of active spiration, the Holy Spirit of Love.

Yes, that small Host, hidden away in the ciborium, shut up behind the golden door of the tabernacle, or perhaps exposed to view in the monstrance for the office of Solemn Benediction or again for the Forty Hours' Devotion, *Dominus est;* it is the Lord, the Lord God, the second Person of the Blessed Three in One; He it is we ought for the moment to visualize by the light of faith, even as though we were with Him and His Apostles on the shores of the Lake of Genesareth, or with Him and His Blessed Angels and Saints in the glory of Paradise. And, of course, as we pay homage to Him, our adoration extends to the Father who eternally begets Him, and to the Holy Spirit whom He, jointly with the Father, is eternally producing.

I and the Father are one (John 10:30), He says—one and the same God—one principle of the Holy Spirit. *My Father worketh until now and I work* (John 5:17), that is to say, the Father is ever begetting His Divine Son, and in His turn the Son is ever producing, in unison with the Father, the Holy Spirit of Love.

When thus engaged in your loving contemplation of the second Person of the Blessed Trinity, then, of course, is also the time of bringing to bear all the affections of your heart upon the sweet mysteries of His sacred Humanity, according to the time of the liturgical year and according to the actual bent of your devotion. I have explained this at great length in my fifth volume, *The Mystery of Jesus.*

Thus will your affective knowledge of the second Person of the Blessed Trinity gain in depth, thereby enhancing also your knowledge and love of the other two Divine Persons.

Finally, as to the Holy Spirit.

Outside of Holy Mass and of the visit to the Blessed Sacrament, when attending to private prayer and to your various occupations through the day, make it a point to address yourself particularly to the third Person of the Blessed Trinity, the Holy

Ghost, who is in the living temple of your own body and soul, who is actually sighing after your recognition of the fact, ardently wishing for you to take proper notice of Him and to turn His presence and omnipotent love to your advantage. Will you not adore this Divine Person? Will you not love the very love of the Father and of the Son? Will you not have something to say to this Divine guest and friend and comforter? Will you not find your delight in Him, and through Him in the other two Persons whose Gift He is?

Now, to do this is to enjoy God. To do this is, indeed, to grow in the knowledge and in the love of the Most Holy Trinity.

CHAPTER VII

THE VOICE OF THE BRIDE

SUMMARY.—Many have erred about the doctrine of the Blessed Trinity, because they have neglected the warnings of Holy Writ. My purpose is not to make theologians. No irreverent curiosity, but simple faith and love. The Church has in her sacred liturgy carefully set down the terms in which we ought to think and speak of the Blessed Trinity. Specially in the Nicene Creed and in the Preface of the Mass of the Blessed Trinity.

AFTER reading the three foregoing chapters some might perhaps accuse me of leading those who follow me into dangerous paths.

It is true that many have erred about this fundamental dogma of our faith, the doctrine of the Most Holy Trinity, for having rashly ventured to scrutinize the depths of the mystery, when they should have been satisfied with believing and adoring.

Such men did not bear enough in mind the caution given by Proverbs thus: *As it is not good for a man to eat much honey, so he that is a searcher of majesty, shall be overwhelmed by glory* (Prov. 25:27). Nor again the warning of Ecclesiasticus: *Seek not the things that are too high for thee, and search not into things that are above thy ability; but the things that God hath commanded thee, think of them always, and in many of His works be not curious; for it is not necessary for thee to see with thy eyes those things which are hid* (Eccli. 3:22, 23).

Now, in self-defense, I protest that my purpose is not to make theologians of my readers, recruited as they are from all ranks of the Christian commonwealth, from the humblest as well as from the middle ranks and from the highest.

No, not theologians in the common acceptation of this word; not theologians, but what is far better, adorers of God *in spirit and truth* (John 4:23). This all may certainly desire and strive

387

after, as they are sweetly invited to do by Our Lord, were they even such as the poor, ill-educated, ignorant and sinful Samaritan woman who met Him at Jacob's well.

The contemplative soul does not approach the infinite Majesty and Sanctity of God with irreverent curiosity, but with humble faith and love. She is thankful that Holy Mother Church has carefully set down the terms within which we are safe to think and speak of the Most Holy Trinity. This the Church has done throughout the whole range of her sacred liturgy, but more particularly in two wonderful official documents, the Nicene Creed, and the Preface of the Mass, of the Blessed Trinity, including the Trisagion which follows.

Every Christian ought to be able to find these in his Sunday Mass-book: nevertheless, for the sake of completeness, we subjoin them here, dividing them into paragraphs and italicising the important words; so as to help the mind of the reader to take in their full import and co-ordination. Thus it will be easier to understand why the Church, the Bride of Christ, makes the Nicene Creed an hymn of triumph, bringing as it does to the Apostles' Creed, after hard conflicts, the precisions and developments which the first heresies had rendered necessary.

As to the Preface, no one needs to be told that it is one of the sublimest lyrical outbursts of the spirit of adoration, at the same time as an absolutely scientific statement of the terms of the mystery of the Blessed Trinity. A rare, combination, indeed, and one which could not .be accounted for but by the direct assistance and inspiration of the Holy Spirit.

That is what I call the voice of the Bride.

I.—THE NICENE CREED

I believe in one God, the Father Almighty, Maker of Heaven and Earth, of all things visible and invisible.
    And in One Lord Jesus Christ,
    The only-begotten Son of God and born of the Father before all ages; God of God, light of light, true God of true God: begotten, not

made, consubstantial with the Father, by whom all things were made.

Who for us men, and for our salvation, came down from heaven, and was incarnate by the Holy Spirit, of the Virgin Mary, and was made man.

He was crucified also for us, under Pontius Pilate, He suffered and was buried.

The third day He rose again according to the Scriptures, and ascended into heaven and sitteth on the right hand of the Father, and shall come again with glory to judge the living and the dead.

Of whose Kingdom there shall be no end.

And in the Holy Ghost,

The Lord and Life-Giver, who proceedeth from the Father and the Son; who together with the Father and Son is adored and glorified, who spoke by the Prophets.

And one, Holy, Catholic, Apostolic Church. I confess one baptism for the remission of sins.

And I look for the resurrection of the dead and the life of the world to come. Amen.

II.—THE PREFACE OF THE TRINITY
WITH THE TRISAGION

It is truly meet and just, right and salutary that we should, at all times and in all places, give thanks unto Thee, Holy Lord, Father Almighty, Everlasting God, who together with Thine only- begotten Son and the Holy Ghost art one God and one Lord,

Not in the singleness of one person, But in the Trinity of one substance. For that which by Thy revelation we believe of Thy glory, the same also we hold as to Thy Son, the same as to the Holy Spirit, without difference or distinction.

That in the confession of the true and everlasting Godhead,

Distinction in Persons,

Unity in Essence,

And equality in Majesty may be adored. Which the Angels and

Archangels, The Cherubim also and Seraphim praise, who cease not daily to cry out with one voice, saying:
    Holy, Holy, Holy, is the Lord God of Hosts,
    Full are the heavens and the earth of Thy glory.
    Hosanna in the heights!

There are many other liturgical texts, such as, for instance, the so-called *Athanasian Creed,* the *Gloria in Excelsis Deo,* the *Te Deum Laudamus,* and an immense variety of Doxologies, which may be pressed into service by the contemplative soul, but the two we have just given will suffice to supply, at least, the framework, so to say, and the keynote for practically endless considerations and affections on the great mystery.

This whole book of mine has no other pretension than to be some kind of unconventional paraphrase of these two wonderful formulas of the Catholic faith and love, the Nicene Creed and the Preface of the Mass of the Blessed Trinity.

CHAPTER VIII

THE MYSTERY OF THE FATHER

SUMMARY.—It is the mystery of the Divine Life which the Father lives within Himself, the Divine operations He performs, the Divine Persons He produces. God speaks His Word. Despair of the man who would express God and love Him adequately. What man cannot do God does. Saying that God is the creator of heaven and earth gives no idea of what God is in Himself, but the Mystery of the Father does.

UNTO *the knowledge* of *the mystery of the Father* (Col. 2:2). The mystery of the Father, what is it?

It is that from all eternity He is begetting a Son, His own living Image: and that this Eternal Father and this Eternal Son do so love each other that, in the act of breathing out their mutual love, they eternally produce a third Divine Person, their Holy Spirit. The mystery of the Father is the mystery of the Divine life He lives within Himself, of the Divine operations He performs within Himself, of the Divine Persons He produces.

One would like to speak worthily of God, to express Him magnificently, adequately, to speak Him out to one's fellow-men in our human language, the only one at hand, in a way that would truly set Him before their eyes. Alas! this is absolutely impossible. Seeing which, the servant of God would fain, even as John in the Apocalypse, when he discovered that no one could open the book with the seven seals, break out into tears (Apoc. 5:4.).

Fain would he remain disconsolate, were it not that a voice whispers to him as one of the Ancients to John: *Weep not* (Apoc. 5:5). Weep not; for what no man can do the Lord Himself does: He speaks one word, only one word, His Word, His own Divine Word, and thereby expresses Himself fully, magnificently, adequately. It takes God to speak worthily of God. Now He does it: He does it from all eternity.

My God, I give Thee thanks! O Eternal Father, I give Thee thanks! And to Thee also, O Divine Word, I give rapturous thanks! Here, then, is the mystery of the Father beginning to unravel itself before our gaze. Let us be bold: let us proceed: let us push forward unto the loving contemplation of the mystery of the Father.

One could wish to love God the Father and His Divine Son as one conceives that such a Father and such a Son are worthy to be loved. Alas! that is absolutely impossible to the creature.

Seeing which, the servant of God again might break his heart, but here also a voice tells him: *Weep not.* Weep not: for what neither thou, nor any creature, or any number of creatures put together could ever achieve, God does perfectly in one single act: God loves God adequately, God loves God even as God deserves to be loved; God the Father loves His Son, His living Image, His Word, who expresses Him so magnificently—He loves Him, I say, to the absolutely full measure of His deserving. And in His turn, God the Son loves the Divine Father, from whom He receives all that He has and is—He loves Him, I say, to the full measure of His deserving, that is to say, infinitely. And in Their mutual infinite love, the Father and the Son breathe out the third Divine Person, the Holy Spirit.

Oh, thanks, my God, Holy Trinity: I give Thee thanks *propter magnam gloriam tuam,* that Thou art thus One God in three Divine Persons; the Lover, the Loved One, the Love: "Amans, Amatus, Amor" as one of the ancient Fathers of the Church has most felicitously expressed it.

This, then, is the mystery of the Father: that God is Love; *Deus caritas est;* God is love in three Divine Persons. This is the mystery that the Father eternally carries in His bosom, which the Son came down upon earth to reveal to us, and which the Holy Spirit brings to pass, even into our very heart and soul and flesh.

When we are told that God is the creator of Heaven and earth, it does not give us to understand what God is. True, none but God could create anything whatever; but God would no less be what He is had He never created anything.

But when we are told that God is the Blessed Trinity of the Father and of the Son and of the Holy Ghost, we come by faith, unto the knowledge of the mystery of the Divine Life and its ineffable operations. The world of creatures is outside the Divine Essence, but the Son is *in the Father's bosom* and is God; then we begin to know God from the inside even as He is in Himself: we come *unto the knowledge of the mystery of the Father.*

The Father is the headspring of the Divine Essence, He is *la Divinité—Source (Fons Deitatis).*

O glory be to the Father!

Glory be to the Father through the Son!

Glory be to the Father through the Son, in the unity of the Holy Spirit. Amen. Amen. Amen.

CHAPTER IX

MORE ABOUT GOD THE FATHER

SUMMARY.—How this should be understood. Whatever is said of the other two Persons and of the Divine Nature as such makes us know more of the Father. The Collects of the Mass. The sayings of Our Lord in the Gospel. How a devotional treatise could be made on .this entrancing subject.

To speak of "more about the Father" is a very human way of expressing ourselves. For, indeed, when we have stated that He is the Father and has ever with Him His Divine Son and His Holy Spirit of Love, all is said completely, adequately.

All is said: yes; but all is not apprehended by our puny minds. It remains for us to open, so to speak, and to unfold this theological statement, and to perceive as distinctly as will be given us all that lies hidden therein, and to give due praise to God the Father for all this.

It must be owned that God the Father is the one of the three Divine Persons to whom most Christians give least attention.

The second Person being Our Lord Jesus Christ, so near to us by means of His Sacred Humanity, arrests our attention much more and almost monopolizes it; though we give also, at least from time to time, some thought to the Holy Ghost. But God the Father, although we are made to name Him first in our every sign of the Cross and every doxology, we can hardly say that we bestow any thought upon Him.

Now this is not all as it should be, nor, indeed, as our Lord and Holy Mother Church would have it.

It is true that whosoever honors any one of the three Divine Persons, implicitly honors, at the same time, the other two; but such implicit worship ought not to satisfy our piety. Both our Lord in the Gospel, and Holy Church in the sacred liturgy, tell us a great deal about God the Father, evidently with a view to lead us into making much of Him.

Unfortunately this twofold, very earnest teaching, most of the time, falls upon inattentive ears. Out of sheer fickleness of mind, men, as a rule, will not give to the First Person what they owe Him, and their piety is impoverished in proportion.

Let us realize that just as it is a sign of a high spiritual life to cultivate an explicit, felt, conscious devotion to the Blessed Trinity, so also is it a sign of real spiritual progress when we come to have a great and enlightened love for the Person of God the Father in particular.

A more explicit and fervent love of the Father, far from diminishing our love of Our Lord, will rather intensify and deepen it, by making it more intelligent, better informed, more theological, more real.

First of all, it must be understood that ' all we are going to say in subsequent chapters about the Son and the Holy Ghost will make us know more of the Father. This is obvious. It will make us know more, and more distinctly, His inner life, with His Divine operations of which these two other Persons are the results. The better we know the Son and the Holy Ghost, the richer, if we will only reflect, grows our knowledge of Him who produces them.

Then (and this may sound like a repetition of what we have just been saying, but it is not) it must also be understood that it is impossible to say anything in praise of the Divine Nature as such, without its resulting, in a most particular way, in praise of God the Father, thereby further enhancing our knowledge of Him; because of His being the headspring from which is derived all that belongs to the Divine Nature, as well as all things created. This has been admirably set forth in the celebrated text of St. James: *Every best gift and every perfect gift* is *from above, coming down from the Father of lights, with whom there is no change nor shadow of alteration* (James 1:17), His *best gift* being His Divine Son, for it is written: *God so loved the world as to give* it *His only-begotten Son* (John 3:16), and His *perfect gift* being His

Holy Ghost, for Our Lord said to His Apostles: *I will ask the Father, and He shall give you another Paraclete, that He may be with you for ever, the Spirit of Truth* (John 14:16, 17). Could a more perfect gift ever be thought of? And now, does not all this increase our knowledge of the goodness of the Father?

In the same strain does St. Paul exclaim: *To us there is but one God, the Father, of whom are all things and we unto Him* (1 Cor. 8:6)—and again: *Blessed be God the Father of Our Lord Jesus Christ, the Father of mercies and the God of all comfort* (2 Cor. 1:3).

We may note also that in all the Masses of the liturgical cycle, the Collects, Secrets, and Post-communions being generally addressed to the Father, they tell us of Him, they mention explicitly some of His Divine perfections.

Finally, do we want still further and still more distinctly to know the Father, we have the short, pregnant sentences of Our Lord about Him in the Gospel, wherein we may find an inexhaustible theme for our pious meditations and ecstatic contemplation. For has not Jesus said: *No one knoweth who the Father is but the Son, and he to whom the Son will reveal Him* (Luke 10:22)—and again: *No man cometh to the Father,* and consequently to the knowledge of the Father, *but by Me* (John 14:6)—and again to the Jews: *If you did know Me perhaps you would know My Father also* (John 8:19).

In this connection perhaps I may be permitted to mention that I had thought of collecting and paraphrasing briefly all the texts of the New Testament where God the Father is mentioned. I thought this would make an illuminating chapter to this present book. Illuminating no doubt it would have been, but I soon had to stop, for I discovered that not one chapter only, but at least one more volume, possibly even two would have to be made out of such a rich harvest of Scripture materials. Now, much as I would like to add this new labor of love to my other works, I am not prepared, nor indeed at liberty, to open such a wide parenthesis in the series of my treatises on Traditional Mysticism, which is not near completion. I can only recommend this interesting side-enterprise to anyone who might have the courage to do it for his own spiritual delight and edification. No telling but that this would even be the making of him as a writer and that he would eventually enrich the world with a precious and beautiful new treatise at once theological and devotional.

Without aiming quite so high as that, any priest or student of theology, or pious educated layman, would certainly increase his knowledge and love of God the Father by simply taking the trouble to look up for himself in his New Testament and to mark, let us say, with red ink, all the passages which refer to the first Person; of the Blessed Trinity, so that he might at any moment lay his hand upon some of them and meditate upon them in a spirit of prayer.

CHAPTER X

THE WORD, THE SECOND PERSON OF THE BLESSED TRINITY

SUMMARY.—A new theological expression peculiar to St. John. Silence of the other writers of the New Testament in this regard. The same appellation is found with the identical meaning of St. John, in several passages of the Old Testament, though it does not appear that the inspired writers of that time, still less the bulk of the People of God, understood its full import.

HAVING now to speak of the second Person of the Blessed Trinity, it becomes necessary to premise a few remarks about the fourth Gospel, that of St. John. It is therein that we find for the first time in the New Testament the peculiar and highly significant new appellation of THE WORD—along with His proper name of the Only-begotten Son—by which this second Person is already known to us. St. John is the only one of the inspired writers of the New Testament to make use of this expression in this sense. None of the three synoptic evangelists, Matthew, Mark, and Luke, nor any of the other writers of the canonical epistles, Peter, James, and Jude, nor St. Paul the Apostle of the Gentiles, ever use the term "Word of God " with any other meaning than the common one of a sound uttered by the lips or the written sign of it. St. John is the only one who uses it as the proper appellation of the very Son of God; and he introduces it in the Scripture vocabulary with such a splendor, such a magnificent insistence and display of pomp and ceremony, if we may say so, that we cannot fail to notice its novelty and paramount importance.

Here are the opening sentences of his Gospel: *In the beginning was the Word, and the Word was with God, and the Word was God. The same was in the beginning with God. All things were made by Him, and without Him was made nothing that was made. In Him was life and the life was the light of men ... the true light which enlighteneth every man that cometh into the world. .*

. . And the Word was made flesh and dwelt among us (and we saw His glory, the glory as it were of the only-begotten of the Father) full of grace and truth (John 1:1-4, 9, 14).

The opening sentence of the first canonical epistle of the same St. John is no less sublime, insistent, and explicit in its identification of *the Word* with the second Person of the Blessed Trinity:

That which was from the beginning, which we have heard, which we have seen with our eyes, which we have looked upon and our hands have handled of the Word of life—for the life was manifested and we have seen and do bear witness, and declare unto you the life eternal which was with the Father and hath appeared to us—that which we have seen and have heard, we declare unto you, that you may have fellowship with us, and our fellowship may be with the Father, and with His Son Jesus Christ (1 John 1:1-3).

This epistle, according to the latest conclusions of exegesis, was evidently written by St. John as a sort of Preface and parenthetical commentary to his Gospel, and must have been sent together with it to different Churches, so that we may well consider it as forming a unique document with this Gospel.

The silence of the other inspired writers of the New Testament about the Word of God as the second Person of the Blessed Trinity is the more remarkable in that the Old Testament supplies us with several striking passages where the expression *the Word of God* is so used, that, with the knowledge we now have of the mystery of the Blessed Trinity, we can apply it but to a Divine Person. Thus in the Book of Wisdom:

While all things were in quiet silence, and the night was in the midst of her course, Thy Almighty Word leapt down from heaven from the royal throne as a conqueror into *the midst of the land of destruction,* with *a sharp sword carrying Thy unfeigned commandment, and He stood and filled all things with death, and standing on the earth, reached even unto heaven* (Wisd. 18:14-16).

It were difficult not to see in this magnificent description a Divine Person, proceeding from God, "God of God" as the Nicene Creed puts it, *omnipotent,* even as He who sent Him, therefore co-equal to Him. The sacred liturgy appropriates the first three lines of the above text to the Introit of the Mass of the Sunday within the Octave of Christmas, thus applying these words to the mystery of the Incarnation, to the Person of Our Lord, God made man.

Then again in Psalm 106:19-20:
They cried to the Lord in their affliction and he delivered them out of their distresses.

He sent His Word and healed them and delivered them from their destructions.

How marvelously literally does this passage apply to the mission of the second Person by the Father, in the mystery of the Incarnation and to His subsequent work of our salvation! This shows that what is said here of the Israelites was only a prophetic figure of what was to be enacted in our behalf by Our Lord, the great Healer and Deliverer and Restorer, therefore there can be no doubt but that it is here really a question of the second Person of the Blessed Trinity.

Again in Psalm 32: 6 we read:
By the word of the Lord the heavens were established and all the power of them by the spirit of His mouth.

The Fathers of the Church are unanimous in seeing in this verse an express mention of the Three Persons of the Blessed Trinity: the Lord, His Word, and the Holy Spirit: the express name of *the Word* being given to the second Person.

A very striking parallel can be established between several passages of the Sapiential books on the one hand and the Johannine statements as to the Word who was made flesh on the other.

Thus in Ecclesiasticus 1:1 we read:
All wisdom is from the Lord God and has been always with Him and is before all time. And in 1:5, *The word of God on high is the fountain of wisdom.*

In Proverbs (1:20-23; 8:1-36; 9:1-7) wisdom is a person, not a mere abstract concept or an empty word, or a purely figurative expression—a real person, nay, a Divine Person. All that St. John in the first verses of his Gospel sings of *the Word* can be and must be attributed to *Wisdom* as she reveals herself to us in the book that bears her very name and in those of Proverbs and Ecclesiasticus. She speaks, she acts, she is *in God,* she plays before Him and *delights to come among the sons of men,* and walks with them *full of grace and truth.*

And yet it must be owned that, for all the magnificent explicitness of these diverse passages as to the Divine Wisdom or the Divine Word being a distinct Divine Person, it does not appear that any of the inspired sacred writers of that time, still less the bulk of the then People of God, understood their full import. If they did understand it at the time, the tradition of such an interpretation did not last long enough to make a deep impression. It had completely vanished at the time of Our Lord; so much so that the main accusation of the Pharisees against Him was that He proclaimed Himself a Divine Person distinct from the Father. They encompassed His death on the very charge that He had blasphemed by proclaiming Himself the Son of God. Our Lord is the King of Martyrs on that very score, that He laid down His life in defense of the dogma of His Divine Son- ship.

But of this more in the next chapter.

CHAPTER XI

THE ONLY-BEGOTTEN SON

SUMMARY.—That the second Person proceeds from the first by way of generation. Testimony of the Father, of the Son, of the Holy Spirit.

IN the course of a most moving description of the Passion of Christ, one of the prophets exclaims: *His generation who shall declare?* (Is. 53:8).

Who indeed? For to do this is beyond the capacity of any created intellect whether human or angelical. Therefore on so sublime a subject we do not want to say anything of our own. God Himself will declare it to us—God the Father, and God the Son, and God the Holy Ghost—God the Father in many passages of both the Old and the New Testament, God the Son all through His Divine Gospel, God the Holy Ghost by the mouth of the Catholic Church in the formularies of the Faith and throughout her sacred liturgy. Says St. John in his first epistle (1 John 5:7): *There are three who give testimony in heaven, the Father, the Word, and the Holy Ghost.*

Of course, we shall have to make a choice among the immense number of these varied testimonies; but the few to which we shall restrict ourselves will amply suffice for our purpose.

The pious reader who is desirous of drawing from this rather long chapter all the spiritual profit possible, will be well advised to read it by small instalments, slowly, prayerfully. Give an opportunity to the Holy Ghost to open the ears and the eyes of your understanding and to inflame your heart. And when you have thus read this chapter a first time and for its own sake, you may perhaps increase your spiritual gain twofold by reading it a second time, in connection with Chapter X of my fifth volume, *The Mystery of Jesus,* which is all about the two nativities of

403

Christ, the one from the Father, from all eternity, the other from the Virgin-Mother, in the fulness of time.

THE TESTIMONY OF THE FATHER.

In Isaiah we read: *Shall not I that make others to bring forth children Myself bring forth) saith the Lord? Shall I that give generation to others be barren) saith the Lord thy God?* (Is. 66:9).

David, raised in spirit in heaven, hears one Divine Person (Dominus) saying to another Divine Person (Domino meo): *Sit Thou at My right hand until I make Thine enemies Thy footstool ... In the splendors of holiness from the womb, before the day star I begot Thee* (Ps. 109:1-3).

The same David in Psalm 2 sings the glories of the Lord and His Christ whom he introduces saying; *The Lord God hath said to me: thou art My son, this day have I begotten thee;* and further down he gives this exhortation (Hebrew text): *Kiss the Son, lest at any time the Lord be angry and you perish from the just way* (Ps. 2:7, 12).

Jesus being baptized . . . lo, the heavens were opened . . . and behold a voice from heaven saying: This is My beloved Son, in whom I am well pleased (Matt. 3:16, 17).

He was transfigured before (Peter, James, and John), *and behold, a bright cloud overshadowed them, and lo, a voice out of the cloud saying: This is My beloved Son in whom I am well pleased; hear ye Him* (Matt. 17:2, 5).

To Peter who made this solemn profession of faith: *Thou art Christ, the Son of the Living God,* our Lord said: *Blessed art thou, Simon Bar-Jona, because flesh and blood hath not revealed it to thee, but My Father who is in heaven* (Matt. 16:16, 17).

When certain Gentiles came to Philip saying: *Sir, we would see Jesus. ... Jesus answered them saying: The hour is come that the Son of Man should be glorified.... Now is my soul troubled, and what shall I say? . . . Father glorify Thy Name. A voice therefore came from heaven: I have both glorified it and will glorify it again*

(John 12:20, 23, 27, 28).

In the first chapter of his wonderful epistle to the Hebrews, St. Paul writes:

God who at sundry times and in diverse manners spoke, in past times, to the fathers by the prophets, last of all in these days hath spoken to us by the Son, whom He hath appointed heir of all things, by whom also He made the world; who being the brightness of His glory and the figure of His substance and upholding all things by the word of His power, making purgation of sins, sitteth on the right hand of the majesty on high, being made so much better than the angels as He hath inherited a more excellent name than they (Heb. 1:1-4).

THE TESTIMONY OF THE SON.

Luke 2:46-49. *It came to pass that after these days they found Him sitting in the temple in the midst of the doctors, hearing them and asking them questions: and all that heard Him were astonished at His wisdom and His answers.... and His mother said to Him: Son, why hast Thou done so to us? Behold Thy father and I have sought Thee sorrowing. And He said to them: How is it that you sought Me? Did you not know that I must be about My Father's business?*

To Nicodemus, who had come to Him secretly, at night, Jesus said, among other striking revelations about Himself and His mission:

God so loved the world as to give His only-begotten Son; that whosoever believeth in Him, may not perish, but may have life everlasting.

For God sent not His Son into the world to judge the world, but that the world may be saved by Him. He that believeth in Him is not judged, but he that doth not believe is already judged, because he believeth not in the name of the only- begotten Son of God.

When Our Lord had healed, on the Sabbath day, the man who had been languishing thirty-eight years, the Jews persecuted Him. But Jesus answered them: *My Father worketh until now and I work.*

Hereupon therefore the Jews sought the more to kill Him, because He did not only break the Sabbath, but also said God was His Father, making Himself equal to God. Then Jesus answered and said to them: *Amen, amen, I say unto you, the Son cannot do anything of Himself, but what He seeth the Father doing: for what things soever He doeth, these the Son also doth in like manner. For the Father loveth the Son, and showeth Him all things which Himself doth. ...*

For as the Father raiseth up the dead and giveth life, so also the Son giveth life to whom He will ... that all men may honor the Son as they honor the Father. . . . Amen, amen, I say unto you that he who heareth My voice and believeth Him that sent Me, hath life everlasting... . The Father Himself who hath sent Me hath given testimony of Me (John 5).

In the course of the passionate altercation which fills the eighth chapter of St. John's Gospel, the Jews said to Our Lord:

We have one Father, even God. Jesus therefore said to them: If God were your Father you would indeed love Me. For from God J proceeded, and came: for I came not of Myself, but He sent Me. Abraham your father rejoiced that-he might see My day: he saw it and was glad. The Jews therefore said to Him: Thou art not yet fifty years old, and hast thou seen Abraham? Jesus said unto them: Amen, amen I say to you, before Abraham was made, I am.

They took up stones therefore to cast at Him, but Jesus hid Himself and went out of the temple.

At the feast of the Dedication at Jerusalem, Jesus walked in the temple in Solomon's porch, and, to the Jews who came round about Him, He said among other things: *I and the Father are one.*

As was to be expected, in His discourse at the Last Supper, which is such an entrancing effusion of the love of His heart to His Apostles, Our Lord gives many most explicit testimonies of His Divine Sonship. Chapters 13 to 17 of St. John should be read attentively from this point of view. For brevity's sake we shall retain but the following passages:

In My Father's house there are many mansions (John 14:2)—*No man cometh to the Father but by Me* (ibid., 14:6)— *Philip, he that seeth Me, seeth the Father also* (ibid., 9)—*The word which you have heard is not Mine, but the Father's who sent Me* (ibid., 24)—*Amen, amen, I say to you, if you ask the Father anything in My Name, He will give it you* (16:23).

I came forth from the Father, and am come into the world; again I leave the world and go to the Father (16:28).

Father, the hour is come, glorify Thy Son that Thy Son may glorify Thee (17:1).

I pray that they all may be one, as Thou Father in Me and I in Thee, that they also may be one in Us, that the world may believe Thou hast sent Me (17:21).

Father, I will that where I am they also whom Thou hast given Me may be with Me, that they may see My glory which Thou hast given Me, because Thou hast loved Me before the creation of the world (17:24).

He that could read these words of self-revelation uttered by the Son of God under the circumstances which we know without being moved to admiration and intensest love must be very dull indeed.

We come now to the wonderful scene in His sacred Passion, when Our Lord gave the supreme testimony as to His Divine Sonship, that of the sacrifice of His life. It is in a way the grandest page of all the Holy Scriptures, and should be read on our knees, with deepest feelings of adoration of His Divine Majesty and tears of sorrow for our sins. Picture Him in your mind's eye as best you can, standing before the High Priest—His Hands bound as a criminal—silent, calm, majestic.

Last of all came two false witnesses and they said: This Man said, I am able to destroy the temple of God, and after three days to rebuild it. And the High Priest said to Him: Answerest Thou nothing to these things which these witness against Thee? But Jesus held His peace.

And the High Priest said to Him: I adjure Thee, by the living God, that Thou tell us if Thou be Christ, the Son of God.

Jesus saith to him:

Thou hast said it. Nevertheless I say to you, hereafter you shall see the Son of Man sitting on the right hand of the power of God and coming in the clouds of heaven.

Then the High Priest rent his garments, saying: He hath blasphemed: what further need have we of witnesses? Behold, now you have heard the blasphemy: what think you?

But they answering said: He is guilty of death (Matt, 26:60-67).

TESTIMONY OF THE HOLY SPIRIT

In the Apostles' Creed:

"I believe in God the Father . . . and in Jesus Christ, His *only-begotten Son.*"

In the Nicene Creed:

"I believe in God the Father . . . and in the Lord Jesus Christ, the only-begotten Son of God, and *born of the Father before all ages:* God of God, light of light, true God of true God, begotten not made, con- substantial with the Father, by whom all things were made."

In the Athanasian Creed:

"The Son is *from the Father alone,* not made, not created, but *begotten. . . .*

"Our Lord Jesus Christ the Son of God is God and man.

"He is God, *begotten before all ages,* of the substance of the Father, and He is man, born in time of the substance of His Mother, a perfect God and a perfect man, made up of a rational soul and human flesh: equal to the Father in the Godhead, inferior to the Father in His humanity, who, although God and Man, is not two but one only Christ; one indeed, not that the Godhead has been changed in Him into flesh, but because His human nature has been assumed into the Godhead: absolutely one, not by a mixture of the substance, but by the oneness of

Person, for, just as a human soul and body make a man, so also God and man make one Christ."

Almost all the prayers of the sacred liturgy are addressed to God the Father and concluded in this set form: "*through Our Lord Jesus Christ, Thy Son,* who liveth and reigneth with Thee in the unity of the Holy Spirit, world without end."

Other prayers, comparatively few in number, which are addressed directly to Our Lord, have a conclusion which by implication proclaims as clearly as the above His Divine Sonship, thus: "Who livest and reignest with God the Father in the unity of the Holy Spirit, world without end."

Though in this chapter our sole purpose has been to put before the reader the dogma of the procession of the second Person from the First by way of Filiation, still it has not been advisable in the above extracts from the Creeds to separate what is said about the mystery of the Incarnation: the quotation would have appeared too badly mutilated.

Besides, what is mentioned of the mystery of the Incarnation, incidentally and by contrast, helps to set forth the Divine Filiation in bolder relief.

.

CHAPTER XII

HOW ST. JOHN CAME BY THE EXPRESSION "THE WORD"

SUMMARY.—He did not borrow it from Greek lore, but it was revealed to him straight from heaven. The Logos of Hellenic literature is an abstraction; that of St. John and of the Old Testament, a living and Divine Person. Striking corollary.

MODERNIST writers, and, I am sorry to say, even some Catholic ones, are at great pains to explain how St. John came by this wonderful expression *The Word*, in Latin *Verbum*, in Greek *Logos*, meaning thereby the second Person of the Blessed Trinity.

We need not trace it to St. John's borrowing from Greek literature. All we need to do is just read attentively a few verses of the Apocalypse. There the riddle is solved for us most satisfactorily. The idea of the Logos—word and all—was revealed to St. John straight from heaven.

Listen: *And I saw heaven open, and behold a white horse, and He that sat upon it was called Faithful and True, and with justice doth He judge and fight. And His eyes were as a flame of fire, and on His head were many diadems, and He had a name written which no man knoweth but Himself and He was clothed with a garment sprinkled with blood, and His name is called the Word of God* (Apocalypse 19:11, 13).

Is this clear enough and express enough? *And His name is called* THE WORD OF GOD. See how well the description fits our Lord. *The white horse* is the image of the immaculate flesh of His sacred Humanity; *He that sat upon it* is the image of His Human Soul, Faithful and True, indeed, and oh! how valiant in the fight against sin and the powers of darkness! Hence the *many diadems* that are on *His Head*; hence also *His garment sprinkled with blood.* But what is that mysterious name which until then

411

no man knew but Himself? Here it is at last revealed: *And His name is called the Word of God.*

There is no middle course left for us but either to range ourselves with the rationalists who, whenever they come upon such luminous texts, invariably shut their eyes in order not to see them—or to walk with the humble believers (so much more reasonable than the rationalists), who gladly receive the light of Divine revelation and adore it.

Yes, the expression the *Word of God* came to St. John straight from heaven, and this ought to make us cease to be surprised at the sublimity of the beginning of the fourth Gospel.

This St. John wrote, as is now well established, not before but after the grand revelation of the Apocalypse; and the same is true, no doubt, of his wonderful first epistle. Previous to that, he had been, during Domitian's persecution, condemned ' to death, and had, in consequence, suffered martyrdom by being immersed in a tank of boiling oil, though he had been miraculously kept alive, nay, he had come out of this terrible ordeal endowed with renewed vigor. Then he had been exiled in the island of Patmos and there it was that he had the grand visions related in the last book of the canon of the Holy Scriptures.

It is natural to conjecture that, after the particular vision related above, St. John was full of the thought of Our Lord as the Word of God. He thought of Him constantly under this novel aspect, freighted with glorious meaning, and by Divine inspiration his meditation blossomed out in those wonderful first verses of both his Gospel and his first epistle.

Until then he had known Our Lord, indeed, as the *Son of the living God,* as *the Lord,* as the Friend with the wonderful loving heart, as the Redeemer, as the Conqueror of death and sin, and the One seated at the right hand of God in glory: but now he is taken and he takes us with himself into the very heart of the Blessed Trinity. He is made to contemplate and to reveal to us the pure Divinity of Jesus, and all this is borne upon us along with the God-given, God-revealed, new name of *the Word.*

From this it follows that, much as it may seem to agree with the Greek concept of the Logos of Plato and Philo, we must not see in the expression "the Word," applied by St. John to the second Person of the Blessed Trinity, a felicitous adaptation from the Hellenic philosophy.

That to a limited extent the "Logos" of the Greeks and "the Word " of St. John should convey identical meaning seems to me a pure coincidence, though a very happy one, for it must have made it more easy for the Greeks to accept the Gospel of St. John. The rich Hellenic expression "Logos" conveys a wonderful multiplicity of meanings, such as those of word, idea, truth, wisdom, order, the reason of things, measure, beauty; but all these in Greek literature are mere abstractions. Not so in our Gospel of St. John, nor for that matter in the passages quoted in the preceding chapter, from the Sapiential Books of the Old Testament. The Word there is a living entity proceeding from the Supreme Living Entity, God the Father, One with Him and with the Holy Spirit, in fact the *Actus Purus.* He is *The Life,* the Uncreated Life, the fountain-head of all created life; and also *The Light,* the very light of God, the light by which the Father sees His Divine Self and all things else, past, present, or future and all things that are merely possible; and He is also the very *light which enlighteneth every man that cometh into the world.*

Now see what this means for each one of us. Follow my reasoning and apply it to yourself.

I seek out for myself before my birth, before the first ancestors of our race, before the very dawn of creation, and I find myself in the Word of God, in that wonderful reservoir or store-room of all the Divine ideas. There am I, a thing that will be, whose idea is adumbrated, nay, well defined; whose realization is freely, if irrevocably, decided upon; and it is He, the Word of God, who will, in due time, bring me into actual existence, and not only me, but as well everything else which shall ever have the tiniest particle of life. *All things were made by Him, and without Him was made nothing that was made* (John 1:3).

O Word of the Father, O Wisdom of the Father, O splendor and loveliness of the Father, second Person of the Most Holy

Trinity! Thee I love, and adore rapturously —Thee and the Father who begets Thee, and the Holy Spirit who receives from the Father and from Thee; I confess Thou art the very light which enlighteneth the eyes of my weak understanding. Oh! when shall I see Thee as Thou art in Thy Father's bosom?

CHAPTER XIII

THE WONDERS OF THE THIRD PERSON

SUMMARY.—The Holy Ghost was known as a Divine Person by Mary and Joseph, though not by the People of God in the Old Testament. Danger of our conceiving the Holy Ghost ns somehow inferior to the Father and the Son. Precisions formulated in the Athanasian Creed. Personal characteristic of the Holy Ghost: He is the substantial sweetness of the Divine Essence. Testimony of Our Lord about Him. Fecundity of the Holy Ghost. How we stand in regard to Him.

IN the historical accounts of the mystery of the Incarnation given respectively in the first chapter of St. Luke and in the first of St. Matthew, we see that both the Blessed Virgin Mary and St. Joseph understood at once who the Holy Ghost was, to whom the operation of the mystery was attributed—namely, a Divine Person.

Although express mention of the *Spirit of the Lord* is so often made throughout the Old Testament, it does not appear that the People of God had any notion that the expression meant anything more than a Divine attribute, that, in fact, it meant a Divine Person. This revelation was reserved for the fulness of time when Christ, the Son of God, should be born; and Mary, His Virgin Mother, was the first to whom it was made. To Mary's query: *How shall this be done, because I know not man? the angel answering said: The Holy Ghost shall come upon thee, and the power of the Most High shall overshadow thee; and therefore the Holy which shall be born of thee shall be called the Son of God* (Luke 1:34, 35). Thus was for the first time the Holy Ghost revealed in His true character of the third of a Blessed Trinity of Divine Persons, of whom the Son of God is the second, and the Father the first; thus for the first time was the whole mystery of the Blessed Trinity explicitly unfolded.

The Holy Ghost is a Person, a Divine Person, the third of the

Divine Persons in the unity of the Divine Essence.

There may lurk in the mind of some Christians an impression, certainly unconscious and unformulated, that the Holy Ghost is somehow inferior to God the Father and God the Son. This erroneous impression may have arisen mainly from the fact that the Holy Ghost is sent to the world by the Father and the Son, and has been manifested under the humble symbols of a dove and of tongues of fire. Now in order to ward off the danger to the purity and integrity of our faith involved in such a frame of mind, the Church gives us wonderful precisions as to the absolute and all-round equality of the Holy Spirit with both the Father and the Son.

Thus in the Nicene Creed we are made to profess:

"I believe in the Holy Ghost ... Who proceedeth from the Father and the Son: who, with the Father and the Son together is adored and glorified."

And in the Athanasian Creed:

"The Holy Spirit is from the Father and the Son—not made, nor created, nor begotten, but proceeding. ... In this Trinity nothing is before or after, nothing greater or smaller, but all the three Persons are co-eternal and co-equal to each other."

This is so true, that we may, to some extent and with due qualification, apply to the Holy Ghost also what St. John tells us of the Word, in the first verses of his Gospel. Thus we shall obtain the following statements:

"In the beginning was the Holy Spirit,

"And the Holy Spirit *was with God.*

"And the Holy Spirit *was God.*

"The same was in the beginning with God the Father and God the Son.

"All things were made by Him and without Him was made nothing that was made."

Thus far, but no farther, as it is obvious, can we literally apply the first verses of the Gospel of St. John both to the second and to the third Divine Persons. The Holy Ghost is God as fully as the other two Persons, from whom He proceeds in a manner which has no parallel among things created.

Now what is the Holy Ghost in Himself? In what relation does He stand to the other two Divine Persons? What is it that differentiates Him from them and makes Him to be what He is?

It is this:

The Holy Ghost is the substantial, everlasting, infinite sweetness, emanating from the Father and the Son in their mutual embrace of love. Just as God the Son is the splendor of the Divine Essence, so is God the Holy Ghost the sweetness of the Divine Essence.

The inspired writer of the Book of Wisdom exclaims: O *how good and sweet is Thy spirit, O Lord!* (Wisd. 12:1)—and in Ecclesiasticus, Divine Wisdom, the second Person of the Blessed Trinity, is introduced speaking in these terms: *I am the mother of fair love and of fear, and of knowledge, and of holy hope. In Me is all grace of the way and of the truth, in Me is all hope of life and of virtue. Come over to Me all ye that desire, and be filled with My fruits, for My spirit is sweet above honey* (Eccli. 24:24-27).

This, then, is the description of the Holy Spirit, which the devout Christian, the mystic, will retain: the Holy Ghost is the substantial, everlasting sweetness of the Divine Essence as emanating from the Father and the Son; the Holy Ghost is THE VERY SWEETNESS OF GOD.

This peculiar and proper characteristic of the Holy Ghost, that of being the substantial sweetness of the Divine Essence as it proceeds from both the Father and the Son, is borne out by the copious testimony which Our Lord in His discourse at the Last Supper gave to His Apostles. A spiritual sweetness absolutely transcending all experiences of sensitive life, an illuminating and invigorating sweetness whose function in regard to men will be to minister to them consolation and keep them united m the love of Jesus.

If you love Me, says Our Lord, *keep My commandments, and I will ask the Father and He shall give you another Paraclete, that He may abide with you for ever, the Spirit of Truth whom the world cannot receive, because it seeth Him not, nor knoweth Him.*

But you shall know Him, because He shall abide with you and shall be in you (John 14:15-17).

These things have I spoken to you, abiding with you, but the Paraclete, the Holy Ghost, whom the Father will send in My Name, He will teach you all things, and bring all things to your mind, whatsoever I shall have said to you (John 14:25-26).

When the Paraclete cometh, whom I will send you from the Father, the Spirit of Truth, who proceedeth from the Father, He will give testimony of Me (John 15:26-27).

I tell you the truth: it is expedient for you that I go; for if I go not, the Paraclete will not come to you; but if I go, I shall send Him to you; and when He is come, He will convince the world of sin and of justice and of judgement (John 16:7, 8).

I have yet many things to say to you, but you cannot bear them now; but when He, the Spirit of Truth is come. He will teach you all truth; for He shall not speak of Himself; but what things soever He shall hear He shall speak; and the things that are to come He shall show you. He shall glorify Me, because He shall receive of Mine, and shall show it to you (John 16:12-14).

Just before His Ascension into heaven, Our Lord, eating with His Apostles, *commanded them that they should not depart* from Jerusalem, but should wait for the promise of the Father, which you have heard (saith He) by my mouth. . . .

You shall receive the power of the Holy Ghost coming upon you (Acts 1:4, 8).

O Holy Ghost, Sweetness of God and my very God, Thou art the substantial Breath of the Father and of the Son. Thou art Their infinite Sigh of contentment in each other's eternal embrace. Thou art Their Joy!

I adore Thee in Thyself.

And I adore Thee in Them both.

And I adore Thee in each of Them, distinct from both and one with Them: one and the same God!

The Holy Ghost is the only one of the three Divine Persons who does not produce another.

Shall we then conclude that He has no fecundity of His own? Far from this being the case, it is He who produces *ad extra* all those other persons who are divine, not, of course, by nature and essentially, but by communication of supernatural grace.

It is the Holy Ghost who produced that masterpiece of Divine grace, the Immaculate Virgin Mary. It is the Holy Ghost who formed in her and of her virgin flesh, the human body of the Son of God at the same time as He created the human soul of the same and united it hypostatically to the Divine Word. To the Holy Ghost likewise must be attributed the production *in esse gratiae* of each one of the blessed children of God, either angels or men, and the gradual formation of the Church, the true Spouse of Christ.

These operations are the proper work of the Holy Spirit and demonstrate His wonderful fecundity which He holds from the Father and the Son. It is through the operation of the Holy Ghost that the diffusivity of the Sovereign Good which God is in Himself is made manifest.

My soul! Let us now try and see in what relation we stand in regard to the Holy Ghost.

Just as the Holy Spirit is the bond of union between the Father and the Son, so also is He the bond of union between both the Father and the Son and my puny self.

It is through Him that the Father loves the Son, and that reciprocally the Son loves the Father; and it is through Him that I am loved of both the Father and the Son and that I love Them in return.

I am dearly loved of the Father and of the Son: to be so loved what is it but to receive Their Holy Spirit? And, on the other hand, could I in any way return Them love for love but through the help of the Holy Ghost?

Let us even go down a little deeper in this consideration.

Between God the Father and God the Son everything begins with love and ends with love: is it not even so with me? Between God and me, everything begins in love. God has loved me first. God has loved me before He made me, and He made me precisely because He loved me. He loved me as God alone could love, that is to say from all eternity, with a view to all eternity; all the charities of my God towards me have followed hence. It is the substantial love of God, the Holy Ghost who brought me out of the depths of pure nothingness, where but for Him I would have slept for ever.

How rightly then is the Holy Spirit called a Gift, the great Gift, the first Gift! He is the Gift which the Father and the Son eternally bestow upon one another, and oh! how wonderful it is to think of it —He is the first Gift which the Father and the Son bestow upon the reasonable creature, upon me, even me, puny me!

My God, before such marvels I am struck dumb. Love is the only word. Love, love, love. Nothing but love!

CHAPTER XIV

THE BLESSED THREE IN ONE

SUMMARY.—A felicitous dogmatic formula. How the three Divine Persons are supremely One. Various images. A mystery it will remain for ever. Unicity of the Divine Essence and three diverse ways of possessing it. In each Person the mystery stands revealed. *Actus Purus* three times over.

AFTER all we have said thus far, it will readily be granted that in the work of contemplating the Most Holy Trinity it is not a question of our trying to understand this, the very greatest of all mysteries, as high above all the other mysteries proposed to our faith as heaven is above the earth. It is only a question— as we have already stated in a previous chapter—of our apprehending rightly the terms in which the mystery is proposed to our belief, so that we may render our acts of faith in it more real, and thus stir up in our hearts the flame of Divine Love.

In the Second Epistle of St. John we read:

There are three who give testimony in heaven: the Father, the Word, and the Holy Ghost, and these three are One.

Some modern exegetists have tried to make out that those words are an interpolation in the sacred text. Even if this were proved to be the case—which is far from being established upon any evidence that is convincing—the fact of the Church having made them quite her own by inserting them in the sacred liturgy would suffice to confer upon them the dignity of a dogmatic utterance. And, indeed, the mystery of the Blessed Trinity could hardly be set forth in a more felicitous formula: *There are three who give testimony in heaven: the Father, the Word, and the Holy Ghost, and these three are One:* three Persons and one only God.

We must not represent to ourselves the three Divine Persons as we would for instance a group of three angels; for three angels have each one a different nature from the other two. Nor as we

421

would a group of three men, for though they have the same human nature, yet each one of them possesses it so individualized in himself that he stands as a separate, complete substance by himself, with an independent life all his own; whilst the three Divine Persons have together one and the same nature, they are together one and the same substance, one and the same *Actus Purus,* the Supreme Being, supremely One.

Three men holding together their arms lovingly entwined behind each other's necks are for the time being as though they were knit together: one of. them cannot take a step but that the other two go with him; and they may very well be but one in heart; still for all that, they have, even then, each his own separate life, and, of course, they cannot remain thus locked together in such a tight embrace, they will have eventually to separate. Not so the three Divine Persons, because the three together are one only, indivisible, incorruptible Divine Essence.

Once I was shown a very surprising piece of workmanship: an ivory ball, or rather shell, of the size of an orange, pierced with a network of holes which permitted one to see within it a second ball or shell, likewise perforated in the same way, and within the second one also a third. Might this serve as a material image of the manner in which the three Divine Persons are one only God, and within each other? No: for the first ball contains the other two, but is not contained within them; the second contains within itself the third one, but not the first; and the third does not contain either of the other two. Moreover, these three balls are not equal but of gradually diminishing size; whilst the three Divine Persons arc so enclosed within one another that each contains within itself the other two, and the three are absolutely equal in all things, possessing each the same infinite perfections.

Says the Athanasian Creed:

"Such as the Father, such is the Son, such is the Holy Spirit. The Father is uncreated: uncreated also is the Son, uncreated the Holy Spirit. The Father is immense; equally immense is the Son, immense the Holy Spirit. The Father is eternal: eternal is the Son, eternal is the Holy Spirit. The Father is God: God is the Son, God is the Holy Spirit, and yet not three Gods but one only God."

Contrasted with the example of the three ivory balls all in one, the popular comparison of the sprig of shamrock, due to St. Patrick, to help rude minds to give their assent to the fundamental mystery of our faith, is a much more felicitous one, though failing in part, as all comparisons cannot but do. At least the three leaves of the sprig of shamrock are equal to each other and stand all three on one and the same stem. That this cannot serve to illustrate the mutual inhabitation of each of the three Divine Persons in the other two is obvious.

When all has been said or tried, we are compelled to confess that this is a mystery and the greatest of all mysteries. We apprehend the terms in which it is expressed, and we believe it upon God's very own testimony, therefore our assent to it is perfectly rational and fully justified; and, moreover, this assent of ours is in the highest degree supernatural and could not be yielded by us but with the help of Divine grace: but a mystery it remains. And though in glory we shall see God face to face, and witness His Divine life as it is *ad intra* and see the Divine operations of the eternal generation of the Son and the eternal breathing out of the Holy Ghost, a mystery it will remain for evermore to all the elect of God. The reason of this is that, although the created intellect may, by grace, or more expressly by the *lumen gloriae,* be raised above itself to the point of apprehending God in an immediate manner, yet it remains fundamentally and everlastingly incapable of grasping His fulness. Only God can fathom God or understand or express Him fully. However, let us hasten to add that it were wrong to fancy that the happiness of the Blessed will, on this score, suffer any curtailment.

On the contrary, this very fact of the absolute infinitude and incomprehensibleness of God will be to them a subject of joy and of praise, for ever fresh and inexhaustible. They would not have it otherwise, being well aware that a God whom they could comprehend would be no God at all.

The unity of God consists in the unicity of the Divine Essence; the Trinity of Persons is founded on the three diverse ways of possessing this one and the same Divine Essence. The Father possesses it as of Himself, and communicates it to the Son by way of generation. The Son possesses it as received from the Father, and together with the Father He communicates it to the Holy Spirit. The Holy Spirit receives it from both the Father and the Son, united in one principle of active spiration, and does not communicate it to anyone soever, because in Him is completed the full cycle of the Divine life.

Therefore the Father is the Divine Essence uncommunicated; the Son is this same identical Divine Essence communicated from the first to the second Person; the Holy Ghost is that same identical Divine Essence as it is in common in the Father and the Son, communicated jointly from these two first Persons to a third one, by way of spiration.

Thus the three Divine Persons have one and the same Divine Essence, which is absolutely incommunicable to anyone else.

So that, to hold the fulness of the Divine Nature from no one but from oneself is to be God the Father; to hold the fulness of the Divine Nature as communicated from the Father alone is to be God the Son; finally, to hold the fulness of the Divine Nature from both together the Father and Son is to be the Holy Spirit.

The Father is the supreme, absolute, infinite Good; the Son is the Splendor of this supreme, absolute, infinite Good; the Holy Ghost is the Sweetness of this supreme, absolute, infinite Good. (We need hardly advert to the fact that here we use the word Good as a substantive noun, not as an adjective.)

In each of the Divine Persons the whole mystery of the Blessed Trinity stands revealed. I cannot view God the Father without being made aware that He has a Son and loves Him and is loved of Him infinitely, thereby producing the Holy Spirit. I cannot view the Divine Son without being made aware that He has a Father whom He loves and of whom He is loved infinitely and therefore also a Holy Ghost. I cannot view the Holy Spirit without being made aware of whom He is the Spirit—namely, of the Father and of the Son.

Although these three Divine Persons are consubstantial, and co-eternal and co-equal in all things, being one and the same Divine Nature, yet there is between them a natural and inviolable order, the Father being the first, the Son being the second, and the Holy Spirit being the third.

1 am who am, says God to Moses, speaking to him from amidst the flames of the burning bush.

By these words God the Father describes the fulness of life with which He produces and carries in His bosom His Divine Word and the Holy Spirit of love. The Bush represents God the Father, the bright flame which shoots forth from it without separating itself from it, represents the Divine Word; and finally, the heat which emanates at the same time from the bush and the flame, aptly represents the Spirit of love.

Actus Purus, what is it again but God the Father who has never been a single instant without begetting His Divine Son, or without immediately producing with Him His Holy Spirit? Does perchance the fact of there being three distinct Divine Persons preclude the Divine Essence in God the Father from being *Actus Purus?* Nay, it but serves to intensify, if one may say so, the pureness of that act which God the Father is. In reality God is *Actus Purus* three times over. God the Father, through God the Son, in the unity of God the Holy Ghost as He is revealed to us in the Catholic dogma, is such an *Actus Purus* as the sublimest among philosophers never could have risen to conceive.

The whole Divine life proceeds from God the Father to His Divine Son and returns to Him through Their Holy Spirit: proceeds from Him without going out of Him: returns to Him without having been separated from Him. He is a marvelous abysmal fountain which ever springs and ever flows within its own Divine Self.

Oh, let us adore in silence!

PART II
GOD IN HIS WORKS

CHAPTER XV

ON THE OPERATIONS OF GOD CALLED "AD EXTRA"

SUMMARY.—What is meant and also what is not meant by "operations *ad extra.*"How numerous and varied. All summed up in the three: Creation, Redemption, Sanctification—appropriated respectively to the Father, the Son, and the Holy Ghost—and further summed up in the fulfilling of Jesus Christ.

N Part I, just now concluded, we have proposed to the devout contemplation of the mystic, the Lord God in Himself, in His operations *ad intra,* as the theologians put it—that is to say, in those Divine operations which give rise to the Trinity of Persons in the unity of the Divine Essence.

We now proceed to the loving contemplation of God in His Works—that is to say, in the results of His operations *ad extra.*

We call operations *ad extra,* those Divine operations whose terms are the things created.

Of course, this expression *ad extra* must not be taken as meaning that God causes anything whatever to exist independently of Himself, for, as the Apostle says: *In Him we live and move and are* (Acts 17:28). All things are necessarily in God and could not otherwise exist. Even sinners at the very time of their committing sin, even reprobate souls and fallen angels, even hell itself, along with the rest of things created, are in God and God is in them. God is in them necessarily, in virtue of His attribute of Immensity, and they are in God as their First Cause, whose creative energy sustains their being.

The operations of God *ad extra,* considered from our human point of view, are almost infinitely numerous and varied—as numerous, indeed, and varied as individual created objects and persons, past, present, and future, and their component parts, and their actions and reactions upon each other, and their mutual relations. For there is not, nor can there be, a single effect proceeding from a secondary cause, which does not constantly require a vital influx from the Primary Cause—that is to say, from God Himself.

Still, infinitely numerous and varied though they be, the operations of God *ad extra* may all be summed up in the three following:

1. Creation and providential government of the whole world of things, visible and invisible.

2. Incarnation of the Son of God and His Redemption of the fallen race of mankind.

3. Sanctification of the predestinate, during the present life under the regimen of faith, in the next world, through the unfolding of the state of glory.

Each one of those three wonderful operations of God *ad extra* is, for reasons of fitness, appropriated, that is to say, assigned particularly, to one of the Divine Persons: Creation to the Father, Redemption to the Son, Sanctification to the Holy Spirit— though each one of them is really, according to a well-known axiom of dogmatic theology, the joint work of the three Divine Persons.

These three Divine operations sum up the whole activity of God as it is poured out of His own Divine life. Nay, even these three are all summed up in the one great work of God, which is the fulfilling of Our Lord Jesus Christ, *the Son of Man,* as He loved to call Himself, for, indeed, the Most Holy Trinity made all things in Him and for Him. The great work *ad extra* of the Blessed Trinity lies in the fulfilment of Our Lord Jesus Christ in time and throughout eternity.

All that this means we shall only know after the general resurrection of the dead and the Last Judgement.

CHAPTER XVI

ON THE PRETENDED PLURALITY OF WORLDS

SUMMARY.—Two attitudes possible in front of the universe. Not a scrap of scientific evidence in favour of the hypothesis of a plurality of independent closed systems of stars, or of planets being inhabited by other human races. Dogmatic revelation dead against the last supposition. We have a better plurality of worlds to consider.

IN front of the flaming hieroglyphics of the universe of things visible and invisible two attitudes are possible.

Bearing in mind that all those wonderful things are the work of God, a man may endeavour to find in them a certain revelation of Him and ever fresh incentives to love Him. That is the right attitude to take.

Or a man may choose, more or less deliberately and consciously, to look upon all this marvellous universe, simply with secularized eyes, not seeking God in it, nor caring to hearken to any supernal message which it may bear to us.

It is to such men that the wise and bitter Ecclesiastes alluded when he penned this sentence:

God hath made all things good in their time, and hath delivered the world to their consideration, so that man cannot find out the work which God hath made from the beginning to the end (Eccles. 3:11).

People talk glibly of a certain plurality of worlds, by them supposed as probable. Some mean thereby to convey the idea that in the starry world at large or even nearer home to us in some planets of our own solar system, there be lands inhabited by other human races different from our own. Others go still further and would have us believe that far away from our visible universe there exist many conglomerations of stars comparable to our nebula of the Milky Way, but separated from it and from each other, forming each a closed system, perfectly independent and autonomous—a world by itself.

Such fanciful hypotheses may serve to amuse people endowed with more imagination than sound judgement, but the truth must be told that not an atom of scientific evidence can be produced in favour of these contentions.

As far as the pretended stellar systems, independent of our own, are concerned, we must note two things: either these new worlds are by us discoverable or they are not.

If they be not, how can one ever-talk of them? To reason about their existence at all is a futile and first-rate absurdity. Only a mountebank bent upon feeding the gullibility of an ignorant and stupid audience of villagers can have the brazen effrontery to hold forth in the name of science on such a topic.

On the other hand, if these pretended new worlds are by us discoverable, it must be by some direct, experimental process; but this would at once do away with the contention that those starry conglomerations form so many separate and independent closed systems, in no way related to our own. For in order to be discoverable by us, they must, of necessity, have a relation of distance and co-ordination and harmony with our own world, and thereby form one universe with it.

It is clear that such wild speculations can in no way contribute to the furtherance of our knowledge of the real state of things in the universe, still less of our knowledge of the good and loving God; rather the reverse. All they are good for is to puff us up with insane pride and feed our hungry souls with wind.

As for other races of men living, either on the planet Mars or on any other sphere of this vast universe, not only is there not the slightest evidence in favour of such a supposition, but the whole weight of the dogmatic teaching of the Divine revelation goes dead against it. True, neither the Bible nor the Church make any pronouncement expressly against this hypothesis: they simply ignore it. But it does look indeed as if what they do tell us authoritatively, of the manner and scope and limits of creation, could in no way be reconciled with such a plurality of human races. One has only to read attentively and with an open mind the first chapter of Genesis in order to see that the hypothesis of other human races besides our own is as inadmissible as that of other closed systems of worlds.

Then the mystery of the Incarnation and what Our Lord tells us of the Kingdom of Heaven, present and yet to come, and of the Last Judgement and of the regeneration of the whole universe when He will make all things new—all this, I say, seems absolutely to foreclose the idea of any other human race being actually in existence besides our own: though it must be conceded that God could, if He saw fit, create such other races. The question is not one of what is possible, but of what is actually a demonstrable fact.

Let us put away all these childish imaginations.

Whilst silly people pursue a shadow they lose the substance. We shall be better advised, if we make use first of all of what we know for certain.

Thereby we shall find so rich, so delightful, so inexhaustible a fountain of knowledge, so marvellous an object of contemplation, so full of God and making us love Him, that we shall have no use for the above-mentioned idle speculations.

We have, indeed, a better plurality of worlds, and immensely more interesting, if only we will attend to it, worlds within worlds, a hierarchy of worlds, admirably co-ordinated, throwing light one upon the other and leading us up to a wonderful increase of knowledge of the good and loving God who made them.

This we now proceed to consider.

CHAPTER XVII

THE GREATEST WORLD UNDER THE BLESSED TRINITY

SUMMARY.—The greatest world under the Blessed Trinity, the Human Soul of Our Lord Jesus Christ. Infinitude of grace and power it derives from the hypostatic union. Divine diffusiveness. The Divine plan. Order of the Divine emanations.

THE greatest of all worlds—this goes without saying—is the Divine Essence, in the uncreated infinite, ineffable Trinity of its Persons, a world which even eternity will not suffice to enable the blessed Angels and men fully to explore; a world compared with which all others, rolled into one, are but a faint shadow.

Next to the Blessed Trinity, the very first and greatest of all worlds is, not this conglomeration of bright spheres which we call our visible universe, nor the dazzling hierarchy of the nine choirs of the blessed angels in glory, but this mightiest and most ineffable of the works of God, the Human Soul of Our Lord Jesus Christ.

In Our Lord two natures are united in one Person; the Divine Nature of the Son of God, and a human soul and body which derive from their hypostatic union with the Word of God an infinitude of grace, and dignity, and power and resources which baffle all understanding.

Our Lord is the first and last word of Creation, the *Alpha and Omega* of it, as He calls Himself in the Apocalypse (i, 8), the reason of it all, the explanation of all.

Let us try and consider this a little more closely.

The very first feature of God, which His works reveal to us, is His diffusiveness, or that perfection of His in virtue of which He loves to communicate Himself and share His own goods with others.

Even pagan philosophers were aware that "bonum est sui diffusivum," and that God, being supremely good, is therefore supremely inclined to spread abroad and communicate to others some emanations of His.

But as these philosophers were ignorant of the supernatural revelation, they missed much of what it is now our privilege to contemplate. They could never suspect how greatly this infinite fire of love, which God is, wants to manifest itself to us in the burning bush or forest of things created, not consuming them, but speaking to us from their midst, and thereby imparting to us even now, and in proportion as we let Him, a share of His own Divine sanctity and happiness.

It was with this end in view that God resolved to create reasonable beings, angels and men, in His own image and likeness, and to raise them, even from the beginning, to a state of grace absolutely above their natural requirements and out of their natural reach.

And now we come to the nucleus of the question, to the core and heart of the subject of this chapter, for in order to carry out His benevolent intentions God decreed, first of all, that His Son, the second Person of the Holy Trinity, should in the fulness of time become man, and that all things should be put under His dominion, that He might bring them all back to God Who made them, that all things might be in Him, with Him, and through Him sanctified, and give glory to the Blessed Trinity: angels from the beginning, men through the succeeding ages. Church history, nay, the history of the whole world is simply the unfolding of this Divine plan.

Obviously, the hypostatic union with which the human soul and body of Our Lord are favoured is a created grace. It is not an essential, necessary, and eternal union like that which exists between the three Divine Persons. It is the union of a created thing—namely, the Sacred Humanity, with the Person of the Word: a union which is not required by the Divine Nature of the Word, nor by the human nature of the body and soul of Christ, but which is wholly the work of the Divine pleasure of the

Blessed Trinity. But it is really the most marvellous work of God, the one which best reveals, by reflecting them, His infinite perfections.

The human soul of Christ is a marvellous mirror of the power, wisdom, and sweetness of the three Divine Persons. In its quasiinfinite amplitude it is a world, a mighty world, the depth and height and length and breadth of which no created intellect, either human or angelical, will ever be able to fathom. By the grace of the hypostatic union, it extends beyond all limits and is able to afford shelter not only to all men of goodwill, but as well to all the blessed angelic natures. We are all in Christ Jesus. We all receive from His fulness. By grace we are made one with Him. The ivory sphere containing yet others, which we have introduced in a previous chapter, might perhaps serve as an apt illustration of the all-embracing capacity of the human Soul of Our Lord Jesus Christ.

Now we may proceed to set down the order of the Divine emanations on things created.

Roughly speaking it is as follows:

1. The fulness of natural perfection and of Divine grace has been poured upon the Sacred Humanity of Our Lord Jesus Christ.

2. Under Christ, the Head, and in Him and through Him, there has taken place a measureless outpouring of Divine grace upon the Church of the predestinate whilst still actually in the making, and which will ultimately consist of the blessed Angels and all the Saints.

3. And first of all, and in an absolutely transcending proportion, there has been made a pouring out of the grace of God through Jesus Christ, upon the first and principal member *of* His Church—namely, the Virgin Mary, His Immaculate Mother, Queen of Heaven, of all Saints, and of ail creation.

4. Then, out of the fulness of grace of Jesus and Mary, the emanations of God, poured forth upon the nine choirs of the blessed Angels, descending as a marvellous waterfall from

the highest through all the intervening degrees, even to the lowest.

5. Then again, out of the same fulness of the grace of Jesus and Mary, and enlisting the ministrations of the blessed Angels, the Divine emanations spread upon all the Saints that have been made up to this present moment, wherever they be, in the bliss of Paradise, in Purgatory, or here on earth.

6. Then also the Divine emanations on the poor sinners.

For, indeed, whatever of natural goodness still subsists in them is evidently a certain emanation of the very goodness of God and is imparted to them through Jesus Christ.

Thus far we have only spoken of the emanations of God which result in the goodness both natural and supernatural of the reasonable creatures. Now we must mention:

7. The emanations of God upon the whole world of Inferior creatures, conferring upon all and each the goodness of some far resemblance to Him, *quasi per vestigia,* say the theologians, "as through His footprints" or the impress of His creative hands, faintly delineating and in various ways expressing His infinite perfections.

8. Finally, there is even in the fallen angels and reprobate men, as well as in all the other creatures, high or low, animate or inanimate, the emanation of the essential, transcendental goodness of God, by which, as philosophers express it, *ens et bonum* are said to be convertible terms. This means that all that God made, all that actually is, in so far as it is, is good.

Evil is not a positive entity, but only a privation.

There is no substantial evil of any kind. Evil is always, in every case, the absence of some quality or perfection which the nature or circumstances of the subject require. In the reasonable creatures—angels or men—evil results from the guilty acts by which they freely put aside the above described supernatural emanations and wrench themselves from the loving grasp of the Sacred Humanity of Our Lord Jesus Christ.

O my God, Most Holy Trinity, how wonderful art Thou in all the works of Thy blessed hands, but most of all in the greatest, which is the Sacred Humanity of Our Lord Jesus Christ. In Him and with Him and through Him, be Thou blessed for ever!

CHAPTER XVIII

THE NEXT GREATEST CREATED WORLD, THE BLESSED VIRGIN MARY

SUMMARY.—The only created world, after Jesus Christ, in which God has not suffered disappointment. The great things God has done to Mary. How we must understand that she is full of grace. A revelation of God's loving kindness and mercy. The universal Mother. The pedestal of the Golden Candlestick.

THE second greatest created world, situate immediately below the Sacred Humanity of Our Blessed Lord, is the marvellous one formed by the Person of the ever Blessed Virgin Mary, with hen immaculate body and soul, in their wonderful relations to each of the three Divine Persons and to all the angels and men and to the inferior material universe.

Mary is, of all pure creatures, the one nearest to God, most like to Him, the one who received most from Him and who renders to Him the greatest glory.

Together with the Sacred Humanity of Our Lord, with which she is so intimately connected and from which she receives all her reflected bright light, even as the moon takes its own from the sun, Mary is the only created world in which God has not suffered some disappointment; for, on the one hand, Our Lord being God and man cannot be ranged among the pure creatures, and, on the other hand, the worlds inferior to Mary, as we shall soon see, have each failed, as a whole, to correspond to the will of God in their behalf.

Mary is, after Our Lord Jesus Christ, the most splendid revelation of God. She herself proclaims in her Magnificat: *He that is mighty hath done great things to me.* No mistake about this; Mary stands as the greatest manifestation of how far the power of God extends in the making of a pure creature like unto Him. This may be put in relief by a few questions. Thus:

Can Divine Omnipotence, out of the whole *massa perdita* of a fallen race, preserve incorrupt and save beforehand, by a higher redemption, one single member to be used for the purpose of the future redemption of the others? Mary is the reply.

Can Divine Omnipotence render a human creature not only immaculate in her conception, but, moreover, without the least interfering with the free play of her will, impeccable? Mary is the reply.

Can Divine Omnipotence raise a pure creature to the very confines or borderland, so to say, of the Godhead, *usque ad fines divinitatis* (to use a forcible and felicitous expression of Suarez); so that she should become the true and natural mother of God, and bring forth in her virgin flesh the Eternal Word of God? Mary is the reply.

Can Divine Omnipotence form a human heart so deep and so strong as to contain, on the one hand, more sorrow at some time of her earthly life than has ever been experienced by all angels and men *in viâ;* and, on the other hand, more joy—at least after her admission to the Beatific Vision—than will ever be imparted to all angels and saints together? Mary is the reply. For, indeed, Mary's joys over her Divine motherhood for ever will be as deep and sublime as heaven itself; and her compassion and sorrow over the passion and death of her Divine Son have been as vast as the ocean, says the prophet Jeremias (Lam. 2:13).

Truly *He that is mighty hath done great things* to her.

The ambassador-angel, speaking in the name of his Master the Tri-une God, proclaimed her "full of grace."

In order that we should realize the significance of this praise, we must bear in mind what a wonderful capacity God has given her. The blessed Angels are all full of grace, so are all the Saints in Paradise, nay, even sometimes whilst still here on earth; but Mary has the capacity of the ocean.

Compared to her the blessed Angels and all the Saints are as so many vessels of all sizes deposited on the sea-shore, which are all filled from its very fulness without causing any appreciable diminution of the same. True, the ocean itself has its limits, and so has the grace of the Blessed Virgin Mary, but those limits can be known but of God.

More than anything else, Mary is to us a revelation of the most touching attribute of the Divine Essence, its goodness, or, in other terms, its loving-kindness, and in Mary this revelation is brought within the grasp of our limited capacity.

God in Himself is far too much above us, too dazzling for our puny understanding, but now behold Mary, a creature even like ourselves—a woman—the Virgin Mother of His Son, bearing Him a little child in her arms, and presenting Him to the loving adoration of the world: Can anything more sweet be imagined? Gould any more touching demonstration of the loving-kindness of God be invented?

And, above all, Mary expresses and puts in strong relief this peculiar aspect of the goodness, of the loving-kindness of God, the Divine Mercy. It is not for nothing, that her heart has been created so deep and wide: it was to embrace in her motherly love, together with her Divine Son, all that are Christ's, both angels and men. More than the first Eve, Mary is the universal Mother, and bears a personal, providential relation not only to each of the redeemed of her Divine Son, but also to each of the blessed pure spirits. This we shall see dearly when we come to heaven. Meanwhile, we believe it and praise the Divine Goodness for it.

She is the created pedestal of the Godhead.

Upon that pedestal stands that seven- branched golden candlestick, the Light of the world, Our Lord, from whom the nine choirs of angels and all the orders of the Saints receive their illumination, in time and throughout all eternity.

Only two virgins ever bore a son— namely, first and from all eternity God the Father; and then, in time, Mary. Thus is Mary a certain revelation of God the Father, and of the Virginal Fecundity that characterizes Him.

The Apostles have duly celebrated the immensity of the grace of Mary when they wrote in the Creed:

"I believe in God the Father ... and in Jesus Christ His only

Son ... WHO WAS BORN OF THE VIRGIN MARY."

O my God, Most Holy Trinity, how admirable art Thou in that masterpiece of Thy creative hands, the ever Blessed Virgin, the unique Daughter of Thee, O God the Father, the incomparable Mother of Thee, O God the Son, the spotless Spouse of Thee, O Holy Spirit! Be Thou, O most Holy Trinity, blessed in her for evermore!

CHAPTER XIX

THE THIRD GREATEST CREATED WORLD

SUMMARY.—The Church of the Predestinate. Of what elements it is made up. God has suffered some disappointment: first in angels, then in the human race. Each predestinate is a little world within the greater one. Each single angel, a whole nature. The first Church Militant. That God reveals Himself in the Saints. Their wonderful personality. Many vessels of gold, adorned with every precious stone. Their various orders.

THE third greatest created world is the Church of the Predestinate. Still in the making as it is, it nevertheless reveals already the glory of the Blessed Trinity—the power, the wisdom, and the goodness of God—to a marvellous extent.

It is made up of the following elements: first, all the blessed angelic natures, then all the departed souls of men who are already in heaven or in purgatory, and, finally, all the men of goodwill on earth.

The Church of the Predestinate was prefigured in the mysterious chariot of which both the prophet Ezechiel, in his first chapter, and St. John the Evangelist, in chapters iv and v of his Apocalypse, give us a description, and which Ezechiel calls *the vision of the likeness of the glory of God* (Ezech. 2:1). It already has a wonderful history in the past ages, and, furthermore, the promises of eternal life, that life of which we sing in the Nicene Creed: *Credo . . . vitam venturi saeculi.*

True, it must be owned that God has suffered some disappointment—to express it in a human way—first of all in the angels, a third part of whom fell away from grace, and then in the human race as a whole, since Adam and Eve fell away from their state of innocence and we all fell away in them (the Blessed Virgin Mary alone excepted), and since even after the Redemption of thè Cross, so many men will not be saved. But

445

this only serves the more to show to us what a wonderful work of God is the Church of the Predestinate; hewn out, so to say, stone by stone, from these two great quarries, the angelic world as God created it in the beginning, and the whole human race as God is creating it through succeeding centuries.

Each of the blessed Angels and each of the Saints, whether already glorified or not, is in himself a revelation of God, a little world within the greater world of the full assembly of them.

A little world which gives to God particular glory, and which adds to the splendour of the whole; a touch, as it were, of colour and a distinct note in the melody, which could not be dispensed with. It is a wheel within a wheel of the mysterious chariot *of the vision of the likeness of the glory of God—rota in medio rotae*—a fixed star out of the dazzling galaxy of the nine angelic choirs and the various orders of the Saints. But what a multitude of them I and how therein also shines the power and the beauty and the love of the Most Holy Trinity who made them!

To speak first of the blessed Angels in particular.

Each of them is a pure spiritual nature, made in the image of God, intelligent and free, simple, incorruptible, inexterminable; raised by grace to the supernatural state, from which not only he never fell away, but did not waver a single instant; destined from the first to eternal glory. He was put upon his trial together with all the other angels, he bravely fought and conquered and was immediately crowned, and is now gloriously employed in active service for the formation of the Church of the Predestinate, as it is to be after the end of the world.

Each of the angels is a whole nature, different from all the others, a world in himself, in which the attributes and perfections of the Blessed Trinity reflect themselves and shine forth with an exclusive lustre, peculiar to that angel. They are all related to one another and co-ordinated into various choirs of dazzling cumulative beauty. They are most noble children of the heavenly Father; willing, whole-hearted servants of the Incarnation, and our own loving elder brothers. Before we came upon this planet of ours they were the first Church Militant, and though their trial was swift, it was keenly searching.

With inexpressible spiritual sadness, they witnessed the defection and fall of those who were their well-beloved brethren, who in their very midst suddenly turned traitors to God, enemies of themselves, tempters of their brethren, in one word devils, and became monstrously malicious and ugly. Under the leadership of Michael, the faithful angels stood the brunt of the battle. With their eyes fixed on God, they bravely fought for justice and truth, without any respect of persons, without false commiseration or unworthy bargaining. They came out of this terrible ordeal, having preserved absolutely unsullied their first sanctity, infused in them at the moment of their creation: nay, it was then and there, by the very act, prodigiously increased, and at once blossomed out into the glory of the Beatific Vision. This much about the blessed Angels in glory.

And now about the Saints, those other living stones of the heavenly Jerusalem that is in the making. By Saints I mean all men of goodwill, wheresoever they be, in heaven or in purgatory or here on earth. But in regard to those on earth I mean particularly Christians who have passed the first two stages of the spiritual life and are arrived at the Way of Union. They are the perfect ones, the heroes of the spiritual life, the ideal Christians.

Now in all these, wherever they be, God reveals Himself, shining forth through their body and soul. God manifests His power, wisdom, and love in each of them, in an original, unique manner according to each one's peculiar character, so that we can truly say of each of them: *There was not found the like of him: Non est inventus similis illi* (Eccli. 44:20).

The Saints are, of all men, the only ones who develop their own personality to the highest degree. Other people servilely copy or plagiarize each other. As for those young and giddy ones who behave outrageously and give as an excuse that they want to live their own lives and are seeking to realize themselves, be it known that they are duping and deluding themselves egregiously. Only the Saints live their own lives and realize themselves, and they do it thoroughly, splendidly, magnificently. And they do it almost unknown to themselves: their only care being to root out of themselves all disordered affections and to allow God to have His own way with them in everything. But the result is marvelous.

The inspired writer of Ecclesiasticus has penned six wonderful chapters in praise of the holy men of old, which I wish I could insert bodily here, were it not for their great length. They are chapters 44 to 50 inclusively. I ask my reader to look them up for himself in his Bible and ponder over them at leisure. I will cull out of them only one verse. In chapter 1, verse 11, it is said of Simon the high priest that he was *as a massy vessel of gold, adorned with every precious stone.* Now this applies as well to each one of the dear Saints of God wherever found, but to each with a difference.

Let us represent to ourselves an immense number of vessels of purest gold, in an infinite variety of forms and sizes, every one chiselled differently.

Each is adorned with the large carbuncles of Faith, Hope, and Charity, and with the four gems of Prudence, Justice, Temperance, and Fortitude, and with the countless precious pearls and diamonds of their own personal merits. The rim of every vessel is outwardly hung round with seven rings or handles of a metal more precious than gold, I mean the seven gifts of the Holy Spirit, inserted in the soul through the sacraments, and ready to the hand of God to lift up the vessel and raise it to any height of heroic sanctity, as soon as it has been emptied of all created affections and has filled itself with God, God, God alone.

I say, represent to yourselves an immense number and variety of such vessels in heaven, in the fiery furnace of Purgatory and here on earth, scattered through the length and breadth of the Church Militant. Now, will not such a magnificent display of the handicraft of the three Divine Persons help us to conceive an exalted idea of Him who made them for His glory? And will it not move us to praise Him and to love Him?

The bare enumeration of the various orders of Saints ought to throw us into raptures, if we will only think over the perfections of God which they reflect and reveal. Innocents, virgins, confessors, penitents, pontiffs, martyrs, patriarchs, prophets, doctors, apostles, and apostolic men. Truly *God is admirable in His saints* (Ps. 67:36).

Join all these to the nine choirs of the blessed Angels, and you have the Church of the Predestinate as it is now, and you obtain a glimpse of what is, indeed, a most marvellous work of the Blessed Trinity.

It takes this great multitude of angels and saints, and those that will in the future be added to their number, somehow to express the sanctity of Our Lord Jesus Christ.

They are the garden of God, where the three Divine Persons take their delight.

They are the sea of glass before the throne of the Divine Majesty, which receives and reflects faithfully the image of the ineffable sanctity of the Blessed Trinity.

They are the living lyres vibrating under the fingers and breath of the Holy Spirit, to form the grand concert of the perfect praise of God.

O my God, Most Holy Trinity, Father, Son, and Holy Ghost, be Thou blessed for ever in this magnificent work of Thine, the Church of the Predestinate!

CHAPTER XX

THE WORLD OF MATTER, FROM STARS TO ATOMS

SUMMARY.—It is the humblest in the scale of worlds as we are considering them, and still very stupendous. The untutored Arab *venus* the European atheist. A starlit night. The atom of hydrogen. The composition of matter, of ether. Man's mind superior to the world of matter. Creation a thin veil on the radiant face of God.

IN the scale of worlds as we are considering them by means of the joint light of reason and revelation, and as so many mirrors which reflect the glory of the. Blessed Trinity, the humblest, the least, and yet, indeed, a magnificent work of God, is this material universe of ours: this stellar world of which our solar system is but a very tiny component, whilst our sphere, the earth, seems to be all but lost in its immensity, as a pebble on the seashore, as a speck in a sunbeam, as an atom, comparatively speaking.

A very beautiful world!

The Church does not hesitate to sing in the *Te Deum:* O *thrice Holy Lord, God of Hosts, full are the heavens and the earth of the majesty of Thy glory.*

Full with the praise of the glory of the majesty of God: yes, so they are, but only for those who have ears to hear and eyes to see.

This stupendous concave, as it seems to us, of the blue firmament overhead, with its myriads of stars and simply inconceivable stellar spaces, which so wrought upon mad Pascal's sensibilities, let us but fill it with the sweet presence of the loving God, and we shall derive from its contemplation an overwhelming torrent of joy.

Here is the *Pensée* of the celebrated man of genius with a strain of melancholy and a touch of Jansenism: "*Le silence éternel de ces espaces infinis m'effraye"* (The eternal silence of those infinite spaces affrights me).

But they are not silent, and he ought to have known it; they speak, they sing, they shout.

From the dawn of creation they sound forth in an unbroken melody, the praise of the Most Holy Tri-une God who made them.

> *The heavens show forth the glory of God,*
> *And the firmament declareth the work of His hands.*
> *Day to day uttereth speech.*
> *And night to night showeth knowledge.*
> *There are no speeches nor languages,*
> *Where their voices are not heard.*
>
> Ps. 18.

The untutored Arab of the desert, the natives of both Americas and of Australia, all hear and understand. It takes a sophisticated and effete civilization as that of Europe nowadays to produce this monstrosity, an atheist, upon whose sensibilities and intelligence the appeal of the firmament by day and night falls in vain.

The most magnificent and entrancing spectacle set before our eyes is, without any doubt, that of a starlit night, especially in those regions where the atmosphere is purest, as for instance in the Sahara Desert. It is far more entrancing and beautiful than the dazzling splendours of midday or the wonderful display of colours of any dawn or sunset, because more mysterious, more awe-inspiring, more heavily freighted with a Divine message.

The splendours of early dawn, or midday, or sunset are, after all, but the illumination of a tiny corner of our solar system, whilst a starlit night seems to open before us a vista of infinitude itself.

And it is not only in its prodigious extent, the dimensions of which we utterly fail to realize, but as well in its every detail, down to the smallest, such as an insect, a blade of grass, a dewdrop, a grain of sand, an atom, that the universe bears the impress of God, the seal of the Most Holy Trinity, showing forth infinite power, infinite wisdom, and infinite sweetness. These tiny objects, each and all, show forth the omnipotence of God. Each of them is a Divine idea realized in a concrete form, a small world in itself; a surprising complex of laws and of actions and reactions; a dosed system: in a word, an abyss wherein man's reason loses itself hopelessly.

Take, for instance, an atom of hydrogen.

It is the most common and best known of all so far. By the complexity of its structure, the intensity of its life, the prodigious swiftness of the movements of its component electrons around a central nucleus, it is, upon an infinitesimally small scale, the very counterpart of any of the solar systems which fill the depths of the firmament.

By methods of observation which it would require a whole volume to explain to the uninitiated, it has been ascertained that in this, the simplest of all atoms, each of the particles which surround its central nucleus performs no less than five million oscillating movements in a second. But that is a comparatively modest number. The atoms of other so-called simple elements show an immense increase of swiftness of movements, and we are yet but on the threshold of the new world of wonders which the discovery of radium and other such substances have of late been opening before us.

From this it will be seen that we are very far, indeed, from having reached the final word on the question of the physical constitution of matter. It seems that the solution of this problem recedes hopelessly as we advance in the path of scientific discoveries. Since atoms are not, as was formerly thought, either homogeneous or insécable—that is to say, indivisible—since they are found to consist of a nucleus around which, as around a central sun, a whole train of minutest satellites oscillate or revolve with stupendous velocity, the question now arises: What is the composition of these nuclei themselves, and what that of their electrons?

We are told by the most eminent and trustworthy physicists that the density of the nucleus of an atom of gold is so prodigious that if a woman's thimble were filled with such nuclei its weight would be something like three hundred millions of kilogrammes. We may well gasp with astonishment. Truly the world of the infinitesimally small is no less marvellous than that of the seemingly infinitely great. Man finds himself poised between these two extremes and it were difficult to decide which gives us a more sublime idea of the omnipotence of its Maker.

Notice that all we have said thus far, and all that our great scientists tell us, leaves absolutely untouched the further question of the constitution of ether, that imponderable fluid in which we are immersed and with which are permeated all the elements of this material universe. Here is, indeed, a beautiful created image of the mysteriousness, omnipresence, invisibility, all-em- bracingness of God and of His sweet way of dealing with us. But, with all its stupendous recent discoveries, will not human science, faced with such enigmas, be well advised to keep an attitude of modesty and humility, and go repeating: 0 GoJ, my GoJ, Aow *admirable, how unsearchable Thou art in all Thy works?*

It is related in the life of St. Benedict that he once had a vision of the glory of God and that the whole universe was shown him as no bigger than a mote disporting in a sunbeam. Now, the mere fact that one is able to take in such a statement shows that the mind of man is superior to the bulk of this mighty universe, and therefore a greater world than it. It is of a different order of greatness. It is made to take in God Himself, the three Divine Persons of the Blessed Trinity; it is destined one day to see God as He is, and face to face.

Meanwhile nature and its immensity, and with the dense forest of beautiful objects it presents to our observation, is for us another garden of God, where He walks mysteriously and wishes to talk to man whom He made in His own image and likeness.

We may well fancy that it is also something like what we may call the playground of the blessed angelic natures, and one day to be also our own playground after the general resurrection, when our regenerated bodies will have put on spirituality.

Then we shall know to what end God has made such a bewildering profusion of stars. The last word about them has not yet been said. What children we are! Can we not make credit to God of a few centuries?

The whole material universe, when we look at it rightly, seems to give us an idea of the exuberant life of God and of His serenity.

It is a veil spread between the majesty of the Lord God and us, His reasonable creatures, a transparent veil, which if it does not allow us to discern the lineaments of His loving countenance, at least allows somewhat of the rays of His glory to pass through, so tempered that we may not be overwhelmed.

O heavenly Father: Most Holy Trinity, who hast made for Thine own glory this wondrous world of matter, I adore Thee, I thank Thee, and I love Thee!

CHAPTER XXI

THE ROMANCE OF OUR LITTLE EARTH

SUMMARY.—The Earth in itself an object full of interest. The abode of Godlike Man, of the Militant Church, of the Blessed Sacrament. Narrow limits within which man can exercise his sovereignty. The mystic has chosen the better part.

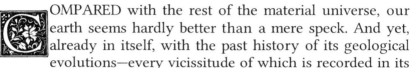COMPARED with the rest of the material universe, our earth seems hardly better than a mere speck. And yet, already in itself, with the past history of its geological evolutions—every vicissitude of which is recorded in its superposed strata, if only we could read them aright— with the deeper secrets it carries in its mysterious bosom, with the wonders and riches it displays on its surface, with its inexhaustible fertility and the marvellous economy of its external structure, with its systems of mountain-ranges and rivers, its teeming manifestations of vegetative and animal life, with the mighty embrace and pulsations of the ocean which covers seven tenths of its surface—the earth, our little earth, is an object full of interest and well worth retaining our attention for its own sake.

It is so situated in the solar system as to make the sun, the moon, and the stars subservient to the needs of its inhabitants. Its movements of rotation on its axis and of translation around the sun give rise to the phenomena of alternate day and night and of the succession of the seasons of the year, which bring about the atmospherical conditions needful to foster and develop the whole scheme of animal and vegetative life as it revolves around man, its central figure: —man who is neither a pure spirit like the angels, nor simply a brute like the dog, the horse, a fish, a bird, or an insect, but composed of an earthly body and an immortal soul united in one person.

The real interest and dignity of the earth come precisely from its being the abode of man, of princely man, of Godlike man.

The earth is the narrow promontory from which man is expected to view the rest of the universe and read the magnificent scroll of its wonders, himself being the greatest of all, and the masterpiece of the world.

The earth is the altar of the material universe at which priestly man is expected to officiate in the name of all nature, to raise the voice of adoration and praise to the Maker of all.

The earth is the abode of the present Militant Church, the stage of the *Divina Comedia* of the dealings of God with fallen man, the place where is now carried on the *praelium magnum,* the mighty struggle between the blessed Angels and the evil spirits, of which struggle the stakes are the immortal souls of men.

The earth has seen Adam and Eve innocents, and the Son of God made Man, and His sweet Mother.

It has been drenched with His sacred Blood.

It is now the abode of His Blessed Sacrament and the scene of the perpetual Sacrifice of the Mass, as had been predicted by the prophet Malachias: From *the rising of the sun even to the going down, My Name is great among the Gentiles: and in every place there is sacrifice, and there is offered to My Name a clean oblation. For My Name is great among the Gentiles, saith the Lord of Hosts* (Mal. 1:11.)

The earth is the place where every man is expected to fit himself for eternal life during the short but eventful span of his temporal one; therefore whence his soul is to take its flight to heaven.

King of this material universe though he be, man at present can exercise his sovereignty but within very precise and narrow limits. This is quite providential, for, as long as we are in our present condition, we are as little children under age, who cannot be trusted, whom it is necessary to surround with all sorts of safeguards— naughty children, *enfants terribles, touche-à-tout,* who still find the means of inflicting grievous harm on themselves and others.

The surface of the earth and of the ocean, and a little below that surface (oh, very little indeed, comparatively), such is the field wherein man is free to carry out his experiments and to exercise his restless activity.

The sun, the moon, and the stars are out of his reach, at a safe distance, so that he can see them and hear their message but not interfere with them, which he certainly would do if he were allowed—with what catastrophic results may be left to our imagination to picture.

Even in his narrow field of action man's control of the elemental forces of nature is but very precarious. The atmosphere, water power, steam, electricity, and all other natural agencies made use of by ourselves in mechanical contrivances, be these as ingenious as they will, ever tend to resume their natural independence, so that if the harness man has put on them happen to be weak at some point and to give way, these elementary forces are liable suddenly to kill him and toss his body away as a dead fly or a straw in a whirlwind.

Much better advised therefore, though greatly daring, the mystic when to these rash experiments he prefers that of seeking after God in the contemplation of the universe. He then finds both God and nature conspiring to forward him in his noble undertaking.

Moreover, at the same time as things visible speak to him of the invisible ones of which they are the signs and figures, he will find that reciprocally the supernatural order of grace and glory, such as it is revealed to us by the teaching of the Church, gives him the key to the great puzzle of the material universe.

In the eyes of the mystic, nature is wholly steeped in the supernatural and illumined with a light which comes from above. Faith holds for him the torch of analogy. Has not St. Paul said: *The invisible things of Him, from the creation of the world, are clearly seen, being understood by the things that are made: His eternal power also and His Divinity* (Rom. 1:20); and again: *By faith we understand' that the world was framed by the Word of God, that from invisible things visible ones might be made* (Heb. 11:3).

The earth is the graveyard of the whole human race, its surface thick with the dust of many thousands of generations. However, the day will come when it will have to give up all its dead. And this will be but the prelude to the earth's own regeneration; for Christ is to say *ecce nova facto omnia— Behold I make all things new* (Apoc. 21:5). I take it that the new earth here spoken of is the same identical planet of ours, but regenerated by fire, purified of all contamination of the sins of men, and made worthy to enter into the new heaven of God, and be a part of it for all eternity.

Were we not right in speaking of the history of our planet viewed from the time of its creation to that of its future final regeneration, as of a romance? And shall we not give due praise to God for it?

Blessed art Thou, O Lord, the God of our fathers, and worthy to be praised and glorified and exalted above all for ever, and blessed is the holy Name of Thy glory, and worthy to be praised and exalted above all in all ages,

O let the earth bless the Lord, let it praise and exalt Him above all for ever.

O all ye things that spring up in the earth, bless the Lord: praise and exalt Him above all for ever.

O all ye beasts and cattle, bless the Lord: praise and exalt Him above all for ever.

O ye sons of men, bless the Lord: praise and exalt Him above all for ever.

O ye servants of the Lord, bless the Lord, praise and exalt Him above all for ever,

O give thanks to the Lord, because He is good, because His mercy endureth for ever and ever (Dan. 3:52-89 *passim*).

After the general resurrection man will no longer be the inhabitant of this small planet, the earth. To that glorified son of God, the whole material universe will be given as His proper abode, to range in at liberty, by means of the wonderful qualities of spiritualized bodies: impassibility, subtilty, and agility, to which will be added that of brightness as of the sun. Through

Jesus Christ, the God-made-mari who is the centre of all things, and for the delight of His redeemed, the whole material universe, and, of course, the earth within it, will be assumed in glory and become part of the heavenly Jerusalem.

CHAPTER XXII

A FALLEN WORLD IN COURSE OF BEING RECLAIMED

SUMMARY.—The human race. How God deals with it. Every man a little world. Worth and capacity of a human soul. Actual population of the globe. Rate of births and deaths. How this works out thus far, for a grand total. Our own image in God. Original sin no obstacle to the plan of God.

WE are too much accustomed to narrow views on the subject of the human race. Scarcely ever do we try to realize of what a vast multitude, actually living upon earth, we are a unit; still less do we extend our intelligent estimation of the bulk of the human race beyond the limits of the present time. And yet, those that have lived before us and died, have not gone entirely out of existence. Their souls are somewhere: even the dust of their dead bodies is not altogether vanished. It is all in the sight of God and ready to His omnipotent hand. All these men and women from the time of Adam to this day, and on to the last day of the world, all these, and we along with them, will be made to live again in the integrity of our human nature.

Thus viewed, is not the human race a great creation of God, a mighty world, a revelation of the power and the wisdom and the goodness of God, of His justice, and of His merciful ways?

God deals with the human race as a whole, and also with each one of its members individually.

God's providence governs the whole race and leads each separate member of it through the various phases of his trial to. his ultimate end.

Each human individual is in himself a little world—little comparatively speaking, and yet great, very great, indeed, very unknown, almost unexplored—with wide stretches of its mysterious body, and of its still more mysterious spiritual essence, lying as so many *terrae incognitae,* which are as yet unmapped.

In this region, as in others, the more we know the more do we find that there remains to be discovered. "Know thyself," urges the ancient philosopher. Ah! we are far from such knowledge. Only after the general resurrection and in the light of the Beatific Vision shall we realize the wonder that each human individual being is. He is a world, I repeat, a vast and deep world; and though his body is a comparatively small, nay, very small organized parcel of the visible universe, in his soul man transcends incomparably the whole universe of matter. A single human soul is of such worth in the eyes of Him who knows, because He made it, because He made it to His own image and likeness, that it took nothing less than the life-blood of the Son of God to redeem it. It is of such vast dimensions that the three Divine Persons want to come into it and make it their abode and take in it their delight, even now—a world still in the making, and it lies with each of us to make it, with God's help, ever so much larger and more beautiful.

And now let me try and realize that I am a mere unit of such a vast multitude of actual inhabitants of the earth; a member of a family of some two milliards of human beings actually living and breathing. Two milliards! In ciphers 2,000,000,000, and this is but an insignificant portion of the total human race, as a moment's reflection will show.

A moderate estimate of the average number of births happening daily is placed at 80,000 a day; the average death-rate being about the same.

Now see how this works out, in a year and then in a century. In multiplying those 80,000 by 360 we obtain as a result the sum of 28,800,000 (twenty-eight million eight hundred thousand) of human births in one year. Multiply this by 100, and you obtain nearly three milliards of human births; in exact number 2,880,000,000 of births in a century. If we are satisfied to stand by the chronology of Usher, the most convervative and moderate of all, and suppose that the age of the world is only 6,000 years, by multiplying these last figures by sixty we obtain the appalling sum of one hundred and seventy-two billions and eight hundred millions of human beings. But if we take into account the fact that the uniform rate of births could not have been realized in the beginning nor directly after the Great Flood, we may, for the sake of stricter accuracy, reduce these figures by two milliards and eight hundred millions, thus obtaining, as our final grand total, the round sum of one hundred and seventy milliards of human beings created thus far.

This, of course, to say nothing of the multitude known to God alone, of those that will be born afterwards, since we do not know how long the present order of things will yet persevere. It may last a great many more centuries.

Well now, what an immense multitude is this of noble servants of God, each with an immortal soul, each made in the likeness of God, each primarily destined to know, love and serve God, each my brother, each dear to God, known of Him by name, and dealt with by Him singly, personally, and for his own sakel But what a grand idea is not this calculated to give us of the power and wisdom and sweetness of the Creator!

We have all been created innocent and holy in Adam, and an object of the love of God from all eternity, in this our primitive innocence, and every one of us destined to eternal glory.

God loved us for what He was to put in us of His own sanctity, first in the present life on earth and then later in heaven. There is in God an image of each one of us men, as God willed us to be, and this ideal image of ourselves is much better than its actual realization in existence.

Whence is this difference? It arises from the fact that on the one hand, in the making of the image of us as God loved us, God alone had a hand, and therefore made it perfect; on the other hand, in the making of our actual selves, not God alone, but, moreover, the first Adam and after him a whole line of our intermediate ancestors, and finally, our very selves, each on his own account, have had a hand.

This applies to all the children of Adam and Eve, to all the tribes of men, past, present, and future; to the white races, to the yellow ones, to the black, and to the red. Etery man of us has his own image or archetype in God, and that image a noble one, and it is quite possible that our judgement will be accomplished simply by confronting what we have made ourselves into, with what God wanted to make us.

The dreadful accident to our nature, of the original sin of Adam and Eve, with its far-reaching consequences, does not stand, nevertheless, in the way of God's plan being realized. It makes it the more wonderful in its execution. All had perished in Adam, Mary, the Immaculate Virgin Mother of the Redeemer, alone excepted. Is it not worthy of the omnipotence and wisdom and sweetness of God to have changed all this *massa perdita* of the human race into a quarry from which to extract the future stones of the heavenly Jerusalem that is a-building?

All had perished in Adam, all are redeemed in Jesus Christ. Redeemed—that is to say, paid for in advance, if they will only consent to be saved. The work of hewing out one by one the elect living stones will never stop until the last of the predestinate in the Divine plan will have been consummated in sanctity.

Then will the present order of things come to an end, at the blast of the angelic trumpet by the command of the Son of Man. Then the *dead shall rise again incorruptible. Then shall come to pass the saying that is written:* Death is swallowed up in victory. *O death, where is thy victory? O death, where is thy sting?* (1 Cor. 15:52, 54, 55).

Well may we exclaim again With St. Paul:

O *the depth of the riches of the wisdom and of the knowledge of God! How incomprehensible are His judgements, and how unsearchable His ways! ... Of Him and by Him and in Him are all things; to Him be glory for ever* (Rom. 11:33, 36).

CHAPTER XXIII

THE TERRIBLE WORLD OF REPROBATION

SUMMARY.—Is God made manifest by it? Emphatically so. True the reprobates arc only spoiled materials and together form a hideous chaos: but Hell itself, that is to say the place where they are imprisoned, is a real world of a stern beauty, and the work of God. The case of the reprobate. God is contrary and a torment to him. No wish to cease to be. Monuments of Divine Justice. Effusions of adoration.

THERE is a last world which we must mention among the works of God, since, indeed, it does exist; a terrible world, the Hell of the reprobates.

Is God also revealed in this work of His? Is the Blessed Trinity in some way adumbrated therein? Can we discover therein a display of the infinite perfections? Most undoubtedly.

We have already explained how each one of the blessed angelic natures, nay, each human soul of good-will, in paradise or in purgatory or on earth, is in itself a world, a real world, a world of immeasurable proportions and wellnigh infinite capacity, because made in the image of God, and possessing already within itself the three Divine Persons. However, the case is altered in the persons of fallen angels and reprobate human souls.

They do not deserve any longer to be considered as worlds in themselves. When we say "world," we mean something not only vast, but also neat and beautiful; something sweet, something organized, co-ordinated, subordinated, harmonious with itself and the rest of things created, and with its Creator; for this is the full import of the Latin term *mundus,* and of the Greek *cosmos,* which we translate by the English term "world." But these fallen ones are disordered, distorted, foul and ugly, each in his own self and all collectively. They are, in their seething multitude, cumulative disorder, carried to an unutterable paroxysm. They are an accumulation of broken worlds, of spoiled materials, absolutely unfit for anything. They are, says St. Jude, *raging waves of the sea, foaming out their confusion; wandering stars, to whom the storm of darkness is reserved for ever* (Jude 1:13). They have made themselves into this, by their own act and free choice, in open rebellion against the benevolent will and loving designs of their Creator.

But if we cannot discover in any of these wretches or their assembled multitudes the least lineament of a world, since they have made themselves into an inconceivable chaos, *a land of misery and darkness, where the shadow of death and no order, but everlasting horror dwelleth* (Job 10:22), nevertheless Hell itself—that is to say, the place which holds them within its fiery prison-walls—is assuredly the work of God, a creation of God, the handicraft of His justice, the protestation of His Sanctity and outraged love; therefore it is, indeed, yet another world, a real world, and serves as much as any of the preceding ones to reveal to us the Omnipotence, infinite Wisdom, and infinite Goodness of the Blessed Trinity.

He that can take this, let him take it (Matt, 19:12).

I know that such a view of Hell does not coincide with a certain mentality, or sentimentality, of our contemporaries. So much the worse for them. Truth must be told, even when it is terrible, nay, the more so that it is terrible. To be silent about it would be wicked, the peril of souls being so imminent and the eventual catastrophe so frightful and irreparable.

Let us try and take a clear, unbiassed view of the case of the reprobate.

First of all let us bear in mind this grand, absolutely incontrovertible principle, that everything created rests necessarily upon God, lives on God, lives to God and for Him; and that it will be so throughout all eternity. *Regem cui omnia vivunt, venite adoremus (Come let ut adore the King for whom all things live);* so sings the Church perpetually.

Now, it is easy for anyone who will reflect to realize that in this necessary and eternal dependence upon God in which they are, for everything they are and have, the blessed Angels and Saints find an inexhaustible fount of joy, admiration, and gratitude. On the other hand, that same Divine fact of their unavoidable dependence upon God will perpetually throw the reprobates into transports of the most violent rage.

The reprobates would like to be absolutely independent of God. They know that He created them—out of love and for the purposes of love—and is, therefore, their great benefactor; but they hate Him most horribly, because they find Him contrary to their perverse will.

They would like to conciliate these two contrary things: to be and at the same time to live separated from the unique wellspring of all existences. So absurd a contradiction can never be achieved in fact; hence, their insane fury. But oh! who could ever have pity on such madness? They are the authors of their own frightful misery. St. Bernard has well and tersely expressed a law of the spiritual world when he said in his treatise *De Consideratione,* Book V, that God is, both at the same time, the reward of the just and THE PUNISHMENT OF THE WICKED.

It will do us good to try to fathom this formidable mystery.

By his own act the reprobate has stripped himself of all the gifts of God but one, that of existence. This last gift God alone could take away, but He never will, because it is inconsistent with His nature to annihilate anything that He has made. And the reprobate, in his own way, appreciates this one remaining gift of God.

He does not wish to return into nothingness, no, not even in order to escape the terrible punishment he has heaped. upon himself, and which will be his lot for all eternity. He would never choose not to be. What he frantically wants, what he strives after with all the inflexible but also impotent strength of his will, is to be otherwise than God would have him; to be both at the same time guilty and happy, a rebel and absolutely free. Such is his craze. He stands obstinately by this perverse will of his; and so it is that God, who is all goodness and all sanctity and love, and precisely because He is all that, is contrary to the reprobate and is a torment to him.

Here below, when a miserable sinner has reached a certain degree of bodily or mental discomfort, he not infrequently lays violent and sacrilegious hands on this work of God that he himself is, in the vain attempt to force it back into non-existence. He only succeeds in making his misfortune incomparably greater and for ever final. But no sooner has he passed the threshold of the spiritual world than on this point, at least, his eyes are open: he sees so clearly what a wonderful gift existence is for a spiritual creature, that on no consideration would he now consent to be without it, were such a thing possible. It is in the realization of this fundamental, ineradicable, incorruptible benefit of existence that he finds the prodigious power of endurance called for by all the harm he has done to himself.

We may notice in this connection that Our Lord, speaking of the awful misfortune of the traitor Apostle, Judas, simply says: *it were better for him if that man had not been born* (Matt. 26:24)— that is to say, if instead of coming to man's estate and incurring such a frightful guilt he had died in his mother's womb. That is precisely what even the holy man Job, in the extremity of his anguish, wished to have happened to himself, to have died before being born (Job 3:11); but he never wished not to have been created or to return to absolute non-existence.

God has made *angels and* men INEXTERMINABLE (Wisd. 3:11).

If they will not, by their own choice, glorify God during their trial state, by turning themselves, with the help of His grace, into monuments of His mercies, then there is no other possible alternative than this: they will have to stand for evermore as monuments of the revenge of order, of the revenge of outraged justice and sanctity.

Such will be their way of glorifying God in spite of themselves.

As I have already treated this painful subject in my third volume, *Mysticism, True and False,* chapter 18, I beg to refer my readers to this. But I cannot leave this tremendous subject, O my God, without unburdening my soul and expressing my feelings about it.

I give thee thanks, O God, Most Holy Trinity, Father of all, our Father in heaven, I return most humble and fervent thanks to Thine infinite goodness for having resolved and decreed from all eternity to create me, to make me in Thine own image and likeness; for having loved me and thus created me and bound me to Thee by the golden and adamantine chains, marvellously supple and yet absolutely unbreakable, of my dependence upon Thee. Those chains I kiss rapturously.

I give Thee thanks also, O my God, for having so loved, from all eternity, every single one of my brethren, whether man or angel, as well the now fallen angels as the blessed ones, as well the sinners and the lost souls as Thy most faithful predestinate servants.

Thou hast created us all in love and for the purposes of Jove. Thou hast willed the salvation of all and each. There will, in the last end, happen to be lost only such as have obstinately refused to do Thy holy will. These wretches will never return Thee thanks; let me do it for them.

Yes, Lord, our God, Creator of heaven and earth, of things visible and invisible, eternal thanks to Thee for the wonderful work of creation, and particularly for the gift of our spiritual nature and the boon of our endless existence!

CHAPTER XXIV

THE DIVINE VIEW-POINT

SUMMARY.—God always right. Two adverse agencies at grips: the virus of original sin and the grace of redemption. Various oppositions. The alternative before us. In the hands of our free will. How sin itself turns to tire glory of God.

HERE is a beautiful saying of Mgr. d'Hulst, the first Rector of the present Catholic University of Paris:

"La sagesse consiste à donner raison à Dieu en toute chose," which means: Wisdom consists in always finding that God is right. God is always right. It must be so, otherwise God would not be God. Therefore wisdom indeed, for a reasonable creature, consists ever and from the very first—3 priori, as the philosophers express it—in taking the part of God, in placing oneself at the view-point of God, for a due appreciation of all things.

It is easy to perceive how such a way of acting is calculated to raise a man above himself and all things created, to flood his mind with light and to pacify him.

For such a man, whatever may betide, all is well and nothing can disturb him. St. Teresa has celebrated this fact in a charming poem of a few lines, beginning, if I remember rightly, with the words: "Nada te disturbe, nada te espanta." The Holy Ghost has put it tersely thus: *Say* to *the just man that it is well* (Isa. 3:10).

It is well; it is well, even though'! may not understand it. I trust it all to God, I know that He knows it all, that He cannot be outwitted by the evil one. My soul, all's well!

When by grace of the Holy Spirit a man finds himself in such a frame of mind, he can face any situation, look serenely upon any contingency whatever, he can meet unperturbed any tragical event, being fully convinced that God, the good and loving God, will have the last word, and that in the end all will turn to His glory and to the good of His predestinate.

As far as we men here below are concerned, it is easy to see from the view-point of God that all the various events of history have reference exclusively to two mighty agencies ever active and ever at grips one with the other—these, namely, on the one hand the virus of original sin; on the other, the grace of Divine redemption.

All the personal sins of men, all the antagonisms of civilized nations, all the degradations of savage peoples, all is explained by the poison of original sin, inoculated into every individual person, manifesting its malignity in various ways according to the diversities of time and circumstance.

Now, God in His wisdom has decreed that the remedy to this virus should come out of the very bowels of humanity, through Our Lord Jesus Christ and His Immaculate Virgin Mother, Mary. And further, it has pleased God to decree that this remedy or counter-poison should be administered by a set of men officially deputed to this work—namely, the priests, and carried to all the ends of the earth by the missionaries of the Catholic Church.

Says the wise son of Sirach in the Book of Ecclesiasticus: *Good is set against evil and life against death; so also is the sinner against a just man. And so look upon all the works of the Most High, two and two and one against another* (Eccli. 33:15).

Against Lucifer and his crew of fallen rebel spirits there stood Michael and the dazzling phalanx of all the blessed Angels.

Adam and Eve, the guilty ancestors of the whole human race, are offset by the new Adam, Jesus, and the new Eve, Mary.

Over against the fatal tree of the knowledge of good and evil which caused our death, there is planted in the midst of the Church the Cross of Our Lord, the fruit of which brings the souls of men to live again, nay, to a higher and more opulent kind of life.

Against the Babylon of this world of sin with the synagogue of the children of the devil, there stands the Militant Church of Christ, made up of all the men of goodwill, who are, indeed, the true sons of God.

To the nefarious maxims of the world is opposed the Gospel

of Our Lord Jesus Christ, with His new commandment of brotherly love, His Counsels of Perfection, and His eight Beatitudes.

To the three concupiscences, that of the eyes, that of the flesh, and the pride of life, are opposed Faith, Hope, Charity, together with the four infused moral virtues and the seven gifts of the Holy Ghost.

Whosoever will not freely receive the mercy of God will perforce experience His justice. Whosoever will not allow God to save him will be damned. Of two things, one, we must embrace either love or hatred; either the glory of Heaven or the flames of Hell; either personal holiness tn the company of all the blessed, or the foul ugliness and incurable perversity of sin in the company of all the reprobates. Such is the alternative.

Thus has the good and loving God placed the angel first and then man, in the hands of their own free will.

Before each one, during the time of his trial, has been set good and evil, and it is for each freely to choose. God wants us to make a good choice; to this end he presses His grace upon all: those who chose aright, owe it to the help of the grace of God; those who chose amiss have only themselves to blame.

But whatever be the choice of the ones and the others, it all turns in the end to the glory of God.

Sin itself turns to the glory of God.

Sin itself, whether in time or in eternity, turns to the glory of God.

It is a great glory to God when, after a long life of evil deeds, a poor sinner does at last repent.

It is a great glory to God that all the sins of the world have been atoned for by the death of Our Lord on the Cross and that reparation has been offered to the majesty of God, infinitely greater than the offence.

It is great glory to God that all those who will not repent will be finally wiped out of the face of the fair world and dumped into the pit of Hell, where they will be for ever punished, although not as much as they deserve.

Let, therefore, no one be scandalized and ask, as casting a doubt upon the goodness of the Supreme Judge: Oh, why has God allowed the great evil of sin to take place?

My son, the good and loving God has permitted the great evil of sin in view of the greater good of the expiation of sin, of the repentance of the sinner, of the display of God's mercies, and for those who will not have mercy, of the display of His justice.

The mystic, the contemplative, the lover of God sees things and judges of them as God sees them and judges of them. He cannot but be right, absolutely right.

O my God, Most Holy Trinity, Father, Son, and Holy Ghost; Creator, Redeemer, and Sanctifier, Thine oracle in the Book of Wisdom (1:1) hath given us this warning: *Think of the Lord in goodness.* This I want to do ever and for ever. Indeed, I confess it with fear and trembling and also with boundless joy: *Thou art just, O Lord, and Thy judgement is right* (Ps. 118:137). Be Thou blessed *in aeternum et ultra* (Exod. 15:18).

CHAPTER XXV

THE DIVINE SOLITARINESS IN THE MIDST OF CREATION

SUMMARY.—Immanence and Transcendence—two aspects of a Divine fact. What these words mean. God ever creating—intimately present in every parcel of the universe. The six days of Genesis and the natural laws. St. Augustine on miracles. God our centre where we can meet. The full import of the term transcendence. Theologians and mystical writers on this subject. Fundamental nothingness of all that is not God. That God is His own all sufficing company in the Trinity of His Persons.

THIS chapter will, unless we greatly mistake, prove to be, at least, as. interesting as any of the foregoing ones, in spite of its being more metaphysical. In order to make it quite easy to understand, I have carefully sifted and separated its various elements and divided it into separate sections, which ought to be read in their order, being careful not to pass to the next until the preceding one has been mastered.

I.

The contemplation of God in His works, in the refulgent mirror of creation, not only bears witness to His infinite perfections, especially to His omnipotence and wisdom and sweetness, which shine forth everywhere and in everything, and to His ineffable justice and mercy in His dealings with angels and men, but it serves, moreover, to manifest and to bring home to our minds the two very striking properties of the Divine Essence which theologians call Immanence and Transcendence.

Let us not be frightened by these two philosophical terms. They have a very beautiful import and are easily understood. They simply mean that God is, on the one hand, necessarily present in all things; and on the other hand, infinitely above all things.

If God had not created anything, or if we had confined ourselves to the contemplation of God in Himself, this twofold sublime property of His would have remained hidden in Him for ever unknown and unknowable. This shows that by our contemplation of God in His works we have gained a distinct addition to our knowledge of Him.

The Immanence and Transcendence of God are two aspects of a Divine fact that will stand for evermore and will be an inexhaustible source of admiration to the blessed in heaven. But there is no reason why we ourselves, while still on earth, should not begin even now to make it also the subject of our loving contemplation.

Immanence, then, is that exclusive property of the Divine Essence by which God is intimately present, of His presence of power, in everything created; Transcendence is that Divine property by which God is absolutely independent of all the natural laws of time and space and is above all modes of being and acting of His creatures, so that He absolutely surpasses them, and, so to speak, extends beyond them infinitely.

II.

God is in the midst of creation, in the whole of it, and in every part of it, not, indeed, as its soul, as though He were a component part of the universe, as the Pantheists would have us believe, but as its first cause, *Prima Causa.*

God is ever creating the world and every separate item of it. *My Father worketh until now, and I work,* replied Jesus to the Jews who were finding fault with Him for having healed on the Sabbath Day a man *who had been thirty years under his infirmity* (John 5:5-17).

It were an error to think that in order to discover God in the act of creating we need go back through all intervening centuries to the work of the six days of Genesis, to the very beginning of all things. Even now, at this moment, at every moment, nothing whatever would persevere in existence were not Almighty God perpetually creating it. Every object in nature, the earth, the sea, the sky, the stars; every person in the world, man or angel, every separate soul, at every moment, in every respect, has need of God in order to continue in being. You, my dear friend, would not be at present reading this, for you would not exist at all, were not God actually creating you at this very moment.

Wheresoever is found some being, spiritual or corporeal, great or small, there God also is with His omnipotence, infinite majesty, ineffable sweetness, in the august Trinity of His Persons. If He were not there, that thing could never be. In order to exist, even the tiniest thing imaginable calls for the previous and simultaneous existence of God, His intimate presence within it, and His perpetual creative action upon it. In order to be at all, that thing has need of God, and, therefore, however insignificant it may be, it is, nevertheless, an irrefutable demonstration of God.

I am, therefore God is.

And, O my God, I confess that I am in duty bound to worship Thee present in me, sustaining me in existence, enveloping me. on all sides, so that I do not know which to admire most, either that Thou, O my God, art in me, or that I am in Thee. *He w not far from everyone of us, for in Him we live, and move, and be* (Acts 17:28).

III.

It might perhaps be asked: What then has Almighty God done in the beginning and in the six days of Genesis more than He is now doing?

The reply is that He then drew out of pure nothingness the materials of this visible universe at the same time as all the angelic natures, and established the order of secondary causes and the harmonious workings of the natural laws.

But, all this notwithstanding, it remains that, under the warp and woof of the secondary causes and natural laws which have held good through so many centuries and centuries of centuries, God stands revealed as the First Cause, whose active influx is perpetually at work and absolutely necessary. *Rerum Deus tenax vigor,* sings Holy Church in the liturgy. God is the Almighty Agent who gives to all things their virtue, at the same time as He is the centre which keeps things in themselves and binds them all in one universe.

Here is the proper place to recall a familiar saying of St. Augustine, to the effect that the natural laws of the world— though we pay so little attention to them through being used to their smooth workings—are much more stupendous than any miracle or all the miracles put together. Miracles, be they ever so wonderful, are after all but casual interventions of God, limited in time and space, whilst the laws of nature and the continuance of the universe in existence call for an active exercise of God's omnipotence, co-extensive in time and space with the whole history of the world past, present, and future.

The forty years' duration of the miracle of the manna was, indeed, a great wonder; so was also the miraculous multiplication of the five loaves with which Our Lord fed the more than five thousand people in the desert: but a far greater wonder is the way in which God feeds all His creatures through the harmonious workings of natural laws. Every day since the beginning of the world, all living things cry out to God, each in its own language: *Our Father who art in heaven, give us this day our daily bread:* and through this long succession of centuries God has never failed to supply the varied wants of this immense family of beasts and men spread over the whole earth.

IV.

The foregoing considerations duly weighed will strike one with awe and reverence. But there is a peculiar aspect of this great truth that God is the centre of all His creatures, which may perhaps more powerfully stir in us feelings of gratitude and tender love towards Him.

Is it not a very touching, affecting thought, to consider that to all His children scattered in the broad expanse of the Church Militant, Suffering and Triumphant, our good and loving Heavenly Father is a trysting-place where we can, with the most absolute certainty, meet and come into contact with one another—under the veil of faith, of course, as far as we on earth are concerned?

Then, from this fact that our good and loving God is Himself the binding force and the link of union of all persons and things, does it not seem that our dear dead are now a great deal nearer to us than when they were in life?

When they were still on earth, a wall was enough to keep them separated from us and to prevent our actual intercourse with them. Still more so if they happened to be at a great distance. But now, îf I so will, I can have speech with my dear departed ones, whenever and as long as I will. Whether they be in Purgatory, or already in the glory of Paradise, makes but little difference, I can meet them in God, and although it is not given me to hear them, I am quite sure to be heard of them, God Himself being our unfailing intermediary.

V.

Now we come at last to the real gist of this chapter, to the summit towards which we have been slowly climbing.

In order to bring home to our reader the full import of the term *transcendence* as applied to God, we cannot do better than reproduce a very apt saying of St. Thomas Aquinas. It occurs in the First Part of his *Summa Theologica* (Quaestio XXXI, art. iii, *ad* i). There the Angelic Doctor explains that if there was not in the Divine Essence a plurality of Persons, we should have to say that God, even in the midst of His blessed Angels and Saints, is alone and solitary. "For," says he, "the solitude of a person is not broken by the fact of his associating with things of a different nature. Thus, we say of a man that he is alone in the garden, although he be there surrounded with numberless animals and plants. In the same way, if there were no plurality of Divine Persons, we should have to pronounce that God is alone or solitary, even though there exist now with Him angels and men in numberless multitudes."

Hence, when we say with Holy Church, after St. Paul (1 Tim.

1:7), *Soli Deo honor et gloria*, it does not mean only: To God alone be praise and glory, to the exclusion of anyone else, but moreover: To God who is alone, to God who has no like. "Who is like unto God," exclaimed the Archangel Michael, when Lucifer would have raised his throne by the side of the Most High (Isa. 14:13; Apoc. 12:7). God is without His like in the majesty of His Divine Essence and Substance and Life. HE TRANSCENDS ALL.

It is also in this sense that we must understand this passage of the book of Job (14:4): *Who can make him clean, that is conceived of unclean seed? Nonne tu qui solus es?* Our Douay version translates the last words thus: "Is it not Thou who only art?" But I think one is justified in finding that this does not render the full meaning either of the Latin, or of the Septuagint, or of the Hebrew original, for they all imply and convey that forcible thought of the absolute transcendence of God as shown by *His magnificent solitariness.*

VI.

In order to do justice, as far as possible, to this wonderful attribute of God, His absolute Transcendence and consequent Solitariness, theologians warn us that all we say of the Divine Essence is said only equivocally, not univocally. This means that, for want of a better mode of expressing ourselves, we are compelled to make use of a word which does not really fit the subject, and which therefore, must not be taken too literally.

This is the reason also why mystical writers like the Pseudo-Areopagite coin very extraordinary expressions when discoursing about God, speaking of His *superessence, supersubstance, supersubsistence,* and so on. All this means that God is a substance in a sense infinitely superior to that of the substances we know; that He has an essence without a parallel; that the words "Persons, hypostases" have here infinitely larger meanings than when applied to man or angel; that the numerals in God denote something transcending our human counting, for, indeed, God is so One that He has no second, and He is Three in

One in a way of which no created things could ever present an example.

My God, O Father, Son, and Holy Ghost, O Thou unspeakable, O Thou "Anonumos, Panonumos, Hyperonumos," as Thy illustrious servant, St. Gregory Nazianzen, tells us Thou art; yes, "The One without a name, in whom all things are named, who transcendeth all names," my God, my God, my God, oh, how I must worship Thee!

VII.

Now, now, indeed, do I begin to understand this great truth that Thou art All, whilst compared with Thee, all things created are simply nothing. Yes, nothing, nothing, nothing!

What dost thou say, O my soul? Has it not seemed to us at times that we were a very big thing, a very important parcel of the universe, a wonderful personage? What a ludicrous error! Before God the whole universe is not even as a drop of water compared to the ocean, not even as a grain of sand. If so of the whole universe, what shall we say of tiny me? I am nothing, I am he that is not: such is the truth; *for,* says St. Paul, *if any man. think himself to be somethings whereas he is nothings he deceiveth himself* (Gal. 6:3).

Greatness of God, nothingness of all that is not God, nothingness of myself. An aboriginal nothingness, a fundamental nothingness, a perpetual tendency to return into nothingness, a perpetual need that God should uphold me and prevent me from falling back into nothingness; such is my case.

VIII.

Now to conclude.

If in the midst of His wonderful works, in the midst of this universe of things visible and invisible, of myriads and myriads of angels and men, God is All Alone, All by Himself, and the Only One that is—even as He proclaims it out of the burning bush in these solemn words *I am who am*—if, I say, there is around His infinite Majesty an awful, unbroken, inviolable solitude, yet let us bear in mind that God is not in loneliness. He is to Himself His own company. The fulness of His own Divine life is such that He subsists in three distinct Persons, most loving and all sufficing to one another's infinite delight.

O God, O Father, Son, and Holy Ghost, *de profundis, out of the depths* of my native nothingness, I cry out to Thee; I adore Thine infinite Being, I love Thy marvellous Life and All-sufficiency to Thyself. I humbly desire to build myself upon Thee. Outside of Thee nothing can stand.

Dominus firmamentum meum (Ps. 17:3). O my great wonderful God!

PART III

GOD IN THE HEART OF THE MYSTIC

CHAPTER XXVI

INTRODUCTORY TO THIS THIRD PART

SUMMARY.—That one does not know God until one has viewed Him under this aspect. This treatise would not be complete without such a presentment of God. Inspired writers and saintly authors have opened the way. A prejudice that has to be broken down.

IN this Third Part I have endeavoured to draw for the edification of my reader some picture, however faint and feeble, of the wonderful familiarity with which the Lord God, so good and loving, is wont to deal with a soul of good-will.

One does not know God until one has viewed Him under this particular aspect.

Among the divinely inspired writers, at least two have shown us, in a lively manner, the loving intercourse which takes place between God and the fervent soul: the first is King David in the Book of Psalms, the second is the writer of the Canticle of Canticles. And then, from among the works of the Saints, let it suffice to name, as specimens of this sort of literature, the celebrated *Confessions* of St. Augustine, the Third Book of the *Imitation of Christy* and the *Living Flame of Love* of St. John of the Cross.

What these authors have so excellently done I have felt constrained, in spite of my own unworthiness and incapacity, to attempt on my own account and in my own way, because a work on the Ecstatic Contemplation of the Blessed Trinity would not be complete without such a description.

I set down some phases of the little drama of Divine love as I have been privileged more than once to see it enacted. I set it down with simplicity, as I understand it, as I have had some personal experience of it. Let people make of it what they please.

There will, no doubt, be those who will think that I have been drawing on my imagination to an unwarranted extent. I can but reply that, on the contrary, I am only too conscious of remaining almost at an infinite distance from the Divine realities of which I would like to give them a taste.

Others may be inclined to take scandal at seeing *the secrets of the King* set down in black and white, in homely phrase, in the vulgar language of our every-day intercourse with each other. They may think this a desecration, even though it be done for their own use and edification. But there can be no greater error than this.

What! *The children of the devil,* as Our Lord calls those who will not follow Him (John 8:44), may describe and sing in prose and poetry, as complacently as they like, their impure love-stories and give to all who read them the thrill of guilty pleasure: and one should not be allowed to make known and to celebrate the sweet, inebriating joys of Divine love; to try and picture them as best one can and make others share them!

O cursed world which has succeeded in deceiving even *the children of light* to such an extent, and imposing on them as an axiom that the beautiful things of God and the good things of God ought to be kept carefully concealed, even as something to be ashamed of! Is it not high time for us to break the despotic yoke of such a prejudice? Is it not high time that we should dare to use our liberty of true children of God, and to make an open profession, not only of our faith and of the hope that is in us, but also of our love, of our love I say, of our love of God who made us and who is so good and loving and sweet?

As on a former occasion (cf. *Divine Contemplation for All,* chapters XXII-XXV), I have been obliged in this Third Part, here and there, to employ figurative language as the best means of conveying my meaning. No one, I am sure, will find fault with me for this, for it is impossible to mistake the true import of it all.

CHAPTER XXVII

THE MARVELOUS ADVENTURE

SUMMARY.—That few seek after God. How thrilling this adventure compared to all others. Its wide range. It captivates the whole man. What it reveals to him.

EW there are, nowadays, who seek after God. People seek after self and after all sorts of consolations from created things. The few, the very few, who care not for such consolations and who do really seek after God are the mystics, the genuine contemplatives. Oh, these are the happy ones!

The earnest search after God, by a pilgrim of the earth, and what follows upon the finding, constitute positively the most marvellous adventure that can ever be thought of.

A thrilling adventure, full of poignant interest, fruitful in unforeseen developments and striking situations, bringing about most sweet and comforting immediate results, to say nothing of its entrancing ultimate consequences which reach out far beyond present and future times, even unto farthest eternity.

In comparison with this, what are the other adventures, mythical or real, of which mention is made in the literatures of the world?

The search of the Golden Fleece by the Argonauts, that of the Holy Grail by the Knights of the Round Table; the conquest of the Holy Sepulchre by the Crusaders of the Middle Ages; the discovery of the New World by Christopher Columbus, that of the Pacific Ocean by Balboa, the conquest of Peru by Pizarro; the search after the so-called Philosopher's Stone, or after the Spring of Perpetual Youth, or after the lost Atlantides; the voyages to the North Pole, or to the South Pole by our daring explorers, the perilous journey to Lhassa, or to Mecca, or to Timbuctu by Europeans, the ascent of Mount Everest, the discovery of the

Tomb of Pharaoh Tutankhamen with its buried treasures; or, on a lower plane, the fast and furious race after fortune, fame, honors, the pleasures of the flesh, or the more refined ones of the mind: what are all those adventures, either in themselves or in their results, that could bear comparison with the marvellous adventure of the search after God?

The search after God ranges all over the earth, all over the stars and goes beyond, and yet is achieved at home, in the secret of the heart, and by men whom one would hardly describe as daring spirits, though, indeed, they are the most daring spirits in existence.

The search after God captivates at the same time the mind, the heart, the senses— the whole man, body and soul—of the searcher. It attunes him to the music of the heavenly spheres and choirs angelical.

It reveals in him depths hitherto unsuspected and capabilities wellnigh infinite; nay, and gives them fulfilment. For it brings that happy seeker suddenly face to face and hand to hand, with Him who is the goal of his fond audacious quest.

CHAPTER XXVIII

WHAT HAPPENS THEN

SUMMARY.—When an earthly lover meets his beloved. With the Mystic in search of God the process is reversed. Beginning of the little love drama.

E all know what does happen when an earthly lover at last meets with the idol of his dreams. Does he not, at once, come to a dead stop? See him stand still, silent, motionless, though bubbling over with hardly suppressed feelings, eagerly gorging himself with the sight. Oh! he is, at least for the time being, a contemplative.

The next stage is for him to impress the image of his beloved deep into his heart, and carry it with him wheresoever he goes, and, losing sight of everything but this object of his adoration, to prostrate before it his whole being.

But the silence cannot last. Soon, very soon, the wounded mortal who has received deeply into his heart the flaming arrow of love cannot bear his joy in silence: he is constrained to give vent to his tumultuous feelings. He must talk, he must sing of her whose charms enthral him.

At this point even the less skilled man will rise to the lyrical mood and show himself both poet and musician. With his heart for a musical instrument, on which are stretched the delicate, strong, vibrating chords of his sensitiveness, he begins to play as never did artist upon flute, harp, or violin, and his whole soul passes in the melody.

Now, this is but a faint adumbration of what happens to the fervent Christian who has really fallen in love with God. Only' in his case the process is reversed: the beauties of God dawn upon him but little by little, and for this reason praise goes first, slowly rising to its climax, and then, at last, at last, there comes silent enjoyment, deep, and inexpressible.

Yes, no sooner has the lover of God been given a taste of the sweetness of the Divine Majesty, than he cannot sing its praise loud enough for his own satisfaction. To relieve his pent-up feelings he must needs proclaim to all the world his passionate love and admiration and overflowing joy. Soon, however, a new mood intervenes: a spell is cast upon him. One by one the chords of his lyre are pressed by the finger of the Spirit and silenced. The hermit-soul withdraws to its cave in the innermost depth of its own self; there to enjoy God in utmost privacy and far from any profane gaze.

Then it is, then and there, and with these circumstances of silence and secrecy, that begins in earnest the little love drama.

CHAPTER XXIX

THE ENCOUNTER

SUMMARY.—What takes place in the secret of the Soul. Transports of joy and illusions. Darkness and Desolation. What to do then. Gold in the crucible.

NOW the fervid lover seizes upon God as upon a prey and gives himself up wholly, unreservedly, to the devouring, all-consuming exigencies of this *Beloved of the beloved.* But oh, with what transports of joy!

Made bold by the darkness, he dares to embrace his All-Beloved, to kiss Him; shedding burning tears and stammering to Him his love in broken accents. He feels also the loving embrace of God, though unable to see Him. He feels His touch and is thrilled to the innermost of his soul. He hears the soft whisper of His voice and catches upon his own lips the breath, the sweet-scented breath of His mouth. *Let Him kiss me with the kiss of His mouth,* exclaims the bride in the Canticle of Canticles. Ah! no wonder, then, no wonder that our Lover should faint, quite overpowered by heavenly delight. Is he still on earth or already in heaven? He could not tell. All he knows is that he has surely found the object of his venturesome, daring quest. All hardships are forgotten. In the wild, extravagant joy of his heart he cries out: *Tenui eum nec dimittam*: I have got hold of my God and my Love; I shall not let him go. No; never!

Puny one, what art thou saying? Does it lie with thee to hold Him fast? Thinkest thou hast already left this land of exile and reached *the land of Promise?* Come down again to the hard and harsh realities of the present life. Behold, all of a sudden thy beloved Lord, the Most Holy God of heaven, disentangles Himself from thy embrace and takes Himself away. Thou art still with Him; He has not ceased to be with thee, but He hides Himself. He seems to have receded far, far away; and thou, in consequence, art left utterly desolate. Oh! this is a cruel turn of affairs. Now what shalt thou do?

Indeed, what is to be done?

Simply this. Thou must begin all over again the search after God: set out again in quest of thy Beloved and spare no pains and give thyself no repose until He be found again. Call for Him unabashed and tireless, and steadily refuse the consolations of creatures. We have had already our experiences of the mysterious withdrawal of the Beloved in our contemplation of the Sacred Humanity of Our Lord (cf. *Mystical Initiation*, chapters XXVIII and XXXII). Now we are dealing with God in His pure Divine Essence: we are made to witness His Divine playfulness with the soul of a lowly pilgrim of the earth. It is almost a repetition of the same incidents, but still more intensely felt, more soul-stirring, precisely because more purely spiritual, nay, altogether Divine. Such a new quest after our All-beloved, begun in sorrow, will yield the more joy when we find Him again.

And so it goes on during the earthly life of the child of Divine love.

In thus passing alternately from intensest joy to deepest sorrow, and back again, in God's good time, into heavenly rapture, followed again by a cruel sense of dereliction sometimes verging on despair, the pilgrim soul is being refined as gold in the crucible. She grows pure, bright, dazzling bright and strong, more and more beautiful in the eyes of God and His blessed Angels, and heaps up a mountain of eternal merits at the same time as she advances in experimental, mystical, intimate knowledge of God.

Never more, after this drastic, energetic treatment by fire, will she yield to the temptation of discouragement, or will she slacken her pace on the rugged path of sanctity, until the shadows of this land of exile retire before the splendors of the Beatific Vision: *donec aspiret dies et inclinentur umbrae* (Cant. 2:17).

CHAPTER XXX

A CHALLENGE

SUMMARY.—The Key of the lives of the Saints. The Soul's reply. The Roman Coliseum. Another Coliseum not made by human hands. The spectators. The spectacle. The Lord is a Warrior. What dost thou say?

N the search after God, such as we have been endeavoring to sketch it out in the foregoing chapters, is found the key to the lives of the dear Saints and of many a great lover of God who has passed away from this world unnoticed and unrecorded. Thus it has been with them in past ages; thus it is at this very moment for generous, souls, known of God alone, scattered all over the world. Thus will it be for ourselves last and least of all, provided only that we be willing.

Nothing more is required of us at the start. We have only to set out on the marvelous quest with a burning desire. The good and loving God who by His prevenient grace gives us already so to will and to set about it is sure to assist us all along and to crown our feeble efforts with a glorious measure of success.

Now what sayest thou to this, O Christian soul?

With utmost alacrity the soul replies: *Dixi, nunc coepi* (Ps. 76:11). I am resolved. I want to attempt the wonderful adventure. Let me set about the quest after God without a moment's delay. I do desire to keep steadily at it, until I have found Him *whom my soul loveth.*

Well said, O my Christian. And now, in order still further to strengthen thee in thy noble resolve, hear something about the scene of thy future valiant deeds and about those who shall witness them. For, indeed, it is a grand sight, a sort of pompous show and exhibition which, all unknown to himself, the fervent Christian is offering to the blessed Angels and the Saints of Paradise —*spectaculum . . . angelis* (1 Cor. 4:9) —when he enters upon the wonderful quest after God. A magnificent spectacle, wholly spiritual, wholly supernatural, wholly Divine.

When, some twenty-five years ago, I was in Rome, I loved to visit the immense ruin of the Coliseum, and each time it was with fresh feelings of wonder. My particular delight was to climb up to the highest tier, where that was still possible, and to reconstitute in imagination the stupendous structure, as it must have looked in the days of its pristine splendor and integrity.

What a genius of a man must have been the Jewish captive who planned this well-named colossus of a building, and who at the same time contrived to give it, both inside and out, the light, airy, elegant form of a flower basket!

Gathered and seated at ease within its prodigious depths, the whole free population of ancient Rome—from the emperor, surrounded with his gilded court, down to the meanest rank of the plebeian in his rags—was wont to forget, at least for the time being, all other business but that of greedily devouring with their eyes the spectacles offered in the arena below: bloody fights of gladiators, or abominable buffooneries, or the much appreciated, toothsome amusement of seeing Christians thrown to the lions and by them devoured alive, as was the case with the aged Bishop of Antioch, the great Ignatius.

When particularly pleasing incidents took place, the applause and vociferations of the immense multitude would break forth and roll out as peals of thunder, to give vent to the feelings of the insane and ferocious enjoyment of these people.

Let us now picture to ourselves another Coliseum, in shape infinitely more noble and elegant and of incomparably vaster proportions—*cujus artifex et conditor Deus* (Heb. 11:10)—whereof Divine love is the architect and the builder. On its lofty steps, tier after tier, range themselves the all but infinite multitude of the blessed Angels and of the Saints, with King Jesus, Our Lord, in their midst, throned under a gorgeous canopy, and having at His right hand our Lady, His sweet Virgin-Mother, Queen of heaven.

All are intently gazing downwards.

What is there in the vast arena so to rivet their attention?

Only this: a solitary man, a fervent Christian, who with burning desire is setting forth upon the great adventure of the search after God; a puny human being in the infirm condition of the present life, bold enough to challenge the Lord of heaven to come to grips with himself.

He goes forth blindfolded, with hands outstretched, seeking his quarry, if we may use the expression. And the Tri-une God, the Lord of heaven, does not disdain to step down into the arena, clad as a warrior, having on the breast-plate of His infinite goodness, and to wrestle with this child of clay. *The Lord is a warrior: Dominus vir pugnator* (Exod. 15:3)—a warrior who not only fights against His enemies, but who, moreover, likes to wrestle with His dearest friends, to play with them the exciting game of love.

Now, God meets halfway the man who seeks Him. He allows Himself to be seized upon, and, in a way, held down, at least, for a short space. Anon He will extricate Himself from the close embrace of His loving adversary and evade for a while his ardent blind pursuit. Then again, at a turn, He will let Himself be overtaken and seized and held captive in the frail bands of a creature's fond embrace.

Who will tell us how such a spectacle stirs to their utmost depths the feelings of admiration and sympathy of the heavenly citizens? They cannot take away their eyes from it. With unstinted applause and loud acclamations, they underline the varying incidents of the little drama as it unwinds itself and progresses to its climax. But our hero, in his present condition of a pilgrim of the earth, neither sees nor hears them.

Well, now, it lies with each of us to offer such a spectacle to the blessed Angels and Saints. I ask yet again: What dost thou say, O soul of good-will? *Amici auscultant* (Cant, 8:13). All heaven is listening, eager to catch every word from thy lips. They have already anticipated what thy ready answer will be. Now what they want is to see thee boldly step into the arena. Are not acts the best proof of our noble intent?

CHAPTER XXXI

GLADNESS IN THE MORNING

SUMMARY.—Weeping in the evening, and its remedy. A vision in a dream. The three Divine Persons and a little boy. A question. The reply. Waking up and after.

AT the end of a long protracted, unbroken period of cruel darkness and desolation, as I was seeking some relief in gathering various texts of Holy Writ to lay as a cordial upon my aching heart, my attention was particularly drawn to that of St. Peter wherein he affirms that we are *made partakers of the Divine nature* (2 Pet. 1:4); and also to this wonderful promise of Our Lord in the Apocalypse: *To him that shall overcome, I will give to sit with Me in My throne: as I also have overcome and am set down with My Father in His throne* (Apoc. 3:21); and to His warning us in the Gospel that unless we become as little children we shall not enter into the kingdom of heaven (Matt, 18:3); and finally, to this oracle of Psalm 29, verse 6: *In the evening weeping shall have place, and in the morning gladness.* At last tired out I fell asleep and had a dream.

I saw a great throne of gold and ivory on which were seated together three Persons, God the Father, God the Son, and between them a lovely little boy of six or seven years:

God the Father, in gorgeous overflowing robes, crowned with a tiara, His face breathing calm majesty.

God the Son, Our Lord, with a glorious kingly crown on His head, clad in loose white garments, which left a good deal of His glorified Sacred Humanity bare; His face radiant with inexpressible benevolence.

The boy, dressed as a little prince, with a graceful countenance, his head crowned with a golden circlet, his curly hair falling on his shoulders. He was straining to his breast, with both hands, a white dove, with wings outstretched, the Divine

Dove, the Holy Ghost.

And it was given me to perceive that from the heart of God the Father, and from the heart of God the Son, and from the heart of God the Holy Ghost, tendrils, as it were, of vine were shooting forth and intertwining around the heart of the little fellow, and he looked the picture of happiness, but of such happiness as is not of this world.

His lips were moving. I intently listened to catch the sound of his words. Then I heard him softly repeating to himself:

"O *Father, Son, and Holy Ghost!*"

Three times he repeated this ejaculation, as one beside himself, and tears of joy, round as pearls, swiftly ran down his cheeks and on his garment.

I could not help it: I had to cry out: "Happy that child! But who is he?" Then a voice behind me (was it that of my guardian angel?) answered:

"It is even thee, if thou wilt."

Whereupon I woke up and found that all my trouble of the previous night had vanished as smoke, or been rolled away as clouds, and it was full daylight and gladness in my soul.

Ever, ever since that blissful dream, I see my God and little me together, and my heart warbles within me as a bird—warbles a wild song of adoration and love, a song of a few notes; no other words than these:

"O Father, Son, and Holy Ghost!"

But oh, with what depth of meaning, and of feeling I with what rapturous melody!

CHAPTER XXXII

THE GOLDEN PYRAMID

SUMMARY.—Gird up thy loins. What for. The Knight in the Palace of Quiet. What he wishes to see. The Holy Trinity under the symbolical appearance of a Pyramid. Petition of Fidelis.

LO, I seem to hear within me again that imperious, most sweet, compelling voice, which I heard at least once before.

"Gird up thy loins like a man" it says (Job 38:3).

And again:

"Thou hast yet a great way to go" (3 Kings 19:7).

With a gladness born of the grace of God, the instant reply rises to my lips:

"Here I am, O Lord, ready to do Thy bidding" (Ps. 118:66)—*Where is Thy servant to go?"* (Isa. 6:8).

And the voice: "Thou art not to go anywhere with thy bodily feet, but to speak to thy brethren, so as to be heard to the farthest ends of the earth. 'Let thy tongue be *the pen of a scrivener that writeth swiftly'"* (Ps. 44:2). Some pages there be which are the very life of the human race, lifting men up to a higher plane. Do thou write such another page.

And I again, with utmost alacrity, not unmixed with a sense of awe and self-abasement:

"O Lord, *da quod jubes et jube quod vis:* Do Thou grant me Thy grace, that I may be able to fulfil Thy command."

It is all about the Knight in the Palace of Quiet, of whom much has been said already in our fourth volume (cf. *Divine Contemplation for All* chapters xxi to xxv inclusive).

He has now for a long time, year after year, enjoyed all the beautiful things which adorn the Palace of Quiet, and thereby come to a deep insight into the mysteries of Jesus, and into the life of the Church in Christ, and into his very own life in the

Church and in Christ. But he is not satisfied with this. His ambition, like that of every true mystic, grows at last until it knows no bounds. Of all things, two in particular he longs to find out.

First, he would like to be shown in what manner he himself is in God.

He has already met with the loving God in the sanctuary of his own soul and contemplated Him there; now what he wishes to see is his own individual self in God.

He does not know whether such a favor can be granted to mortal man or how; but he feels inwardly urged to sigh after it and humbly begs for it. He is aware that in so doing he is only yielding to a pressure coming from within him, though not from himself, but—as he is intimately convinced' —from the Holy Spirit.

And then, the second vehement desire, which is growing and ripening in his heart of hearts, is so sublime, so absolutely supreme, that he hardly dares to put it, even to himself, into words. It is to see God in Himself, in His very Self, in His Divine Essence—if this could be granted him here below, in howsoever small a measure—or else he feels he will die of longing and sorrow.

Now, these holy desires please God so much that He vouchsafes to grant them some fulfilment.

One day Fidelis—for such was the name now given him from above—was reading some verses of Exodus, as illustrated on the mosaic pavement of the Palace. He began to ponder deeply over the words which God spoke to Moses from the midst of the burning bush: I *am who am* (Exod. 3:14). Suddenly a wonderful thing happened.

The Palace of Quiet—pavement, walls, columns, fountain and all—vanished. There he stood on the naked earth and in front of him rose a huge pyramid of gold, or of fire, or of some unknown material, incandescent, piercing the sky. Its brightness was such that nothing already known to him could give an idea of it. And he felt that this was no inanimate object, but living, intensely living, nay, Life itself— essential, superessential, supersubstantial life—the very headspring of all life, the only true life, in one word, God, the Most Holy Trinity, expressing Himself under this symbolical appearance, to the eyes of his intellect even more than to those of his senses.

To throw himself prostrate on the ground was the work of an instant; but though our Knight hid his face in the dust before the tremendous Majesty of God thus revealed, he did not cease a single instant to see the vision.

It was a perfect pyramid, self-contained, and self-sustaining, for it did not rest on the ground. And it had no aperture of any kind in the shape of either door or window. And from it floated (how shall I describe this?), as it were, a stream of harmonious sound inexpressibly sweet, and a cloud of perfume so exquisite that it did not seem' a man could breathe it for any length of time and live. *Sound, perfume,* did I say? But these are coarse figures, though the best at command, to give an idea of what was an absolutely spiritual, nay, a Divine phenomenon.

The whole Palace of Quiet had melted away, it would seem, and our Knight was alone, all alone, with God alone, but instead of terror, this filled him with the deepest feeling of joy he had ever experienced in his life.

There he was, groveling on the ground, telling God his adoration in inarticulate speech, broken by sighs. There he was in presence of the Infinite Majesty—alone, wretched, void of merits, and yet beloved! Oh the Divine irony of the situation!

And yet he realized that this was as it should be. He felt it was right that these two extremes should meet. He exclaimed between sobs: "My God, my dearly loved God, Most Holy Trinity, such as I am, wretched as I am beyond all words, I long to be united to Thee as Thou art, O Infinite Goodness; that the flames of Thine Infinite Sanctity may consume the rust of my sins and vices. Oh that I may at last be one with Thee in perfect love for ever!"

CHAPTER XXXIII

THE SUPREMEST EXPERIENCE

SUMMARY.—The living Crucifix. Through Him into the Golden Pyramid. What then? How long? Limitations of the transforming Union. Feelings of the Soul about it. Back into the Palace of Quiet. The soul enlarged and what it sighs for. Last days of St. Thomas Aquinas. Knight Fidelis will die of his wound.

AS he concluded this prayer our Knight scrambled to his knees, and fastening his gaze in an ecstasy of adoration upon the bright vision, he stretched out his arms in the form of a cross, and lo and behold, he had no sooner unconsciously struck this attitude, than he descried in front of him at the foot of the Pyramid, a cross, a wooden cross, with its burden of suffering, agonizing humanity.

The representation of the Lamb of God, bleeding away His sacred life, was so vivid, so pathetic, so irresistibly attractive, that he could not repress the impulse: he dragged himself on his knees close to the cross, embraced the feet of his Savior, bathing them with tears of love and sorrow, then, plucking courage, he arose and cast himself upon the breast of Our Lord, and embracing Him in a transport of love, he strained Him with incredible fervor to his heart, which he felt as though ready to break.

But oh! what was this new marvelous impression?

Whilst thus embracing his crucified Savior, our Knight felt as though he were passing wholly into Him, nay, through Him and beyond Him and into the very interior of the Golden Pyramid.

It had not been opened to let him in, nor had it closed behind him, and now he felt he was simply engulfed in its infinite depths.

There he was, in the pure, naked, simple Divine Essence, separated from every created thing, dazzled by the infinite splendor, speechless, imageless, motionless as one dead. And, indeed, dead he was to all the world outside, though, in himself, or rather in God, more quick and alert and loving than he had ever been before.

But what did he see in that sanctuary which the blessed Triune God is to Himself? in the primordial, transcending, infinitely pure Divine Essence?

He saw and he saw not. He saw Nothing and he saw All things. He was seized upon and he gave himself up utterly. He saw himself in God as a tiny spark of the same fire as the pyramid itself. One word was spoken to him, only one word, uttered in the midst of an ineffable silence. He himself, in reply, said one word, only one word, not as coming from himself, though his whole self passed into it; one word, not out of the human vocabulary. It was given him; he received it rapturously and hastened to give it back to the Giver: *arcanum verbum,* too sacred to be repeated.

How long did this ecstasy last?

Ah! Who can tell? A passing moment or a century? Was he rapt only in the spirit or also in the flesh? *Nescio, Deus scit: God alone knows* (2 Cor. 12:2). It was certainly as near an approach as possible on earth to the bliss of eternity which theologians describe, after Boethius, as "the full and perfect possession, all at once, of a limitless life: *Interminabilis vitae tota simul et perfecta possessio"* (*De Consol. Philos.*, Tit. iii, Pr. 2).

There are no successive moments in such a duration: all is given in an immutable Now. God is to Himself His eternity, His own duration, absolutely changeless. Now, it seems that something of this immutability of God enters into the contemplative during such moments of ecstasy, almost as though he were turned into God.

Of course, we must not fall into the error of pantheists: we must admit that this sort of Divine visitation with which some devout persons have been sometimes favored is, of its nature, purely accidental, ft in no way affronts the inviolable Divine Essence, nor, either, does it alter the fundamental limitations of the man rapt in God. A created thing can never become the

Uncreated, nor could a secondary cause become one essentially with the *Causa Prima.* The finite spirit for ever remains within its own finite boundaries, nor would he be content, if—by supposition of an impossible thing— it were offered to him to become anything but what it is. In this firm, humble attitude, he renders to God a noble tribute of adoration. It is as though he protested: *Loquar ad Dominum meum cum sim pulvis et cinis.* Indeed, I *am but dust and ashes, but let me say this:* Thou my God, art the only Holy, the only Lord, the only Most High: *Tu solus Sanctus, tu solus Dominus, tu solus altissimus!*

When he came to himself again, Knight Fidelis found himself once more in the Palace of Quiet. But although every object in that palace had, from the fact of his recent experience, put on, so to speak, a fresh meaning, at once deeper and more delightful, nevertheless he found it difficult, nay painful, extremely painful, to readjust himself to it.

Long ago, quite at the beginning of his sojourn in that blessed, enchanted abode, it had seemed to him that for the remainder of his life (were it even to be prolonged to the years of Mathusala), never would he tire of the holy delight of the Palace of Quiet: but what he then judged impossible is now happening to him. More than ever does he enjoy its delights; he penetrates into the meaning of every single detail of its wondrous architecture and ornamentation, and they stir him as never before; but somehow himself is changed.

Through burning contact with the Divine Essence, his soul has become so enlarged that nothing on earth will any longer be capable of filling and satiating it, not even the full banquet of religion as the Catholic Church spreads it before the children of Divine grace. The soul that has gone through the supremest mystical experience craves for more than this. Yes, for more than faith and hope. Even for more than charity as it is to be had here below; for more than the precious life-giving Sacraments; more than the veiled presence of her Beloved in His Holy Eucharist; more than the actual communion of His living flesh and blood;

more than the enjoyment of the perpetual presence within her of the Holy Ghost, with all His gifts and fruits and beatitudes. My God! even more than all these? What then? What?

Oh! nothing less than the vision of God, face to face.

Nothing short of this will now satiate the hunger of that man, the sublime ambition of his soul, aroused to its highest pitch.

He has lost all interest in what goes on around him; lost interest in his former occupations, in his dearest works. Thus, St. Thomas Aquinas, in the last days of his life, when urged by his faithful amanuensis to add something to his unfinished *Summa Theologica,* would reply: "Oh! I can no more. Brother Reginald, all this looks to me now as mere chaff."

So Knight Fidelis drags himself along, sighing incessantly. The daintiest food of Christian piety which he used to relish so much, the Divine Scriptures, the lives and writings of the dear Saints, the flesh and blood of his Savior, offered upon the altar and received in Holy Communion, do but exasperate his hunger and heighten the fever that is consuming him. He is languishing for heaven, fainting away; sorely smitten with the golden arrow tipped with flame from the altar of God. Oh! he will die, he will surely and swiftly die of his wound.

Blessed death! May mine own be like unto this!

EPILOGUE

I ASK again: "My soul, what have we done?

"Can it be that we set out to attempt this impossible task of declaring God?"

God!

A short word. Three letters and that is all. One syllable. A breath!

But the Thing, ah! the Thing it means; the One, the Tri-une, *He that is,* and nothing else is in comparison; have we succeeded in bringing Him to view before the mind's eye?

We wished to. Have we succeeded?

No! no! A thousand times no! It were too egregious a delusion to believe it. Indeed, how could we expect to succeed in this rash enterprise—especially we, we of all men?

The last four chapters of the Book of Job contain a Divine rebuke to that holy man for his failure to speak of God and His works worthily. A few short extracts will here serve our purpose Then the Lord answered Job out of a whirlwind and said:

Who is this that wrappeth up sentences in unskilled words?

Gird up thy loins like a man. I will ask thee, and answer thou Me.

Where wast thou when I laid the foundations of the earth? Tell Me if thou hast understanding.

Who hath laid the measure thereof, if thou knowest? Or who hath stretched the line upon it?

Upon what are its bases grounded? Or who laid the corner-stone thereof,

When the morning stars praised Me together, and all the sons of God made a joyful melody?

Didst thou know then that thou shouldst be born? And didst thou know the number of thy days?

Hast thou entered into the storehouses of the snow? Or hast thou beheld the treasures of the hail?

Shalt thou be able to join together the shining stars the Pleiades, or canst thou stop the turning about of Arcturus?

Canst thou bring forth the day star in its time, and make the evening star to rise upon the children of the earth?

Dost thou know the order of heaven? And const thou set down the reason thereof on the earth?

Job 38, *passim.*

Then Job answered the Lord, and said: What can I answer, who have spoken inconsiderately? I will lay my hand upon my mouth.

One thing I have spoken, which I wish I had not said: and another, to which I will add no more.

Job 39:33-35.

And I also, in my turn, will answer the Lord and say with a deep sense of my utter failure and asking pardon for my rashness: *One thing I have spoken,* in the first part of this treatise—namely, the mystery of the Most Holy Trinity—*which I almost wish I had not said. And another*—in the second and third parts, about the works of God and His wonderful dealings with a fervent soul—to *which I will add* no *more.*

THE END

Printed in Great Britain
by Amazon

60734714R00306